ERIE LACKAWANNA

Death of an American Railroad, 1938–1992

H. Roger Grant

ERIE
LACKAWANNA

Death of an American Railroad,
1938–1992

Stanford University Press
Stanford, California 1994

Stanford University Press, Stanford, California
© 1994 by the Board of Trustees of the Leland Stanford Junior University
Printed in the United States of America

CIP data appear at the end of the book

Stanford University Press publications are distributed exclusively by
Stanford University Press within the United States, Canada, and Mexico;
they are distributed exclusively by Cambridge University Press throughout
the rest of the world.

For
Bernard Donahu
and
Harry Zilli

PREFACE

WHY WRITE A BOOK about a defunct railroad of moderate size? I do so for several reasons. Admittedly, I find the Erie, which became the Erie Lackawanna after 1960, a fascinating firm. Since it never enjoyed robust health, it often had to live by its wits. The Erie's innovative operating procedures at times reflected a troubled economic situation. No wonder this company became a darling of railroad enthusiasts who adore the unusual and pine for the past! Yet nostalgia should not be ignored; after all, the Erie was "a beautiful road. . . . It had fascinating motive power, interesting depots, some of the best scenery in the country and great employees." Such attractions are mostly memories today and therefore require a permanent form of memorial.

The Erie story also has not been extensively told. In fact, of the four principal carriers that once linked New York City with Chicago—the Baltimore & Ohio, the Erie, the New York Central, and the Pennsylvania—only the B&O has received much scholarly attention. Of these four, however, the Erie has had the best journalistic account, *Men of Erie* (1946). A popular but badly flawed book, *Men of Erie* suffers from more than a politically incorrect title; it contains too much of the colorful and episodic and it is badly dated.

I expect that *Erie Lackawanna: The Death of an American Railroad* will be a building block for future studies on railroad history. The Erie and Erie Lackawanna railroads illustrate, in a particular way, critical developments and themes, including dieselization, corporate merger and dissolution, regulatory mismanagement, and changing patterns of travel and business. This 50-plus-year saga of the "Weary Erie" illuminates much about the national railroad enterprise.

The initial idea for studying the Erie was not, in fact, mine. In January 1987, I received a message at my office to call "Mr. Donahue at Erie Lackawanna." I thought it either a joke or a mistake since I remembered that the company was what the late David P. Morgan, Jr., veteran editor of *Trains*, labeled a "fallen flag." The carrier had disappeared into the quasi-public Consolidated Rail Corporation in 1976. Nevertheless, I contacted Mr. Bernard ("Barney") Donahue. I quickly learned that a remnant of the former railroad existed: the "Estate," Erie Lackawanna Inc. Barney, a member of the board of directors, had read one of my railroad books and realized that I lived less than an hour from the firm's office in the Midland Building near Cleveland's Public Square. A chat with Barney and Harry A. Zilli, Jr., the Estate's chief executive officer, convinced me that I should study this company in some fashion. Barney promised me access to the records in Cleveland, ample funds for research elsewhere, and a generous honorarium. Moreover, he guaranteed me absolute control of the manuscript; in fact, I need not write anything. Excited by this not-to-be-missed opportunity, I pragmatically placed a study of the Chicago & North Western Railway on the back burner.

No book is a single-handed effort. My obligations are numerous. In the course of my research I had help from scores of people, including archivists, librarians, and persons associated with the company and the railroad industry.

There have been many high points in my research. I enjoyed examining materials held by the Erie Lackawanna Historical Society, which are stored in the home of Larry DeYoung, in suburban Philadelphia, Pennsylvania. I have vivid, pleasant memories of a spring day in 1990, when I talked with nearly a dozen former Erie Lackawanna employees in the living room of John R. Michael in Huntington, Indiana. Memorable, too, was the visit paid me by Jervis Langdon, Jr., former president of the Baltimore & Ohio and Chicago, Rock Island & Pacific railroads, trustee of the Penn Central Transportation Company, and a participant in the Erie's reorganization from 1938 to 1941. At the age of 85 he piloted his own aircraft from his retirement home in Elmira, New York, to Akron.

What surprised and pleased me about interviewing was the remarkable cooperation I received. Of the more than 50 people with whom I spoke, only one, a former officer, refused to answer all of my questions, but even he provided me with insights. Perhaps my timing was right. Although the Erie Lackawanna disappeared as a railroad nearly two decades ago, a variety of individuals who knew the road intimately and who retained their mental acuity felt unrestrained about telling the story "the way it was." Some had even kept valuable records. Among them was Perry Shoemaker, who served as Lackawanna's last president and chairman of the board of the Erie-Lackawanna

Railroad and who shared with me an assortment of documents, including confidential memoranda.

I have been fortunate with funding for this project. Unlike some earlier ones, my labors on Erie Lackawanna have not been conducted on a shoe-string. It is easier to gather materials when travel costs are less an issue. In addition to the support given me by Erie Lackawanna Inc., I also received a Faculty Summer Fellowship from The University of Akron. This grant, awarded for 1992, gave me a large block of uninterrupted time to complete my work.

Finding the appropriate publisher can be tricky. In this case Mary Lincoln, who heads the Northern Illinois University Press and with whom I have worked extensively, mentioned my project to Norris Pope, acting director of the Stanford University Press. Fortunately, he contacted me, and our relationship has been a productive one.

Lastly, I wish to thank those individuals who assisted me in the preparation of the manuscript. My department head at The University of Akron, Keith L. Bryant, Jr., a talented historian of American railroading, critically commented on chapter drafts. William D. Burt, an industry expert and student of the Erie and Erie Lackawanna, also reviewed the manuscript. Bernard Donahue and Harry Zilli, as well as Joe Allen, a former Erie and Erie Lackawanna locomotive engineer and Brotherhood of Locomotive Engineers official, and Gregory W. Maxwell, the last and now deceased president of Erie Lackawanna, examined selected chapters. Those individuals and organizations who assisted me with illustrations deserve recognition. They include the Broome County Historical Society, Binghamton, New York; John F. Humiston, Olympia Fields, Illinois; David McKay, Cleveland, Ohio; Dorothy Maxwell, St. Louis, Missouri; Bob Pennisi of Railroad Avenue Enterprises, Flanders, New Jersey; Perry Shoemaker, Tampa, Florida; Charles Willer, Fort Wayne, Indiana; and Harry Zilli for Erie Lackawanna Inc. The history department's former secretary, Edie Richeson, typed portions of the early chapters with skill and dispatch; she also helped me to solve the mysteries of my new personal computer. And once again my wife, Martha Farrington Grant, proved to be my best copy editor and critic. This is *our* twelfth book; I hope more will come.

H.R.G.

CONTENTS

1 Weary Erie, 1832–1937   1

2 Bankruptcy, Reorganization, and War, 1938–1945   20

3 Postwar Railroading, 1946–1957   40

4 Merger, 1958–1960   75

5 Enter the Erie-Lackawanna Railroad, 1961–1962   101

6 The William White Revival, 1963–1967   123

7 Dereco, 1968–1972   155

8 "Erie Lack-of-Money" and the Coming of Conrail, 1973–1976   178

9 The Estate, 1977–1992   210

Notes 231
Selected Books 271
Index 277

MAPS

1. Proposed Merger, 1920's   xiv–xv

2. Delaware, Lackawanna and Western Railroad   xvi–xvii

3. Erie Railroad Suburban Lines   xviii–xix

4. Erie Lackawanna Railroad, 1974   xx–xxi

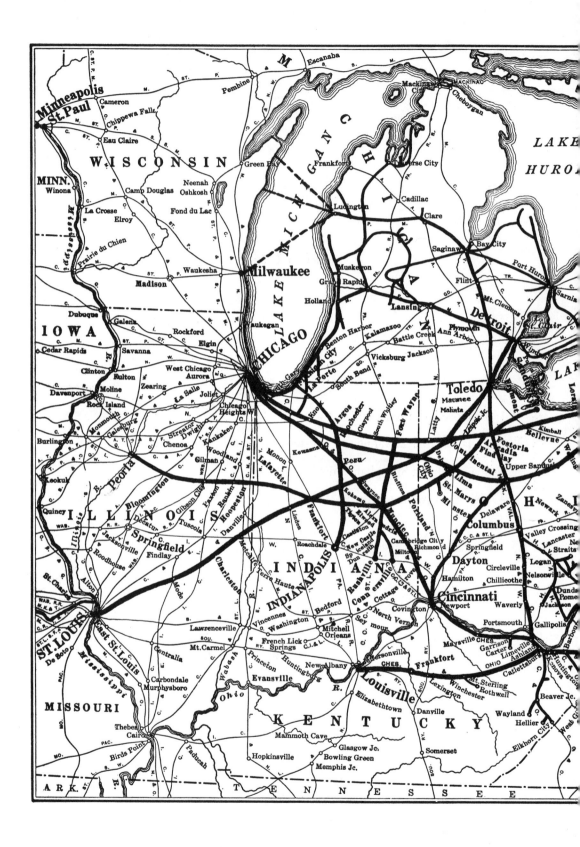

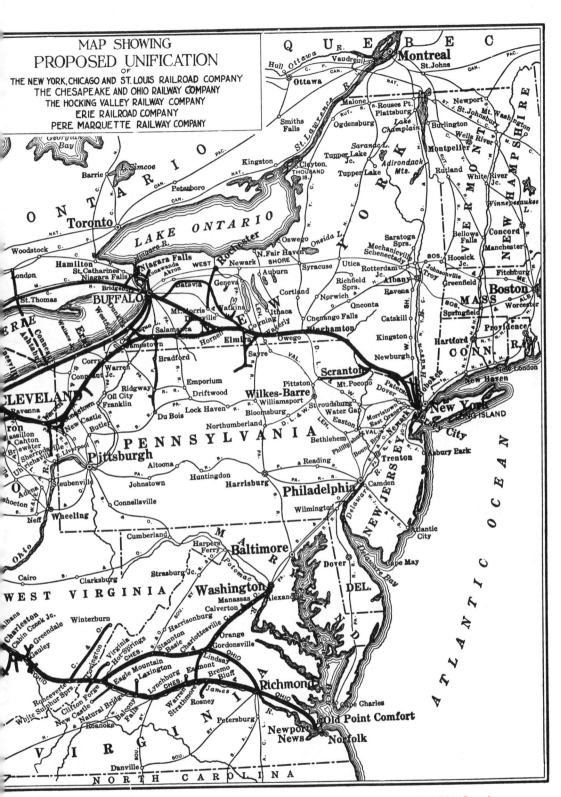

Map 1. Proposed merger, 1920's. In the mid-1920's Cleveland railroad titans O. P. Van Sweringen and M. J. Van Sweringen expected to merge the Erie Railroad with their other controlled properties. Although they failed because of shareholder and regulatory opposition, the brothers retained financial hold over these carriers for another decade. Had the Erie joined the super-railroad depicted on this map, published in 1925, its history would have been dramatically altered. (Erie Lackawanna Inc.)

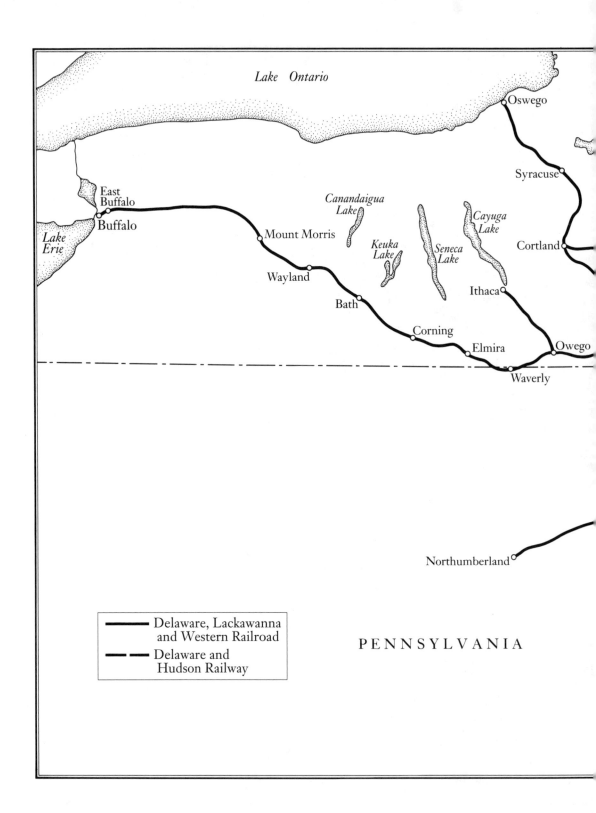

Lake Ontario

Oswego

Syracuse

East
Buffalo

Buffalo

Lake
Erie

Mount Morris

Canandaigua
Lake

Keuka
Lake

Seneca
Lake

Cayuga
Lake

Cortland

Wayland

Bath

Ithaca

Corning

Elmira

Owego

Waverly

Northumberland

Delaware, Lackawanna
and Western Railroad

Delaware and
Hudson Railway

PENNSYLVANIA

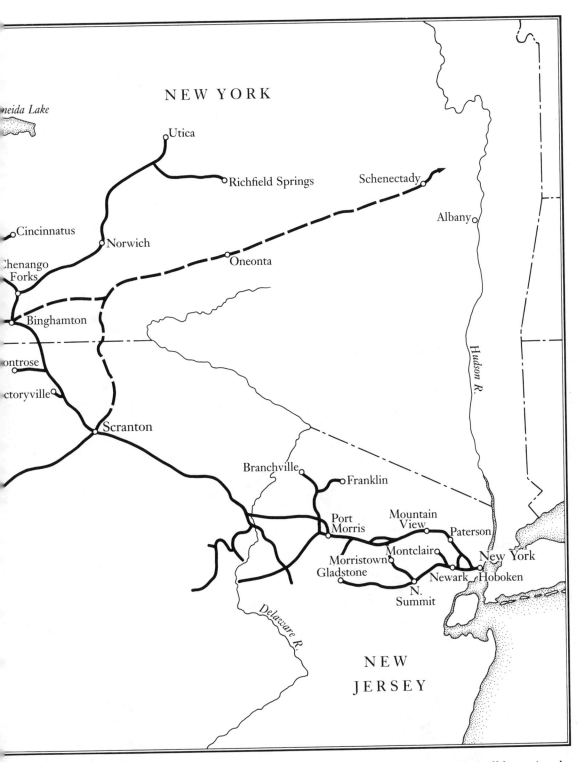

Map 2. Delaware, Lackawanna and Western Railroad. Although chiefly a New York–Buffalo carrier, the DL&W operated an impressive network of commuter/feeder lines in northern New Jersey and several strategic branches in New York and Pennsylvania. This simplified map shows how the Lackawanna tapped Pennsylvania's coal fields. (Erie Lackawanna Inc.)

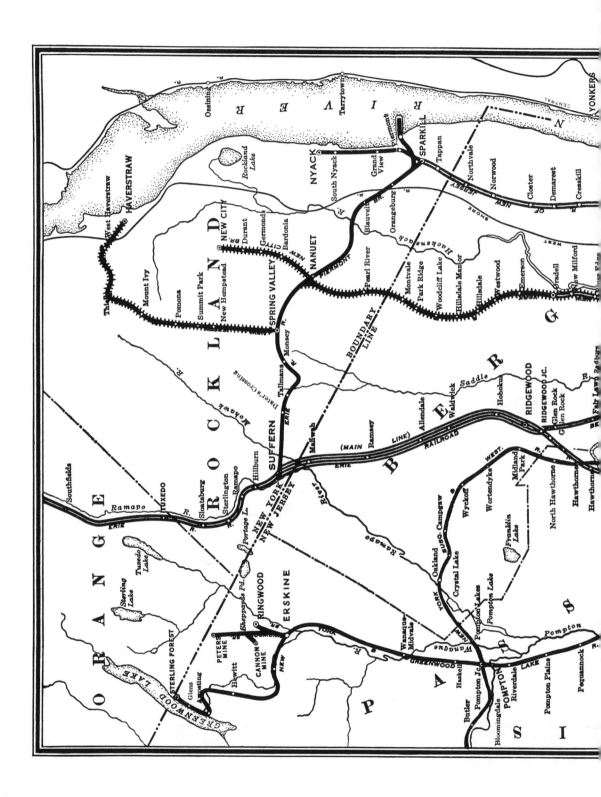

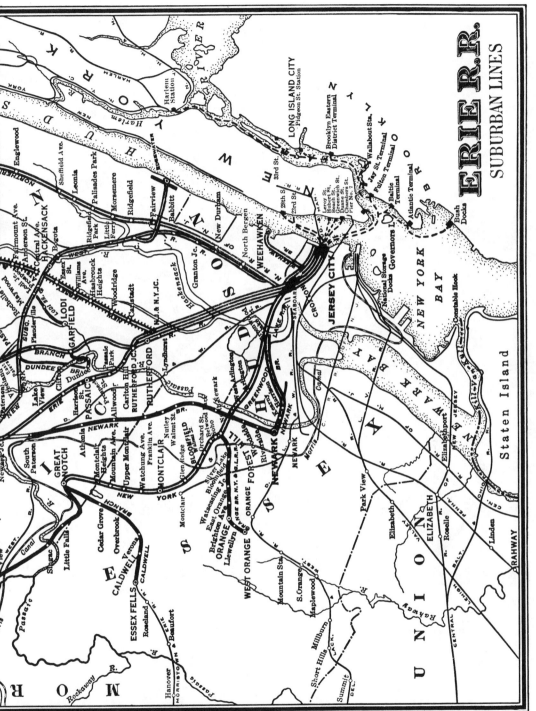

Map 3. Erie Railroad suburban lines. By the late 1920's the Erie Railroad had cobbled together an extensive network of lines in the metropolitan New York City area. This system included both wholly owned and leased properties for freight, passenger, and commuter service. This modified map does not show the New York, Susquehanna & Western, which left the orbit of the reorganized Erie in 1941. (Erie Lackawanna Inc.)

Erie Lackawanna
Railway Company

Passenger and Freight
Freight Only
Trackage Rights

The Friendly Service Route

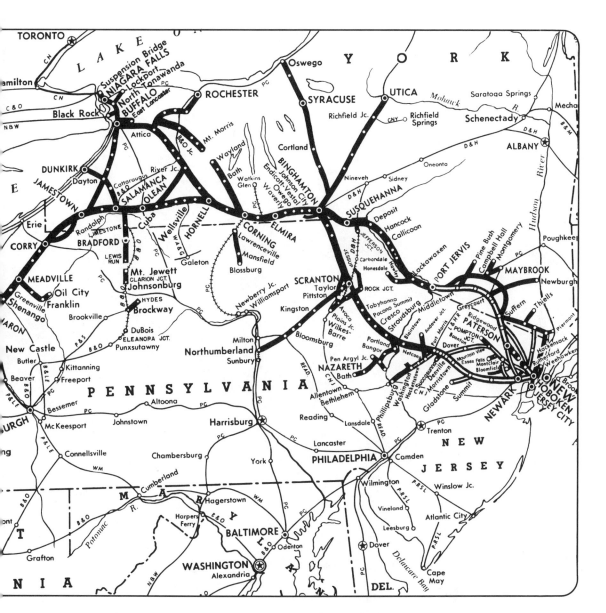

Map 4. Erie Lackawanna Railroad, 1974. On the eve of Conrail, the Erie Lackawanna operated mostly main lines between its principal terminals of Hoboken and Jersey City, New Jersey, and Chicago, Illinois. Unlike many major railroads the Erie was not burdened with a large number of low-density branch lines. Its several appendages handled mostly coal and other bulk commodities by the time this map was issued. (Erie Lackawanna Inc.)

ERIE LACKAWANNA

Death of an American Railroad, 1938–1992

WEARY ERIE,
1832–1937

THE ERIE RAILROAD had an uncommon past, claiming, in its formative years, several distinctions. It was briefly America's longest rail artery. Instead of being a gradual assemblage of little roads, it was intelligently envisioned from the start by promoters as a single system; they built it "with a view to through traffic." Under the corporate banner of the New-York & Erie Railway, chartered in April 1832, the company held its groundbreaking ceremonies in November 1835, but did not open its initial stretch of track until 1841. After several additional interruptions because of inadequate funding, its backers finally completed a 447-mile route between "the Ocean and the Lakes" a decade later. This pioneer carrier linked the New York communities of Piermont, on the Hudson River about 25 miles north of New York City, and Dunkirk on Lake Erie.[1]

This new long-distance road offered much to the public. It dramatically improved transportation to large sections of the Empire state that had failed to benefit directly from the opening of the more northerly Erie Canal in 1825. This meant in part that much of the territory's economy quickly began to base itself on cash, not barter. The road also strengthened New York City's control of internal commerce by being "the easy and quick thoroughfare for the trade and travel of the East and West." This helped Gotham to become the continent's most populous urban center and meant secondary places for longtime rivals Baltimore, Boston, and Philadelphia. Most New Yorkers agreed that a viable network of canals, improved natural waterways, and railroads was the sine qua non for a prosperous market economy.[2]

The finishing of the New-York & Erie in 1851 was a joyous occasion. "On the 22d of April, the first Train of cars, containing the officers of the road, passed over the line from Piermont to Dunkirk," proudly noted the annual *Report of the Directors for 1851*, "and on the 15th of May, the event was celebrated at the latter place, honored by the attendance of the President of the United States [Millard Fillmore], and a portion of his Cabinet, and a large number of other distinguished guests." One dignitary, Daniel Webster, toured the line in an odd way: the elder statesman took advantage of delightful weather and his desire "to better see and admire the scenery along the route" by riding on a rocking chair placed on a flatcar. Because the completion of this "iron highway" was worthy of a grand celebration, railroad brass permitted Webster's peculiar request. The Erie claimed to be the longest railway in the world and readily accepted the accolade of New York City's aldermen as "The Work of the Age." Even 35 years later the company reminded readers of its public timetables that "at the time it was constructed it was the most stupendous engineering feat ever attempted in America." The road's breathtaking and strikingly beautiful Starrucca Viaduct, near Susquehanna, Pennsylvania, composed of 100-foot-high bluestone arches, testified to this statement.[3]

The railroad also extolled its distinctive broad or "Erie Gauge," the impressive six feet between its iron rails rather than what emerged as the standard width of four feet eight and one-half inches. Influenced by the wide-gauge (7′¼″) Great Western Railway of England, the Erie thought that a broad width held several advantages. "These dimensions admit of wider and more commodious cars being used with safety, than can be adopted for roads of the ordinary width," explained company president Eleazar Lord in February 1841. Lord and his associates concluded that this larger rolling stock, with its greater overall carrying capacity, would increase operating efficiency; larger cargoes meant fewer trains and employees. They also believed that an odd gauge would prevent diversion of freight shipments to connecting standard-gauge lines and would insure the Erie's hold on trans–New York rail traffic. Public officials especially liked the wide gauge because it would not permit the Erie to "mate" with other lines beyond the borders of the state. If other roads of Erie's width reached the company's main stem, the established company might reasonably expect to control the interchange traffic.[4]

Erie personnel refrained from commenting much on a more bizarre aspect of the road's construction. When the company pushed westward through New York's "Southern Tier" of counties, it built more than a hundred miles of wooden pilings upon which it planned to install track. This "railroad-on-stilts" scheme, not unknown to the railway world during its demonstration period, seemed to offer advantages over a graded roadbed. Argued an adviser in January 1840: "[A piled roadway] . . . is not liable to de-

Locomotive No. 144, in Susquehanna, Pennsylvania, in 1862, shows the broad gauge of the Erie. The company retained its unusual width until the early 1880's. (Grant)

rangement by frosts; it is not liable to be obstructed by snow; it is free from dangers of a graded road in consequence of the washing of the banks by flood and rains, and settling when set up in soft bottom, thereby requiring constant expense to adjust the road and replace the earth materials." Enthusiasts suggested that "the interest on the money saved by building a pile road instead of a graded road will renew the piles, if necessary, every five years." Sensitive to political forces, Erie leaders felt that their sputtering project might be speeded to completion by employing stilts, and that those local suppliers of timber and their neighbors might become more supportive; after all, some residents of the Southern Tier viewed the railroad as of benefit principally to citizens of New York City and its environs.[5]

The piling strategy failed miserably, however, as construction difficulties increased costs; the Erie spent about $1 million on this ill-fated endeavor. Officials finally conceded that a graded roadbed was the practical alternative. When the line eventually opened in 1851, it cost several times the original estimate; mile after mile of rotting oak posts understandably contributed to this overrun. "For many years after the railroad was competed," observed Edward Harold Mott, the Erie's first chronicler, "long rows of these piles could be seen, . . . mournful monuments to misdirected effort in furthering a worthy cause."[6]

Although the stilt fiasco suggested unconventional thinking by the management, more accurately it predicted the Erie's innovative bent, a company hallmark. Early on the road showed a remarkable knack for being the "railroad of firsts." For example, the Erie gained much positive notoriety when in September 1851 its resourceful general superintendent, Charles Minot, conceived the idea of using the newly perfected magnetic telegraph for traffic control. Soon thereafter Minot placed a dispatcher with access to telegraphic communications in charge of train operations for each division, something that quickly became common railroad practice. The proclivity to innovate probably resulted from the company's often woebegone condition. "The Erie needed to be forward looking if it wished to survive as a company," remarked an official in the mid-1890's. "You must use your wits when you are poor."[7]

This different railroad also had a dark side, and it involved much more than funds wasted on wooden pilings. The building process took nearly a generation, in part because self-serving politicians, who made possible $3 million worth of state loans, forced the road to push through the rugged and sparsely settled Southern Tier. The railroad's largest on-line community, Elmira, had a population of only several thousand. These lawmakers hoped to please voters and spur the region's economic development, and they and their constituents wished to match the advantages other New Yorkers received from the expenditures of public funds on the Erie Canal. The company, moreover, lacked direct entrée to the burgeoning cities of New York and Buffalo and skirted the traffic centers of northern Pennsylvania, thus significantly weakening its earning capabilities. The road's terminals were dreadful: the village of Piermont abutted a desolate marsh and Dunkirk, another hamlet, lacked a developed harbor. Admittedly, the Erie corrected its mistake of an eastern terminus in the boondocks by piecing together a line into northern New Jersey opposite Manhattan Island. "[Passenger] trains now run without change of cars between Jersey City and Dunkirk," the company happily noted in November 1853. Yet there was still some truth to the popular adage that "the Erie ran from Nowhere-in-Particular to Nowhere-at-All." Everyone agreed that the railroad had less than ideal geographical positioning.[8]

The property was hardly a model for emulation. In the 1850's its spindly line was in such wretched shape that it "became notorious for the insecurity of travel upon it." The Erie's virtual physical collapse gave way to financial failure in 1859, the first of five bankruptcies. Further, the great promise of its subsequent reorganization, brisk oil traffic from the newly developed fields in northwestern Pennsylvania via the broad-gauge Atlantic & Great Western Railway, and record Civil War–era business proved to be a cruel mirage.[9]

The Erie Railway, its second corporate name, soon became the "Scarlet

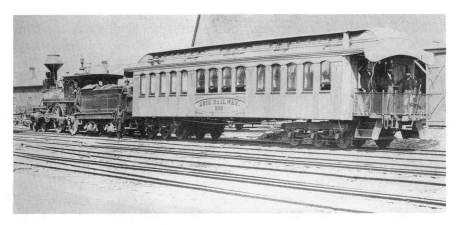

An Erie Railway office car and locomotive pause along the road during the late 1860's. The bearded man standing on the right of the car platform is probably Jay Gould. (Grant)

Woman of Wall Street." This image forever haunted the firm; indeed, its reputation became so sullied that what Credit Mobilier did to the Union Pacific and what Jay Cooke & Company did to the Northern Pacific were not as bad in comparison. The troubles began when a bevy of personalities—what iconoclast Ambrose Bierce would call "railrogues"—entered the picture. Unscrupulous speculator Daniel Drew, "the leading brigand of the Wall Street pirates," discovered the Erie and cleverly manipulated its stock to his advantage. Then, in 1867, a three-way battle erupted for control of the property, with interests represented by Drew; by John Eldridge of the mostly "paper" Boston, Hartford & Erie; and by "Commodore" Cornelius Vanderbilt of the New York Central. Two other financiers then joined the fray: the creative Jay Gould and the flamboyant Jim Fisk. When the smoke cleared, Vanderbilt had lost, although subsequent negotiations between Drew, Eldridge, and Vanderbilt produced a satisfactory compromise agreement. "Having scraped the oyster clean," observed historian Maury Klein, "the participants were content to toss the empty shell to Gould and Fisk."[10]

A silver lining of sorts came with the "Erie War." The able Jay Gould, the epitome of American get-up-and-go, took charge, and he immediately sought to rehabilitate the road rather than destroy it. Notwithstanding the company's poor overall condition and its heavy burden of fixed charges—the conflict alone cost more than $9 million—Gould's guidance made it a better property.[11]

Jay Gould, however, was no magician, and the Erie failed to emerge as a powerful concern. Most of all, he could not expand permanently the company's sphere of influence into the Old Northwest and beyond. But he tried mightily. Gould's efforts to buy or lease the Cleveland & Pittsburgh; the Columbus, Chicago & Indiana Central; the Pittsburgh, Fort Wayne and Chicago; and the Lake Shore turned out badly. The Erie's ever more powerful and aggressive rivals won the prizes: Pennsylvania took the former three and New York Central got the latter. Only briefly did Erie control the Atlantic & Great Western, its important interchange partner at Salamanca, New York. Gould was right when he said (perhaps apocryphally), "There will be icicles in hell when Erie common pays a dividend!" Gould did not have enough time to work wonders; his enemies ousted him from the presidency soon after colleague Jim Fisk died at the hands of his mistress's lover in early 1872.[12]

Much of the decade of the 1870's proved to be troublesome for the company. It limped along under ineffectual leadership until its second bankruptcy in the wake of the Panic of 1873. Yet the Erie bravely put on a good public face. An advertisement, typical of the time, called "Why Travel By the Erie?" suggested two compelling reasons: "Because it daily runs Four First-Class Express Trains through, without change, between New York, Cincinnati, Cleveland, Dunkirk, . . . in direct connection with all Eastern and Western Lines[, and] Because its Passenger Coaches, being of the broad-gauge pattern, and over a foot wider than those in use on competing lines, afford the most commodious and pleasant means of transit to and from the seaboard." While the Erie had expanded only modestly beyond its original core, namely branches to Buffalo and Rochester, New York, it benefited from physical connections with the broad-gauge Atlantic & Great Western and Ohio & Mississippi railroads for Cleveland, Cincinnati, Dayton, and St. Louis.[13]

A better day seemed to have dawned for the Erie by the late 1870's; reorganization in 1878 as the New York, Lake Erie & Western Railroad boded well for the struggling road. Modernization of the rail and rolling stock, standardization of gauge and creation of an expanded, albeit patchwork, system that included a 998-mile main line from Jersey City, New Jersey, to Chicago, Illinois (much of which was leased, including the long-desired Atlantic & Great Western) and important coal-carrying appendages in Pennsylvania highlighted the capable administrations of Hugh Jewett (1874–84) and John King (1884–94). In fact, the Erie's new artery into Chicago, opened in 1883 by its subsidiary, the Chicago & Atlantic Railway, between Marion, Ohio, and Hammond, Indiana, featured "airline" qualities. It is likely that this 250-mile extension could claim to be the best-engineered right-of-way between Ohio and Illinois.[14]

But the Erie stumbled again. When the deadly Panic of 1893 made a shambles of American business, it sent the company into a third bankruptcy. The Erie, though, had plenty of company, including the Santa Fe, the Union Pacific, and a host of eastern carriers. Two years later, in 1895, the New York, Lake Erie & Western became the Erie Railroad Company. The reorganized property, however, lacked a financial structure that would have enhanced its chances of avoiding future problems. Bonded debt skyrocketed from nearly $79 million to more than $238 million. This meant a goodly increase in annual interest payments, amounting to more than $8 million. No wonder Edward Harold Mott asked in 1899, "Can the Erie earn this appalling sum? Can it pay this terrible penalty that its misguided past has doomed it to—and live?" A capital structure too heavy on debt forever plagued the road.[15]

Still, the Erie once more entered an optimistic phase. Now part of one of several strong "communities of interest" backed by powerful investment bankers, the Erie profited from being a "Morgan property." The mighty house of J. P. Morgan & Company, for one thing, sought unity among the anthracite roads, and specifically controlled the Erie and the Lehigh Valley. Although the 2,166-mile Erie suffered from a complex and restrictive financial structure and faced keen competition from the New York Central on the north, from the Pennsylvania on the south, and encountered a more vigorous Baltimore & Ohio in its western territory, ever-increasing freight and passenger business as well as good leadership augured well for the future. Being largely free from unreasonably restrictive government or labor-union interference helped, too. Of course, the vibrant national economy after 1897 did much to aid the Erie. Wrote an official in 1900, "The Erie is filling her great trains with goods and her passenger cars with people for everything in the regions of the East and the Middle-West is on the move." In 1895 the Erie hauled 11,402,000 tons of freight and 7,456,000 passengers; ten years later the figures swelled to 31,561,000 and 20,755,000 respectively. Freight revenues surged from $11,843,000 to $32,181,000 and passenger income rose from $2,907,000 to $8,397,000. Net earnings and income from other sources, mostly from company-owned coal mines in Pennsylvania, paid fixed charges and left a regular surplus.[16]

By the late 1890's the Erie showed greater strength as a hauler of coal and merchandise. It unquestionably had established itself as an important carrier of the former. The company's 1900 annual report indicated that the railroad transported more than 12.7 million tons of "black diamonds," and this considerable volume represented about half of its total freight tonnage. The Erie's through-freight trains moved more shipments between Chicago and Jersey City, although the road could not claim to operate a premier freight artery until later in the twentieth century. "Prior to 1902," concluded the *Railway Age Gazette* in 1916, "shippers in Chicago were hardly aware that the Erie was a competing railroad with the other trunk lines." Yet to bolster its competitive stance, the company operated a fleet of tugs and car floats across the Hudson River to serve customers on Manhattan Island and in the Bronx and Brooklyn. It also dispatched "time freights," and they carried high-revenue cargoes such as perishable merchandise from the West and Midwest destined for New York markets.[17]

Erie passenger operations also lacked great distinction. Nevertheless, the company attempted to accommodate patrons. This occurred partly because management recognized the marquee value of such service. Since most individuals had contact with the road as travelers, good passenger service might create good will, which could then be converted into freight business. The Erie's rolling stock represented this commitment to good public relations. *The Vestibuled Limited*, the road's most luxurious train, contained by the 1890's "Smoking Car, Day Car, Pullman Cars. . . . Meals in Dining Car," equipment that mostly equaled those used by competitors. Unlike early long-distance trains that consisted of only a few cars, "the regular through passenger trains on the Erie to-day (1898) average seven cars, and seventeen cars in a train are not unusual." While these Erie trains resembled those of other eastern roads, they set no speed records. By way of illustration, the *Official Railway Guide* for June 1898 indicated that the best Erie "varnish" between New York and Chicago took three to eight hours longer than name-trains on the New York Central and Pennsylvania systems. Although the public often clamored for speed, some lauded the company for its refusal to practice "ballast scorching." "While their direct competitors have been engaged in a reckless attempt to make speed at all hazards," editorialized the *Phoenixville* (Pennsylvania) *Republican*, "the Erie has apparently cared more for the safety of the passengers. . . . We don't remember that they have had any wrecks of serious consequence in many years." With slower service, Erie's managers wisely decided to focus on short-haul traffic. "The policy of your officers for some time past," related the *Annual Report for 1898*, "has been to encourage and build up the local passenger business." Whether attracting through or local riders to its leisurely runs, the Erie rightly ballyhooed the spectacular scenery along its original core; this self-proclaimed "Landscape Route of America" offered a smorgasbord of natural delights.[18]

As the twentieth century began, an unusually capable president, Frederick Underwood, took charge of the Erie. An experienced railroader who had worked his way through the operating ranks of the Chicago, Milwaukee & St. Paul, Soo Line, and Baltimore & Ohio railroads between 1870 and 1901, "He is a graduate of the University of Hard Knocks," observed writer-philosopher Elbert Hubbard, "a product of storm and stress, of difficulty, trial, hardship, high endeavor and noble achievement." James J. Hill, the "Empire Builder," had more specific thoughts about Underwood several years before he joined the Erie. "Mr. Underwood in all matters pertaining to the operation of a railway, rolling stock, equipment, and its economical use and maintenance, is better informed than most railway men in the country. In matters of construction, building and doing heavy work, he has had large experience and has profited by it so as to bring the cost of his work much below the ordinary prices paid by railways." Concluded the founder of the Great Northern, "You will find him perfectly straight-forward in speech and manner and in every way a manly man."[19]

The Erie Railroad needed a "manly man," and Frederick Underwood did yeoman service for the company during much of his 26-year tenure as president. He led the road's participation in the Age of Reconstruction, which occurred on a colossal scale after 1900, when most carriers rebuilt their principal rail lines and facilities. Convinced that a more competitive and efficient plant would be the Erie's salvation, Underwood oversaw an impressive list of betterments, ranging from completing the double-tracking of most of the main line to replacing a longtime traffic bottleneck west of the Jersey City terminal, the Bergen Hill Tunnel, with a mile-long cut. His desire to offer dependable service at low cost also resulted in the purchase of some of the world's largest and most powerful steam locomotives, Mallet-type 0-8-8-0's and 2-8-8-2's, and innovative internal-combustion passenger equipment. The Erie president was so proud of the renaissance that he endorsed publication of a documentary pamphlet, *Erie Railroad: Showing Changes from 1901 to 1914, Inclusive.* This work extolled recent accomplishments; one sample reads: "Bridges: Since 1901, the carrying capacity of Erie Railroad bridges has been increased 31%, and 814 new Main Line bridges have been erected; [and] Automatic Block Signals: In 1901, there were no automatic block signals on the Erie Railroad; in 1914, there are 1,452.2 miles of track so equipped." The old wheeze, "I want to go to Chicago the worst way." "Take the Erie!," seemed less apropos than ever, as did composer Irving Berlin's slight "He may be as slow as the Erie," in his hit song "You'd Be Surprised." Underwood concluded correctly that starving the property into prosperity was impossible.[20]

The job of president challenged Underwood continually. Financial matters taxed his skills, and yet he extinguished some potentially fatal fires. During the brief but sobering Panic of 1907 the Erie required a cash infusion of $5,500,000 to retire short-term notes due to mature in early 1908. Underwood grasped the severity of the situation and marshaled the necessary support to pay off the bonds, but it was difficult. J. P. Morgan & Company, the Erie's principal financial partner since the 1895 restructuring, refused to lend another dime and so Underwood turned elsewhere. He convinced the railroader, banker, and board member Edward H. Harriman to give assistance. With the help of another loyal board member, financier George F. Baker, they averted a fourth bankruptcy. The resourceful Underwood also negotiated another financial rescue during World War I when a dramatic increase in wages and material costs left the Erie's treasury nearly empty. Finding that the company could not market short-term collateral notes, Underwood con-

Crew members of an Erie Railroad passenger train in West Orange, New Jersey, about 1915, pose with their vintage locomotive and service-worn wooden coaches. (Erie Lackawanna Inc.)

vinced Elbert Gary, head of United States Steel Corporation and a former Erie director, to have his firm provide a $5 million bridge loan. The Erie weathered the crisis and subsequently repaid its benefactor with interest.[21]

Even though Underwood successfully coped with Erie's money woes, the railroad's financial structure remained troublesome. The company's flock of mortgages severely limited its borrowing power. This was especially critical in the early 1920's, when competitors spent heavily on modernization following the period of federalization between 1917 and 1920. And the Erie needed more than most to upgrade its property, for the government had returned it in a "battered" condition.[22]

The Erie's financial problems appeared to be solvable. In a memorandum to Underwood shortly before the president's retirement, New York banker Henry S. Sturgis shrewdly assessed the road's financial picture and offered a blueprint for a better tomorrow. He correctly indicated that the Erie was not a ramshackle property, like the Chicago, Rock Island & Pacific or the Denver & Rio Grande Western ("Dangerous & Rapidly Getting Worse!"), but that it needed financial rehabilitation. "The Erie Railroad traverses a rich territory, it commands a large tonnage which it carries economically, its property and equipment are in good shape, and it owns valuable terminals. In other words, the Erie has everything which goes to make up a good railroad, except sound credit—the ability to finance a fair proportion of its needed additions and betterments at a fair rate of interest." Added Sturgis, "Unless some effort is made to overcome this obstacle, the Erie will be forced to continue to devote all its surplus after charges to property improvements and to the rehabilitation of its cash position, or in any consolidation to accept a price which will be lower than is justified by its strategic position, property values, and earning power."[23]

The Sturgis scheme focused on restructuring Erie's numerous bond issues, which had been superimposed one upon another for decades. These bonds, with one exception, lacked provisions for refinancing at lower rates of interest. Sturgis thought the finance and executive committees of the railroad, and large investors too, would readily embrace his proposal. "[It would] build a foundation under the capital structure which would raise the value of all Erie securities . . . [and] it would discharge all short term debt and put the treasury in easy cash position." But he was wrong; no one showed much enthusiasm. The economy of the twenties was booming and most investors seemed content with the status quo. Also by this time, a new financial force had entered Erie's world. Two prim and reserved bachelor brothers from Cleveland, Ohio—Oris Paxton Van Sweringen and Mantis James Van Sweringen—had acquired a substantial interest in the company. (To the Van Sweringens' associates they were "O.P." and "M.J."—always in that order—or simply "the Vans.") For more than a decade the Erie would be part of the brothers' remarkable railroad empire.[24]

<hr/>

The Vans' interest in the "Old Reliable," as they called the Erie, began less than a decade after they entered railroading. These rags-to-riches Ohioans had already prospered in Cleveland-area real-estate ventures when, in 1916, they acquired the lackluster though strategic New York, Chicago & St. Louis Railroad. The majestic New York Central controlled this 523-mile route, universally called the "Nickel Plate Road," which paralleled its main line from Buffalo to Chicago. But because of the federal government's threat of antitrust action under the Clayton Act of 1914 and the friendship between New York Central president A. H. Smith and the Vans, the Central gladly allowed the Nickel Plate to become the first component of the brothers' future rail domain.[25]

Although the Vans sought only several miles of the Nickel Plate as access into downtown Cleveland for an electric railway from their planned community of Shaker Heights, they nevertheless acted to make their acquisition profitable. They borrowed heavily and their holding company, Nickel Plate Securities Corporation, became highly leveraged. Still, the brothers' financial strategy succeeded. They raised sufficient capital to modernize the property and they hired, at Smith's suggestion, an able up-from-the-ranks railroader, John H. Bernet, to guide the road. By the early 1920's this quiet, firm-jawed man had molded the Nickel Plate into an efficient and prosperous carrier. Some commentators called Bernet "the Miracle Man," and rightfully so.[26]

The flourishing Nickel Plate whetted the Vans' appetite for more railroads and made it possible for them to push ahead with acquisitions. With Interstate Commerce Commission (ICC) approval in 1923, the Vans merged the Nickel Plate with two adjoining properties, the Toledo, St. Louis & Western ("Clover Leaf Route") and the smaller and less attractive Lake Erie & Western ("Leave Early & Walk"), creating a 1,700-mile system and the only important formalized railroad merger of the twenties. The brothers then purchased from Henry E. Huntington and his associates controlling interest in the Chesapeake & Ohio (C&O), a thriving 2,100-mile-long coal-hauler. Next they acquired a major position in the 2,250-mile Pere Marquette, a mostly Michigan road with a prime Chicago connection, and then bought heavily into the Erie. By the mid-1920's they controlled more than 9,000 miles of rail line. Their holdings stretched from the Atlantic ports of Jersey City and Hampton Roads to the primary gateways of Chicago and St. Louis, the rail crossroads of America, and served scores of industrial centers as well as the expanding bituminous coal fields of the central Appalachians. The Vans had assembled the fourth largest eastern trunk network and challenged the long-established Baltimore & Ohio, New York Central, and Pennsylvania systems.[27]

Although the Erie lacked the luster of a Chesapeake & Ohio or even a Pere Marquette, its location made it attractive to the Vans. The Old Reliable interchanged with the Chesapeake & Ohio, Nickel Plate, and Pere Marquette, and the Erie (via the Nickel Plate at Buffalo) provided a direct eastern connection for New York and New England traffic. There was another important consideration; "No other railroad into . . . Chicago has as easy grades as [the] . . . Erie route," observed railroad executive and consultant John W. Barriger III years later. "In fact these favorable physical characteristics were among the reasons why the Van Sweringen brothers acquired control of the Erie for C&O back in the 1920's." And he added, "After that had been accomplished, C&O's large coal traffic moving into the Chicago gateway was diverted from interchange with Nickle [sic] Plate at Fostoria, Ohio, to Marion and the Erie."[28]

The Vans' timing for bringing together the several trunk roads was superb. The decade of the 1920's was a period of business consolidation, and not since the turn of the century had political, economic, and social factors created an atmosphere so exhilarating to promoters of vast enterprises. In the case of railroads, Congress instructed the Interstate Commerce Commission in the Transportation Act of 1920 to prepare a unification plan that would eventually form a limited number of competitive systems of approximately equal financial strength. The scheme never materialized, but Congressional intent unmistakably favored massive system-building.

The transactions of the Vans became progressively complex as they built their empire. They grasped the economic forces at work and controlled their railroads largely through holding companies rather than by mergers. The brothers dissolved the Nickel Plate Securities Corporation in 1924; its original purpose had been served, and they transferred its assets to other companies created to facilitate expansion of their investments. Among these firms was the Vaness Company, incorporated in 1922, the affiliate that later acquired Erie securities. The Vans embraced this holding-company strategy for several reasons. Such business arrangements gave them control in an extremely leveraged fashion, yet they could attract investors through financial inducements: the Vans held the majority of the voting common stock while others owned nonvoting preferred shares with attractive fixed dividends. The brothers also could assemble rail carriers with these mechanisms without approval from the Interstate Commerce Commission. Similarly, domination of a rail system through holding companies meant that they might later present a formal merger application to regulators as a fait accompli.[29]

In the spring of 1925, the Vans believed it auspicious to consolidate their affiliated properties. In order to achieve that objective, they required permission from the Interstate Commerce Commission. They also needed to make additional stock purchases to strengthen their position. The brothers asked the ICC to allow them to merge the Chesapeake & Ohio, Erie, Nickel Plate, and Pere Marquette, but a year later the Commission said no. While the Vans' proposal appeared to be in the public interest, financial considerations, most of all complaints from C&O minority stockholders who fervently maintained that their equity in a strong road would be diluted by the weaker carriers, especially the Erie, led to the negative decision. The Vans continued, however, to use holding companies to circumvent the ICC, to generate additional capital, and to make further rail acquisitions.[30]

Undaunted by the earlier Commission decision, the Vans returned to that body in February 1928, and asked to merge the Chesapeake & Ohio with the Erie and Pere Marquette. But fifteen months later the ICC authorized only a C&O–Pere Marquette union. Once again concern about the financial condition of the Erie precluded a full merger. Frustrated, but still anxious to expand their empire, the Vans formed a master holding company, the Alleghany Corporation, in January 1929. This firm immediately absorbed all of the brothers' railroad assets, providing them with personal control while its capital came from nonvoting preferred stock, bonds, and notes.[31]

By 1927 Erie management reflected the Vans' financial involvement. The year began with retirement of 77-year-old Frederick Underwood. The Vans put in "the old man's place" John J. Bernet. While an experienced and competent railroader, Underwood had grown weary and seemingly lacked the skills necessary to energize the road. On the other hand, Bernet, dynamic at 59 years of age, knew the industry well, and had the Vans' ears as well as access to their pools of capital. While at the Nickel Plate, Bernet had observed closely the Erie's strengths and weaknesses, and he believed that the latter dominated. "Bernet used to say, when first he came to [the company], that the only good thing about the Erie was its roadbed."[32]

Bernet initiated his program of reform and betterments almost immediately. After a rapid, though thorough, examination of the road's daily operations, he ordered a drastic overhaul of its bureaucracy. Management had long endorsed the so-called "regional system of control." Under this arrangement each regional district—the Erie had three—was essentially a separate railroad with a complete staff of regional officers and department heads who reported to a vice president. Bernet thought such a structure was fine for a railroad with the mileage of a Pennsylvania or the geographic scope of a Canadian Pacific, but the Erie operated mostly as a trunk artery with minimal branch line appendages. As he said, "The structure is too top-heavy and cumbersome." Bernet opted instead for the "departmental plan," a reasonable response since it functioned well on the somewhat similar Nickel Plate. The Erie retained its three operating districts, but each one was assigned a general manager instead of a vice president, who reported to the operating vice president at corporate headquarters in New York City. The general manager focused his attention solely on transportation matters. Newly created administrative positions in New York handled traffic, maintenance-of-way, and mechanical duties. The company thus abolished two vice presidents and eliminated scores of clerical personnel. Moreover, Bernet, who "was unusually good with the men," made this reorganization surprisingly popular. Restructuring led to few dismissals of officers and "practically all the important [personnel] changes were in the nature of promotions."[33]

Considerably more conspicuous to employees and the public alike was new rolling stock. In his annual report to shareholders, Bernet explained tersely: "Your Company at the beginning of the year [1927] had many units of equipment which were obsolete or could not be economically maintained." No knowledgeable observer would have disagreed. By year's end the Erie had retired nearly 9,000 units, including more than 7,000 freight cars, approximately 250 passenger cars and 367 steam locomotives. The replacements ordered were larger, heavier, and with greater carrying capacities, so fewer pieces were necessary.[34]

The most heralded acquisitions were fifty powerful and highly efficient steam locomotives. These were Berkshires, with a 2-8-4 wheel arrangement, and they soon appeared in fast through-freight service between Jersey City and Marion, Ohio. "Fewer locomotives but better ones was the credo of Bernet," observed one Bernet-era railroad official. He wisely junked "a weird lot of old teakettles." The new motive power reduced expenses and produced more competitive freight-train schedules. As the Berkshires arrived, costs per locomotive mile dropped from 95.75 cents in 1927 to 91.35 cents a year later, and average speeds rose dramatically from 11.5 mph to 16.4 mph, a 65 percent increase.[35]

Mighty road locomotives reduced freight schedules. For one thing, faster time freights from Chicago connections meant a growing Erie share of the profitable perishable traffic bound for eastern markets: carloads of fruits and vegetables from California and meat products from Midwestern packing houses "customarily were routed via Erie." The company could truthfully tell readers of its June 7, 1931, public timetable that "Manufacturers with delivery problems are taking advantage of the modern equipment of the Erie in safely and swiftly moving their wares."[36]

A symbol of the Erie's renaissance during the Bernet regime came with the introduction in June 1929 of a new passenger express, the *Erie Limited*. Originally the Jersey City–Buffalo *Southern Tier Express*, the run was extended by Bernet's order to Chicago through Jamestown, New York, and he had it completely reequipped. The flagship of the Erie passenger fleet acquired state-of-the-art steel, heavyweight cars. "A touch of luxuriousness is added," observed a writer for *Railway Age*, "by the use of carpeted aisle strips across the vestibules of the coaches, diner and Pullman cars, thus providing a completely carpeted passageway throughout the train." The *Erie Limited* operated on a convenient overnight schedule between its two terminals, and the public responded positively to "the lowest fare now available on any 25-hour train [between New York and Chicago]." Its surcharge of $4.80 was $5.20 less than the New York Central's *Twentieth Century Limited* and the Pennsylvania's *Broadway Limited*. Employees, too, admired the train. "I can't help but think that the Erie Limited made the men all along the route feel that the Erie was a less dreary place to work. It was sure good to see her speed by."[37]

The Vans felt that Bernet had performed so admirably on the Erie that in mid-1929 they sent him to head the jewel in their railway crown, the Chesapeake & Ohio. Fittingly, the brothers saw that Bernet's replacement possessed comparable skills. They placed at Erie's throttle a proven railroad officer, Charles E. Denney, whose career paralleled Bernet's. Denney had worked his way through the ranks of the New York Central before he joined the Vans' Nickel Plate in 1916. He served as Bernet's principal assistant, first on the Nickel Plate and then on the Erie. "[Denney] was bright, gregarious, a tremendous salesman and worker. . . . He surely had the right sort of stuff to be a great railroad president."[38]

Despite having the "right sort of stuff," Denney could not save the Erie from a rapid downhill slide once the Great Depression, triggered by the thundering stock-market crash of October 1929, settled over the nation. "Erie's business just went to hell," recounted a future officer. Gross revenues stood at a respectable $129,230,000 in 1929, plummeted to $90,154,000 two years later, and hit bottom at $72,086,000 in 1933. Income remained near that depressed level in 1934 and 1935. Fortunately, earnings for the Erie and most carriers rose significantly in 1936 as industrial production increased. That year the road generated revenues of $85,005,000. Then a national recession began in August of 1937, one of the worst short-term economic downtrends in history. A sudden decline in business orders, plant investment, and optimism devastated both the country and the company. Industrial production declined dramatically and the Erie's gross revenues fell sharply from $83,925,000 in 1937 to a dismal $69,509,000 a year later. "The last few months of 1937 really hit the Erie hard," recalled a former official, and it took the road down. "The company could not recover. . . . Damn, we were bankrupt again."[39]

Charles Denney and the Erie's management responded as best they could during the economic troubles of the 1930's. Money was tight and, like other business leaders, they "slashed expenditures to the bone." This meant curtailed purchases, furloughed employees, and reduced salaries. But the Erie needed to do much more. Traditional sources for cash and credit offered limited opportunities, and the company's chances for successful sales of securities were "virtually nil or less." No longer could the carrier tap the resources and skills of the Vans; their railroad empire lay in ruins and they would both be dead by 1936. Fortunately, the railroad received an infusion of cash; it borrowed heavily from the Reconstruction Finance Corporation (RFC). Launched by the federal government in January 1932, the RFC loaned money to railroads, banks, insurance companies, and industrial firms. The self-help Railroad Credit Corporation, a fund created by carriers to pool freight-rate increases granted by the ICC in the early thirties, also provided some assistance.[40]

The Denney administration did more than retrench and increase debt. It valiantly sought to boost traffic. Since the physical plant and equipment remained in good condition as result of the Bernet-era improvements, the company ballyhooed its "Fast Erie Service." "We really gave shippers fine, dependable service," remembered one official. "The Erie was a friendly road . . . , and new customers soon came to understand that fact of railroading." And he noted, "With those big Berks [Berkshire-type locomotives] on the hills east of Marion, we could wheel the tonnage over the road as well or better than our competition."[41]

One way for the Erie to fill freight cars was to improve its less-than-carload (LCL) business. Following the lead of the Chicago Great Western Railroad and several other hard-pressed carriers, the company inaugurated an expanded freight collection and delivery program on December 1, 1933. "Today a phone call to your Erie agent solves *all* your problems on less-than-carload shipments." A few years later this became a "no extra charge" service. Customers liked the Erie plan: income from LCL traffic rose most years during the remainder of the Depression.[42]

The Denney regime did not ignore the passenger sector even though it was less important, accounting for approximately 6 percent of gross operating revenues during the 1930's. The Erie's principal competitors, on the other hand, depended more heavily on passenger operations: the figure stood at about 15 percent apiece for the New York Central and Pennsylvania. Already smarting from the sting of increased automobile use and bus competition because of new bridge and tunnel construction in the New York City area and better roads generally, the Erie worked hard to attract riders, most of all on the more profitable long-distance runs. Sensible scheduling of trains especially helped to mitigate losses. "The Erie did a good job serving its on-line towns with good passenger service," remembered a former employee, "so that there was always convenient service between any two local points at decent hours." But the company needed to do more than arrange its timetables in an attractive fashion. While the *Erie Limited* continued to roar through the night between the railroad's major terminals, enjoying a loyal and steady clientele of sleeping-car patrons, coach traffic dropped noticeably on the *Limited* and on companion trains. Management tried various incentives to regain coach business. It slashed rates to special events, including the popular Century of Progress Exposition in Chicago during the summer of 1933, and promoted budget "coach luncheons" where attendants "carrying baskets containing various kinds of tasty sandwiches, pies, fruit, etc., also hot coffee, pass through the coaches at frequent intervals."[43]

And the Passenger Department vigorously promoted escorted trips over its superb steel highway. The Erie's "4-Way Tours" (Railway, Airway, Waterway, and Highway), for instance, offered opportunities for a pleasant, moderately priced six-day outing via the *Chicago Express* from New York City to Cleveland, sightseeing in the Ohio metropolis, an airplane ride to Detroit and more sightseeing, an overnight lake steamer to Buffalo, a side trip by bus to Niagara Falls, and a return to Gotham on the *Erie Limited*. As a descriptive folder proclaimed, "The Erie Railroad has succeeded in creating a spirit of camaraderie in its personally conducted parties that permits of no wall flowers." It added, "No one travels 'alone' on an Erie tour. Whether you are a youngster, oldster or an in-betweener, you are with friends." Management's response to the decline helped to halt the slide. While passenger revenues dropped 50.5 percent between 1929 and 1932, they slipped a mere 2.9 per-

Members of the Susquehanna, Pennsylvania, shops band assemble at an outing about 1920. By the early twentieth century scores of Erie employees belonged to brass bands in various division and shops towns. Largely subsidized by the company, these musical groups participated in annual competitions and provided entertainment for community events, which surely contributed to strengthening the bonds of commitment among the "Erie family." (Erie Lackawanna Inc.)

cent between 1933 and 1936. "Being aggressive prevented a major disaster in the passenger area. . . . The Denney people did a good job considering the circumstances."[44]

Hard times produced more than red ink and creative responses. These years of struggle meant sacrifices by employees, whether caused by layoffs, at times for extended periods, or by substantial salary cuts. Yet morale remained remarkably high. A good esprit de corps had existed for decades among members of "our railroad family" and there were "few chronic kickers." In 1946, Edward Hungerford, the pioneer editor of the *Erie Railroad Employee Magazine*, the railroad industry's first employee publication, and author of a well-received company history, reflected on the railroad he knew so well: "Erie was a funny old road, rather decrepit in many ways, but its patrons, after they had ceased poking fun at it, liked it. And the most of its employees adored it." One engineman echoed this perspective. "Yes, we used to call it [Erie] the 'f——old Erie,' but she was loved and I really mean that." He recalled that "The boys during the Depression often had a rough time of it and still they wanted to work for the Erie in the worst way. It was more than a job for many . . . and they had a special place in their hearts for it. I rather doubt that was the case on the [New York] Central or Pennsy." This latter observation may have been correct. The Erie was smaller and more homogeneous. Yet a strong "rah-rah" spirit existed on the neighboring Baltimore & Ohio, due largely to its employee-sensitive president, Daniel Willard, who headed that company from 1910 to 1941. Loyalty of B&O workers probably equaled or even exceeded that of those on the Erie.[45]

Through the decades strong bonds of commitment had developed at Erie, nurtured by a hardworking management and even the popular company magazine. The "Weary Erie" was blessed with a loyal work force, who toiled vigorously to keep the company running. While bankruptcy loomed, it seemed to be nothing more than another hurdle to jump.

BANKRUPTCY, REORGANIZATION, AND WAR, 1938–1945

PRESIDENT CHARLES DENNEY'S special message to the nearly 21,000 employees of the Erie Railroad in the February 1938 issue of the company's monthly magazine surprised no one: "It became necessary on January 18th for the Erie Railroad Company to file a petition under the Federal Bankruptcy Act." He explained that "the shortage of funds was primarily due to a marked decline in earnings during the latter part of 1937 and increases in expenses beyond our control. The Company was unable to borrow funds to meet its requirements." While hardly good news for the Erie's work force, court protection meant little in the day-to-day affairs of the railroad. Rather, it signified another chapter in the history of the "Weary Erie." As most employees expected, trains continued to run, payrolls were met, and the company survived.[1]

Denney's somber report aptly summarized why the Erie had tumbled into its fourth bankruptcy. In the fall of 1937 the nation slipped rapidly into the recession of 1937–38, the worst economic decline since 1933. Between October 1937 and May 1938, industrial production fell more than a third, durable goods production sank more than half, and business profits plummeted by more than three-quarters. The service territory of the Erie "took a beating," and these hard times had a crippling effect. Denney told the trade press that the company experienced a "tremendous drop of earnings" between August and December of 1937.[2]

Another reason for the company's financial woes was the unfavorable decisions made by the National Mediation Board. Reflecting the prolabor stance of the Franklin D. Roosevelt administration, this federal body ordered nationwide wage increases of five cents per hour for members of fourteen nonoperating unions, effective on August 1, 1937; two months later the Board hiked by five and one-half cents the hourly income of those who belonged to the five operating unions. This meant a 5 to 10 percent raise for most employees. These rulings cost the Erie approximately $2,700,000 annually, or about 5 percent of its yearly operating expenses.[3]

But it was a combination of interrelated decisions made by other government agencies and another railroad that landed the knockout punch. The Erie asked the Interstate Commerce Commission (ICC) in early December 1937 to approve its loan request to the Reconstruction Finance Corporation (RFC) for slightly more than $6 million. The railroad planned to use this money to pay vouchers, taxes and, most of all, interest on maturing bonds and equipment trusts. Although the Commission endorsed the loan application on December 28, it made a crucial stipulation: the Chesapeake & Ohio Railway (C&O), Erie's principal stockholder, must either guarantee payment of this loan or deposit collateral, which, taken with Erie's collateral, would satisfy the RFC. A few days earlier, however, the C&O board decided not to honor any request to underwrite loans for the Erie. The day after the ICC revealed its special requirement, the C&O board, meeting in Cleveland's Terminal Tower, reaffirmed its unwillingness to come to "Old Reliable's" aid. The board argued that "its first and most important duty to the public and to security holders is to maintain unimpaired the C.& O. resources, especially in view of the uncertainties of business conditions, and their relation to the railroad situation."[4]

Unwilling to accept defeat, Denney and his fellow Erie directors responded swiftly. While these men did not relish the Commission's demand for Chesapeake & Ohio involvement, they knew that their property desperately needed government money. At a special meeting of the Erie board held in the Midland Building in Cleveland on December 30, 1937, Denney reviewed the disturbing events of the previous weeks and won approval to ask the ICC and the Reconstruction Finance Corporation to accept the Erie's own collateral alone in lieu of any financial backing from the C&O.[5]

Denney took the Erie's case personally to Jesse H. Jones, head and guiding spirit of the Reconstruction Finance Corporation, the lender of last resort for the New Deal.[6] Denney did so with good reason. On December 31, Jones sent him a telegram in which he shared his comments from a previous message to C&O board chairman Herbert Fitzpatrick. Jones told Denney and Fitzpatrick that "I AM STRONGLY OF THE OPINION THAT THE DIRECTORS OF THE C&O WILL BE PURSUING A SHORTSIGHTED POLICY IF THEY PERMIT THE ERIE, IN WHICH ACCORDING TO MY UNDERSTANDING IT OWNS 55 PERCENT OF THE CAPITAL STOCK, TO GO INTO RECEIVERSHIP OR TRUSTEESHIP. IF THE C&O WAS NOT IN A STRONG FINANCIAL POSITION THE SITUATION MIGHT BE DIFFERENT. BUT OWNERSHIP CARRIES RESPONSIBILITY AND THE C&O THEREFORE

CANNOT DENY RESPONSIBILITY FOR THE ERIE." Since Jones planned to return by train to his office in Washington, D.C., from his home in Houston, Texas, over the New Year's weekend of January 1 and 2, 1938, Denney rushed to St. Louis to ride with the RFC chairman to Columbus, Ohio. They talked for five hours.[7]

Charles Denney realized that the results of his conference with Jesse Jones were not encouraging. The next day he received a letter from the RFC head that repeated the loan body's position. Jones told Denney (with a copy to Chesapeake & Ohio's Fitzpatrick) that the C&O held the key to Erie's financial fate. "You are advised that the RFC will make the loan for $6,006,000 upon the collateral listed in the Commission's order, and other acceptable collateral to be furnished by the Chesapeake & Ohio Railway Company having a market value of $3,000,000, or if, in the opinion of our Board, the collateral furnished by the C&O is of unquestioned value equal to $2,500,000, we will regard that as acceptable." Jones closed with these comments: "You have advised us that it will be necessary for you to know by noon tomorrow [Monday, January 3, 1938] that the loan . . . has been approved, otherwise you will be unable to pay interest due on that date. If the C&O advises us tomorrow morning that it will assist you in the manner outlined herein, we will be willing to disburse $3,000,000 of the loan on your own collateral listed in the Commission's order, and the money will be available upon execution and delivery of your note and the collateral. The balance of the loan will be available to you upon demand after deposit of the additional collateral by the Chesapeake & Ohio Railway Company."[8]

Jesse Jones did more than send board chairman Fitzpatrick a carbon copy of his message to Denney. Jones wrote a straightforward cover letter in which he reiterated his belief that the C&O should assist. "In my opinion your Board can do no greater dis-service to the railroad situation, including the systems of which your road is the principal, than to refuse help to the Erie at this time." He reminded Fitzpatrick that the Erie was not hopeless. Although the company had encountered deficits during some of the years since the Depression began, its net income for the period mostly had covered its fixed charges. Jones added that he did not foresee a crisis with Erie bonds. "[T]he only important maturities prior to 1953 are $4,616,000 New York & Erie Railroad Company Bonds due March 1, 1938, and $2,148,000 due September 1, 1939." He also repeated what Denney had told him on the train: "Because of the position these bonds occupy in the road's debt structure, there should be no difficulty in extending them."[9]

President Denney and the Erie board seized the initiative. Hoping that Jones's arguments would help, Denney and Erie board chairman Charles L. Bradley met with C&O's board on the morning of Monday, January 3. They explained once more the Erie's case and asked for collateralization of the loan. The directors refused. That afternoon the Erie defaulted on $1,800,000 in interest payments for six bond issues and the New York Stock Exchange suspended trading in the company's securities.[10]

Discouraged, but determined to save the Erie from bankruptcy, Denney left Cleveland by train late Monday for the nation's capital. The next day he met with Jesse Jones and representatives of the Interstate Commerce Commission. Jones and the ICC remained adamant concerning the additional collateral. Denney's trip to Washington did focus national attention on both Erie's plight and the role of the Chesapeake & Ohio. Jones grabbed this opportunity to blast the parent company publicly. "[I]t is well known that the Chesapeake & Ohio is easily able to assist the Erie in this small way, and its failure to do so brings into serious question its right to own control of the road." Jones recalled "Letting the Erie Sink" years later in his memoirs. "In 1937 . . . the C. & O. declared cash dividends of $29,000,000 and also a 4 per cent preferred stock dividend of $15,000,000. Probably if the directors had been less interested in fattening the Alleghany Corporation, the holding company which received a large part of the road's dividends, their course with the Erie might have been different."[11]

Refusal by the Interstate Commerce Commission and the Reconstruction Finance Corporation to alter their requirements for the $6,006,000 loan and the Chesapeake & Ohio's determination "to refuse this baby a milk bottle" led to an emergency meeting of the Erie board on January 18. The directors made one decision; they voted unanimously to file for bankruptcy. Later that day, S. W. West, a judge for the United States District Court of the Northern District of Ohio, Eastern Division, in Cleveland, approved Erie's application. A few weeks later Judge West named two trustees, President Denney and Cleveland attorney John A. Hadden, to begin the process of reorganization.[12]

Judge West chose well. Denney was an experienced railroad executive and a logical choice. John Hadden was a surprise, but was nevertheless a capable appointee. A Cleveland native, Hadden graduated from Harvard College in 1908 and the Harvard Law School two years later. By the 1930's he was "well established in general corporation law." A family connection may also have led to his selection. His father, Alexander Hadden, a longtime probate judge in Cuyahoga County (Cleveland) had been "close to West." Denney and Hadden had different personalities. The former enjoyed golf outings; the latter's game was bridge ("an exceptional player"), and Hadden was more even-tempered and meticulous than his co-trustee. Yet both men worked hard and well together. Hadden liked his new role: "It was a challenge to head the Erie," recalled his wife, "and he enjoyed that part of his life."[13]

The process of Erie's fourth reorganization differed significantly from the other three. Worsening economic conditions prompted President Herbert Hoover to sign a major and much-needed business reform, the Federal Bankruptcy Act, during the final days of his administration. For railroads this meant that a company in bankruptcy would no longer have a court-appointed receiver who then sold the property, usually to a group of bondholders. Under Section 77 of the new statute, a bankrupt carrier operated under the aegis of one or more trustees whom the court and the Interstate Commerce Commission supervised. The latter for the first time played an active and positive role. "In the entire history of the ICC," commented transportation economist George W. Hilton, "probably nothing that the Commission undertook has met with such general approval as its behavior in reorganization of the bankrupt carriers of the 1930's." Argued Hilton: "The Commission helped bring about the reorganizations quickly and typically with conservatism concerning the railroads' future prospects." His conclusions fit the Erie perfectly.[14]

The Erie, of course, was not alone in experiencing financial woes. The architects of the 1933 bankruptcy measure likely did not expect the Great Depression to send scores of railroads into bankruptcy. But it did: mileage in receivership peaked at a record 77,013 route miles in 1939, or nearly a third of the nation's trackage. Of this, 2,432 miles belonged to the Erie. But unlike most Depression-era railroad bankruptcies, Old Reliable did not remain long under the court's thumb; the company completed the process of reorganization in less than three years. The Erie could claim the distinction of being the last major railroad to go into reorganization and the first to emerge. Compared to the Missouri Pacific, another carrier dominated by the Alleghany Corporation, this seemed only momentary. In 1933 the Missouri Pacific became the first major railroad to file for legal protection, and 23 years later it was the last to emerge from a Depression-era bankruptcy.[15]

Word of the Erie's plight triggered a swift response from investors. While several blocs of security holders emerged to protect their financial interests, the first to appear was the Group of Holders of Erie Refunding and Improvement Bonds. "The Group," which consisted of fourteen institutions that held less secure "junior" bonds, or about $100 million of the company's nearly $270 million of debt, feared that unless it took the initiative, its members ultimately would be forced to make substantial financial sacrifices. It became the driving force behind the reorganization. For leadership the Group quickly selected Wilfred Kurth, chairman of the Home Insurance Company; Henry S. Sturgis, vice president of the First National Bank of New York; and Daniel C. Bordon, vice president of the National City Bank of New York. Speedily it formulated a plan to present to the regulators.[16]

Before submitting a proposal, the Group wisely discussed its collective thoughts with large holders of other Erie bond issues. It focused attention on the principal senior bondholders, four life-insurance companies: Metropolitan Life, Northwestern Mutual Life, Prudential Life, and Massachusetts Life. The Group's position was straightforward: it would yield on some matters in order to speed the process (a protracted dispute would accumulate unpaid interest on senior securities, to the detriment of junior issues); the Erie's credit had to be restored completely; and the new capital structure should guarantee the railroad's prosperity. The company's interest charges and lease rentals had been excessive, about $15 million annually, and this had to be reduced. The Group scored its first triumph when the four insurance firms agreed to cooperate.[17]

Modest opposition did develop. One disapproving group was a protective committee designed to defend the interests of owners of small numbers of junior refunding and improvement bonds. It charged that the Group represented the "big fellows" and was "not interested in the little ones." This organization, however, had little impact except to increase the cost of the case. A more congenial group of dissenters worried that some senior securities might not be treated fairly under the Group's plan. In time this faction came to accept the thrust of the reorganizing efforts.[18]

The Group worked diligently, taking six drafts to create a plan acceptable to the dominant junior and senior bondholders. The Interstate Commerce Commission received this document on October 18, 1938, exactly nine months after the filing of the bankruptcy papers. The plan represented what largely became the financial reorganization of the "new" Erie Railroad Company. The co-trustees submitted their own proposal to the Commission on December 19, 1938, and while these two plans differed on the proposed capital structure, they resembled each other on the treatment of the underlying bonds.[19]

The Group's plan contained an assortment of financial provisions. It left undisturbed several important security issues, including $12 million of Chicago & Erie Railroad first-mortgage bonds due to mature in 1982. "These were very good bonds," concluded Henry Sturgis, "and there was no real reason to disturb them." The document also proposed the issuing of two mortgages, a first consolidated mortgage with a fixed 4 percent interest and a general mortgage with the interest on the original series contingent upon the road's earnings. The company would also have two equity issues, a 5 percent preferred stock and common stock. The Group believed that the four types of securities, together with cash generated from the sale of collateral trust notes, would satisfy all claims against the railroad. Except for the holders of the undisturbed bonds, remaining debt and equity owners would be issued a combination of securities. Those who held better-grade bonds would receive the consolidated mortgage and income bonds and preferred stock, while those with less valuable securities, including the refunding and improvement bondholders, would be issued mostly common stock. Surprisingly, existing common stockholders would not have their equity destroyed; both they and junior bondholders would get an attractive and ingenious offer. "The refunding and improvement bondholders, who were to receive common stock to the extent of roughly 70 percent of their claim, would place their stock under option to the stockholders for a reasonable period at the price at which the bondholders were taking it in satisfaction to their claim," explained Sturgis. "In effect, the owners of the property [stockholders] were being given an opportunity to redeem their property by the payment of a part of their junior debt." Later, too, the Group endorsed the proposal that old stockholders should be given 20 percent of their holdings in new common stock in addition to the stock warrants.[20]

The Group showed considerable shrewdness with its offer to stockholders. Since the Chesapeake & Ohio Railway owned a majority of Erie common, the Group feared that unless it could win this powerful investor's support early on, reorganization might be delayed indefinitely. "Sturgis was an able negotiator and the Erie wanted a settlement," recalled onetime C&O counsel Jervis Langdon, Jr., "and so he brought in the opposition [C&O]." The strategy worked. After some disagreements, the C&O endorsed the Group's plan, and for this cooperation the C&O "came out about $35 to $38 million ahead."[21]

Formal hearings before the Interstate Commerce Commission began in Washington, D.C., on January 4, 1939. After the introduction of the customary exhibits, Henry Sturgis presented the Group's position and John K. Thompson, the Erie officer who chaired the Debtor's Reorganization Committee, offered the company's plan. Following less than three days of testimony, the presiding commissioner called a short recess to allow a discussion between the various parties. The Group surrendered little, however, as its coalition of bankers and insurance executives remained firm. The proceedings reconvened on January 30. The Chesapeake & Ohio argued that the Erie was of "considerable value," and its management hoped to enhance its own position. Yet the sessions went quietly and predictably. The commissioner adjourned the hearings after three days and the participants awaited the report.[22]

The wheels of the federal regulatory machinery turned slowly. The Commission did not reveal its hand until August 21, 1939. The ICC modified or opposed several features, but after rebuttal arguments in November the Group plan largely prevailed. In early 1940, the ICC formally approved a reorganization scheme that seemingly satisfied the principal parties.[23]

A Berkshire (2-8-4) steam locomotive, purchased during the John J. Bernet administration, wheels a long freight made up mostly of refrigerator cars, or "reefers," on a curve on the Delaware River near Callicoon, New York, about 1940. (Erie Lackawanna Inc.)

Additional steps remained to be taken. The Federal Court in Cleveland needed to endorse the Commission's actions. After the bankruptcy filing Judge West had died and an equally competent jurist, Robert Wilkin, had assumed his duties. Judge Wilkin's court held the prescribed hearings on August 12, 1940. The Group, the Erie, and the Chesapeake & Ohio made no objections, although the pesky protective committee of junior bondholders, the self-proclaimed "little fellows," protested that they would not escape the bankruptcy unscathed. After several additional albeit minor legal hurdles, the court, on December 17, 1940, concluded the reorganization plan to be "fair and equitable." The Erie's security holders received ballots on the document in early February 1941, and they completed their voting by mid-April. No class of creditors rejected the plan, and Judge Wilkin confirmed it on July 17, 1941. The last legal paperwork followed and the Erie Railroad Company, its corporate name unchanged, emerged from court protection on December 22, 1941.[24]

The Erie reorganization entailed more than juggling stocks and bonds. The process also included modernization of the railroad's corporate structure. When the company achieved its freedom from Judge Wilkin's court, it stood as a financially manageable property.

The most striking event in this streamlining process involved the Erie's formal acquisition of the strategic 123-mile-long Cleveland & Mahoning Valley Railroad (C&MV). This carrier, which had been leased since the 1880's, served the area of its corporate title and gave the Erie access to Ohio's largest population center. The C&MV likewise provided a direct route between Cleveland and Pittsburgh, via Youngstown, Ohio, and the Pittsburgh & Lake Erie Railroad, a New York Central affiliate. While Erie trains traveled over the C&MV with carloads of general freight and high-rated merchandise, the most important commodity was iron ore that moved from the Port of Cleveland to the teeming steel mills of the Mahoning Valley (Girard, Niles, Warren, and Youngstown) and the greater Pittsburgh region. When the steel industry boomed, business on the C&MV soared, but when a bust cycle occurred, as happened in the 1930's, traffic dropped markedly. "It is very much like the steel business it serves," observed banker Henry Sturgis, "a prince and pauper railroad."[25]

Ownership of the Cleveland & Mahoning Valley was centered abroad. Since the 1880's it had been in English hands, namely the London-based Atlantic Leased Lines, Limited. The Erie rented this property through a controlled company, the Nypano Railroad (née the New York, Pennsylvania and Ohio Railroad, successor to the Atlantic & Great Western Railway), and the charges were considerable. The Erie paid Atlantic Leased Lines more than half a million dollars in 1937, even though income derived from this trackage had fallen considerably from the pre-Depression years.[26]

Through contact with the English owners, the trustees learned that they might renegotiate the lease arrangement. The investors wanted to protect their rental income, of course, but their position was not rigid. Fortunately for the Erie, the English investors felt the sting of their country's high tax on rental income and favored American dollars because of the tense European political situation. John Hadden became intrigued with the possibility of a cash buyout, although he knew that the purchase of a large leased line by a railroad in bankruptcy had never occurred. "That did not bother Mr. Hadden, who expressed himself as quite willing and anxious to explore the question." Hadden met with a representative of the owners and subsequently struck a deal for a purchase price of $7 million. Although the Erie could not raise the money itself, the court responded favorably. In October 1939, Judge Wilkin authorized the necessary trustees' notes and Hadden then convinced the Reconstruction Finance Corporation to acquire them. This restructuring led to a cash savings of nearly $200,000 annually, and soon the Cleveland & Mahoning Valley Railroad became part of "Old Reliable."[27]

Simplification of the Erie's corporate structure involved a myriad of other matters. Before the bankruptcy, the carrier consisted of an unusually large number of railroad and terminal companies, 38 of them, of which the parent held either most or all of the stock or part or all of the debt. The Erie also leased 18 properties, mostly branch lines, and their status required serious financial scrutiny. The reorganization process did not follow the standard modus operandi. Traditionally questions of control become part of the core plan, but in the quest for speed the principal parties agreed to allow "reorganization managers" to have power to affirm or deny previous commitments and to acquire properties with the new securities of the company. Still, approval from the Interstate Commerce Commission and the court was needed.[28]

The five reorganization managers worked as an effective team. The Metropolitan Insurance Company, the Prudential Insurance Company, the Reconstruction Finance Corporation, the Group, and the railroad each appointed one manager, and they eventually folded into the parent Erie 18 companies and reduced the number of leases by 8. They also allowed the 144-mile New York, Susquehanna & Western and the 42-mile New Jersey and New York railroads, both wholly-owned subsidiaries of the Erie but in separate receiverships, to go their own ways.[29]

The reorganization went well for the Erie, although some analysts in the financial world criticized the results. "They didn't reduce the debt enough," argued railroad bond specialist Isabel H. Benham years later. "It was the most liberal [high debt] reorganization of the time." Liberal or not, the "new" Erie encountered a dramatic decrease in its fixed expenses. The railroad's debt prior to 1938 was slightly more than $275 million, but the plan cut it to less than $150 million. Annual fixed charges dropped correspondingly, from $14.5 million to $7.6 million.[30]

The return to prosperity during World War II further strengthened the company. "At the end of 1937, the railroad had quick liabilities equal to $9,253,802 more than it had quick assets," explained Henry Sturgis in 1948. "Now the road has an excess of quick assets of $21,752,472. To this must be added $10,000,000 of United States Treasury bonds tucked away among investments for a rainy day. This nest egg will take care of about two years of fixed charges." Banker Sturgis hoped that by squirreling away this reserve, the Erie would survive one of those periodic net-revenue famines that it had experienced with some regularity. Other railroads, too, commonly employed such a strategy.[31]

Those associated with the Erie rightly felt encouraged by 1941. The company proclaimed this positive feeling at the time bankruptcy officially ended:

"The Erie Railroad is in the best physical and financial condition in its long and spectacular career." The *Marion Star*, the unofficial voice of the Erie in Ohio, added its own upbeat comments. "The railroad has ceased to be a gag for any Vaudeville team. The old jokes are out." The paper also detected a "new spirit" at Erie. "Everyone from the lowliest track walker up to the president has caught it and is proud of the new Erie."[32]

Charles Denney did not continue to lead the reconstructed Erie. He resigned as co-trustee and director on September 30, 1939, to assume the presidency of the giant Northern Pacific Railroad. A longtime employee, Robert E. Woodruff, then vice president in charge of operations and maintenance, replaced him. Like Denney and most railroad officials of the day, Woodruff had worked his way up through the ranks. Born in Green Bay, Wisconsin, on September 11, 1884, and raised in Benton Harbor, Michigan, Woodruff studied civil engineering at Purdue University. He graduated in 1905, and joined the Erie upon the advice of his department head, Professor William D. Pence. "I wouldn't apply to the New York Central or the Pennsylvania," Woodruff remembered Pence saying. "They are old established railroads, everything is systemized, and you have to wait until somebody dies before you get anywhere. Why don't you tackle the Erie? They are an old broken-down road . . . but who now have a new management [Frederick Underwood] and it looks as if the road is some day going to amount to something." Woodruff agreed.[33]

In proper railroad tradition the future Erie president started at the bottom with the expectation of steady advancement; he joined an Erie track gang on the Kent [Ohio] Division in June 1905. "I soon found that a job on a section was not a 'bed of roses' but, at the same time, it was very interesting. The hours were long—ten a day—from six in the morning to five at night, with an hour for lunch. The pay was thirteen cents an hour. I am happy to say I lived on my income but that took some close figuring." Woodruff did not remain long in that lowly position. After several supervisory assignments, he entered the superintendent's office at Rochester, New York, in December 1910. A decade later Woodruff served as manager of the busy Hornell (New York) region, and on December 1, 1928, following two additional positions, he became assistant vice president for system, based in New York City. Six months later Woodruff moved into the company's number two job, the one Denney vacated when he became Erie's twenty-fifth president.[34]

Robert Woodruff possessed the necessary operating experience to head the Erie. "Woodruff knew his stuff about everyday railroading," commented a fellow president. News of Woodruff's elevation pleased employees. The gregarious Woodruff had traveled the property frequently and remembered the first names of hundreds, perhaps thousands, of workers. "Mr. Woodruff made you feel comfortable," recalled an associate. "He was very well liked by all."[35]

One explanation for Woodruff's considerable popularity stemmed from his interest in, even obsession with, improving employees' skills. Both before and during his presidency, he promoted personal improvement, especially self-help training. "Men have been encouraged to study," he wrote in his unpublished autobiography. "As a matter of fact, every higher officer and most of those of middle rank have taken some correspondence school course, similar to Alexander Hamilton Institute. We have never asked a man to take it but have from time to time given lists of names to a sales representative and let him sell the individual. The net result is that all our higher officers and most junior officers, as well, have had the benefit of business training, enabling them to look beyond their own departments and beyond their own jobs and know something of the other fellow's problems and the principles which guide the business."[36]

Woodruff also launched a much-publicized apprenticeship training program for employees in the mechanical and marine departments in the late 1930's. "Candidates for apprenticeship training," he explained in the *Erie Railroad Magazine*, "are carefully examined and only the best are hired." The railroad painstakingly supervised these individuals for a four-year period and, in the process, moved them around the system to provide a variety of work experiences. Although some foremen complained ("They were not especially pleased with change"), most graduate apprentices believed they profited. "I know Woodruff's program developed young men in the company," observed electrician John Ray. "It did that for me."[37]

While widely acclaimed, and Woodruff's pride and joy, the Erie apprenticeship program had apparent flaws. The company accepted the debatable concept that "first hand knowledge of the kinds of work involved in maintaining railroad rolling stock and motive power was the sine qua non of a successful career in the mechanical department." This philosophy led apprentices to do unrewarding tasks. "I was generally shunted around to places where they needed an extra and a willing hand to take up the slack in the schedules," related Robert Aldag, a mechanical engineering graduate of Purdue University. "In retrospect I see the Erie's apprenticeship program as being part and parcel of the obsolescence of that railroad. We put our minds and our backs into it with a fair amount of enthusiasm, but we were learning yesterday's technology and work methods." Added another Purdue graduate, G. J. Weihofen, "[The program] neither used nor furthered my engineering education except for a couple of months in counterbalancing, five or six weeks installing power plant machinery, and another six or eight weeks off and on doing drafting work." Concluded Aldag, "There was nothing in the program that was designed to prepare [Erie's] future managers for the diesel-electric revolution that was just around the corner."[38]

Woodruff hardly ranks as either the industry's or the Erie's best chief executive. While he cannot be faulted seriously for his failure to develop a fully forward-looking apprenticeship program, he had other glaring shortcomings. Woodruff had little knowledge of or interest in financial matters. Instead, he initially relied heavily on trustee John Hadden, whom he admired. After the reorganization Woodruff depended upon the considerable expertise provided by the powerful and aggressive board members Henry Sturgis and Harry Hagerty, treasurer of the Metropolitan Life Insurance Company. While dedicated to boosting the Erie, Woodruff was relaxed about his work. At times he appeared casual about his obligations. He loved leisurely golf outings; "his clubs were always close at hand," remarked one acquaintance. Woodruff took extended trips to his lavish winter home at Delray Beach, Florida, for he found his mansion in Shaker Heights, Ohio, unattractive during the long gloomy spells of late autumn, winter, and early spring. On a pleasant Friday afternoon in summer, Woodruff commonly dismissed his staff on the executive floor at Cleveland headquarters. "The place just shut down and no wonder people adored Mr. Woodruff." A trim though balding six-footer, Woodruff fancied himself a "ladies' man." Married three times and divorced and widowed once, he seized every opportunity to mix pleasure with work. "Woodruff had great fun in that [business] car of his . . . and that meant more than having plenty of drinks, good meals and friendly games of poker and occasionally tending to railroad business," recalled an employee. "Once while he [bedded down] . . . the wife of a wealthy Hornell manufacturer in his business car there in the Hornell yards, the irate husband burst into the car with a gun and the frightened Woodruff fled outside without a stitch of clothes."[39]

One Woodruff shortcoming benefited the Erie. This self-confident and rodomontade railroader considered himself to be the personification of the company. Whenever possible, he referred to "our big, happy Erie family," suggesting that he was the good father. This sentiment undoubtedly was received warmly by employees, particularly when he spoke at the gala company-sponsored annual picnic at Conneaut Lake Park in northwestern Pennsylvania. Woodruff personally advanced the railroad, especially in business circles, and proudly promoted a pet project, the "I Worked on the Erie Club." The idea came to him during the early part of World War II when he chatted with Major General Richard Donovan, commander of the Eighth Army, on a visit to Dallas, Texas. Donovan indicated that he had spent six months with a survey crew on the Erie before he entered West Point. Soon thereafter Woodruff started to issue printed identification cards to Erie alumni, although initially they needed to have some prominence. He noted with pleasure in his autobiography, appropriately titled, "I Worked on the Erie," that "At one time, at an Eastern Presidents Conference, every man at the table was an Erie alumnus but one, the exception being General [William W.] Atterbury [of the Pennsylvania Railroad]; the others were Daniel Willard of B. & O., [Edward] Loomis of Lehigh Valley, [John] Davis of Lackawanna and [Patrick] Crowley of N.Y.C., and J. J. Bernet of the C. & O." Woodruff proudly concluded, "once an Erie man, always an Erie man."[40]

Woodruff constantly strove to improve the Erie's public image. He authorized advertisements about the road's "personalized" freight and passenger service in such mass circulation magazines as *Collier's*, *Cornet*, and *Saturday Evening Post* and on radio shows in Chicago, Cleveland, and New York City. He had a field day when the Board of Directors decided in 1942 to pay a dividend on the company's common stock. Woodruff worked closely with the railroad's public relations officer in preparing this clever news release, "Icicles Froze in Hell Today":

The Erie Railroad Company declared a dividend on its common stock.

The dividend of 50 cents a share payable July 10 to Stockholders on record June 30 is the first Common Stock Dividend ever paid by the present Erie Railroad Company organized in 1895 and the first paid by any Erie Company in 76 years. . . .

Thus Wall Street tradition was shattered and Brokers were dazedly groping for reliable replacements for the immemorial dictums—When Erie Common pays a dividend there'll be icicles in hell—and three things are certain—Death, Taxes, and no dividends for Erie Common.[41]

The buoyancy of the "icicles froze in hell" statement reflected accurately the Erie's strengthening financial position. Although the United States did not enter World War II officially until December 8, 1941, the conflict had been raging in Europe since September 1939. As the American defense industry increased production, freight traffic burgeoned, in part stimulated by orders from Britain in 1941 and then "lend-lease"–financed goods, especially in 1942 and 1943. The Erie, among Eastern roads, won more than its share of this business. Shippers regularly designated Old Reliable to receive thousands of carloads of oversized cargoes because of the Erie's advantageous and extensively advertised wide right-of-way clearances, a legacy of its broad-gauge construction. "As the Coueites [followers of philosopher Emile Coue, 1857–1926] would say," happily noted an official in the fall of 1941, "day by day, and in every way, the Erie is getting better and better." Freight revenue statistics bore him out: $70,605,713 in 1939, $76,243,627 in 1940, and $95,798,571 in 1941. The latter represented a hefty 26 percent increase over the previous year.[42]

War shook the nation. As the country battled Japan, Germany, and Italy, it participated in a conflict that was global in the truest sense of the word. Rival military forces encountered each other in Africa, Asia, Europe, and the Pacific islands. Americans united for war as never before: eligible men and women rallied to the colors, civilians in unprecedented numbers labored on the home front, and the government marshaled resources to ensure victory for the Allies. America's railroads responded to enormous demands. "Without transportation we could not fight at all," observed Joseph B. Eastman, director of the Office of Defense Transportation in 1943. "In these days there is nothing which enters into war, from troops to bullets, which is not dependent absolutely on transportation. Everyone must concede that they [the railroads] have done an outstanding piece of work." Because of rationing of gasoline, tires (rubber was in especially short supply), and replacement parts, motor carriers could not maintain their previous levels of transport, let alone cope with the increase. Moreover, the presence of German submarines in the waters of the Atlantic and Caribbean disrupted the flow of goods through the Panama Canal and along coastal shipping lanes between Texas and New England. As a result, railroads handled 83 percent of the increase of *all* traffic between 1941 and 1944, and they moved 91 percent of all military freight within the country and 98 percent of all military personnel. Freight traffic, measured in ton miles, soared from 373 billion in 1940 to 737 billion in 1944 (the industry would not pass the latter record figure until 1966). Passenger traffic, expressed in revenue passenger miles, skyrocketed from 23 billion in 1940 to 95 billion in 1944, and that peak figure would never again be equalled.[43]

The Erie carried an enormous volume of goods and passengers during World War II. The road's traffic largely mirrored national trends, although 1943, rather than 1944, was the busiest time: 16.8 billion ton-miles of freight and 15.1 million passengers. In that hectic year Old Reliable claimed one of the highest traffic densities in the nation. Only the Chesapeake & Ohio and Norfolk & Western had slightly greater figures.[44]

The Erie coped magnificently with these burdens. "We could handle almost everything they threw at us during the war," remembered a dispatcher. "When troop trains got bogged down on the New York Central or Pennsylvania, we took them." Yet wartime railroading challenged the work force. Recalled a trainmaster assigned to the Kent Division, "You bet we were damn busy. . . . At times it was downright hell getting the trains made up and out of town. We always seemed to have the yards full of cars, but we got the job done."[45]

While the Erie moved everything from Sherman tanks to fresh produce, it became a principal conduit for petroleum products that moved from the oil

A "Heavy K-5 Pacific" locomotive, No. 2936, built by Baldwin in 1923, pulls a mainline passenger train, perhaps the *Erie Limited*, in 1943. (Erie Lackawanna Inc.)

fields of Louisiana, Oklahoma, and Texas to the Northeast before construction of the "Big Inch" and "Little Inch" pipelines by 1944 reduced the need for rail transport. In August 1942, John Grover, a writer for the Associated Press, rode a 60-car oil train from Port Arthur, Texas, to Providence, Rhode Island, and his trip included an 800-mile ride over the Erie between Huntington, Indiana, and Maybrook, New York. Grover wrote, in part:

The oil's going through. It's a gigantic effort that compares with the great sagas of our pioneer days. It's the toughest kind of work, because railroads are short-handed, like every big outfit. That means hours up to the limit of Interstate Commerce Commission rules, a quick flop and bath, and back again for a new assignment. . . . Railroaders are working the hours it takes to move the freight that's got to move.

This conversation, in the Marion, O., yards of the Erie, is typical.

"Yay, Smitty, How y' doing? Playing the horses lately?"

"Playin'em hell. I'm the horse. I've had one day off since April."

"Ya big sissy. What's a day off? I don't remember." . . .

Everywhere among the nation's railroad men, the clock is the enemy. They're always fighting time. They hauled a crippled tank car out of the line at Marion . . . , slapped a new set of wheels on it and had it ready to go along with us by the time our engine was serviced.

This wasn't extraordinary, just routine. Tank car movement of oil makes a terrific job for railway shopmen. Every rusted, busted tanker that will hold oil has been rounded up and sent flying East. . . .

Our oil train gunned 2,500 miles at three times the normal, pre-war speed of freight. That sort of thing is being done every day. We couldn't fight a war without it.[46]

Journalist Grover correctly sensed the wonderment of these oil-train "moves." Railroads, including the Erie, toiled mightily to transport countless commodities, and they did so with fewer and often less-experienced employees. "[T]he Board of Directors wishes to acknowledge the continued efficiency and loyalty of the employees whose efforts have contributed so much to the results that have been achieved," wrote President Woodruff in February 1945. "Never have the demands upon them been greater and never have they responded more capably. 5,428 employees of the Company [approximately a quarter of the work force] have entered the Armed Forces and are serving in all parts of the world." In addition to hundreds who enlisted or were drafted, the Erie fielded two Army railroad operating battalions, the 735th and 765th, both of which played important roles in the European theater, and Paul W. Johnston, a high-ranking official, left the company in March 1942 to command a large unit in Australia that had a staff of fifteen Erie men.[47]

To keep the freight and passenger trains running, the Erie tapped sources of nontraditional and often unskilled labor. The company magazine frequently published stories about "new members of the Erie family." In September 1943, for example, it described activities of four Alfred (New York) University professors, "three of them Ph.D.'s," who joined the railroad's maintenance-of-way forces. The location of the college, nine miles west of Hornell, a division point and locomotive repair center, made commuting to work practical. "We were happy to do our bit, for we felt by helping the Erie Railroad keep 'em rolling we were hastening an Allied Nations victory," commented Harold Boraas, an instructor of education and psychology. "When our regular term of school ended, we four men decided to try for jobs in the war effort." The Erie also hired scores of women to perform duties normally done by men. For instance, the company employed several African-American women as full-time delivery clerks in its busy 14th Street freight station in Chicago and used additional women, both black and white, in similar types of low-paying work, including wiping locomotives, cleaning passenger coaches, and guarding grade crossings. The railroad increased its work force of 22,481 at the outbreak of the war to a wartime high of 24,714 in 1944, the largest figure since 1931, although far from the record of 47,676 in 1918.[48]

The war created an enormous spirit of patriotism through the Erie ranks. There were, of course, those heavy enlistments, and cases where individuals gladly "went railroadin'." Management especially waved the flag. It continually pushed the purchase of war bonds and peppered employees with reports on such sales. The company noted proudly in February 1943 that the "December war bond campaign was so widespread, involving, as it did, all employees, on line and off, that tabulation of the figures is still being made. However, we can say that 96.81 per cent of Erie employees are now subscribing to the payroll deduction plan." The Erie, like some other carriers, even ordered the painting of rolling stock to stimulate bond purchases. Several cabooses sported red, white, and blue stripes with large "BUY WAR BONDS" emblazoned on their sides, and an ancient switch engine, "little No. 2," an 0-6-0, chugged around the Jersey City yards with a side banner urging, "BUY BONDS AND KEEP THEM FLYING."[49]

While Erie men and women backed the war effort and contributed "100% to the operations of the company," they rightly grumbled about their wages. The outbreak of hostilities in Europe produced a sharp rise in the cost of living before the United States became directly involved, and Washington moved slowly to set fair maximum prices. By May 1943 the cost of living had risen 27 percent since September 1939, but the Office of Price Administration (OPA), created in 1942, succeeded in restricting the rise in living costs during 1944 and 1945 to a modest 1.4 percent. Although OPA applied the brakes, an Erie trainman recalled, "I still remember how expensive everything got during the war. . . . My family was squeezed really hard. It sure was a big change from those Depression years of the 1930's when a few dollars in your pocket meant a good chunk of money."[50]

Workers across the country understandably protested the wage-price squeeze. On January 25, 1943, operating personnel—engineers, firemen, conductors, trainmen, and switchmen—asked the railroad industry for a wage increase of 30 percent in their basic daily rates and a minimum of three dollars per day. After intense, protracted, and unsuccessful negotiations, the employees called for a strike on December 30, 1943. Simultaneously nonoperating railroaders demanded a wage increase; they sought a 20 cents an hour hike and 70 cents an hour minimum wage. Once again negotiations, at times bitter, failed to produce a settlement, and these railroaders, too, issued a strike order. With a transportation crisis looming, President Roosevelt signed an Executive Order on December 27, 1943, seizing at least in name the country's rail network. Federal control lasted briefly and ended when labor and management came to terms on January 18, 1944. Operating employees won an increase of 32 cents per day, retroactive to April 1, 1943, and effective December 27, 1943, an additional 40 cents a day. Nonoperating personnel saw their paychecks increase 10 cents an hour for the lowest hourly rated persons to 4 cents an hour for the highest hourly rated ones, retroactive to February

1, 1943, and effective December 27, 1943, they received a graduated scale of hikes ranging from 9 to 11 cents an hour.[51]

Erie's work force generally endorsed the outcome of the midwar wage disputes, but the company did not. "This hurts," asserted President Woodruff. The bill exceeded $4 million in 1943 and then rose to approximately $7.5 million a year later. The railroad, however, had no alternative and industry-mandated wage increases, according to Woodruff, "seemed always to happen."[52]

The interventionist role of the federal government took on various dimensions during the conflict, although the seizure grabbed the headlines. While federalization had occurred during the Great War, carriers in World War II remained in private hands, with, of course, that one brief episode. Yet the Erie and other railroads faced rigid government supervision. Soon after Congress passed a declaration of war, it created the Office of Defense Transportation (ODT). This agency quickly produced a blizzard of bureaucratic paperwork, including scores of "service orders" that required heavier loading of equipment and the conservation of fuel. For example, one important directive, issued toward war's end, led to the withdrawal of all Pullman sleeping cars from commercial service on trips of 450 miles or less and assigned them exclusively to carrying troops. While the ODT order did not affect Erie's trains from New York to Chicago or New York to Cleveland, it meant an end to Pullmans traveling the 425 miles between New York and Buffalo. (The equipment returned to regular service in early 1946.)[53]

Erie officers cooperated fully with the government, and there is no evidence to suggest that either management or labor felt unduly coerced. When the military faced the critical need for additional ground storage for war materials in the spring of 1942, the Erie gladly responded to the emergency. "Your company constructed open storage yards at four widely scattered locations along its line with a short space of time having a capacity of thousands of carloads," wrote an appreciative Major General C. P. Cross, chief of transportation for the War Department, to President Woodruff. "The selected properties were cleared and graded and track construction started in some cases within forty-eight hours. The necessary organizations were established and crane equipment made available so that actual unloading was begun within a very few days. All employees, including carefully selected and trained guard organizations, were hired by your company. All equipment, such as cranes and special handling devices, was furnished by the Erie Railroad so that the entire operation was under your supervision and responsibility." Added Gross, "As the entire project was handled by private enterprise, the Army was relieved of the countless details involved in the construction and operation during this emergency period."[54]

While the war years taxed the capabilities of the Erie, its Weary Erie image diminished. Even though wage hikes and wartime inflation hurt ("We paid $3,318,739 more for coal [in 1943] than in 1942, of which $1,860,746 was due to increased prices") and the Interstate Commerce Commission failed to boost freight and passenger rates, the Erie by V-J Day in August 1945 was "sort of fat and sassy." Its balance sheets "were so different from those of the 1930's," remarked a financial officer, "that I couldn't believe that they were for the same company." Operating ratios (the ratios of expenses to revenues) were solid, especially for 1943 and 1944 (69.63 and 65.95 respectively), and the company even generated considerable passenger income. This was unusual, since the Erie had long been "a first-class freight railroad but a second-class passenger one." In prewar years passenger revenues represented about 6 percent of total operating revenues, but in 1945 they rose to nearly 10 percent. Not surprisingly, the Erie continued to pay annual dividends, five dollars on preferred shares and one dollar on common.[55]

The future looked promising. President Woodruff was particularly sanguine when he considered the Erie's substantial reduction in its fixed charges: $14,546,710 in 1937 (the last full year prior to bankruptcy) to $5,682,158 in 1945. "Erie's credit is good," he happily told employees in early 1946. "We have paid our way since our reorganization and are able to borrow money at cheaper rates now than five years ago. We paid off many of our old loans and replaced them with new loans at cheaper rates." The company wisely exploited falling interest rates, and railroads regularly restructured their debt during and immediately after the war. Understandably, Woodruff expressed his belief to a reporter from the *Cleveland Press* that "the Erie Railroad is in its spring-time of life. . . . We are a new company with a successful reorganization behind us." Yet in reality the Erie's immediate future seemed more akin to Indian summer than spring, and in time the railroad would drift steadily toward a bitter winter.[56]

POSTWAR RAILROADING,
1946–1957

LIKE MOST AMERICAN RAILWAYS, the Erie Railroad entered the post–World War II period in an expansive mood. "The future is bright," predicted board member and former trustee John A. Hadden in early 1947. "Last year the Erie Railroad moved the greatest volume of freight traffic in any peace-time year in its history." President Robert E. Woodruff also expressed confidence. "A decade from now our railroad will be much better than it is today," he told employees in 1946. "The wear-and-tear caused by the war will be gone as will be the great age of steam." And he added, "We will spend what it takes to make the Erie one of America's finest railroads."[1]

With strong financial reserves and ample credit, Woodruff's noble objective seemed plausible. Spending for future greatness started quickly after 1945 and moved forward at a brisk pace. In the three years after V-J Day the Erie invested $36 million in equipment and improvements. "The railroad was like those postwar consumers," recalled an Erie official, "just spending on anything and everything." Most of all, these capital expenditures went for acquisition of diesel-electric locomotives and the necessary support facilities for this innovative motive power. The Erie retired hundreds of steam locomotives and abandoned the plethora of related structures—water towers, coal chutes, and roundhouses—that served them.[2]

By the mid-1940's diesels had demonstrated their superiority over steam locomotives, and this replacement technology radically changed the Erie and the industry. Diesels excelled in every respect except romance. "Old timers . . . miss the bell and the deep steam whistle, the puffing of the smokestack and hiss of the exhaust," remarked a writer for the *Erie Railroad Magazine* in March 1947. "Alas, the diesel only goes 'shoosh-throom.'" But an Erie locomotive engineer told a reporter who covered the inaugural run of a diesel-powered passenger train that same year, "I'll gladly trade glamour for comfort." Woodruff, too, was impressed, and he could not resist commenting on this wonderful invention: "[Diesels], of course, have changed the entire picture," he concluded in 1953, a few months before the Erie retired its last steamer. "A steam engine could only work about 16 hours a day. A Diesel works 22 [average utilization was never this high] and can be turned around immediately upon refueling. The Diesel produces its greatest tractive effort at low speeds and so is a greater hill climber as compared with a steam engine. The employment of strong Diesels . . . has made possible better handling of trains in starting and stopping and getting up speed." Diesels were superior in other aspects: they required no water stops; could operate hundreds of miles without refueling; demanded less overall maintenance; and could function in multiple-unit combinations with only a single crew. As historian Maury Klein has cogently argued, "The diesel locomotive revolutionized the way railroads performed their work; reconfigured the physical landscape of railroads; redefined the role of labor in this most traditional of industries; . . . and consigned to the realm of nostalgia an entire subculture rooted in a shared passion for that dominant symbol of nineteenth-century America, the steam locomotive."[3]

The Erie readily recognized the value of diesel-electric technology. Although the road was both a producer of coal (principally through its subsidiary, the profitable Pennsylvania Coal Company) and a hauler of coal, management willingly embraced motive power fueled by petroleum products. Some railroads had postponed dieselization, fearing they would offend powerful coal shippers. Indeed, the Erie had long used various forms of locomotion. Shortly after the turn of the century the company surprised the industry when it electrified with single-phase alternating current 38 miles of its Rochester Division for passenger service. (This operation lasted until 1934.) In 1908 it acquired its first self-propelled passenger car, and by the early 1930's nearly a score of these gasoline- or oil-powered units hauled hundreds of patrons on daily runs. Then in May 1926 the Erie gained acclaim for being a pioneer in another area, diesel ownership. It bought a 300-horsepower unit from the American Locomotive Company, Number 20, and placed it in its busy West 28th Street yards (Pier 67) in New York City to satisfy a local smoke-abatement statute. The company added a similar locomotive in September 1928. Before the decade ended, it bought three more diesel switchers for assignments on Manhattan Island, two 600-horsepower units and one rated at 800 horsepower. The Erie acquired three additional diesels in 1931, and placed them in switching service in Akron, Ohio, partly to solve a smoke

The Erie established itself early on as an industry innovator. An example of the company's creativity was the acquisition of gasoline and diesel-electric passenger motor cars. One of these practical and economical "Go Devils" waits at the station in Hackensack, New Jersey, on July 11, 1940. (Grant)

problem. And at the end of the 1930's the road invested in another seven locomotives to assist in the busy Jersey City terminal complex. "They gave such excellent service and played such a big part in handling wartime traffic that 20 more diesel switchers were put into operation by the end of 1946." Diesel switchers soon appeared system-wide: in addition to those in the earliest locations, they shunted cars in Buffalo, Chicago, Jamestown (New York), Kent (Ohio), and Mansfield (Ohio). Predictably diesels first appeared in switching service, where their characteristics of smokeless operations, easy maneuverability, high traction at low speeds, and ability to operate almost continuously made them incontestably better than their steam counterparts.[4]

Before World War II ended the Erie also began to operate diesels on through freight runs. In October 1944, it took delivery of six 5,400-horsepower four-unit diesel sets, commonly called "F" (for freight) units, from the Electro-Motive Division of General Motors, and placed them on the rugged main line with its sawtooth profiles between Marion, Ohio, and Meadville, Pennsylvania. "[The Kent and Mahoning] divisions are the traffic bottleneck which the Diesels will help to eliminate," explained George C. Frank, Sr., the

The Erie pioneered the use of internal-combustion locomotives like No. 20, a 60-ton diesel-electric switch engine built jointly in 1926 by the American Locomotive Company (Alco), General Electric, and Ingersoll Rand, shown here at the 28th Street Terminal in New York City in May 1930. (Erie Lackawanna Inc.)

railroad's manager of public relations, shortly before these locomotives went into service. "No longer will it be necessary to split eastbound freights at Marion and westbound freights at Meadville and tie them together again. . . . This will mean that for the first time a solid train with full tonnage can be run from one end of the [road] to the other without splitting it up at intermediate terminals on account of grade changes. The result will be a saving in time and serious traffic delays." This operating improvement appealed to federal authorities who encouraged expediting war-related cargoes, and so Erie won authorization to buy these scarce locomotives.[5]

With return to a peacetime economy, the Erie could more easily add to its small fleet of diesel-electric locomotives. Orders were placed for both switchers and road units. By 1947 diesels pulled "hot-shot" freights between Croxton Yard (Jersey City) and Marion, a distance of 725 miles, on expedited schedules. Also in 1947 the company acquired seven 4,500–horsepower three-unit diesels from Electro-Motive Division to speed its principal passenger trains between Jersey City and Chicago, *The Erie Limited* and *The Mid-*

Introduced for the New York World's Fair in 1939, *The Midlander* served as one of
Erie's workhorse passenger trains during the 1940's. Train No. 16, pulled by Alco-
built Pacific No. 2907, rolls along Chicago & Western Indiana tracks at 87th Street
in Chicago, on August 25, 1946. (John F. Humiston)

lander. It dieselized the less important *Atlantic Express* and *Pacific Express* only
between Jersey City and Marion.[6]

The Erie did not buy all its diesel locomotives from General Motors. It
also placed orders with American Locomotive Company–General Electric
(Alco-GE) and Baldwin Locomotive Company. This buying policy, common
throughout the industry, occurred for several reasons: no dominant manufacturer had yet emerged; the Erie wished to spread its business, and it had a
burning desire to dieselize. Recalled Erie executive Milton McInnes, "Sometimes we bought diesels after the war where we could find them." Diesels
from different builders created a more complicated program of maintenance
and repair, required a larger inventory of parts, and raised operating
expenses.[7]

Regardless of the source, Erie welcomed its ever-growing fleet of diesels.
These units performed well and increased operating efficiency and income.
Diesel sales representatives faced little challenge whenever they called at cor-
porate headquarters. After all, the railroad had traditionally experimented

The Erie proudly posed the old and the new of motive power for newsreel, magazine, and newspaper cameras a few days before its centennial gala of May 14 and 15, 1951. The steam locomotive *William Mason*, a classic American 4-4-0 borrowed from the Baltimore & Ohio, stands beside No. 711, an Electro-Motive diesel built for the Erie in 1950. (Erie Lackawanna Inc.)

with motive power and it liked its early diesels. Furthermore, Erie's steam power needed to be retired; it was not modern in terms of the steam-locomotive technology of the 1940's. The last steamers, 20 2-8-4's (Berkshires), had arrived in 1929, and the roster contained a number of pre–World War I locomotives, including 38 2-8-2's (Mikados) built between 1911 and 1913. Wartime service likewise hastened the need for replacements. "By the end of the war [1945] most of these old engines were ready for the junk heap," remembered an Erie shopman. "It was time for diesels."[8]

When the Erie celebrated the centennial of its core route in 1951, it owned an extensive fleet of diesel-electric locomotives. It operated 339 units, 306 more than it had in 1945, and they represented an investment of more

THE ERIE LIMITED One of six daily passenger trains operated by the Erie Railroad between New York and Chicago. Powered by 4500 H.P. Diesel locomotives built by Electro-Motive Division of General Motors Corp.

The Electro-Motive Division of General Motors issued this advertising card in the early 1950's to promote its diesel-electric locomotives. The Erie was one of many roads honored in this fashion. (Grant)

than $60 million. The company expected to dieselize everything except the Mahoning and New York divisions where it would operate some steam locomotives until the final order of diesels arrived. The twilight of steam, however, lasted longer than planned. The outbreak of the Korean Conflict in June of 1950 increased traffic significantly, and the company prudently retained the core of its steam-locomotive fleet. (The Erie owned 235 steamers in 1950, but only 141 a year later; there had been 750 steam locomotives in 1945.) By October of 1950 diesels accounted for 63.7 percent of the freight-locomotive miles, 81.7 percent of yard-service locomotive miles, and 87.2 percent of passenger-locomotive miles. At the end of 1952, the Erie retired its last steam locomotive from freight service. "The Erie is the first major railroad operating between New York and Chicago to use diesel locomotives 100% for freight service," announced the company in a series of nationwide advertisements. A year later, but without fanfare, it dieselized completely. The last steamers, which operated occasionally on commuter trains out of Jersey City, became scrap metal. The Erie was not sentimental about the end of steam; it saved no steam locomotive, nor did it give or sell any to communities along its lines, as many other carriers did.[9]

The process of dieselization involved more than buying sparkling black-and-yellow freight, switching, and passenger locomotives. In the early 1950's the Erie moved rapidly to improve its aging fleets of steam-powered cranes and tugboats. The company replaced 30 obsolete cranes with 26 diesel ones,

An Erie employee checks a 1,500-horsepower diesel engine unit in one of the road's new three-unit Electro-Motive 4,500-horsepower locomotives about 1946. (Erie Lackawanna Inc.)

The Erie operated car floats between Jersey City and New York City for many years. This one, guided by a company tug, contains refrigerator cars bound for New York's fruit and vegetable market. The Delaware, Lackawanna & Western's passenger ferry *Binghamton* moves across the North River in the background. (Erie Lackawanna Inc.)

and it also acquired 5 diesel-powered tugboats. "Boy! you sure couldn't smell smoke around the Erie by then [1954]," remarked an employee. "But the company still had those steam ferryboats, . . . only they made you think of the past."[10]

The Erie's modernization efforts included much more as the company upgraded its rolling stock, especially freight cars. Since freight traffic remained the road's bread and butter, it strove mightily to keep its fleet of nearly 25,000 units well maintained. Generally the freight cars had withstood the war years reasonably well, in part because they were relatively new. In 1946, 64 percent of freight-car equipment was less than 21 years old, compared to the national average of 45.3 percent. As the peacetime economy improved, the Erie bought thousands of new cars and rebuilt thousands more in its Dunmore, Pennsylvania, carshop. In 1947, for example, the road acquired 500 boxcars, 300 hopper cars, and 200 gondola cars, and it repaired or rebuilt a comparable number. Although all rebuilding and general repairs occurred at Dunmore, less extensive work took place at three other shops, each specializing in one type of equipment: boxcars went to Port Jervis, New York; hopper cars to Avoca, Pennsylvania; and gondolas and flatcars to Brier Hill

(Youngstown), Ohio. The company also "tore down" obsolete cars on a regular basis.[11]

This program of buying, repairing, and rebuilding worked well. In 1951 the percentage of "bad-order" or out-of-service cars in the freight fleet stood at a modest 3.9 percent, significantly better than the industry's average. Moreover, the average age of these cars was fifteen years, with nearly a quarter being less than five years old. "The Erie not only has brought about a considerable modernization of its freight car fleet in the past decade," observed *Modern Railroads* in May 1951, "but it also has established a highly efficient system of maintaining its cars in high grade condition."[12]

Old Reliable did not ignore its passenger equipment. Although the company refrained from purchasing expensive, modern stainless-steel streamlined pieces (unlike its vigorous competitors), it did more than just dieselize its main-line and then branch-line and suburban trains. Immediately after the war, the Erie embarked on a twofold plan to improve its passenger-train rolling stock. Convinced that "there is a market for the intermediate traveler, . . . one who wishes to go from some point on our main line to either New York or Chicago," the road purchased some new equipment. This included 7 lightweight "all-room" sleeping cars, 22 baggage and express cars, and 8 baggage and mail cars. But unlike the freight story, here the Erie relied much more extensively on its own refurbishing abilities. The reason was simple: the company could not afford dieselization and freight-fleet improvements and still buy extensively for its passenger service. Furthermore, the road's existing passenger equipment was in good condition. "Only 8.4 percent of our [passenger] cars are over 30 years old as compared with the average for all railroads of 38.2 percent," noted President Woodruff in March 1947. "As a matter of fact, there is no other railroad in the country which has a smaller percentage of passenger equipment in this age bracket than does the Erie." Nevertheless, this rolling stock, while hardly museum-quality, "looked old" and needed to be upgraded. This the shopmen at the Susquehanna, Pennsylvania, coach shops did with imagination and skill. By 1951 they had rebuilt 35 coaches and 8 diners, transforming them thoroughly. These "new" cars featured flush-rounded roofs instead of dated clerestory ones and contained extra-large "picture" windows, and air conditioning. Shopmen also added to the coaches reclining chairs (seating capacity dropped from 84 to 52), wide aluminum baggage racks, and individually controlled overhead lights. Contemporary color schemes were selected for the cars. The Susquehanna facility likewise modernized more than 200 commuter cars; this meant better ventilation, reupholstered seats, and bright interior decor.[13]

The process of rehabilitation was manifested throughout the system. The ten-year period between the end of Erie's bankruptcy and its centennial recorded capital expenditures of $114 million. Although the lion's share, ap-

A commercial photographer from Cleveland clicked this staged photo of the "New Luxury Coaches for Erie's Diesel Passenger Trains" placed in service in 1947. The skilled craftsmen of the Susquehanna shops gutted fifteen older steel coaches "from car roof to floor" to create ones with "newest seats and broad view windows." (Erie Lackawanna Inc.)

In 1946 a company photographer recorded the developing revolution in motive power at the recently opened diesel-maintenance shop in Marion, Ohio. (Erie Lackawanna Inc.)

proximately $60 million, went for diesel locomotives, the company spent widely on other betterments. Some costs involved maintenance that may have been deferred since the 1920's. Gangs of workers from the Bridge and Building Department, for example, painted trackside and support structures. "You could really see this in the New York City area," remembered a long-time employee. "For one thing, the Erie docks were repainted, and they looked great in comparison with those of the Lehigh Valley and other roads."[14]

Much less mundane than cosmetic improvements were the major adjustments to the physical plant that dieselization demanded. The Erie not only built several diesel-locomotive repair facilities—one of the nation's first specialized diesel shops opened in Marion in March 1945—but it also modernized classification yards and terminals, lengthened sidings, and replaced and respaced signals. The longer freight trains, some reaching 150 or more cars, that diesels made possible necessitated many of these changes.[15]

Capital expenditures also included a vast array of modern machinery. The railroad purchased more efficient and cost-effective equipment for track maintenance. Between 1945 and 1950, for example, it bought 16 mechanical spike hammers, 12 bulldozers, and 4 "Power Ballaster" ballast cleaners. Office work likewise benefited from the latest technology. Several varieties of electronic calculators and sorting machines hastened such functions as equipment accounting, payroll, and stores record-keeping. The general public heard little about these advancements.[16]

Improved communications through technological change, however, drew considerable attention. The Erie had long been in the vanguard of such progressive measures. At the turn of the century it pioneered the use of telephones for train dispatching; in the 1920's it led with the "printing telegraph," a forerunner of the teletype; and after the war it employed some of the earliest commercial "walkie-talkies" for yard operations. Then in 1951, the company became the first major railroad to have its entire main line served by radio. Known as the "four-way train radio-telephone," this VHF system allowed static-free voice contact from train cab-to-caboose, train-to-train, train-to-station, and station-to-station. "The Erie should be congratulated for continuing to set a progressive pace for American railroading," editorialized the *Cleveland Press* in 1950. "[Radios offer] unending possibilities for increased safety and convenience."[17]

New passenger stations also caught the attention of journalists and the public. They lauded the opening of several structures after the war, such as facilities in Akron, Ohio, and Paterson, New Jersey, and the relocation of the downtown Cleveland station from an old and inconveniently situated building to the massive Cleveland Union Terminal on Public Square. The construction of the Akron depot typifies the philosophy of the Erie during the postwar years; namely, it sought to provide a good but economical facility.[18]

A bustling city of more than a quarter-million people, Akron was the largest intermediate community on the Erie main line, and it badly needed better depot facilities. Since 1891 a small union station had served the community, but Akron's spectacular growth during the 1910's boom in tire production made that building obsolete. (The Erie had become a terminal tenant in 1901, when it joined the Baltimore & Ohio and Pennsylvania railroads.) Moreover, the depot showed signs of wear and was poorly placed. In the early twenties civic leaders pushed unsuccessfully for a modern facility to be shared by the "Rubber City's" three principal carriers. Although increased use of automobiles and the Great Depression that followed lessened demands for improvement, the wartime surge of travelers sparked another drive for a better depot. Soon the New Union Depot Civic League, composed largely of local businessmen, pressured government authorities and railroads for action. Success, of sorts, followed. After nearly twenty years of foot-dragging, the Ohio Public Service Commission ordered a replacement structure in 1942, and the Erie quickly announced that it would construct its own facility. Tired of fuss-

Arthur W. Baker (*left*), the Erie superintendent at Hornell, New York, watches a demonstration by a Federal Communications Commission representative of a two-way radio in a caboose in December 1950. The old technology—the venerable kerosene lamp—is only inches away from the new. (Erie Lackawanna Inc.)

ing with its rivals, the B&O and the Pennsylvania, the company concluded that a separate depot would be less expensive. President Woodruff publicly argued, and with good reason, that a separate new station "could establish [the Erie] as a greater competitive factor and provide better [passenger] service for this area."[19]

Dreams of an improved passenger facility took shape soon after the war. In August 1946, the federal government's Civilian Production Administration gave the Erie a green light for construction. The architectural plans had been drawn, two months later the company awarded the general contract, and in less than a year the $350,000 facility opened. Hardly an example of imaginative styling, this 30-by-80-foot bilevel masonry box contained an office, ticket-counter, and waiting room on the street level and express, mail, and baggage-handling sections at trackside.[20]

The day of celebration was July 16, 1947, a rainy but pleasantly warm Wednesday. The *Akron Beacon Journal* cheered: "At Last! Akron Has a New Depot," and it commented that "No longer will Akronites have to apologize to visitors who come to town on Erie trains." The Goodyear blimp hovered over the downtown trailing a huge banner, CONGRATULATIONS—ERIE—ON YOUR NEW STATION. The company, too, "went all out" for the occasion. It hosted a luncheon for about 400 community leaders in the ballroom of the city's finest hotel and President Woodruff, publicity-conscious as ever, seized the opportunity to "put the Erie Railroad on the map." He subsequently delivered a well-attended dedication speech, oversaw public inspection of a diesel-powered passenger train, and assisted "Miss Erie," a seventeen-year-old Akron high school student, in the official ribbon-cutting ceremony. "The money we have spent here in Akron . . . is proof that we want to build for our patrons. . . . The future success of American railroads requires this level of investment."[21]

<hr/>

Woodruff's remarks at the Akron gala suggest much about the Erie's thinking: an upgraded and well-groomed property would create corporate prosperity. In the words of the *Annual Report* of 1951, "A railroad must make constant improvements if it is to progress and keep pace with an expanding . . . economy." This was the automatic response of the past; but unfortunately the company failed to consider carefully the rapidly changing nature of postwar transport, most of all ever-increasing truck competition and automobile usage. "The Erie just assumed that if it could get the tonnage delivered in a decent fashion then it would be in fine shape," argued a prominent railroad consultant. "It mostly ignored ways of how to combat the erosion of lucrative traffic and all of those problems that plagued railroading after its monopoly was lost." Perhaps it was the prosperity of the 1940's that distracted the company's leaders, and if so, they left the Erie unprepared for what happened in the 1950's and 1960's.[22]

Old Reliable showed some innovative tendencies. The Erie earned a reputation for embracing change, albeit mostly in the realm of technology. Still, the road sought to understand customers' needs. In 1942, President Woodruff tapped Eugene Root, an accounting department officer, to head the newly created Research Department, one of the first in the industry. Root and his small staff at the Cleveland headquarters examined traffic patterns and conducted some modest forecasting. The office worked closely with the Traffic Department, relying heavily upon its sales force to gather information. "The whole thing was pretty amateurish," recalled M. Fred Coffman, Root's principal assistant, "but it was a big improvement over the past. . . . We got some useful data about shippers and we could better predict our equipment needs." The Research Department also painstakingly studied which types of freight showed net profit or loss, and theoretically this information guided traffic personnel in their solicitations.[23]

The Erie approached the freight business in a traditional way and remained a substantial transporter of goods. The company hauled a significant volume of freight after the war: an average of 43.5 million tons moved annually between 1946 and 1951, peaking at 48.3 million tons in 1947. But the combination of a general business recession and prolonged strikes in the coal and steel industries in 1949 hammered traffic: volume that year slipped to 35.4 million tons, the lowest since 1939. Fortunately, the company hauled a diverse traffic mix, and it did not depend upon a limited range of cargoes. Management extolled this diversity: "Commodities moving over our railroad are a mixture of products that make up the general everyday commerce of our American economy."[24]

The commodity mix remained much as it had during earlier decades, with mining products making up the greatest volume, about half of the tonnage. The Erie ranked as an important coal carrier, although it was neither as famous nor as successful as some other Eastern roads. Old Reliable, for example, never matched the Norfolk & Western, "a conveyor belt for coal masquerading as a railroad." Still, Erie trains of hopper cars rumbled over its heavy-duty branch lines in Pennsylvania to other parts of the system and for interchange, especially to destinations in New England. The road's highest volume originated in the rich soft-coal fields of the Clearfield and Reynoldsville districts of west-central Pennsylvania and the celebrated, albeit fading, hard-coal deposits of the Keystone state's northeastern corner.[25]

The Erie also transported large amounts of iron ore. Delivered to company docks in Cleveland mostly from mines at the head of the Great Lakes by giant ore boats, "freshwater whales," and transferred to hopper cars by three monster Hulett unloaders, this red mineral was then moved by Erie crews to nearby points in Ohio and Pennsylvania.[26] Much of the iron ore fed hungry steel furnaces in the Mahoning Valley, a region employees aptly dubbed "the breadbasket of the Erie." Since the Erie commonly moved this ore on an intrastate basis, it could cut rates without approval from the Interstate Commerce Commission. The railroad's efficiency, coupled with competitive tariffs, enhanced its market share, largely at the expense of the Pennsylvania Railroad, and still produced profits.[27]

Also vital to Erie revenues were goods described as "Manufactures and Miscellaneous," about 37 percent of tonnage in 1951. This catchall category included automotive vehicles and parts, chemicals, iron and steel, and petroleum. Much of it either originated or terminated online, for (as the company bragged), "The Erie Area is the nation's largest single market. One third of America's people live, work and buy there—the greatest concentration of industry in the world."[28]

The third major category of freight, roughly 10 percent of tonnage, involved "Animal and Farm Products." Since June 28, 1887, when the Erie hauled a shipment of 806 boxes of California-grown plums, apricots, and peaches over its main line, a substantial amount of fresh fruits and vegetables, largely from the Far West, had moved over the line to New York City and points in New England. By the late 1940's this totaled about 35,000 to 40,000 cars annually. The Erie also hauled thousands of cars of meat products from the Chicago packing houses of Armour, Swift, Wilson, and others. For years the company proclaimed itself to be "The Route of the Perishables," and many shippers agreed. Since the Erie passed through some rich agricultural land, mostly in western Ohio and sections of Indiana, it also moved a variety of local crops, including corn, soybeans, and wheat. "We sure did a good grain business west of Marion," remarked a dispatcher in Huntington, Indiana. "The Erie sort of looked like a granger road out here."[29]

The remainder of Erie's freight tonnage consisted of "Forest Products" (3 percent) and less-than-carload (LCL) merchandise (about 2.5 percent). Fortunately for revenues, a substantial portion of both types moved on a "long-haul" basis rather than for only short distances. The road did not transport "piggyback" truck trailers until 1954, although two interchange partners, the Chicago Great Western and the New York, New Haven & Hartford, had begun promoting this intermodal service in the 1930's.[30]

Old Reliable long considered itself to be an "eastbound" freight hauler, and this pattern generally continued after World War II. The freight flow was generally directionally balanced between Chicago and eastern Ohio, but then became predominately eastbound to Jersey City. Eastward overbalance also characterized tonnage on the road's two principal non-coal-carrying appendages, the Hornell-to-Buffalo and Youngstown-to-Cleveland lines. Coal traveled from Pennsylvania mines and usually toward eastern on-line destinations and interchange points.[31]

Whether east- or westbound, the Erie operated its freight service expeditiously, and the company's locals and "coal drags" resembled those of comparable roads. More than twenty "hot" manifest freights sped cargoes between major terminals; they matched the best trains operated by competitors in the East and even by trunk lines west of Chicago. Carson S. Duncan, director of Competitive Transportation Research at the Association of American Railroads, described the road's freight operations in this 1948 statement: "The Erie's movement of freight reminds me of a western road. The railroad's wide clearances and well-engineered rights-of-way make it possible for [it] . . . to wheel goods rapidly between Chicago, New York and New England."[32]

Management worked diligently at "wheeling" freight tonnage; it made up almost all the road's income. In 1950, for example, freight accounted for 88.4 percent of total traffic handled and nearly 93 percent of revenues. Seizing the opportunity to bolster business, the road ballyhooed the introduction of its *Flying Saucers* in April 1949. While hardly UFOs, these two new diesel-powered freight trains, officially numbered 99 and 100, gave second-morning delivery in both directions between New York and Chicago of less-than-car-load and forwarder freight (the latter being carloads of goods shipped by freight-forwarding companies). The *Flying Saucers* also provided similar service to certain New England cities by connecting carriers. These trains pressed both the New York Central and Pennsylvania and forced them to speed up their schedules for movement of similar traffic. Overall, dieselization slashed transit time, as did the upgrading of terminal practices and facilities. "We did all that we could think of to get the freight trains over the road. That meant using diesels, two-way radios and experienced crews," said M. Fred Coffman. "We were a first-rate freight railroad that had the customer in mind."[33]

The Erie felt enormous competitive pressure to be a "first-rate freight railroad." Not only did freight generate most income, but this business was never guaranteed. The company depended considerably on "bridge" or interchange traffic. It originated less than half of its freight tonnage while industry folk wisdom considered it necessary for a carrier to generate at least half of its own freight business. Lumber, for example, typically moved from mills in the Pacific Northwest through the Chicago gateway for delivery at various eastern and northeastern destinations. Although possessing wide clearances and other attractive features, the Erie did not have the shortest route between Chicago and New York: it was about 100 miles longer than the Pennsylvania, 50 miles longer than the New York Central, and even somewhat longer than the Nickel Plate–Delaware, Lackawanna & Western "fast freight line" through Buffalo. To obtain those carloads of Pacific Northwest lumber and similar traffic, Old Reliable had to be just that and more.[34]

Unmistakably, the Erie was a strong freight road, but it never ranked as a premier passenger carrier. The company operated no train comparable to either the New York Central's crack *Twentieth Century Limited* or the Pennsylvania's equally smart *Broadway Limited*. Its flagship train, the *Erie Limited*, was neither as fast nor as elaborate. Both the *Twentieth Century* and the *Broadway* traveled from New York to Chicago in 16 hours by 1950; the *Erie Limited* took nearly 24. While the *Erie Limited*'s consist included Pullman sleeping cars, it was not an all–private accommodation train like its famous rivals. Nevertheless, the Erie offered a clean, comfortable, and dependable service. The *Erie Limited* left Jersey City in midmorning so that its passengers, unlike those who chose the overnight *Twentieth Century* or *Broadway*, enjoyed the spectacular scenery of the Delaware and Susquehanna river valleys. "This trip gave you some wonderful vistas," recalled a Connecticut resident, adding, "The Erie was a very pleasant but leisurely way to go to Chicago." When the Erie promoted its postwar passenger service, it could not claim a fleet of streamliners, so advertising copy told prospective patrons that "almost the entire main line between the Ohio and Pennsylvania state line and Jersey City runs along glistening rivers through green valleys and along colorful ranges of wooded hills." The company remained "The Scenic Route of the East."[35]

The Erie maintained quality intercity trains and sought, in a publicist's words, to "treat the traveling public right." Dieselization and new and remodeled equipment underscored the company's philosophy as expressed by President Woodruff: "that if you're hauling people, you had better keep up your trains. . . . The public, rightly or wrongly, judges a railroad by its passenger service." Introduction on May 2, 1950, of the *Steel King*, a new name-train that linked Cleveland and Pittsburgh (via the Pittsburgh & Lake Erie Railroad at Youngstown), represented this commitment to "treat the traveling public right." The *Steel King*'s schedule of two hours and forty minutes bettered the fastest times offered by competitors Baltimore & Ohio and Pennsylvania, and its equipment "is fully modern and appealing." As the train passed along this 131-mile route, its noisy regularity was a Big Ben of sorts to the area. The attractiveness of Erie's passenger service became more pronounced as the character of other roads' trains began to deteriorate. "I want to tell you how much I enjoyed a ride to Chicago on your Train No. 5 [*The Lake Cities*]," wrote a New Jersey resident to company brass. "The equipment was in fine condition; the food and service excellent; the train was handled smoothly; and no one could have asked for a more pleasant and friendly set of train crews." And he concluded, "the trip home on the Pennsylvania [Railroad] brought into sharp focus why so many travelers refer to that line as the 'Public Be Damned.'"[36]

While the long-distance passenger business eventually turned to dross, the Erie did not foresee that outcome, and for good reason. Although automobile ownership increased rapidly after 1945, reaching 49 million vehicles by 1950, not everyone owned a car; the census of 1950 revealed only slightly more than one automobile per household. Even if individuals drove at home, they might not take their cars on out-of-town trips. Traffic was heavy and road conditions were poor; drivers commonly jostled with one another for space on narrow, rough, and winding highways. And other nonrailroad options were limited. Although commercial aviation expanded after the war, plane travel remained costly and novel. Buses, while hardly expensive or unfamiliar, encountered the same problems that plagued motorists. The Erie thus attracted an array of patrons; its trains played a part in their lives that at the time seemed indispensable. By way of example, Alfred University students from the New York City area concocted this bit of doggerel:

> Ten More Days of Starvation
> Before We Go Back to Civilization

The STEEL KING *Erie Railroad's newest name train leaves Cleveland Union Terminal for its daily run of One Hour 18 Minutes to Youngstown and Two Hours 40 Minutes to Pittsburgh.*

The Erie ballyhooed its new name-train, *The Steel King*, which first linked Cleveland and Pittsburgh on May 2, 1950. The company operated this convenient and comfortable train jointly with the Pittsburgh & Lake Erie. (Grant)

> Then We Go Down to the Station
> The ERIE Will Take Us Home![37]

"We were in pretty good shape in the passenger area for some time into the 1950's," remembered an Erie executive. Passenger revenues remained relatively stable after the war, although patronage eroded gradually after 1948. The company made adjustments beyond upgrading long-distance service. It wisely pushed hard to discontinue money-losing runs, and unlike most Eastern carriers, the Erie quickly extricated itself from the branch-line passenger quagmire. When it abandoned its last two trains on the Buffalo-and-Hornell line on February 12, 1951, the Erie ended branch-line operations west of the New York City commuter zone (Suffern, New York), except for the Cleveland and Youngstown operation, which resembled the main line. The railroad's only real concern involved ever-mounting deficits run up by its considerable commuter operations. Management, however, responded slowly to the problem, although it petitioned to abandon the runs losing the most money, namely those on its Greenwood Lake Division in New Jersey.[38]

Although passenger revenues did not portend robust financial health, they suggested no immediate crisis at the Erie headquarters. Indeed, these were golden years. "We prospered after the war and especially in the early 1950's," recalled a financial officer. Operating revenues reached a record

Engineer Edgar Staley (*left*) and conductor John Chaney perform the railroading ritual of checking timepieces for on-the-second synchronization before the departure of their passenger train from Kent, Ohio, in the late 1940's. (Erie Lackawanna Inc.)

Optimistic about long-distance passenger service immediately after World War II, the Erie repeatedly sought to build up its Chicago–New York trains. Newspaper advertisements, radio spots, and even ink-blotter cards such as this told potential patrons about the company. (Grant)

$178,857,243 in 1951, and operating ratios looked good; they fluctuated from a high of 85.83 in 1949, a recession year, to a respectable low of 73.18 in 1950. With fixed charges of approximately $5 million (they stood at nearly $14 million in 1941) and no major bond maturities until early 1953, the company repeatedly declared annual dividends. It paid five dollars per share on preferred stock and continued to pay on its common, increasing the dividends from one dollar in 1946 to $1.75 in 1950.[39]

In the midst of these flush times, the Erie experienced a change of leadership. Approaching the company's mandatory retirement age of 65, Robert Woodruff notified the Board of Directors that he planned to leave the presidency on October 1, 1949, several weeks after his birthday. (Woodruff would then serve as chairman of the board.) Few expected anyone other than executive vice president Paul W. Johnston to be his successor, and they were right. Woodruff had groomed this accomplished railroader to be his heir for some time. One official, Harold Dale Barber, a vice president since 1939, had pressured Woodruff and several board members for the job, but "[Woodruff] liked Johnston and believed that he would be a better president." (Later Johnston fired Barber because he "was still angry about the slight and questioned Johnston's authority.")[40]

The Erie's twenty-seventh president was a solid choice, for Paul Johnston possessed numerous positive attributes. Fellow Erie employees and many

The leaders of the Erie Railroad during the 1940's and 1950's, Paul Johnston (*left*) and Robert Woodruff, stand by a commemorative bronze plaque honoring the dedication of Woodruff Yard in Hornell, New York, on September 30, 1953. "Not until President Johnston unveiled the plaque did Mr. Woodruff realize that the ceremony was in his honor," reported the November 1953 issue of the *Erie Railroad Magazine*. "His expression then changed to one of amazement and pleasure." (Erie Lackawanna Inc.)

from the industry described him as "a fine, outstanding man," "knowledgeable about railroading," and a "natural leader of men." Paul W. Johnston, Jr., who also served the Erie as an officer, recalled that his father was a "private, compassionate, intelligent, organized person, with a keen sense of humor and a stable disposition." It is not surprising then that one acquaintance observed: "Paul was the best president at Erie since [Charles] Denney and until Bill White took over as chairman of the board in 1963."[41]

Johnston came from an Erie family. He was born on July 5, 1892, in a house across the street from the Erie depot in Transfer, Pennsylvania, where his father worked as agent. "The first sounds that he heard, besides his mother's lullabies," wrote the company's public relations officer, "were the whistles of Erie locomotives approaching the station and the click of the train wheels over the rail ends as trains rolled over the main line." As a child Johnston helped his father at the depot, and in time became a full-time employee. The young railroader left the Erie to enroll at nearby Allegheny College, graduating with honors in 1914. Although Johnston subsequently spent a year in divinity school at Boston University and became an ordained minister in the Methodist Church, he decided to return to the Erie. Johnston steadily advanced through the ranks and in 1948 became the second highest officer, executive vice president. Like thousands of other Erie employees, Johnston had joined the military during World War II, and he served on the staff of General Douglas MacArthur in the South Pacific. He was discharged as a brigadier general.[42]

The formative years of Johnston's presidency reveal continuity rather than change. Like Woodruff, Erie's new head believed firmly in technological advancements. He happily informed stockholders in February 1951 that the $114 million invested in modern equipment and facilities during the previous decade had been spent wisely; the road's annual net income was the highest in history. Johnston also liked to boost the company: "Erie's bad old reputation is a thing of the past," he told the press shortly after he took office. "We in management will continue to promote this progressive railroad and its vibrant service area to the best of our ability." Sounding like his predecessor, he added, "I believe that if the public knows about the Erie that it will prosper even more."[43]

⌇

This feeling of accomplishment and dedication to corporate advancement found expression in a well-orchestrated celebration. With much fanfare, the Erie observed the centennial of the completion of the New York & Erie Railroad's main line from the Hudson River to Lake Erie in 1851. "We'll turn the spotlight on our railroad," Johnston declared, and the Erie did just that.[44]

Corporate centennials and related celebrations proliferated among the nation's railroads following World War II. Several factors contributed to this phenomenon: carriers were flush with funds; many were founded a century earlier; and most strove to enhance their images. The Erie was no exception. Like dozens of other trunk roads, it spent heavily on this form of self-promotion. The company had joined a score of major roads in sponsoring the highly acclaimed Chicago Railroad Fair in 1948 and 1949. More significantly, the Erie decided to exploit a forthcoming "Milestone in American History," the centennial of its core trackage between Piermont and Dunkirk.[45]

George C. Frank, Sr., assistant to the president and editor of the *Erie Railroad Magazine*, took charge of this celebration. An able and affable promoter, he spent months preparing for two principal activities, a two-day reenactment of the first through train between the Hudson River and Lake Erie, and a two-month tour of the system by a special eighteen-car exhibition train. Frank did not work alone; the company contracted with a New York City public relations firm, Steve Hannigan and Associates, for assistance.[46]

Frank and his public relations allies developed a theme for the observance: "Progress and Service." As Frank explained to colleagues in late November 1950, "We want to plant firmly in the public's mind the point that the Erie Railroad is the route of PROGRESS AND SERVICE." Frank also listed the expected benefits of this anticipated investment of $200,000:

1. Increased knowledge about the Erie
2. Demonstrate Erie's progressiveness
3. Build faith and confidence in Erie's management
4. Strengthen employee morale and pride in the company
5. Add increased recognition of Erie's service to communities
6. Stimulate business, both passenger and freight
7. Establish Erie's improved credit position in financial circles
8. Associate Erie's history with free enterprise principles
9. Show importance of strong, healthy railroads in peacetime and for national defense
10. Promote desirability of Erie Area for plant location.[47]

The centennial festivities went well, with hundreds of thousands of "very pleased visitors" flocking to various activities and attractions. The media provided extensive coverage. "I couldn't imagine that we could have done a better job in bringing attention to the Erie," recalled a board member; that was the universal consensus.[48]

The cleverly staged reenactment of the 1851 journey from New York City to Dunkirk captured the most attention. George Frank and his associates closely followed the itinerary of the historic trip. It took two days—May 14 and 15, 1951—and involved several hundred guests. The excursionists traveled by boat from New York City to the rail connection at Piermont, where they boarded the "Centennial Train." The consist of this special was memorable: two diesel locomotives, ten cabooses, and four flatcars on which were placed Daniel Webster and his famous rocking chair, an 1851-era steam locomotive, and a vintage baggage car and passenger coach. As the train moved toward an overnight stop at Elmira, New York, it paused in several communities where "Mr. Johnston made a speech [and] . . . always called for a speech from Daniel Webster, this is to say from his impersonator . . . [actor] Dallas Boyd, who himself looked like the photographs of this great orator and Secretary of State. . . . He always made a great hit." (Nearly forty years later Frank recalled that "Boyd's speech at Deposit [New York] was so moving that it even brought tears to my eyes.") The public response to the Centennial Train was impressive. "[T]here were enormous crowds at the stations awaiting the train,

The Erie spent heavily on its celebration of the centennial of its original core line between Piermont and Dunkirk, New York. The company distributed thousands of these souvenir color postcards with the official centennial logo. (Grant)

especially at Port Jervis, Deposit and Susquehanna," reported one rider. "All schools were closed and even storekeepers and others closed to give their employees an opportunity to view the proceedings. . . . Children were lined up by the thousands under the control of a probably greatly enlarged police force and their teachers. Bands of Music, High School Fife and Drum Corps of boys and girls, all in colorful regalia and the air was filled with music, noise and loud cheers." After an elaborate banquet in Elmira, the train continued to stop at various communities until it reached Dunkirk shortly after 6 P.M. There the Erie hosted more speeches, a parade that featured a motorized replica of an early steam locomotive and coach, and a massive public "feast." More than 40,000 individuals attended. The festivities ended by ten and the traveling guests boarded a Pullman-equipped train for their return to New York City.[49]

Although less spectacular than the reenactment, the "Erie Centennial Exhibition Train" (dubbed the CET) attracted hordes of visitors from throughout the system. Between its debut in Hammond, Indiana, on June 18 and its final stop at Jersey City 53 days later, 354,285 people inspected the train. Resembling the Piermont-to-Dunkirk consist, the CET included flatcars with antique rolling stock, but it also featured display equipment: sleeping, dining,

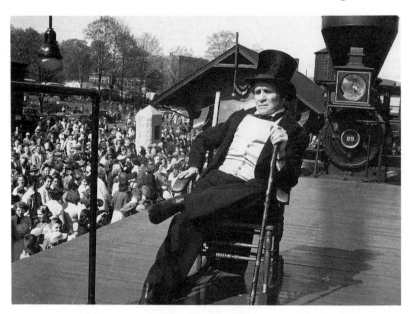

Actor Dallas Boyd, who portrayed Daniel Webster in the reenactment of the opening of the "Ocean to the Lakes" route, rests in a rocking chair during centennial ceremonies in Deposit, New York, on May 14, 1951. The Erie paid special attention to this small New York community, where dignitaries had turned the first ground for the New York & Erie on November 7, 1835. (Erie Lackawanna Inc.)

and refrigerator cars, another flatcar with the "biggest and latest Army tank—the 73-ton 'experimental heavy,' " (chosen to demonstrate Erie's ample clearances and the road's importance to national defense), a museum coach, and a radio-equipped caboose.[50]

And the Erie did more. It distributed cartons of folders, scores of press releases, and thousands of souvenirs such as pins, window decals, and postal cards. The company even installed bronze hundredth-anniversary plaques at stations along its principal lines. The only negative note was cost; it exceeded the original budget by nearly a third. When accountants made their final audit in 1952, the gala's price tag stood at $280,080.67. Yet, to use Frank's words, "It was worth every penny." The company charged the amount to operating expenses and nobody objected.[51]

These centennial festivities represent Erie's zenith between its reorganization a decade earlier and its merger with the Delaware, Lackawanna & Western nearly a decade later. Milton McInnes correctly spoke of the importance of the celebration: "I can't recall when the Erie felt better about itself or the public about it than during the summer of 1951. . . . We were on cloud nine." Surely the hundredth anniversary of "the Great Lakes to the Sea" rail route symbolized the new Erie more than did the end of bankruptcy. That event offered hope; the centennial proclaimed the arrival of prosperity.[52]

An objective of the centennial celebration had been to "strengthen employee morale and pride in the company." There is no way to measure whether this occurred, but workers viewed the road positively; most considered themselves members of the Erie family. Although this feeling apparently had existed for generations, the centennial probably reinforced these strong bonds.[53]

Why "Eriemen" showed loyalty to the carrier, even during its darkest days, can be explained partially by the continuing and widespread practice of nepotism. Family members received favored treatment at all levels, whether in train service, shop work, or office jobs. This had been traditional throughout the industry. In his examination of railroad work in the nineteenth century, labor historian Walter Licht discovered that "family connection represented probably the most important asset in securing employment for all grades of railway workers." James H. Ducker, another labor scholar, reached a similar conclusion about employees on the Atchison, Topeka & Santa Fe Railway: "Favoritism and nepotism [were] major factor[s] in hiring throughout the [nineteenth] century." The importance of kinship knew no geographical bounds.[54]

Nepotism continued in the hiring practices of carriers into the twentieth century, and the Erie must have been a leader. Retirees agreed: "Most fellows who got jobs had railroad connections." Explained a former telegrapher and dispatcher, whose father was a longtime station agent, "Having Dad there with the Erie was the only way I got the position [agent-telegrapher] during the Depression of the 1930's." Remembered another Erie worker, "The company was so full of related employees that you had to watch what you said in the locker rooms. . . . Most men had relations there in the shops." Executive positions were not exempt from nepotism. For example, President Frederick Underwood named his stepson, Franklin Robbins, to head the Elmira, Corning & Waverly Railway, an Erie subsidiary, in 1913, and William White, later chairman of the Board of Directors, but then trainmaster on the Kent Division, got his younger brother Garret a clerk's job in November 1925, and subsequently his sibling became a top official.[55]

Nepotism on the Erie may have been more a blessing than a curse. "You really felt part of the team if you came from a railroad family," remarked a locomotive engineer. Recalled another employee, "You wanted to be sure that the equipment and track was good and that safety was always followed, . . . for you might have a family person's life in danger if things were not up to snuff." An office worker who came from an extended Erie family in Hornell, New York, observed, "I thought of the Erie as part of my home life. . . . You know, they spoke Italian on the job, maybe not to the boss, but to each other. That made them feel good about their work and the Erie." There is additional evidence to suggest that nepotism created better morale. In a survey of employees' attitudes in 1947, management found that "among those who thought the Erie was better than most companies were many who had fathers and grandfathers working for the company; and many of the 6 per cent who said it was 'not so good' were individuals who just had a job and had not been with us very long and had not yet acquired the typical Erie spirit."[56]

Management repeatedly buttressed the "family" atmosphere. During the Woodruff and Johnston regimes especially, the company zealously supported the annual picnic held in August at Conneaut Lake Park, Pennsylvania, which consistently drew large, spirited crowds. Similarly, the road backed the Erie Veterans' Association, launched in 1926; it publicized the group's numerous social events in the monthly employee magazine and provided speakers and transportation. The Erie also "made a big deal of everybody's retirement. . . . The boys liked that." And the road backed other spirit-boosting activities, including brass bands (the one at Huntington, Indiana, even outlasted the Erie Lackawanna Railway) and athletic teams. Winning the coveted "R. E. Woodruff Bowling Trophy" in the late 1940's and the 1950's meant much to hundreds of employees. Members of the Erie family likewise warmly endorsed the company's college scholarship program for children of its employees.[57]

The railroad's structure fostered an esprit de corps. Beginning with the Bernet reorganization, the company, unlike other large Eastern carriers, permitted junior personnel to participate in making day-to-day decisions. Operating employees could exercise their own judgment within the constraints of the Book of Rules and other directives. Examples abound. "We got the trains over the road efficiently and safely," recalled a freight conductor. "It was a good job because the big shots encouraged you to use your best judgment and you had a say on how things ought to be done." Added an office clerk, "Local people could settle labor matters like time slips, just so long as no precedents were set." Division officers met regularly with their workers and an open line of communication linked all levels of command, from trainmen to trainmasters to superintendents and even to the president.[58]

The labor-movement system at the Erie was hardly utopian. Just as corporate welfare programs in larger businesses failed to eliminate conflicts between workers and managers, even the Erie family had its spats. All the same, labor unrest never plagued the company as it did some roads after the war. The Chicago Great Western, for example, experienced a walkout by its operating unions for 43 days in early 1953, and the wounds healed slowly. The Erie and other carriers both benefited from and were cursed by the passage of federal mediation statutes, including that which created the National Railroad Adjustment Board in 1934.[59]

Petty wrangling occurred throughout Erie ranks and seemed continuous. While there were many such cases, the attack made by the general chairman of the Brotherhood of Railroad Trainmen against the behavior of the terminal trainmaster at Jersey City is typical of the genre. That officer allegedly bullied a yard conductor and charged openly that "the Brotherhood of Railroad Trainmen would never get anything on the Erie Railroad, and if a member got discharged, the Trainmen could not get him back to work, that they were throwing their money away by belonging to the organization and that once in a while the railroad gave the organization a claim just to pacify them." The trainmaster's conduct produced only angry words, however, and these "minor disputes" were resolved either internally or through federal mediation.[60]

Serious controversies did erupt. Workers' discontent did not focus singly on Erie management, but rather was part of the national brotherhoods collectively battling the rail industry. After World War II employees of Old Reliable and other carriers felt the sting of inflation; heavy postwar spending by the federal government, especially during the Korean Conflict, reduced the purchasing power of the dollar. Railroad workers demanded higher wages and were encouraged by hefty pay hikes granted to coal miners and steelworkers in early 1947. Railroaders pushed hard for increased income, and between 1947 and 1953 they won several major pay raises. The process involved strike threats, wildcat work stoppages, and ultimately government intervention. Conditions became so unsettled that twice the nation's railroads fell briefly under federal control.[61]

The labor agreements subsequently drafted cost the Erie dearly. President Woodruff lamented in 1949 that "as a result of settlements reached with some of the unions and the acceptance of [Presidential] Emergency Board decisions in the case of other unions, . . . wage costs [for the Erie] increased $8,166,000 in 1948 over 1947." Carriers, including Erie, asked the Interstate Commerce Commission for rate increases to pay for the new wage levels, and they enjoyed some success. Fortunately for the Erie, the portion of its income that workers received remained relatively constant: it stood at 47.5 percent in 1947; reached a high of 49.5 percent two years later; and declined to 46.9 percent in 1953.[62]

If management had been able to eliminate "featherbedding," or make-work, its financial position would have improved noticeably. Dieselization made firemen redundant. Since there were no fires to tend, these crewman mostly watched for dangers; indeed, a federal fact-finding board appointed by President Harry Truman in 1949 concluded that work in a diesel cab was "considerably less than a full-time job." Similarly, a comprehensive investigation made by a Canadian commission in 1957 found that the fireman's functions "have either totally disappeared, as in the case of production of power, mechanical assistance and inspection, or are a mere duplication of what is discharged by another or others, as in the case of lookout functions performed by the head-end trainman and engineman." "Full-crew laws" in several states further hurt the Erie. These statutes required the company to employ three brakemen on long freight trains, when they needed only one or perhaps two at most. Such requirements did not reflect the realities of postwar railroading, but rather the era of the steam locomotive and handbrakes. "After the war we really didn't try to reduce the labor force to cut costs like we should have," admitted Milton McInnes. "The unions and their friends, the politicians, just had too much power." Organized labor's dogged defense of outdated work rules discouraged railroad officialdom and roads like the Erie failed to benefit fully from technological change. The corporate response was, whenever possible, to pass increased operating costs on to customers.[63]

By the mid-1950's Erie management considered industrial development to be the "best way for us to generate traffic and heighten revenues." The company had a long-established program to increase on-line business from existing firms and attract new industries to Erie sidings. "An important asset to any railroad is the number of individual plants located on its lines," argued President Woodruff. He noted with satisfaction that "a continued and intensive effort is being maintained to increase the number of industries which can be served by the Erie." The company's small but aggressive Industrial Development Department worked effectively to that end. As the result of personal contracts and other strategies, the department greatly expanded the base of shippers. Between 1946 and 1957, 1,235 companies either opened new plants or expanded operations along the Erie. Railroad representatives gave these firms considerable assistance: they provided up-to-date information about locations, labor supplies, tax rates, available electric power, natural resources, and, of course, how the Erie might serve their transportation needs. "We hit hard the point that we cared about our customers," remarked a traffic executive, "and that we'd do all that was humanly possible to move their goods on time and in a careful and professional fashion." By 1950 "nearly every industrial building adjacent to our lines has been taken up and is occupied by active industry," and so the Industrial Development Department arranged for the railroad to sell unneeded yet suitable real estate and to aid groups in creating industrial parks. By decade's end the latter became centers of manufacturing and commercial activity along the system. Especially successful were efforts in New Jersey, including sites in East Rutherford, Fairlawn, Secaucus, and Teterboro.[64]

When President Johnston boasted in the mid-1950's that the company had been "unusually successful in attracting new industries which it can service," he merely stated a fact. The road profited not only from a talented development staff and its well-established reputation for personalized service but also from its location. Before the region fell victim to the "Rust Belt" phenomenon, the Erie served the "Heart of Industrial America." These factors collectively helped it to win a spectacular plum in 1953: the world's largest automobile assembly plant, causing "quite a stir" in railroad and business circles.[65]

The Ford Motor Company in early 1953 decided to locate the principal assembly plant of its Ford Motor Division on the Erie main line near Suffern, New York. The selection of Mahwah, New Jersey, several miles southeast of Suffern, for the expansion became a sensation, and construction of what journalists called "Boomtown on the Erie" began immediately. The multimillion-dollar state-of-the-art single-story facility opened in July 1955. Board member John Hadden discussed the coup: "[W]hen we first got in touch with the Ford people they were already two-thirds sold on a site on the Pennsylvania [Railroad]. . . . so there were really two jobs—unselling Ford on the Pennsylvania and selling them on the Erie site. The thing that impressed me as much as anything else was . . . that one or two of the key men in the Ford organization were already very much sold on Erie service—nevertheless, the job required a high order of salesmanship and Erie had it." Added Hadden, "I was amused to learn that one of the things that seemed to please the Ford people on one of their first trips to the property was the suggestion of Vice President McInnes that he run them up from New York in the business car—the luxury of the business car seemed to please the Ford people very much. It is often the little things that count."[66] This decision by Ford meant much to the Erie, as Mahwah produced a solid increase in freight revenues, about $9 million in 1956, and the Erie held exclusive rail rights to the sprawling complex.[67]

While Old Reliable failed to duplicate the Mahwah feat, it lured several other large manufacturers to sites along the system. The most important in terms of income generated was the choice of Mansfield, Ohio, on the main line, as location for a large stamping plant of the Fisher Body Division of General Motors. Begun in 1955 and completed a year later, this facility produced body parts and subassemblies for automobile plants nationwide, and these components moved mostly by rail. "This was good, profitable business," recalled a traffic specialist. The Erie believed that this business meant "solid income for years to come." This expectation made sense during the 1950's and even later, for the domestic automobile industry prospered. General Motors, America's largest automaker, averaged profits of nearly 20 percent on net worth between 1946 and 1967; its factories generally hummed with activity.[68]

Hand-in-hand with industrial development went efforts to improve freight service. With much press notice, the Erie entered the trailer-on-flatcar (TOFC) field: its first piggyback shipment, a trailer loaded with cleaning compound, moved from Chicago to Croxton Yard in train number 100, the *Flying Saucer*, on July 14, 1954. Initially, the company limited TOFC to the route between Chicago and metropolitan New York, but expansion soon followed. This meant adding more terminals, including facilities on principal branch lines, and agreements with connecting carriers. The Erie and New Haven, for example, launched a joint service on December 20, 1955, that linked Erie territory with southern New England. Both traffic departments discovered that businesses in Chicago and northeastern Ohio (Akron, Cleveland, and Youngstown) customarily shipped freight by motor carriers in and out of the Boston and Providence areas. Some of these destinations were "truck plants," facilities not located on rail sidings. "With the new piggyback service the Erie is definitely going after this business," reported the *Erie Railroad Magazine*, and it did so with some success.[69]

Unfortunately, the Erie, and most roads too, equated piggyback traffic with increased profits. Carriers, including Old Reliable, seldom conducted accurate cost analyses, for the economics of piggyback were still poorly understood and would remain so on most railroads until the industry achieved partial deregulation in 1980. By pricing TOFC service at the lowest truck rates, freight often moved out of boxcars into lower-revenue truck trailers, conferring unintended windfalls on customers. The Erie also may have blundered in the TOFC business by using commercial freight forwarders rather than its own equipment. The New York Central ran counter to the Erie and the industry when it astutely formed a motor subsidiary, New York Central Transport Company, in 1956, and its program of retailing TOFC prospered. Wholesale piggyback operations on the Erie probably earned less than if the road had embraced a retail approach.[70]

━━━

The Erie generally held its own financially during the 1950's until the national recession of 1958–59, together with an upward spiral in operating expenses, dramatically slashed net income. These factors forced cuts in expenditures, employee layoffs, and drastic reductions of dividend payments. Net income in the early 1950's had stood at respectable levels, remaining strong and stable in 1952 and 1953 at $13.2 million and $12.6 million. Suddenly net income plunged in 1954 to $6.4 million, largely because of a drop in traffic caused by the end of hostilities in Korea. Net income rose in 1955 to $7.9 million, even though Hurricane Diane in August of that year did more than $2 million in damages to the Delaware and Wyoming divisions; a year later net income reached $8.2 million. But net income dropped to $3.6 million in 1957, a harbinger of the approaching financial crisis. Owners of preferred stock had continued to receive annual checks of $5 per share; holders of common got $1.75 per share in 1952 and 1953, and $1.50 in 1955 and 1956, but only $1 in 1957. These payments soon ended altogether.[71]

The company profited from a generally strong national economy during

President Dwight Eisenhower's first term when the gross national product increased from $363.2 billion in 1953 to $412.4 billion in 1956. The country's employment in 1956 reached an all-time high of 65 million—a rise of 3.7 million over 1953. Ike and his probusiness administration could also boast that during their first three years in power inflation, a problem that haunted the Truman presidency, had been halted. From 1953 until early 1956 the consumers' price index remained firm. Unfortunately economic problems reappeared after 1957, and the "Eisenhower prosperity" was not as permanent as many Americans thought.[72]

Initiative also helps to explain Erie's prosperity. Being an important carrier of raw materials and finished products aided the company, but so did aggressive marketing, dieselization, and good maintenance. No one contested President Johnston's statement in 1956: "By continually improving the dependability of our service, we are benefiting not only our customers, but employes and shareholders as well."[73]

Creative financial strategies likewise helped. The company offered preferred shareholders the opportunity in 1955 to exchange their stock for 5 percent income debentures. Nearly three-quarters of these equity owners agreed. "We went out and talked to as many of them as we could possibly find," noted a financial officer. "The old preferred stockholders did not lose anything, but we told them that the company would really benefit." The reason was a simple accounting gain. Interest paid on debentures, unlike payments on stock, could be deducted on corporate federal income tax returns. "This transaction, based on current tax-rates," noted the *Annual Report* of 1955, "produces net savings of approximately $777,000 a year."[74]

The Erie also gained from several increases in freight rates. Railroads did experience difficulty winning timely approval from the Interstate Commerce Commission to adjust charges in order to offset higher costs. The ICC granted a significant, albeit temporary, hike of 15 percent effective May 2, 1952. Although in force only until February 28, 1953, the Commission later extended the deadline to the end of 1955. Another freight-rate boost came in 1956, but it was not as large as the carriers sought. Better news, at least for the Erie, had come from Washington in June 1953. Officials smiled when they learned that the Commission had sided with eastern roads in their long and hotly contested battle with southern and southwestern carriers over divisions of freight rates. For years southern and southwestern roads had taken a larger slice of income generated from their interchange traffic with the eastern carriers, this share amounting to as much as 25 or 30 percent. Eastern roads in the late 1940's made a careful cost study and developed convincing evidence that an *equal* division of revenues should become regulatory policy. The ICC's decision meant about $50 million annually in additional income for the victors; Erie estimated that its yearly increase would exceed $1 million.[75]

The heavy repair area of the Marion, Ohio, diesel maintenance facility had state-of-the-art equipment when this image was made in January 1954. The worker is installing a newly wound armature into the magnet frame of a traction motor. (Erie Lackawanna Inc.)

Even though the Erie prospered during the post–World War II period, it began to feel squeezed by 1957. The economy soured; the regulatory process was more of a hindrance than an aid; and competition with motor carriers, notwithstanding growth of piggyback operations, continued unabated. "By the late 1950's we were sliding into a hole," recalled Milton McInnes. "Something much more spectacular needed to be done than what we were then doing." The answer appeared to be a corporate merger.[76]

MERGER,
1958–1960

S HORTLY BEFORE THE ERIE RAILROAD encountered formidable financial problems and sought relief through a merger, the company experienced a major change in leadership. On November 1, 1956, President
Paul W. Johnston, who was nearing his sixty-fifth birthday, the mandatory age
for retirement, surrendered his duties to Harry Von Willer, the company's
ranking traffic officer. Johnston then took the place of 72-year-old Robert E.
Woodruff as chairman of the Board of Directors, a position not considered
active service. There were other promotions at the senior level: Milton Mc-
Innes assumed the number two post of executive vice president; David
Thompson, a career traffic specialist, took Von Willer's job as vice president
for traffic; and Garret "Gary" White became vice president for operations.[1]

Unfortunately, the Erie assembled a management team ill-suited to face
the difficult times ahead. Its new officers knew traditional railroading, but
collectively they lacked imagination. One industry expert said it well: "They
were not like the creative group that Al [Alfred E.] Perlman hired at the [New
York] Central about the same time or the people that Ben Heineman was
bringing in at the [Chicago &] North Western." And, he concluded, "Paul
Johnston had been a reasonably good president for the times, but Harry Von
Willer was not much more than a good traffic man from the old school and a
swell fellow."[2]

Like his immediate predecessors Johnston and Woodruff, Harry Von
Willer, Erie's twenty-eighth president, reached the last rung of the company
ladder shortly after his sixtieth birthday. Born in Greensburg, Indiana, on Au-

Harry Von Willer, the last president of the Erie Railroad, sat for this portrait about the time he took charge of the company in November 1956. (Erie Lackawanna Inc.)

gust 11, 1896, Von Willer attended grade school and a manual-training high school in Indianapolis. Entering Purdue University in 1914 to study electrical engineering, he had to withdraw in his sophomore year when his father, a conductor on the "Big Four" Railroad (New York Central system), died suddenly. Compelled to leave college, Von Willer took a clerical job with the Big Four in its Indianapolis freight office. A few days after the United States entered World War I, Von Willer eagerly left railroading for soldiering. Discharged in 1919 as a sergeant first class, he returned to his former employer in Indianapolis. In 1923 Von Willer moved to a similar job with the Erie, which provided freight service to the Indiana capital from Dayton, Ohio, under a trackage-rights agreement with the Baltimore & Ohio Railroad. Von Willer subsequently joined the traffic department and advanced steadily, becoming its head in 1942.[3]

Harry Von Willer's choice of traffic work suited his personality; he was a gregarious, tenacious, and hardworking young man. He happily endured thousands of nights in Pullman berths and hotel beds. A feature writer for *Business Week* noted in 1953 that "[Von Willer] travels 150,000 miles a year, makes more than 100 speeches, and visits hundreds of customers." His hobbies—baseball, cards, and golf—appropriately complemented his professional life, but rather than smoke a cigar, the trademark of a salesman, he puffed on a favorite pipe.[4]

While labeled "old school" and blasted by some ranking industry officials for his background—"A traffic man doesn't make a good president"—Von

Willer showed more foresight than most colleagues during the postwar years. He realized that the Erie had to compensate for changing patterns of freight; anthracite loadings had declined dramatically, and more powerful trucks and improved roads had increased competition from motor carriers. "We need to provide stimulus to growth," Von Willer told the Board of Directors in April 1956, and he recommended a threefold plan: "1) Intensification of direct selling efforts [of which he was a master], 2) the development of piggyback service, and 3) industrial development." Although hardly earth-shaking, these suggestions, hallmarks of his forthcoming presidency, surely helped to generate additional revenues. Von Willer understood that intermodal traffic would take on added importance, in part because the Erie functioned as a fast-freight route and lacked an extensive network of industrial branches.[5]

Harry Von Willer endorsed another method to improve Erie's balance sheets. This involved coordinated services with the Delaware, Lackawanna & Western Railroad (Lackawanna), a high-speed 962-mile railroad that paralleled much of the Erie main line between metropolitan New York and Buffalo and a road that wished to reduce its operating expenses. Both companies correctly sensed that coordination offered a practical way to pare excess capacity. Furthermore, the amount of red tape involved would not be burdensome.[6]

Even before Von Willer had moved into the presidential office, the two railroads began to consolidate facilities. They both served the southern New York communities of Binghamton and Elmira, and they combined their freight houses in these two cities in 1955; the roads used the Lackawanna station at Binghamton and the Erie's building at Elmira. This venture produced modest savings.[7]

A year later the Erie and Lackawanna created considerably more benefits by implementing the first phase of merged passenger operations in Hoboken, New Jersey. At 4:01 A.M. on October 13, 1956, the Erie shifted most of its non–rush hour trains, including all of its long-distance service, from its scruffy Pavonia Avenue station in Jersey City to the larger, more efficient, and better equipped Lackawanna Terminal about 3,000 feet to the north. The second phase began on March 22, 1957, when remaining commuter trains, except those on the Northern Branch (Jersey City to Nyack, New York), switched to the Lackawanna in Hoboken. Although consolidation cost about $1 million, mostly for track connections and signal changes, savings exceeded $1 million annually. Patrons, too, blessed the union. The Hoboken facility provided faster and easier loading and unloading of ferryboats, more frequent service (the Erie added two ferryboats to the Lackawanna's fleet) and easy access (a minute and a half walk) to "tube" trains of the Hudson & Manhattan Railroad to New York's midtown and Wall Street districts. As the Erie and Lackawanna docks in Manhattan were less than 1,000 feet apart, few patrons lamented changing from the former's Chambers Street facility to the latter's

we're changing stations

Effective Saturday, October 13, all Erie and N. J. & N.Y. trains will use the **Erie-Lackawanna Terminal at HOBOKEN,** (with ferry service to and from Barclay Street, New York, instead of Chambers Street).

EXCEPT "rush hour" commuter trains, Monday through Friday. . . Arriving Jersey City between 7:55 and 8:59 a. m. (local time) Departing Jersey City between 5:03 and 6:13 p. m. (local time)

and *all* Northern Branch trains, which will continue to use the *Jersey City* and *Chambers Street Stations.*

See your local ticket agent for details.

There will be minor time changes. New timetables will be available October 1.

To announce consolidation of the Erie and Lackawanna commuter service in the latter's elaborate terminal at Hoboken, New Jersey, on October 13, 1956, the Erie issued this notice to patrons. (Grant)

Barclay Street terminal. After an extended but victorious battle with New Jersey authorities, the Erie on December 12, 1958, ended both its remaining passenger activities at Jersey City and its ferryboat runs to and from Chambers Street.[8]

The efforts of the Erie and the Lackawanna to slash expenses did not end with combined freight and passenger facilities. The companies agreed in June 1957 to seek regulatory approval to share a 75-mile stretch of main line between Binghamton and Gibson, New York, two miles west of Corning. This was a sensible decision: the roads were often in sight of each other and eliminating the parallel plant would reduce the high fixed-cost aspect of railroading. After extended discussions, the companies rejected a scheme to use roughly half of each route and decided to dispatch all Lackawanna trains over Erie trackage. The Lackawanna, however, would continue to serve two segments of its former main line: Binghamton to Vestel, New York, and South Waverly, Pennsylvania, to Nichols, New York. The decision to select the Erie reflected on-line traffic rather than engineering. While the Lackawanna's route was better physically, more rail customers dotted Old Reliable's right-of-way. Also, the Erie dominated negotiations. "The Erie people wanted to run the whole show," contended Lackawanna's Perry Shoemaker, "and I guess we let them on that Southern Tier line consolidation." This concession foreshadowed later merger tensions between the two companies.[9]

The joint agreement surprised many railroaders. In the 1950's few companies showed enthusiasm for shared trackage. Most feared that the owning road might harass a tenant; the host carrier might give its trains priority, thus disrupting the other road's schedules. Friction might develop if the owning company upgraded the line and passed along expenses that the tenant opposed, or the tenant might demand betterments that the owner refused. But these possibilities did not deter the Erie and the Lackawanna, although for mutual protection they signed a contract that detailed matters of usage, maintenance, and liability. The roads needed savings. "This project is an excellent example of what can be done through mutual agreement to effect economies and strengthen railroad properties by eliminating costly duplicate expenses," explained Harry Von Willer. The Erie president also knew that his road had been aided historically by trackage-rights agreements; for example, the Erie entered Cincinnati and Indianapolis over the tracks of the Baltimore & Ohio. The Southern Tier understanding appeared to be devoid of inherent flaws, and offered attractive cost benefits. The principal expense—installation of a common signaling system—amounted to a one-time expenditure for the Erie of $815,000, but the company estimated annual savings of about $500,000. The Interstate Commerce Commission gave its approval and the physical alterations began quickly. The changeover occurred on August 31, 1958, and Erie officials expressed no regrets.[10]

These cooperative cost-cutting efforts represented tangible steps toward merger of the Erie with the Lackawanna. Discussions about union, however, actually predated coordination. Paul Johnston and Perry Shoemaker, the roads' respective presidents, launched the process with informal talks in 1954, and they were among the first railroad executives to contemplate unification. The men were friends, having known each other since the late 1930's. "I started the merger ball to roll," Shoemaker asserted, and Johnston endorsed the concept. Since the late 1940's the Erie had worried that the Lackawanna might merge with the Nickel Plate Road and forge an aggressive single-company route between Chicago and New York.[11]

The Lackawanna management moved with haste. Perry Shoemaker had good reason to find a potential suitor, for he felt the winds of economic change. By the mid-1950's the "Road of Anthracite," rebuilt to exacting engineering standards early in the century, had lost its economic prowess. Gone were the halcyon years when bankers deemed this Hoboken-to-Buffalo carrier's securities appropriate to protect the assets of widows and orphans. Earnings during the pre–World War I years, derived largely from hard-coal traffic, general merchandise tonnage, and a brisk passenger business, supported exceptionally high dividends. In 1914, for example, the company paid

This portrait of Perry M. Shoemaker, the last president of the Lackawanna, was taken at the Peter A. Juley studio in New York City about 1957. (Perry M. Shoemaker)

a 10 percent return on its common stock and also distributed an extra 10 percent dividend. And it spent much of its surplus for betterments; the figure exceeded $40 million between 1901 and 1914. As a symbol of its might, the Lackawanna popularized the mythical Phoebe Snow. This beautiful young woman, who wore white linen, selected the road because its anthracite-burning passenger locomotives never showered her clothing with soot and ashes:

> Says Phoebe Snow
> About to go
> Upon a trip to Buffalo:

"My gown stays white
from morn till night
Upon the Road of Anthracite."[12]

But Phoebe Snow's railroad started to decline in the 1920's and then slipped badly during the Great Depression. Gross revenues plunged from $81.7 million in 1929 to $43.3 million four years later, and they remained at a reduced level through 1940. While the company avoided bankruptcy, its administration, led by the folksy and financially naive John M. Davis, lacked vision. "It was a typical old-fashioned railroad," recalled a Lackawanna executive. Davis cared so little about his job that he allowed Charles Hubbell, the purchasing agent, to handle much of the road's daily affairs.[13]

The Lackawanna's fortunes improved dramatically in the early 1940's. War-related traffic burgeoned, and its new leader William White (see Chapter 6), a perspicacious railroader, made a positive impact. White accepted the presidency of the Lackawanna in 1941, and he accomplished much during his eleven-year tenure. He assembled a skilled management team; spearheaded modernization of the property, including dieselization; and filled some of the void created by the declining coal business with increased merchandise traffic, especially from the Nickel Plate, its principal interchange partner.[14]

White strengthened the Lackawanna in two additional ways. Between 1942 and 1946 he orchestrated acquisition of an assortment of leased lines; this produced more than $1 million in annual savings. Later he convinced the Board of Managers to buy Nickel Plate stock, to lead to eventual consolidation, or at the least to ensure this vital connection in Buffalo. White also envisioned control of the 771-mile Delaware & Hudson Railroad (D&H), a strategic link for New England and eastern Canada traffic, with a merged Lackawanna and Nickel Plate, and "had conversations with Joe Nuelle [D&H's president] about it." When White resigned in 1952 to head the New York Central, the Lackawanna owned nearly 15 percent of Nickel Plate's common; these shares had appreciated greatly in value and had paid handsome dividends.[15]

William White could not create corporate bliss; nevertheless, this able railroader did much for the Road of Anthracite. "Bill White put the Lackawanna in about as good of shape as anybody could have," reflected Robert Fuller, a banker and member of the executive committee of the Board of Managers. Perry Shoemaker, White's successor, echoed Fuller's comments: "I inherited a good organization from Bill, and that helped the company a great deal during those difficult times in the 1950's."[16]

While lacking the star status of a White, Perry Shoemaker did a capable job. This is understandable, for he enjoyed his work: "I always wanted to be a railroader even when I was in knee pants." And he knew the nuts-and-bolts of railroading. A graduate of the University of Michigan's College of Engineering in 1928, and Yale University's advanced transportation engineering program a year later, Shoemaker took an entry-level position with the Erie in 1929, and soon became a general yardmaster. After a few years he left the company to operate his family's cold-storage firm in Elmira, New York. He returned to railroading, his love, in 1934 when he joined the New York, New Haven & Hartford Railroad. In 1941 Shoemaker entered the management of the Lackawanna; seven years later he became its second-ranking officer.[17]

The presidency of the Lackawanna taxed the considerable skills of Perry Shoemaker. "I felt at times as if I were the captain of a sinking ship." He selected an appropriate metaphor, as the company coped with a series of financial setbacks. Income generated from the road's once enormous anthracite business declined strikingly, dropping from $10.3 million in 1952 to $5.1 million five years later. By 1957 the dirty, gritty business of hauling stone coal seemed to be nearly a thing of the past. Exacerbating that loss were exorbitant (Shoemaker characterized them as "confiscatory") property-tax assessments in New Jersey; continually unprofitable commuter operations in the metropolitan New York City region with losses exceeding $3 million annually by 1957; high costs of handling freight in the New York City area (these problems also affected the Erie); and a bill of more than $8 million from damages inflicted by Hurricane Diane in August 1955 to trackage between the Water Gap of the Delaware River and Scranton, Pennsylvania. The Lackawanna also reduced its capital reserves greatly to retire $5.45 million in Morris & Essex bonds in 1955, and to pay $5.5 million in 1957 for a replacement of its Hackensack River bridge at West Secaucus, New Jersey, which the Army Corps of Engineers had condemned. Ironically, the replacement span immediately raised the company's property-tax assessments! The road confronted growing problems: increased competition from motor carriers, especially those operating over newly completed limited-access highways, siphoned off lucrative merchandise traffic; the opening of the St. Lawrence Seaway diverted bulk cargoes from the New York harbor to Great Lakes ports; disruptive strikes by longshoremen, steelworkers, and others periodically reduced shipments; and a recession in the late fifties, particularly severe in the Northeast, inflicted considerable financial damage. Conditions worsened so much that the Lackawanna encountered an operating loss of $1.47 million in 1958, and the future "looked pretty damn bleak."[18]

The Lackawanna coped well, however, inaugurating piggyback service in 1954 to enhance revenues and by working closely with the Nickel Plate and Wabash railroads for interchange of trailers-on-flatcars through the Buffalo gateway. "[Piggyback] has brought business back to the Lackawanna that has not been handled in 20 years," Shoemaker happily reported in 1956. "The tremendous appeal of this service is due largely to its dependability and convenience." The company also reduced operating costs, increased efforts to attract customers to trackside locations, and sold surplus real estate. The most dramatic response involved the sale in 1958 of the Lackawanna's principal liquid asset, its 628,722 shares of Nickel Plate common stock. This generated $18,908,814.15 and permitted the company to pay for the Hackensack bridge and to "bring our unpaid bills to a current basis."[19]

The Lackawanna had good reason to sell its block of Nickel Plate securities. The company badly needed cash and by the late 1950's hopes for unification with its favored interchange partner had been dashed. The Lackawanna had begun protracted efforts in 1952 to elect two members to the Nickel Plate Board of Directors but vigorous opposition from that road and a negative decision by the Interstate Commerce Commission thwarted the scheme. The Nickel Plate board opposed any step toward merger. "[It] was scared of the losses being generated by the Lackawanna's commuter service," revealed Shoemaker, "and the high tax policy of the State of New Jersey worried them, too." Another Lackawanna official suggested that President Lynne L. White was the culprit. "He was jealous of the Lackawanna's people and feared that he'd not be the top dog of the merged company." Apparently prospects for closer ties with the prosperous Norfolk & Western Railway intrigued the Nickel Plate. "If the Nickel Plate people thought they couldn't go it alone, then the N&W looked a lot better than we did," recalled Robert Fuller. Whatever the explanation, William White's dream of union with the profitable and superbly positioned Nickel Plate would not be fulfilled.[20]

With prospects dimmed for closer ties with the Nickel Plate Road, the Lackawanna turned to the Erie and the Delaware & Hudson. This decision shocked no one. "The Lackawanna knew that its days were probably numbered by 1956," recalled one transportation consultant, "and that it had to consider a merger partner or partners." Coordination with the Erie moved smoothly, and a close relationship, both in management and traffic, existed between the three carriers.[21]

The Delaware & Hudson entered the merger picture because of the interest of its recently hired president, William White, and its physical relationship with the Erie and Lackawanna. White knew intimately the officials and board members of both roads, and he wished to play a larger role in the industry. He took charge of the D&H in October 1954, several months after he lost a bitter proxy fight with financier Robert Young for control of the New York Central. White's D&H operated a main line from Wilkes-Barre, Pennsylvania, to Rouses Point, New York, via Albany, with connecting trackage to Montreal, and served as a major bridge route between the mid-Atlantic region and eastern Canada and New England. It interchanged with the Erie and Lackawanna at two principal points, Binghamton and Scranton, with the "Binghamton Gateway" vital to each carrier. Although the D&H was an anthracite road, it enjoyed a longer and hence more profitable haul for this commodity. Further differing from its hard-coal colleagues—Central Railroad of New Jersey, Erie, Lackawanna, and Reading—the D&H was not burdened with money-losing commuter operations. "The D&H was a jewel. . . . For an eastern road it was sound financially and Bill White made it stronger every day." The company's balance sheet for 1955 bore out this observation: it had a net income after federal income taxes of $9,081,347; the Erie, approximately three times its size, earned $7,897,354, and the somewhat larger Lackawanna lost nearly $1 million, due partly to the ravages of Hurricane Diane.[22]

The first public announcement of the intention of the Delaware & Hudson, Erie, and Lackawanna to study merger came on September 10, 1956. In a statement made the next day to Lackawanna security holders, Perry Shoemaker succinctly summarized the situation: "Preliminary talks between President Johnston of the Erie, President White of the D&H, and myself, have indicated that there may be opportunities for economies and service improvements. The possibilities are sufficiently substantial to present an obligation in the public interest and an obligation to our security holders to thoroughly explore the possibilities." The companies created a committee from their boards to investigate the matter and arranged for New Jersey–based Wyer, Dick & Co., an eminent transportation consulting firm, to conduct the preliminary examination.[23]

The carriers selected wisely. Wyer, Dick & Co., originally Wm. Wyer & Co., dated from 1940 when William Wyer and Corwin Dick formed their widely respected partnership. The philosophy of the two men was simple: "You must be able to do what you say." Wyer, Dick was "honest, conservative, and well-staffed," and it developed a substantial business, most of all during the railroad merger craze of the 1960's.[24]

William Wyer, the senior partner, possessed considerable talents: he was bright, highly educated, and knowledgeable about railroading, especially engineering matters. He held undergraduate degrees from Yale University and the Massachusetts Institute of Technology, had taken courses at the Harvard Business School while a student at MIT, and later attended the Cleveland Law School. After a stint with the Army Corps of Engineers during World War I, Wyer joined the Norfolk Southern Railroad, a 900-mile regional carrier that linked Norfolk, Virginia, with Charlotte, North Carolina, as its assistant superintendent of transportation. He then served successively as statistician to the president and assistant to the chairman of the Board of Directors of the Missouri Pacific Railroad, and later he became that company's secretary and treasurer. Wyer undertook a number of studies as a consulting engineer on transportation problems beginning in the mid-1930's; headed the bankrupt Central Railroad of New Jersey from 1943 to 1947; and served as trustee of the Long Island Railroad from 1951 to 1954. His only noticeable weakness was women; "he changed wives like you would change locomotives."[25]

Corwin Dick was likewise intelligent and able. A graduate of Harvard College and the Harvard Graduate School of Business Administration, he spent three years in the operating department of the Chicago, Rock Island & Pacific Railway before he joined the Missouri Pacific. There he began his association with William Wyer. While Wyer's forte was engineering, Dick was the "cost guy." His knowledge of passenger-service expenses made him a leading specialist; his extensive studies of commuter operations for the Long Island Railroad and the Port of New York Authority during the 1950's sharpened these skills. Unquestionably, the complementary talents of Corwin Dick and William Wyer gave their firm strength and credibility.[26]

Wyer, Dick & Co. launched its extensive study of the Delaware & Hudson, Erie, and Lackawanna soon after it received the contract. The firm examined traffic and operations to determine how merger would affect net income. Wyer, Dick used both its seven-member professional staff and personnel from the three railroads. "Hundreds of officers and employees gave freely of their time and cooperated in the study," reported William Wyer. An associate, Charles J. Meyer, argued that "we did our work, we did it well, and at a price that was competitive [about $300 a day]."[27]

At the urging of the merger committee, Wyer, Dick made a preliminary estimate of savings. In a letter dated April 2, 1957, William Wyer predicted that merger would generate substantial returns. Based on five factors, the amount would reach $14 million annually. Savings would accrue in this way:

Common points	$3,750,000
Duplicate lines	1,400,000
Marine operations	1,100,000
Shops	550,000
Organization	
Traffic	2,000,000
Operation	1,800,000
General	3,400,000

"The word 'estimate' lends too much dignity to these figures," explained Wyer, "which in the absence of field inspections or more detailed consideration by the department heads involved, partake more of the character of 'guesses.'"[28]

More firmly grounded figures came in on July 1, 1958, when the three carriers received copies of Wyer, Dick's final findings, *Report on Economics of Proposed Merger*. This document encouraged unification. It anticipated an increase in the net income level from merger that was considerably higher than the first rough calculations; the figure could exceed $29 million annually. Yet this optimistic report came with clarifications. "This total should be reduced by 15% as an allowance for contingencies," and "of the total savings, $12,326,641 or approximately 42% are dependent upon a cash expenditure." It explained that the "gross cash expenditure is estimated to be $42,139,004, which would be reduced by salvage, elimination of extraordinary expenditures and non-recurring income tax savings to a net figure of $10,462,399." The report concluded that "in one sense all of the savings are dependent upon cash expenditures as the merger would not be practical or possible without some capital expenditure." Wyer, Dick expected that most of the increase in net annual income would be achieved within five years. Allowing 15 percent for contingencies, the estimated enhancement during this period would be:[29]

	Estimated increase in net income	Percentage of ultimate increase realized
First year	$2,891,492	12
Second year	10,775,370	44
Third year	17,232,273	70
Fourth year	22,460,540	91
Fifth year	24,147,043	98

The fifteen-member merger committee gathered in New York City on July 15, 1958, to discuss the Wyer, Dick document. "All agreed that Mr. Wyer's report of July 1, 1958, was an excellent job," observed P. D. Jonas, Lackawanna's vice president and comptroller, "and that the estimated net savings were substantial enough to further progress merger possibilities of the three Companies." Remembered Perry Shoemaker, "We were really pleased." The committee authorized presidents Shoemaker, Von Willer, and White and Erie chairman Johnston to hire the prestigious First Boston Corporation to study the financial aspects of merger. Specifically, it would examine: "1) Relative values and contributions of each company and 2) Terms of exchange to be made to stockholders." The report would cost $125,000, and the three roads would pay for it on an equal basis.[30]

It took considerably less time for the First Boston Corporation to report than Wyer, Dick & Co.; in fact, First Boston used information gathered by Wyer, Dick. In December 1958, First Boston presented a 95-page comparative analysis of the three railroads. Based on material for the period 1948 through 1957, the study offered data in a uniform fashion in order to provide better, more revealing comparisons. "[The report] emphasizes very much earnings before Federal Income Taxes and then appl[ies] income taxes against the earnings at the corporate rate in effect during the various years," explained William White to members of the D&H merger committee. "This helps to get away from the distortions that result from carryback, carry-forwards, lack of uniformity in connection with accelerated amortization, tax losses due to property retirement, etc."[31]

The First Boston study pleased White in another way; it concluded that the D&H was unmistakably the strongest company. The report revealed, for example, that the working capital of the Erie and Lackawanna had deterio-rated markedly during the mid-1950's, while the D&H had built up a healthy position. As of December 31, 1957, White's road showed an excess of $22.8 million of current assets over current liabilities, compared with $9 million for Old Reliable and only $900,000 for the Road of Anthracite. The D&H also had less debt. The company had only one bond issue outstanding while the Erie had seven and the Lackawanna fifteen. If merger occurred, D&H secu-rity holders deserved a substantial position in the new corporation, even though their road possessed the least mileage. First Boston informally con-cluded that an equitable participation in the combined company would be 60 percent D&H, 27 percent Erie, and 13 percent Lackawanna.[32]

Even before First Boston Corporation issued its findings, the three com-panies asked Wyer, Dick & Co. to prepare a supplemental report. They wanted to know what changes in net income might be expected from merger of only the Erie and Lackawanna. Privately William White began to express misgivings about D&H's participation. The negative impact the recession of 1958 was having on the other two carriers worried him, and so he insisted that such revised data be presented. Neither Erie nor Lackawanna merger com-mittee members protested; they "realized that they might have to go it alone."[33]

Wyer, Dick's study of the Erie and the Lackawanna indicated that even a smaller merger would be prudent. Presented on September 26, 1958, this re-port estimated that the increase in net income before payment of federal in-come taxes would be slightly more than $16.6 million. But the consultants again emphasized that "all savings are dependent on cash expenditures since merger would not be practical or possible without some capital expenditures." Of course, the better scenario involved participation of the D&H, for Wyer, Dick concluded that "on this basis it might be said that for every dollar of net cash cost, $1.09 would be realized annually in the Erie-Lackawanna merger as compared with $2.36 in the three-way merger."[34]

The Delaware & Hudson would have enhanced the merger significantly, but it withdrew formally from the talks on April 13, 1959. "After . . . a very sincere effort and a great deal of work, the D&H, Erie and Lackawanna mu-tually agreed that a formula for merger was impractical at this time," argued the public explanation. "The work was terminated, in the friendliest possible atmosphere between the three companies, and certainly with disappointment on the part of all three." To this commentary a diplomatic Harry Von Willer added, "[I]t would be impossible to arrive at merger terms which would be fair and equitable to all parties." This statement contained the crux of the problem. William White opposed reducing the First Boston ratio for the D&H, and neither the Erie nor the Lackawanna wished to accept such a small position in the combined company. The matter involved "how to cut the pie."[35]

William White had dug in his heels for several reasons. The 1958 recession ripped into the earnings of the Erie and the Lackawanna like a buzz saw, and he wondered if they could recover quickly. Moreover, White had misgivings about the reports' data, as much of the statistical information gathered by Wyer, Dick and First Boston predated the economic downswing. White additionally was troubled that the Lackawanna had sold its Nickel Plate holdings. He told D&H investors that this "creates an altered situation in the midst of our negotiations." Recalled Perry Shoemaker, "Bill never forgave me for selling the Nickel Plate stock"; but White, he explained, "was not close enough to the Lackawanna's situation to understand its necessity." Still, White publicly expressed his regrets that a union was unlikely: "In a day when mergers are in the air, we don't take lightly the fact that no merger can be worked out."[36]

The decision of the D&H not to participate deeply disappointed the Erie and the Lackawanna. "It's like your nice, rich uncle deciding to leave you out of his will. . . . You know that you're going to have to be on your own," said Harry Von Willer. In a less metaphorical fashion, Perry Shoemaker remembered worrying about the economic viability of merger without the D&H. "We really needed the east Canada and New England traffic to prosper. . . . An independent D&H could solicit traffic away from the proposed Erie Lackawanna." But the two roads put a good face on it. Paul Johnston told *Railway Age* that merger between the Erie and Lackawanna "should move a lot faster than any consolidation proposal yet made. All we have to do is sort figures."[37]

The final merger study involved more than the two companies sifting through previous data. The roads again turned to Wyer, Dick & Co. In their April 29, 1959, request, they specifically asked the consulting firm to report on the "economics which would result from merger . . . , using a basis which would require as little capital money as possible." The roads wanted this material swiftly; they wished to file a merger application with the Interstate Commerce Commission "as soon as possible."[38]

The Erie and Lackawanna received copies of Wyer, Dick's second *Report on Economics of Proposed Merger* fifteen weeks later. The Wyer staff presented the obligatory bare-bones blueprint for unification; it kept costs to a minimum. For instance, the study eliminated expenditures for an electronic hump yard at Binghamton, general office space in Hoboken, and an insurance company subsidiary, items previously included. Wyer, Dick estimated that the increase in net income to be gained from merger might approach $16 million. "[W]e believe that this total should be reduced by 15% as an allowance for contingencies," explained William Wyer, "so that our final estimate of the ultimate increase in net income is $13,542,038, which is a net figure reduced by a 5% carrying charge on the net non-recurring cash expenditure required to effectuate merger." As in the three-way study, Wyer, Dick thought that Erie-Lackawanna could achieve these anticipated savings within five years.[39]

Wyer, Dick personnel realized that they lacked clairvoyant powers, and leaders of the Erie and Lackawanna knew that the report only estimated the savings unification could create. "Folk wisdom told us that this data was in the ballpark," recalled Perry Shoemaker. The Wyer, Dick findings understandably encouraged the prospective couple. "We got the ammunition we need to battle the ICC and others for our badly needed merger," said a heartened Harry Von Willer. "It's a sure bet that we'll be the old weary Erie again if this doesn't go through, but I think now that it will."[40]

Even before Wyer, Dick delivered its report, the two roads had decided to merge. On April 17, 1959, the Lackawanna Board of Managers approved Perry Shoemaker's recommendation that the "Merger Committee actively progress merger negotiations between the Erie and Lackawanna," and Erie's merger committee concurred. Then on April 22 three representatives from the Erie and four from the Lackawanna met in Cleveland's Midland Building and decided the critical matter of a stock-exchange formula. The two parties, after "extended" discussions, arrived at 65.14 percent for the Erie and 34.86 percent for the Lackawanna. To achieve this ratio the Erie agreed to declare a 25 percent stock dividend, amounting to 612,522 shares, which would increase its outstanding common stock from 2,450,090 to 3,062,612 shares. Both boards consented to these terms and signed a "Joint Agreement of Merger" on June 24.[41]

The 65-35 formula made sense. Robert Fuller readily admitted that "the Lackawanna, smaller and an ailing company, couldn't dictate a 50-50 proposition. . . . That would defy logic." Perry Shoemaker argued in an April 29 "Memorandum concerning unification negotiations between Erie and Lackawanna" that the final arrangement was "wholly appropriate." While the precise figure of 65.14 to 34.86 was the ratio of the two roads' earnings per share of common stock for 1953 through 1957, he listed other factors that made this a sensible figure. The First Boston study of 1958 concluded that the ratio between Erie and Lackawanna would be 67.6 percent Erie and 32.4 percent Lackawanna. Also, the market value ratio of publicly held common stock of the two firms as of April 21, 1959, produced a relationship of approximately 62 percent Erie and 38 percent Lackawanna. "Most any way you compared

the two companies it came out about two-thirds Erie and one-third Lackawanna," recalled Lackawanna's Fuller. "I think we did just fine in Cleveland."
Erie's executive vice president Milton McInnes, who participated with Fuller
in the discussions, concluded in like fashion: "Our investors got a fair deal.
. . . Even later the formula seemed to have been the right one."[42]

The formalities of merger were cumbersome, however, involving more
than the endorsement of corporate committees and boards of directors. The
procedure required approval from shareholders and the Interstate Commerce Commission. The latter, rather than the former, could be glacially
slow. Mandated by Congress to protect the public interest, the ICC was notorious for being a lethargic, bureaucratic agency.[43]

Still, the Erie and the Lackawanna willingly endured the process. "We
were weak financially and really we didn't have much of a choice by that
time," recalled Milton McInnes. "I wouldn't say that we were desperate, but
we were close to that." Or as David P. Morgan, Jr., editor of *Trains*, viewed
the situation, "[I]t amounts to a man in a leaky boat lending a hand to a swim-
mer in shark-infested waters." Earnings remained poor as a combination of
continuing recession, flood damage, and a 116-day steel strike battered the
companies. The Erie's gross revenues of $154.2 million for 1959 were slightly
better than those for 1958, but they were $18.9 million less than in 1957; the
carrier employed red ink in 1958 and 1959, posting negative net incomes of
$3.6 million and $5.6 million respectively. The Lackawanna's gross revenues
of $71.8 million for 1959 represented a recurring decline; they stood at $76.2
million in 1958 and $85.9 million in 1957. The company likewise saw red ink;
it recorded net income losses of $3.9 million in 1958 and $4.3 million in
1959.[44]

Money woes affected more than the Erie and the Lackawanna railroads;
carriers nationwide encountered financial difficulties at the end of the decade.
Although net incomes remained acceptable during most of the late 1940's and
into the mid-1950's, in part because of massive savings derived from dieselization, conditions worsened by the late fifties. Increased modal competition
reduced revenues; railroads steadily lost business, some of their most lucrative, to airlines, automobiles, barges, buses, pipelines, and trucks. The industry's share of intercity freight dropped from 68 percent in 1944 to 44 percent
in 1960, and its portion of commercial intercity passenger traffic plunged
from 74 percent to 27 percent.[45]

Labor matters also affected income negatively. Dieselization and other
technological advancements reduced the need for tens of thousands of workers, but the railroads encountered stiff resistance from unions in their efforts
to trim employment and thus to cut payroll expenses. Firemen on diesel-

electric locomotives emerged as the most publicized illustration of redundancy. In its hard-fought, albeit unsuccessful, campaign against archaic work rules, the Association of American Railroads, the industry's principal advocacy group, argued during the late 1950's that since there were no longer fires to stoke, the coal shovel was an "expensive antique."[46]

Governmental regulations further reduced earnings. Even though Congress passed the Transportation Act of 1958 to relieve the "deteriorating railroad situation," this measure failed to become the industry's Magna Carta. Admittedly, the new law created a more progressive approach to rate-making. No longer were charges to be placed at a particular level in order to protect the traffic of other modes of transportation. The act also guaranteed loans to carriers in serious financial condition. Nevertheless, argued one transportation consultant at the time, "The railroads remain bound by horse and buggy–era restraints." Companies, for instance, continued to find it difficult to win speedy approval to remove money-losing passenger trains, close little-used depots, and abandon lightly trafficked branch lines.[47]

An indication of the malaise that gripped American railroads, most of all those in the East, can be seen in their physical deterioration. Class I roads, identified by the Interstate Commerce Commission in the mid-1950's as having annual operating revenues of $3 million or more, had 4.5 percent of their total fleet of freight cars in "bad order" or out-of-service condition on August 1, 1956. Two years later that percentage nearly doubled. Representative of railroads in the East, the once-mighty Pennsylvania saw its freight cars in bad order increase from 7.4 percent in January 1957 to 11.2 percent a year later. The Southern Pacific, on the other hand, reflecting the greater financial strength of Western roads, had only 2 percent of its freight-car fleet in the bad-order category as of January 1958.[48]

Pressing financial problems understandably heightened talk of mergers. By 1960 scores of companies either conducted merger studies or discussed consolidation informally. Thus the urge to merge was not limited to the Erie and the Lackawanna. In the ten-year period that began in 1955 the Interstate Commerce Commission received 47 merger applications, although the request from the Erie and the Lackawanna was one of only four filed in 1959 and only the ninth since 1955.[49]

Work on merger consumed the managements of the Erie and the Lackawanna during the summer of 1959. They performed numerous tasks, ranging from organizing proxy materials to filing the formal application with the Interstate Commerce Commission. "We had to get our ducks lined up," remembered Perry Shoemaker, "and most of all that meant getting ready for the ICC."[50]

The first major step toward unification went smoothly. The two companies called the mandatory special meetings of investors and they assembled in their respective offices in New York City on September 22, 1959. Shareholders of both firms speedily and overwhelmingly approved the terms of merger and bondholders endorsed changes in certain mortgages. Although these sessions lacked drama, an annoying, albeit minor, event occurred at the Lackawanna gathering. Some pesky speculators, the "Serlin Group," led by New York investor Howard H. Serlin, which owned about 14,000 shares or 0.1 percent of the company's total common stock, opposed the plan. They charged that the "shareholders . . . were not receiving proper protection." But as Robert Fuller correctly concluded, "This was only a tempest in a teapot. . . . Their allegations were nonsense."[51]

The next step in the process proved to be more involved and nerve-racking. "I sort of worried about the proceedings before the ICC," recalled Milton McInnes. While there would be grounds for this Erie executive's concern, the hearings started auspiciously. The Commission selected Buffalo, New York, as the site and September 29 as the date. About 100 people assembled in the ballroom of the Hotel Buffalo on that Tuesday morning for the opening testimony. The dominant individual was the Commission's chief emissary, Hyman J. Blond, the hearing examiner. Considered "good" and "reasonable" by the Erie and Lackawanna, Blond knew both roads well; he had overseen their recently completed coordination projects. This nearly all-male audience also consisted of the officers, staff members, and advisors of the applicants; "interveners," representatives of other railroads and the railroad brotherhoods, and their associates; and various clerks, stenographers, and observers. "We knew many of these people," said Harry Von Willer. "I felt comfortable with the group in Buffalo."[52]

During the first part of the hearings, representatives of the Erie and the Lackawanna, under oath, presented reasons why merger should occur. Mostly, they restated and clarified the recently completed Wyer, Dick report; as expected, it served as the core of the proposal. Harry Von Willer cogently argued the public-interest perspective:

It must be born in mind that our rail system generally is in a weak condition and that its position has been deteriorating. This is shown by the fact that during 1958, the last full calendar year, the Class I railroads of our country as a group earned a rate of return on net investment of only 2.276%, which was the lowest for any year since 1939. . . . Our estimate is that the Erie in 1959 will earn a rate of return of only 0.84%. Obviously, these rates of return are grossly inadequate to enable the railroads to keep pace with the country's development and to perform the improved kind of transportation service which the nation's economy requires. . . .

From the standpoint of the Erie and Lackawanna, the most fruitful way to reduce costs on a large scale is through this merger. . . .

The tremendous importance to the Erie and Lackawanna properties of an annual increase in income available for fixed and contingent charges (before federal income taxes) of more than $13,500,000 a year [anticipated by Wyer, Dick] is obvious, and is highlighted by the fact that such an amount is actually greater than the combined 1958 fixed charges and contingent interest of the two railroads.

This additional income will help substantially to provide the money necessary for improved facilities and better service, for protection of bondholders, for fairer treatment to stockholders, and for keeping the railroads in sound competitive position—all greatly in the public interest.[53]

Von Willer expanded upon the public interest issue, arguing that the prospective merger partners would extend certain considerations toward rivals, including the Chesapeake & Ohio, Nickel Plate, and Wabash, roads that stood to lose the most from traffic diverted by the union. "The Erie and Lackawanna lines now maintain many through routes and joint rates with other carriers," explained the Erie president. "It will be the policy of the merged company to maintain such through routes and joint rates, and we are entirely willing that the Commission attach appropriate conditions to its order herein requiring their maintenance." He added in the same conciliatory manner that "the merged company will recognize all trackage rights under existing agreement, assuming, of course, that the other party desires the agreement to continue, and we have no objection to the Commission's imposing such a condition."[54]

The Erie and the Lackawanna continued to hammer the point that a financially healthy railroad would benefit the public. Typical testimony came from Stanley F. McGranahan, a retired Erie operating official who served as a consultant to the applicants in the merger proceedings. He argued that unification would aid customers in various ways. An electronic freight yard planned for East Buffalo, New York, would substantially improve switching for traffic using that gateway, and through-freight shippers would benefit from routings over the Erie main line between New York City and Binghamton, thus avoiding the 1.4 percent grades in and out of Scranton on the Lackawanna, and would also gain from the Erie's better profile between Corning and Buffalo. A stronger financial position, moreover, would permit the merged management to take advantage of future technological improvements to a greater degree than each road could do singly. McGranahan also contended that the elimination of duplicate facilities would free real estate for industrial sites; such development would yield jobs and tax revenues for scores of communities.[55]

Shippers generally accepted the argument that merger would produce better service. The assistant general traffic manager of Union Carbide Corporation, Edmund A. O'Brien, was one who endorsed the proposal before the Commission examiner: "We approve of this merger because we believe the

unified operation of these railroads will provide a more efficiently functioning operation which should reflect beneficially on the rate structure." O'Brien
testified that Union Carbide used both the Erie and the Lackawanna: "It appears to me that this merger should result in the elimination of unnecessary
duplication of services and facilities without in any way destroying or adversely affecting existing routes or services used by our corporation. We are,
therefore, willing to lend our support to this proposed merger because we
believe it will result in improved service." Joseph C. Murray, assistant to
the president of Endicott-Johnson Corporation, a footwear manufacturer,
echoed O'Brien's statements: "As an important rail shipper on both the Erie
and Lackawanna, Endicott-Johnson Corporation has a substantial interest in
the continuation of dependable rail service in the areas served by these railroads." Added Murray, "It seems clear to me that this merger should result in
the elimination of unnecessary duplication of services and facilities without in
any way destroying or adversely affecting existing routes or services used by
Endicott-Johnson Corporation." With plants in the New York communities
of Binghamton, Endicott, Johnson City, and Owego, this manufacturer had a
direct stake in the future of the two railroads.[56]

The merger hearings, which subsequently moved from the Hotel Buffalo
to the chambers of the Interstate Commerce Commission in Washington,
D.C., also won public backing from a powerful railroader, James M. Symes,
president of the Pennsylvania Railroad, whom the Erie's public relations officer described as a "surprise witness." "Here are two railroads, both operating in the red with the future outlook not very encouraging," the Pennsylvania executive told examiner Blond. "They are endeavoring to solve their
problems by merging and if approved, probably will solve them. This should
be a good example to encourage other railroads to do the same thing."
Symes's latter comment fit his own agenda; he sought to pave the way for another union. On March 9, 1962, the Pennsylvania and its archrival New York
Central would petition the ICC for authority to merge, an idea conceived by
Symes.[57]

However, President Symes's testimony before the Commission was
mostly insincere. Behind the scenes he orchestrated *opposition* to the Erie-
Lackawanna merger, again for selfish reasons. Symes saw the proposed union
adversely affecting the "Pennsylvania Empire"; he wished to bolster two
Pennsylvania affiliates, the Lehigh Valley and the Wabash.[58]

James Symes's concerns about his satellites might have seemed unwar-
ranted. Union of the Erie and the Lackawanna appeared likely to help and not
injure the Lehigh Valley, an ailing anthracite road that linked Jersey City
(New York City) with Buffalo. As the sole "independent" road (the Pennsylvania controlled 51 percent of its common stock) between these major centers, Lehigh Valley was expected by Wyer, Dick to reap a bonanza from

freight traffic diverted by roads serving Buffalo from the west, including the Wabash. This increase in Lehigh Valley's annual income might approach $5 million. On the other hand, the Wabash, a strategic carrier that connected Buffalo, Chicago, Kansas City, and Omaha, in which the Pennsylvania had an even larger financial stake, probably would experience a sizable loss of income, perhaps as much as $1 million annually. Symes did not dwell on these prospects; rather, he realized that a combined Erie-Lackawanna would offer stronger competition. More important, he saw an opportunity to strengthen significantly the Lehigh Valley and Wabash and hence his financial world. If the Erie and the Lackawanna could be forced to provide a better physical connection between the two Pennsylvania satellites in Buffalo, then another potentially profitable route for the parent would exist between New York and Chicago.[59]

Symes did not operate as the point man in this plan. He preferred to work behind the scenes. Symes told Herman Pevler, the Wabash president, to discuss the Buffalo matter with Erie and Lackawanna personnel. But as Perry Shoemaker recalled, "We knew he [Pevler] was a stalking horse of Symes and the Pennsy." Prior to the ICC hearings Pevler asked Harry Von Willer and Shoemaker to grant concessions; they refused. So at the hearings the Lehigh Valley and the Wabash demanded access to Erie-Lackawanna facilities in Buffalo. Later, Shoemaker explained to a group of New York security analysts the applicants' feelings: "The . . . opposition . . . from Wabash and Lehigh Valley . . . reflected no credit upon the industry. . . . I know of no precedent for the price of merger being the supplying of property investment and property rights to improve a competitor's product, even if it is a product badly in need of improvement." And he continued, "It was, of course, rejected by us, and much time was spent on what was basically a phony issue having no proper part in the merger proceedings." Later on April 26, 1960, the parties reached "terms mutually satisfactory" and the Lehigh Valley and Wabash gave the merger their blessings.[60]

Other railroads outside the Symes orbit also sought concessions. The New York Central and Nickel Plate demanded that the Commission impose conditions, which, according to Perry Shoemaker, "would essentially freeze existing traffic through the Buffalo Gateway and prevent the merged company from achieving longer haul upon important traffic now moving [on the] Lackawanna." These complainants wanted to maintain the premerger level of service. This meant retaining the frequency and schedules of connecting trains in Buffalo. Both carriers, most of all the Nickel Plate, did a brisk interchange business with the Lackawanna, and they expected it to diminish when their favored partner entered the merger. "The Erie-Lackawanna would not be so dumb as to short haul itself," predicted Lynne L. White, Nickel Plate's chief executive officer. Of course, he was correct. The Erie and the Lackawanna, nevertheless, contended that these demands were unfair: "[They] would impose inflexibility upon future management and seriously impair the potential earning power of the merged company." This clash prompted a writer for *Trains* to conclude, "The layman is appalled by the contradictions in all of this testimony, but the legal mind will see that the Nickel Plate is asking for everything possible in order to get what it can from the I.C.C. Nickel Plate men are duty bound to work out the best deal they can for their road. The incredible rules of the transportation laws are the rules of the proceedings."[61]

These railroads were not the only ones who expressed to the Commission their concerns about the merger. A small number of Lackawanna shareholders, the Serlin Group, continued to allege that the stock-exchange ratio established by the boards of directors in June was unfair. These dissidents charged that their Lackawanna shares were worth considerably more than the established ratio of 65.14 percent Erie and 34.86 percent Lackawanna. They also blasted management for the recent sale of the Nickel Plate stock. Even before the hearings convened, the Serlin Group, through its attorney Arnold Fein, protested the merger. In a telephone conversation on September 21, 1959, between Fein and Rowland L. Davis, Jr., the Lackawanna's vice president and general counsel, the group's spokesman indicated that it "would make application to the ICC that the hearings in Buffalo be adjourned." On several occasions Lackawanna officials explained the rationale for both the exchange ratio and the Nickel Plate sale, but the group remained unmoved. At the hearings the Serlin interests attempted to show that the Lackawanna was worth more than the ratio and that merger would affect adversely *all* holders of Lackawanna common. Yet these protesters were not friends of the stockholders; they followed their own schedule of affairs. According to Robert Fuller, they were speculators who had only lately acquired their holdings and who sought to strike a "profitable deal" with the company. The Serlin Group promised to "disappear" if it received $20 per share, "take a point or leave a point." Its members presumably paid considerably less; the trading range of Lackawanna stock during 1958 fluctuated from $6.37 to $11.62. The railroad rightly refused this greenmail scheme, and so the carriers had to endure the tedious effort by the group to damage their case publicly.[62]

The proceedings before the Interstate Commerce Commission included complaints by still another group, organized labor, represented by the Railway Labor Executives' Association (RLEA). While the Association's involvement was less extensive than either the protesting railroads or the stockholders, its impact upon the merger was considerable.

The RLEA's participation was understandable. Although it had not objected to the recent merger of the Norfolk & Western (N&W) and Virginian railroads (these roads filed their request with the ICC in April 1959 and it was approved six months later), the Association worried about the overall impact a rash of rail consolidations might have on union members. The Erie-Lackawanna's bid for unification seemed likely to be the harbinger of many more. The RLEA had refrained from a showdown with the combined N&W-Virginian because it liked the company's treatment of the brotherhoods; this wealthy coal hauler had made "certainly unprecedented concessions" to its employees.[63]

Yet if the RLEA planned to make the Erie Lackawanna merger a test case for future corporate marriages, it failed to fire its opening salvos at either the hearings in Buffalo or those in Washington. The Association's attorney, William C. Mahoney, refrained from entering the cross-examination process until the third day, and he only sprang to life when Perry Shoemaker used the word "featherbedding" in his testimony. Recalled a participant, "the railway labor people were real pussycats." Unfortunately for the applicants, that posture would soon change.[64]

Even though public hearings ended on October 22, 1959, the slow process of winning approval for the merger continued. The Commission required briefs of objectors by November 23, and the Erie and Lackawanna had until May 17, 1960, to make replies to any "exceptions."[65]

During the post-hearing months, the RLEA formulated its position on the Erie-Lackawanna application. The Association decided that it would not acquiesce to a possible wave of mergers without demanding extraordinary protection of workers' jobs. It feared that as many as 25 percent of positions nationally might be lost. Railway labor asked that if the Commission blessed the merger, it do so with "important conditions prescribed." When revealed publicly, RLEA's battle plan shocked the applicants and the industry, too. "Von Willer and Shoemaker were furious," recalled Milton McInnes, "and they were also badly worried. I think every railroad president had the same reaction." What stunned these officials was not organized labor's concern for the well-being of its membership but its desire to freeze *every* position for a period of four years. During this time jobs could be ended only through natural attrition. If organized labor prevailed, mergers would produce substantially less savings.[66]

Observant railroad officials had seen an indication of potential labor problems on matters of job security several years earlier. In September 1956, a few months after the creative and hard-driving Ben W. Heineman won control of the sprawling Chicago & North Western system, he sought to trim its work force. This immediately raised the ire of organized labor. Eleven brotherhoods demanded that the company give each dismissed employee severance pay equal to the total wages earned during the employee's service with the road. These unions charged that "ruthless" laying off of workers had occurred and they threatened a strike. "We weathered that storm," recalled Frank Koval, the company's public relations head, "but the brotherhoods seemed pretty determined by 1956 to do everything possible to save their jobs, even though these jobs might be useless."[67]

In the case of the Erie and Lackawanna merger, the RLEA based its argument on its peculiar interpretation of the law. Specifically, it charged that the amended Interstate Commerce code, commonly called the "Harrington Amendment," gave workers uncommon protection. According to Section 5(2)(f): "In its order of approval [of mergers] the Commission shall include terms and conditions providing that during the period of four years from the effective date of such order such transaction will not result in employees of the carrier or carriers by railroad affected by such order being in a worse position with respect to their employment." In the eyes of railway labor, this provision prevented dismissal of *any* employee for four years. The RLEA, therefore, requested that the Commission impose this restrictive condition: "The Erie-Lackawanna will take into its employment all employees of the Erie Railroad Company and the Delaware, Lackawanna and Western Railroad Company who are willing to accept such employment, and none of the present employees of either of said carriers shall be deprived of employment . . . for a period of four years from this Commission's order."[68]

The Erie and the Lackawanna had no intention of treating their employees shabbily. The companies' managers, most of all, "had lived with unions all of their professional lives" and "they didn't have the stomach to wage an all-out war on the brotherhoods, partially because of the 'family' nature of both roads." Furthermore, railroaders had long enjoyed considerable protection. Prior to inclusion of Section 5(2)(f), part of the Transportation Act of 1940, most carriers, including the applicants, had signed the "Washington Agreement" of 1936. This understanding provided benefits for employees adversely affected by consolidations, namely an allowance equal to 60 percent of their average salary in the year prior to their discharge. And the Commission had subsequently imposed similar conditions, most notably with the New Orleans Union Passenger Terminal Company in 1952. In this case the ICC ordered extensive employee protection. A worker hurt by merger within a four-year period received a monthly dismissal allowance equal to the average monthly pay received during his last year of service, and this compensation continued for four years, unless the individual had been employed for less than four years. In that situation the protective period covered only the length of his prior service. If an employee found another job, his dismissal allowance, according to the New Orleans Terminal decision, "shall be reduced to the extent that his combined monthly earnings in such other employment, any benefits received under any unemployment insurance law, and his dismissal allowance exceed the amount upon which his dismissal allowance is based." The ICC thus concluded that compensation in lieu of employment satisfied the law, and the Erie and Lackawanna agreed wholeheartedly.[69]

The carriers understandably challenged organized labor on its view of Section 5(2)(f). Much of "The Applicants' Replies to Exceptions" focused on this controversial matter. "[I]t is patently unfair and inequitable to require a carrier to retain an unneeded employee if he could find a job doing useful work with another carrier or in another industry," charged attorneys M. Cayley Smith, Jr., for the Erie and Roland L. Davis, Jr., for the Lackawanna. "Such a condition [the four-year freeze on jobs] has never been imposed by the Commission in the past. Moreover, . . . labor organizations have never before even asked the Commission to impose a requirement like that which the RLEA now asserts is an indispensable minimum under the Statute."[70]

The companies offered a convincing position based on how the Commission had interpreted previously the issue of employee protection. When examiner Blond presented his report on March 28, 1960, he accepted their arguments. "Employee protective conditions the same as those prescribed in *New Orleans Passenger Terminal* case . . . would fully comply with the statutory standards requiring fair and equitable arrangements to protect the interests of railroad employees affected." Blond added, "Nothing contained in the arguments of the labor association disproves the adequacy of such conditions in terms of employment or compensation. . . . The New Orleans conditions will be included in the certificate and order recommended herein."[71]

Blond's stance on the job-freeze issue delighted the Erie and the Lackawanna. But it was the examiner's decision to approve the application of merger that elated them. "I wasn't that surprised when I heard the good news," recalled Perry Shoemaker, "but it made me feel that there was some hope for our situation." The conclusions that Blond reached on other matters, likewise, cheered Shoemaker and his colleagues. The hearing examiner endorsed the financial arrangements; approved the modest reductions of the physical plant; and sided mostly against carriers who had sought to protect their interchange traffic. In this regard, Blond argued that "it is not practicable, nor would it be in the public interest, to impose conditions calculated to freeze the flow of traffic into a pre-existing pattern or to protect competing and connecting carriers against all possible adverse effects which might follow from the unification and resulting improvements in service by the surviving corporation."[72]

Finally, on September 13, 1960, the Commission endorsed Blond's work; the merger would become effective at 12:01 A.M. on Monday, October 17. Any opponents would need to take court action. Only the brotherhoods fumed, and then sued. Two weeks before the ICC's order took effect, labor, specifically the Brotherhood of Maintenance of Way Employees, with the

RLEA as intervenor, filed suit in Federal District Court for the Eastern District of Michigan in Detroit, challenging the Commission's position. The petition asked that merger be postponed until the legal questions dealing with employee protection could be settled. The court heard the case on October 12; two days later it ruled that merger could proceed, but the new company could not abolish any jobs or transfer workers until additional hearings took place.[73]

With the employee retention issue in legal limbo, the mood of the management of the Erie-Lackawanna (the hyphen remained until 1963) Railroad Company was subdued. The new carrier, the twelfth largest in the nation with 3,031 route miles, remained for the time being partially "un-merged." Yet Harry Von Willer, president, chairman of the board, and chief operating officer, and Perry Shoemaker, vice chairman of the board and chief administrative officer, met the press with broad grins and assurances that their company had a bright future.[74]

Even before merger day ("M Day"), Harry Von Willer, the master promoter, asked James D. McFadden, superintendent of the Kent Division, to deliver a letter of congratulations, with appropriate press coverage, to division employee Truman G. Knight. This locomotive fireman from Stow, Ohio, had designed the road's new herald, imaginatively using a version of the old Erie diamond emblem by restructuring the Erie E so as to form both an E and a L by setting off the top two arms. (Some said that the design reminded them of the largest character on an eye chart.) Perhaps to appeal to Lackawanna employees Knight selected that road's maroon color scheme rather than Erie's black and yellow combination. Von Willer praised the delighted fireman for winning a contest that had generated nearly 2,500 entries and promised him twenty shares of common stock in the soon-to-be-created railroad.[75]

Truman Knight could take pleasure in more than a stock certificate; he soon saw his emblem affixed to boxcars, tugboats, timetables, stationery, and other rolling stock and documents. "That sure made me proud," he told the editor of the *Erie-Lackawanna Magazine*. Knight probably never imagined that sixteen years later his handiwork would symbolize another "fallen flag." Rather, he probably accepted the official company pronouncement that "merger of the Erie and Lackawanna Railroads is an answer to the challenge of the times. The future for all concerned will be brightened by the greater strength that merger produces in earning potential, purchasing power and modern improvements, all of which contribute to growth and progress."[76]

ENTER
THE ERIE-LACKAWANNA
RAILROAD, 1961–1962

THE EMBLEM THAT fireman Truman Knight designed for the Erie-Lackawanna Railroad did more than cleverly incorporate the initials of its corporate name. As a modification of the seven-decade-old Erie diamond herald, Knight's creation suggested that the carrier was more Erie than Lackawanna. He rightly conveyed the image of an Erie-dominated merger; former Erie officials generally held key positions in the new firm until a sweeping administrative reorganization took place in 1963.[1]

Even though Lackawanna personnel knew that "the Erie and the Lackawanna were historic rivals," they accepted former Erie president Harry Von Willer as the chief executive of the combined company. In fact, Perry Shoemaker, last head of the "Road of Anthracite," promoted Von Willer's election. "Putting an Erie man in charge first," recalled Shoemaker, "might smooth out some of the people problems." Moreover, neither Shoemaker nor his Lackawanna colleagues expected Von Willer to remain in office long; he was nearing 65, the traditional age for retirement, and his health was declining. (Von Willer's constant worry about the company's economic prospects aggravated a chronic heart condition; "at merger time he wasn't operating at full speed.") The Lackawanna contingent believed that Shoemaker would succeed Von Willer; premerger discussions among members of the two boards pointed to Shoemaker's appointment. But when Von Willer resigned in November 1960 "for reasons of health," the board of directors, dominated by former Eriemen, instead tapped Milton G. McInnes, a career Erie official, as his replacement. Shoemaker remained as vice chairman of the board, but on August 31, 1961, he became chairman, a post held by the retiring Von Willer. "I received a

Erie Lackawanna officials examine a recently painted Erie Lackawanna boxcar soon after the merger. The maroon and grey car sports the new corporate trademark, a modification of the old Erie diamond logo. (Erie Lackawanna Inc.)

sop," explained Shoemaker. "I was made chairman, but I certainly didn't run the railroad." Efforts by former Lackawanna directors Harland C. Forbes and Lewis G. Harriman, who both served on the Erie-Lackawanna board, to increase Shoemaker's powers and duties largely failed.[2]

Most observers initially believed that the second president of Erie-Lackawanna, Milton McInnes, possessed skills necessary to guide the company. His career largely paralleled that of the talented Perry Shoemaker; McInnes, too, knew railroad operations intimately. And his educational and work record corresponded to that of Paul W. Johnston, "Erie's best president after the reorganization."[3]

Life had been good to "Mac." McInnes was born in Boston, Massachusetts, on March 17, 1905, into a comfortable middle-class home. His contractor father won acclaim for building the Mother Church for Mary Baker Eddy's Christian Science faith, and "that helped his business greatly." The McInneses sent their bright, earnest son to Dartmouth College, where he earned a B.A. degree in 1930. He enjoyed his liberal arts studies, most of all courses in English and history, and has said of that time, "I thought that I would be a teacher." But when the stock market crash of 1929 limited opportunities in education, McInnes looked elsewhere for a career. By good luck his room-mate, Clark Denney, the older son of Charles Denney, the recently appointed president of the Erie Railroad, provided the needed contact. During a cam-pus visit, McInnes asked the senior Denney if he could give him a job, but he received only this curt reply: "We are laying off people." Then the day before commencement, McInnes got a telegram that asked him to report to 50 Church Street, the Erie's main office in New York City; he gladly obliged. Apparently the railroad did not have a specific slot for the new Dartmouth graduate, but "the old boy connection certainly paid off for me." The presi-dent's office sent McInnes to the fruit pier to do manual labor. "I was called a clerk but I unloaded perishables at Pier 20 in New York harbor." McInnes did not remain there for long. Although he subsequently worked as a laborer in several other assignments, he rose steadily through the operating ranks. Jobs included stints as yardmaster, trainmaster, assistant superintendent, superin-tendent, assistant general manager, and general manager. In 1955 McInnes became Erie's executive vice president, and he continued in that post with Erie-Lackawanna.[4]

"Mac should have been a college professor," concluded a longtime col-league. That remark conveyed McInnes's strengths and weaknesses as Erie-Lackawanna's ranking officer. No one questioned his intellectual prowess or his commitment to the railroad, but close observers felt that he lacked a burn-ing desire to lead. McInnes admitted that "I never really wanted to become president. . . . I didn't want the responsibilities." Observed another associate, "Mac was a good lieutenant, but he wasn't a commander. . . . He wasn't what you would call a street fighter."[5]

Yet a street fighter of sorts inhabited the executive floor in Cleveland. He was Garret ("Gary") C. White, vice president for operations, the alleged power behind the throne and a "horse for work." This younger brother of William White joined the Erie in 1925 as a clerk and rose to be operations head in 1956. White's basis of support was not so much his brother (although "that did count for something at headquarters") as it was Harry C. Hagerty, the powerful if not dominant member of the merged road's board of directors and its Executive Committee. A veteran Erie board member, the 68-year-old Hagerty also served as a director of the Metropolitan Life Insurance Com-pany, where he had formerly been financial vice president and vice chairman of its board. His company long had owned a large percentage of Erie bonds; "the Erie was a Metropolitan Life property."[6]

White and Hagerty had their own agendas. The former wanted the pres-idency and the latter craved power. They had blocked Perry Shoemak-er's promotion and considered Milton McInnes "their man." "Gary and Ha-gerty . . . would pull Mac's strings as need be," remembered a former Erie-Lackawanna officer. "Mac was really their stalking horse." Few questioned

The Erie's top operating brass, some with their sack suits from Brooks Brothers, assemble for a systemwide service and policy meeting in a Jamestown, New York, hotel in June 1950. Two men who guided the company in later years attended this gathering: Gary White (*front row, fifth from left*) and Milton McInnes (*front row, third from right*). (Erie Lackawanna Inc.)

Hagerty's business acumen. "He was the dominant force on the financial side of Metropolitan Life," recalled fellow board member Robert G. Fuller. "He knew railroad finance. . . . He had the experience." Still, Hagerty was widely despised and feared, mostly by former Lackawanna employees. "He was not a modest fellow," were Fuller's temperate words, but another associate said bluntly: "He always had a swelled head . . . [and] he was unethical as hell!" White, too, was an "egomaniac" and a "slippery" and "manipulative fellow." While Hagerty worked largely behind the scenes, White usually did not. His ubiquitous staff meetings revealed his personality and style. "Those [sessions] . . . were for Gary, and they were also boring," charged Curtis F. Bayer, director of purchasing and stores. "He went over train movements. . . . It was a waste of time. He had everybody in there. . . . The idea was to show the Erie-Lackawanna people, including McInnes, that he was the big cheese. People were in there on camp chairs, even Mac, who sat in front and only asked for a cigarette. White was building up his ego and wanted to show that he was the boss." Added Perry Shoemaker, "It was impolite to ask questions."[7]

While White and Hagerty sought to become puppet masters, the rest of management concentrated on consummating the corporate marriage. Although the Erie and Lackawanna united officially on October 17, 1960, an injunction granted the Railway Labor Executives' Association (RLEA), which represented twenty brotherhoods, temporarily delayed any job changes. The RLEA sought to protect union members through a four-year employment freeze. Organized labor bitterly resented the company's plan to eliminate 1,600 jobs and transfer 1,700 employees to other positions over a five-year period. Because a federal district court ruled on October 14, 1960, that no jobs could be abolished or transferred pending further judicial consideration, the railroad initially failed to benefit from a reduced and reorganized work force. Good news for management finally came from a three-judge statutory court in December 1960; these jurists rejected the RLEA's position. "A requirement that carriers retain employees following mergers would sterilize provisions of the [Transportation] Act [of 1940], which is designed to promote economy partially through the reduction of personnel," argued the judges. "It seems to us that if Congress had intended such a result, it could have, and would have, said so in unequivocal language."[8]

But organized labor fought on. Early in January 1961, the RLEA filed a "Notice of Appeal" with the United States Supreme Court, which soon agreed to consider the matter. The high court in a six-to-three decision on January 23 refused to restrain the company from melding its work force. As it turned out, this was a fleeting victory for Erie-Lackawanna. The railroad could not proceed with its merger plans because the Supreme Court, on February 20, 1961, reinstated the restraining order. "The labor people were all smiles." The tribunal announced, however, that it would review the case on March 27.[9]

The Supreme Court ultimately resolved the employment issue in favor of Erie-Lackawanna. On May 1, 1961, it concluded that conditions prescribed by the Interstate Commerce Commission provided adequate compensation for affected workers. The court thus rejected the RLEA's contention that Erie-Lackawanna must guarantee employment for four years. A week later it vacated the restraining order that had prevented the abolishment or transfer of jobs. Then on June 12, this court of last resort denied labor's petition for a rehearing. Finally, some eight months after merger, Erie-Lackawanna won permission to proceed with the consolidation of its personnel in offices, shops, stations, yards, and train service. "June 1961 and not October 1960 was the real date of the merger," noted Milton McInnes.[10]

While the company's triumph improved the legal climate for later railroads that merged, it smacked of a Pyrrhic victory. The necessity of operating mostly separate entities during the interim hurt. As the case moved through the courts, connecting carriers often delivered freight equipment to interchange points that "happened to be handy," whether they were the best locations or not. In communities with both Erie and Lackawanna yards, these cars might appear at the former Erie facility although bound for a point along the old Lackawanna. This required extra switching, and "it cost us a bundle both in terms of dollars and cents and in good will we lost with customers because of delays." Yet hope remained. "[The RLEA suit] has been a bothersome struggle lasting far too long," admitted McInnes, "but we anticipate that the future will be better."[11]

Nonetheless, when the Supreme Court removed the last hurdle for merger, Erie-Lackawanna failed to experience the better times that Milton McInnes expected. The opposite occurred. The company came dangerously close to bankruptcy only two years after "M-Day." The road lost a staggering $26,488,759 in 1961 and $16,608,069 a year later. Besides, it faced a substantial maturing debt, including $1.5 million of notes in January 1963, $5.7 million of equipment obligations the same year, and $11.6 million of Erie bonds in 1964.[12]

Individuals close to the faltering railroad began to throw up their hands in dismay. William White, for one, who headed the Delaware & Hudson, concluded by autumn 1961 that Erie-Lackawanna was "a basket case." He wired Perry Shoemaker to confer with him at the Mayflower Hotel in Washington, D.C., about the road's deteriorating situation. Shoemaker consented. They discussed the Erie-Lackawanna at length, but concluded that there "wasn't anything that we could do about it." Management was in place and only the Board of Directors could institute sweeping changes. "Hagerty wasn't about to fire Mac or Gary White at that time." With the crisis mounting, those in industry and financial circles started to dub the road "Erie-Lack-of-Money" and "Erie-Lack-of-Wampum" and understandably so.[13]

⁓

Admittedly, the railroad could not control all its financial woes. A soft national economy, plant closings and cutbacks, and increasing modal competition hurt earnings. These factors also adversely affected most carriers in the region. During the first five months of 1961, for example, principal eastern roads showed deficits of more than $100 million: New York Central lost a staggering $25.3 million, Pennsylvania $18.3 million, and Baltimore & Ohio $17.5 million. (Erie-Lackawanna's loss exceeded $15 million.) While a strong economic upswing characterized the mid-1960's and eastern carriers thought bankruptcy and even nationalization were less probable, they still worried about their fate.[14]

So much was changing. "The traffic base in the Northeast is really starting to erode," remarked a spokesman for the Association of American Railroads in 1963. "Traffic is going to other railroads, especially in the South, and heavily to roadways and waterways." Traditional railroad freight business in the East declined widely: hard- and soft-coal traffic continued to slide, largely because of alternative fuels; poultry feed production and consumption shifted from New England, New York, Pennsylvania, and New Jersey to Delaware,

Virginia, North and South Carolina, and Georgia; export grain dropped with the opening of the St. Lawrence Seaway in 1959; the steady post–World War II diffusion and decentralization of industry accelerated; increased European manufacturing output hurt export tonnage; and finally, erosion of iron and steel traffic intensified. The ferrous-metals story was particularly multifaceted. Obsolescence of many plants created relocations of heavy production away from established centers such as the Cleveland-Youngstown-Pittsburgh axis; some increased efficiency in steelmaking resulted in the use of fewer raw materials; imports of steel, via the St. Lawrence Seaway, further curtailed carloadings; substitute materials, mostly aluminum and plastic, reduced steel consumption; and high-quality foreign iron ore began to move through the ports of Baltimore and Philadelphia and thus lessened ore tonnage moving from the upper Great Lakes. The latter worked to the advantage of some railroads, but not others, including Erie-Lackawanna.[15]

With all of these uncontrollable and troubling developments, Erie-Lackawanna also stumbled for reasons of its own making. Revenues should have been larger and realized sooner. The explanations for the company's inabilities to bolster income extend beyond Milton McInnes's flippant comment that "if you merge two losers, you get a bigger loser."[16]

Lack of detailed premerger planning is one reason Erie-Lackawanna's fortunes fell. Perhaps this happened because the merger trend had only begun and executives failed to grasp the importance of such preparation. Furthermore, both companies wanted the deal done quickly; the impetus to unite increased markedly after the Delaware & Hudson withdrew from negotiations and the roads' economic health worsened. Argued an Erie official, "We were under the gun to merge." And he revealingly added, "I assumed that the Erie way of doing things would be carried over in the new company." This vitiated much of the Lackawanna's own premerger planning. "The Lackawanna's points of view," remembered Perry Shoemaker, "weren't given much weight." If the Erie and Lackawanna had been more alike in their operations and procedures, their inadequate preparation for union might not have been so bothersome.[17]

Although the Erie and Lackawanna both belonged to the anthracite grouping, served similar territories between New York and Buffalo, and provided commuter service to Gotham, titanic differences existed. A fundamental distinction was organization. In the 1930's the Erie once more became decentralized; the Lackawanna was not. Their respective operating departments illustrated this difference. The Erie was organized on a division basis. Its master mechanics, for example, reported to division superintendents. The Lackawanna used a departmental structure, and its master mechanic reported directly to the chief mechanical officer. So unlike were the practices employed by the engineering and maintenance-of-way departments that after the merger one worker asked, "Isn't there anything that we do or use that is the same?" This was hardly a naive or foolish question. For instance, the Erie selected 110-, 112-, and 115-pound rail for sidings and branch lines; the Lackawanna used 105- and 118-pound steel. While both companies utilized similar heavier rail (130, 131, and 132 pounds) for its "high iron," each had a special way of drilling rail that necessitated different angle bars. Tie plates used on curves also varied; the Erie chose a thirteen-inch plate while the Lackawanna picked one that measured sixteen inches.[18]

A wonderfully comprehensive description of how corporate practices differed appeared in a speech given by Curtis Bayer to the New England Railroad Club, a professional group, in 1962. This former Lackawanna purchasing agent, who headed Erie-Lackawanna's purchasing and stores operations, reviewed how accounting methods, as they pertained to his job, varied:

To begin: In the one company the monthly inventory balance statement was prepared in its entirety by the Accounting Department [Lackawanna].

In the other company this statement was prepared in the Stores Department [Erie].

In the one company the preparation of vouchers covering invoice payments for materials purchased, was jointly done by both the Stores and Accounting Departments [Lackawanna].

The Purchasing Department of the other company carried out this function [Erie].

In one company credit memorandums were held in the Purchasing Department to be deducted from the next invoice of the supplier concerned [Lackawanna].

In the other company the Stores Department issued collection bills against credit memorandums received [Erie].

One company's Accounting Department priced the charge-out tickets received for materials issued [Lackawanna].

In the other company the Stores Department priced the charge-out tickets [Erie].

In the one company invoices received were forwarded to the department receiving the materials for certification or approval [Lackawanna].

In the other company all departments receiving materials prepared a receiving record which was forwarded to the Stores Department for matching with the invoice covering such material [Erie].

Both companies followed an entirely different policy for placing a value on secondhand and repaired materials. In this way they were as far apart as the poles.[19]

Bayer then enumerated additional differences he found in the operations of the companies' purchasing and stores organizations:

In the one company the department was recognized as one of the most important in the over-all organization [Lackawanna].

In the other company not nearly as great a recognition was given to the Purchasing and Stores function in the general organization of management [Erie].

In one company the department head was responsible only to the Chief Executive Officer [Lackawanna].

In one company the department head reported to a top line officer who was not the Chief Executive [Erie].

In one company the purchasing function was literally free from the influence of other departments [Lackawanna].

In the other company the purchasing function was subordinated in many ways to the wishes of other departments [Erie].

In one company there was longstanding recognition that Purchasing and Stores complement each other and should be consolidated into one department under a common head [Lackawanna].

In the other company there existed a tradition of independent operation, broken on occasion, but with emphasis on Stores being the dominant factor even as to certain purchasing functions [Erie].

One company had a highly centralized Stores organization, which may also be explained as the "Mother Store Theory" [Erie].

The other company leaned more to a decentralized Stores operation emphasizing direct shipments to the using points wherever practical [Lackawanna].

In one company there was a highly organized reclamation operation [Erie].

In the other company there was little or no reclamation responsibility [Lackawanna].

In one company virtually all unapplied materials were the trust and responsibility of the Stores Department [Lackawanna].

In the other company less than one-half of the unapplied materials were in the custody of its Stores Department [Erie].

In one company stationery and printed material requirements were met almost entirely within the Stores Department [Lackawanna].

In the other company a large part of such requirements were satisfied by placing contracts outside of the railroad [Erie].

The one company operated its own laundry, buying and washing its requirements of wiping towels [Erie].

The other company rented its requirements [Lackawanna].

One company used the medium of competitive bids more extensively than did the other, particularly in the field of fuel for heat, [Lackawanna] and so on, and on . . . [20]

Bayer argued that these dissimilarities should have been considered before merger. Though officers of the combined department "picked out what we felt to be the better way of doing business, borrowing freely from both companies," this after-the-fact planning caused difficulties. "The result was frequently chaotic," explained Bayer, "and certainly worked a hardship upon the people in the organization."[21]

The overall failure to plan ahead affected other departments, most notably accounting and treasury. They also faced the necessity of blending procedures and selecting those that seemed appropriate. "You can't expect a merger to work smoothly and to save you money if you throw together different approaches," remembered Milford Adams, then the assistant comptroller. "It sure took us a long time to get things sorted out." He could have added that there was no guarantee that *better* methods and traditions would survive.[22]

Erie-Lackawanna suffered greatly by not always embracing the better ways. The Lackawanna usually surpassed the Erie in its business practices, but it, of course, did not dominate the merger. Therefore, only a limited amount of "Lackawannization" occurred. Purchasing and stores was a noteworthy exception, probably because Bayer, a former Lackawanna officer, took charge.[23]

An ironic twist to Erie's past involved its less-than-stellar corporate customs. These shortcomings became public knowledge during the mid-nineteenth century, and they surfaced again, albeit less conspicuously, during and after the Robert Woodruff regime. The railroad admittedly possessed a scrappiness that commonly characterized underdogs, a spirit that yielded benefits. No one, for example, berated the Erie's reclamation operations for obsolete equipment; its "waste-not-want-not" program rightfully won praise. When Woodruff spoke about "Old Reliable," he repeated a perception that most accepted. "As the poor kid on the block, we're very frugal [and] conscientious."[24]

Reality differed somewhat. The Erie created a pleasant environment for its executives. "If you played the game, you had a comfortable job." Examples abound. Top employees enjoyed club memberships that were gratis, whether or not these perks fostered business. The treasurer, Jasper Van Hook, for one, belonged to a prestigious Cleveland country club, but he never entertained anyone who generated income for the railroad. Excessive drinking and gambling routinely occurred in office cars, even during inspection trips. Attendants "pulled the blinds and the good times began, . . . not a great idea if the point was to see the property." Apparently few officers paid for their meals. "[They were] just put on Uncle Erie's tab." The head of the dining car service for years sent turkeys at Thanksgiving and Christmas to officials and then billed the company.[25]

And related problems plagued the road. The Erie had long accepted nepotism at all levels and this practice led to less-than-capable employees remaining on the payroll. "Sons were hired because of their father's role with the railroad and guys married their secretaries." Cronyism ran rampant. Friends of officers received jobs or won contracts for supplies or services. One "incompetent" minor executive "went whoring around with Gary White, but he couldn't be touched because he was White's buddy."[26]

Perks, nepotism, and cronyism carried over into the corporate culture of Erie-Lackawanna. "The place was just like the old Erie," happily commented an operating officer. "The good things about the way of doing business and treating people were there at first." And he added, "I felt good at that time because I knew it was not really a merger, but only a takeover of the DL&W."

Conditioned by different business mores, ex-Lackawanna officials disliked the "bloated" system and the "immoral" atmosphere. Perry Shoemaker told several of his former Lackawanna colleagues a few months after the merger, "I feel terrible. I sold all of you down the river."[27]

Attitudes of the former Eriemen further exacerbated this despair. Collectively they thought that the "DL&W fellows had chips on their shoulders because they didn't run the show," and frequently shunned them. This was most evident at Cleveland headquarters. The Lackawanna officers ate alone and even feared to be seen together. They gathered for luncheon clandestinely at a downtown club. "We took separate routes from our offices and at different times," remembered Curtis Bayer. When they met, they paid for their own meals. "The ex-Erie people let the company pay for their lunches in the fancy Oak Room in the Terminal Tower." Shoemaker, who theoretically held the second highest position, recalled that some ex-Erie people would not speak to him and "many . . . who liked me personally were afraid to come into my office." Moreover, the Gary White–Harry Hagerty–Milton McInnes triumvirate denied Shoemaker access to much of the property; they severely restricted his actions.[28]

Failure of Erie leaders to bring in Lackawanna brass wasted talent, hurt morale, and resulted in a costly brain-drain. Even before the railroads united, Lackawanna's capable vice president for operations, William Gregg White, decided to leave. "He was promised a good job, but Gary White [not a relative] already held the top operations post and he didn't know what was in store for him. But he could probably guess." Rather than accept that fate, William Gregg White left railroading for trucking, and soon headed Consolidated Freightways, one of the nation's largest motor carriers.[29]

Other talented former Lackawanna executives changed jobs once they encountered "that Gary White crowd." Roland L. Davis, Jr., who served the Lackawanna magnificently as its general counsel, was the first important officer to depart. But the resignation of Perry Shoemaker in November 1962 shocked many and discouraged even more. "That was a troubling loss," asserted Charles Shannon of Wyer, Dick & Co. "I sometimes think that if Perry . . . had landed on top then the company might have gotten off to a much better start." Shoemaker accepted a salary cut of $20,000 a year to become president of an old and sickly anthracite line, the Central Railroad Company of New Jersey (CNJ). "I got a call from Earl Moore, who was retiring from the CNJ . . . and [he] said, 'How would you like to come back to work?'" Shoemaker jumped at the chance and took with him two former Lackawanna executives: James L. Barngrove, Jr., Erie-Lackawanna's assistant vice president for staff and a "crackerjack traffic man," and Richard H. Wackenfeld, the road's able assistant general counsel. "Both were tickled to death to work for the CNJ."[30]

Erie-Lackawanna management expressed little concern about the departure of Lackawanna executives. "It was probably for the better," recalled Milton McInnes. "Perry Shoemaker and the others weren't really happy with us." Shoemaker's resignation ended the plan to "pension him off." About this time the Board of Directors offered to place $500,000 in a special trust account in a New York City bank that would pay him $30,000 annually for fifteen years. For once the company saved precious funds, but it lost an able executive.[31]

Inefficiencies further explain why Erie-Lackawanna faltered. Coupled to inadequate premerger planning and ghastly personnel problems, these shortcomings nearly derailed the road. One publicized problem involved the technical incompatibilities of diesel-electric locomotives. Units of the former Erie used electric devices to sand tracks and ex-Lackawanna diesels employed pneumatic ones. "[When] the two fleets began to mingle, . . . individual units had to be kept separate . . . it was a headache and it was expensive." The problem would not be solved until 1963; proper reassignment of these diesels meant that "you didn't have to worry too much about the lack of compatibility, but management couldn't figure that out."[32]

A yet more costly albeit less reported stumbling block plagued Erie-Lackawanna. When Wyer, Dick made its merger study, it assumed that the new carrier would be operated effectively, but the road "never made adjustments for inefficiencies." Because the Lackawanna was the better-run road—"You could get your hands on it"—the problem once more involved the former Erie management. "They were in charge and they had some awful ways of doing things."[33]

Charles Shannon recalled the nightmare at Hornell. The McInnes-White regime concluded that to make the railroad work, it needed to rebuild the yard at this strategic Southern Tier point. More than the site of a major shops installation, Hornell was the junction where the Buffalo extension left the main line, vital since the company downgraded the Lackawanna's route to Buffalo. While admittedly a focal point of system operations, management assigned too many switch engines to work the yard, and this escalated labor costs tremendously. "Just to keep switchmen busy," explained Shannon, "they would make up a train in Hornell and send it to Buffalo. And often Buffalo couldn't take it, so they put diesels on the end and took it back to Hornell."[34]

Unnecessary rentals for equipment also damaged the balance sheet. Railroads made per-diem payments to owners of noncompany or "foreign" cars, but more so than most, Erie-Lackawanna "spent far too much money on car rentals." While an inadequately maintained fleet of rolling stock partially explained the problem, inefficient switching operations, lack of supervision, and sloppy record keeping contributed to the mounting deficit. Since the company was slow to return equipment, the meter kept running until deliveries occurred at the appropriate interchanges.[35]

The company's infatuation with its less-than-carload (LCL) operations further depleted earnings. This business, also known as merchandise or package traffic, involved "freight in one car from more than one shipper or destined to more than one receiver." Carriers historically liked LCL: heavy volume and high rates made it attractive. Erie and Lackawanna each developed extensive LCL networks, involving specialized equipment, stations, and trains. Even after World War II this activity remained strong for both roads and much of the industry. In 1946, railroads transported 24 million tons of LCL cargo, ten times the figure of the early 1960's. Conditions, however, changed strikingly during the fifties. Construction first of high-speed tollways, including the New Jersey, New York, and Pennsylvania turnpikes, and then freeways, financed by the National Defense Highway Act of 1956, drained much of this traffic to trucks. And this competition from motor carriers proved aggressive, innovative, and reliable. When other railroads, notably the New York Central, decided either to end or curtail LCL, Erie-Lackawanna sought to maintain it. Management seemingly failed to recognize the fate of LCL and ignored the time-consuming inefficiency of LCL consolidation. Yet the company's LCL volume shrank steadily (193,645 tons in 1960; 144,270 tons in 1961; and 102,387 tons in 1962), and it lost heavily—several millions of dollars annually in wages, taxes, and maintenance expenses. "The LCL business by the early 1960's was a dinosaur and should have been canceled. . . . Gary White loved it, probably because it had always been part of the Erie."[36]

Another waste-maker came from a badly disrupted bureaucratic function: the company's botched accounting operations could hardly support its obsolete LCL business or anything else. In what may have been unique in American business, Erie-Lackawanna divided its accounting work between two cities. It consolidated revenue accounting employees in the Columbia Building, "a decrepit pile of bricks" in Cleveland, and its disbursement staff in the former Lackawanna offices in Scranton. Management's rationale involved two factors: its commitment to Scranton officials that the merged firm would keep a substantial work force in this depressed Pennsylvania community (the quid pro quo meant that Scrantonites would endorse the merger), and the desire to minimize the movement of people and disruption of family ties.[37]

The physical separation of these vital tasks did more harm than money being squandered on duplicate facilities; it resulted in lost income, reduced employee morale, and a damaged corporate image. Work rules worsened the situation tremendously. Since former Erie and Lackawanna revenue and disbursement clerks shared different seniority rosters, this meant that relocated personnel would lose seniority rights. A move also would disrupt their domestic lives. "Nobody that I knew wanted to leave Cleveland for Scranton, nobody," remembered accountant Milford Adams of Cleveland. Most of these clerks acted predictably; they bumped junior clerks once the court settled the RLEA's suit. "Supervisor or experienced employees will train an individual; a better job opens and he bids into it, and we have to start all over again." Inexperienced people then performed much of the revenue and disbursement tasks. "As of August 15 [1961] we still had sixty-five unfilled jobs in Cleveland in revenue and machine accounting," noted Perry Shoemaker two weeks later. "On the other hand, we had all the jobs filled in Scranton, but 70% were filled by people who had not worked on that kind of accounting." Since this work was highly specialized—"Revenue and disbursement clerks use languages foreign even to public accountants"—chaos reigned. "There were physical monies actually lost," recalled Adams. Remarked Harry Zilli, Jr., a colleague, "I-and-Cs [individual and company receivables] just piled up. There were some that were not acted upon for a couple of years." Bills, too, went unpaid. Irate creditors harassed officials for their money. Some suppliers shied away or refused discounts. "This was a hell of a mess," charged Shoemaker. "People just wouldn't trust the company. . . . It took a long time to straighten this all out."[38]

The work-rule bugaboo similarly affected blue-collar employees and contributed markedly to inefficient, expensive operations. The activities of the Brotherhood of Locomotive Engineers (BLE) illustrate the problem. Together with other unions, the BLE showed less preparedness for the merger era than did most carriers. Not until its national convention in 1966 did engineers amend their constitution and bylaws to allow their president to consolidate separate BLE units, if necessary, in the wake of a rail merger. Before that time, bodies remained mostly unchanged. In the case of Erie-Lackawanna, its two BLE committees did not merge until 1968; the thirteen former Erie locals and the six former Lackawanna locals finally agreed to unite.[39]

As the Erie and Lackawanna moved toward corporate marriage, the general chairmen of the respective committees of the Brotherhood of Locomotive Engineers eagerly sought to protect their turf. "In no way did we want to lose out to the Lackawanna fellows," admitted Erie chairman J. D. Allen. "We naturally wanted to protect our financial security." That is what happened initially and "it was quite a mess." Almost immediately hard feelings developed between Allen and his counterpart on the Lackawanna, William Thomas. Under terms of the merger agreement, a specified number of jobs went to former Erie and Lackawanna operating personnel in joint terminals. This was determined on the percentage of work that had been performed there prior to "M-Day." In Elmira, for example, there were five yard jobs given to former Erie engineers and seven to former Lackawanna engineers. When a vacancy occurred among the Erie contingent, the policy called for an Erie engineer to come from Hornell, even though a Lackawanna engineer might be found locally. The time and expense of bringing an engineer the nearly 60 miles to Elmira annoyed the company and angered Lackawanna's BLE membership. "It was a ridiculous situation when you think about it," remembered Charles Shannon, "but that's what happened and the company was largely helpless." Understandably Thomas protested, and Allen threatened a strike. Representatives from BLE's national headquarters in Cleveland intervened; they backed Allen because the "agreement must be honored." Thomas conceded defeat but tensions continued between the two arms of this brotherhood. "There were some pretty hard feelings among the Erie and Lackawanna engineers for a long time afterward."[40]

Hard feelings about employment policies had other ramifications. Like every railroad in the United States, Erie-Lackawanna felt the burden of "featherbedding" caused by outmoded work rules. By the early 1960's the price tag for the company exceeded $7 million annually. The railroad industry battled organized labor over the issue of firemen on diesel-electric locomotives for years and finally won a decisive victory in the Supreme Court in 1963. This would be the beginning of the end of the superfluous and expensive crewmen. And the industry made similar gains in altering other contractual arrangements.[41]

State-enacted work rules, however, took longer to modify or repeal. Various legislatures, imbued with the anticorporate, proconsumer spirit of progressivism, decided early in the century to require extra brakemen on longer freight trains. Unfortunately for Erie-Lackawanna it encountered these "excess" or "full crew" laws along much of its main line: New York, Ohio, and Indiana had such statutes. (In the latter state, for example, an Erie-Lackawanna freight train needed a six-person crew if it were longer than seventy cars.) Although radical changes in freight-train operations brought by technological improvements relegated these statutes to featherbedding status, labor fought for their retention. Union leaders privately admitted that the issue was largely self-interest, but publicly they charged that removal of trainmen would impair safety. The brotherhoods held fast to their position, even when New York's Public Service Commission studied the matter and reported in 1960 that the state's 1913 law, amended in 1921 and twice during the 1930's, was unnecessary for the "safety of railroad operations, employees engaged therein, and the public."[42]

The McInnes administration recognized featherbedding, but it did little. Continued support of the railroad industry for reform and modest lobbying efforts were its principal responses. McInnes, for one thing, explained the company's position to his former classmate at Dartmouth College, Governor Nelson Rockefeller of New York, but the issue remained unresolved. McInnes preferred moral suasion. He used the company's annual reports to explain the evils of these make-work statutes and asked investors to take positive action: "Shareowners residing in those States [New York, Ohio, and Indiana] once again are urged to write their state legislative representatives requesting repeal of these laws." Observed a disgusted outsider, "Mac thought he was the schoolteacher . . . and lo the whole featherbedding thing could be solved once people knew the facts of the matter."[43]

Another albatross hung around the neck of Erie-Lackawanna; its New York City suburban commuter operations. For years the Erie and Lackawanna lost millions of dollars providing these vital trains for thousands of mostly New Jersey residents. Due partly to earlier lobbying by Paul Johnston, lawmakers in Trenton authorized the state shortly before the merger to contract with commuter railroads for this service. They also appropriated funds. While the Erie and Lackawanna together received approximately $2 million for a ten-month period that began September 1, 1959, this support was inadequate. "The railroads are simply providing an essential public service under contract with the State and are being paid for it, although the payments unfortunately do not fully eliminate the commutation deficit," wrote McInnes. "In effect, the commuters are being subsidized as the fares they pay do not cover the cost of providing the service." New Jersey continued subsidies: Erie-Lackawanna received more than $2.5 million for the operation of certain "essential" trains in 1962. Yet this was only a stopgap; a financially realistic plan needed to be implemented.[44]

Although Erie-Lackawanna management announced repeatedly that it sought to end the commuter drain, little happened during McInnes's tenure. According to Charles Shannon, "Mac seemed resigned to the status quo, believing that some public monies were better than none." Years later McInnes had no regrets about his lack of action. "It was a lost cause," he concluded, "It would have been virtually impossible to get New Jersey officials to let the Erie[-Lackawanna] get out of the business."[45]

Even if McInnes were correct, his administration still should have controlled costs. Wyer, Dick subsequently discovered that the commuter service was burdened with too many stations and auxiliary facilities, inefficient deployment of workers, and antiquated ticketing procedures. The latter alone wasted thousands of dollars yearly. This was understandable, since the road used 82 different ticket forms, including 5 for cash receipts. "The multiplicity of . . . tickets used and their obsolete design and characteristics," argued Wyer, Dick in October 1963, "have resulted in unnecessary accounting, more collectors on trains than would otherwise be necessary and loss of revenue through refunds and failure of riders on both trains and ferries to pay proper transportation."[46]

"The Erie-Lackawanna . . . is about at its lowest point since the Erie Railroad failed in the 1930's," observed a financial writer for the *Cleveland Press* in late 1962. "Conditions look poor, at least for the near term." Those who knew the company agreed. Negative external and internal factors combined to produce a raft of problems and to point toward a fifth bankruptcy. The decision by a federal Emergency Board early in 1962 to grant a 10.28 cents an hour hike to nonoperating employees in the railroad industry, which cost Erie-Lackawanna approximately $2.8 million annually, seemed to be "another nail in our coffin." Remembered Milton McInnes, "We just about threw in the towel at that time." Declining operating revenues characterized the years 1960 through 1962; they dropped from $226.1 million in 1959, a poor year for both the Erie and the Lackawanna, to $220.4 million in 1960, $211 million in 1961, and $210.9 million in 1962. In fact, these figures had shown a consistent decline since 1956. Deficits mounted: they exceeded $62 million for the three-year period. Long-term debt, including equipment obligations, at the end of 1962 stood at $322.7 million, "far too much for the company to handle comfortably."[47]

The railroad still invested in its physical plant. The philosophy of its capital budget program was straightforward and sensible: "The only projects undertaken were those that would produce a high rate of return in reduced operating costs, or would increase revenues." The company built track connections and installed signals to join parts of the property, usually with materials salvaged from downsizing former Lackawanna routes; replaced tens of thousands of rotten ties with used ones from abandoned lines; ballasted hundreds of miles of track and ground even more miles of rail to prolong its life; and improved facilities, including rehabilitating piggyback ramps in Chicago and Croxton and conversion of the Hornell yard from a manual-hump operation to a flat-switching yard. The firm also upgraded rolling stock in a modest fashion. This involved purchasing or reconditioning nearly 400 flatcars for piggyback service, rebuilding several hundred boxcars and gondola cars, and ordering 15 second-generation 2,400-horsepower diesel-electric locomotives.[48]

Bison Yard near Buffalo highlighted improvements during the McInnes regime. Management wanted a modern electronic freight yard at this strategic gateway. A state-of-the-art switching terminal would replace two smaller, less efficient yards; this promised considerable savings, perhaps exceeding $3 million annually. Shortly after work started in 1961, the company felt even better about this multimillion dollar project. The Nickel Plate agreed to participate; it would pay half the cost of the land and betterments. The Nickel Plate concluded that this commitment served its best interests: it needed to upgrade its terminal operations in Buffalo, and there existed the real chance that if the Interstate Commerce Commission approved the contemplated merger between the Nickel Plate, Norfolk & Western, and Wabash, it would add the "feeble" Erie-Lackawanna. Not only did the Nickel Plate provide needed financial support, but it brought in the Wabash as a rent-paying tenant. Yet Bison Yard failed to be the "good thing that we expected." Construction of this 3,000-cars-a-day facility was not completed until July 1963, and joint operations did not begin because of work-rule disputes with several brotherhoods.[49]

Erie-Lackawanna scrambled for cash throughout the McInnes regime. Efforts to improve its financial health involved various tactics, including an old favorite—retrenchment. Upon assuming the presidency, McInnes, with board approval, slashed salaries of executives and supervisory personnel and stopped dividend payments to holders of preferred stock. (The Erie had paid three quarterly dividends on these securities in 1959, but skipped payouts for the last quarter.) Additional salary cuts occurred in 1961. Other "morale busters" included the end of company-sponsored college scholarships for children of employees, a program launched in 1952, and reduction in the frequency of the *Erie-Lackawanna Magazine* from monthly to bimonthly. Management also limited circulation to active and retired employees and paid subscribers.[50]

The firm also liquidated assets. It raised more than $800,000 in January 1961 from sale of its stock in U.S. Truck Lines, Inc., a profitable Cleveland-based motor carrier. And it launched an active campaign to sell surplus real estate. Not only did this scheme generate several million dollars between 1960 and 1963, but also lowered the real-estate tax bite. Such measures, however, failed to generate enough working capital. The amount had dropped dramatically from $22.5 million for the combined roads as of December 31, 1959, to less than $5 million a year later. So the road borrowed heavily. It received $15 million from four financial institutions, made possible by a federal loan guarantee, and took these monies in three installments: $6.2 million on June 15, 1961; $2.5 million on November 30, 1961; and the remainder on January 3, 1962. Yet working capital continued to decline; it stood at only $4.1 million as of December 31, 1962.[51]

⌇

While the fortunes of Erie-Lackawanna sank to dangerous levels after the merger, experts still considered it to be an important railroad. "The Erie-Lackawanna is a vital part of the great central corridor between the East and West," argued railroad executive and consultant John W. Barriger III at the road's nadir in 1963. Few questioned his assertion. Significance of the road's main line between America's two largest metropolitan centers convinced

Spector Freight System, Inc., an aggressive Chicago-based motor carrier, to invest more than $1.2 million in Erie-Lackawanna stock in 1960. This enabled Spector to name attorney William J. Friedman, a company director, to the railroad's Board of Directors a year later.[52]

Spector recognized the possibility of expanded intermodal operations over Erie-Lackawanna. "It thought that its overall service could be improved with piggyback service, not unlike what the United Parcel Service would do on the EL a decade later." Spector also viewed the property as a way to battle New York Central's popular retail "Flexi-Van Service." Beginning in January 1958, the Central used special equipment to capture lucrative freight business. "Our Flexi-Van car is a 79½ ft. flat and will carry two cargo units," the company told shippers. "These units . . . are trailer bodies without wheels: The wheel assembly is dropped at the loading point. We won't need special terminals to load or unload our cars." By the early 1960's the road had increased its Flexi-Van business substantially, which included a "Super-Van" schedule between Boston and Chicago, providing the "fastest freight service ever offered between those two cities." Although Spector liquidated its position at a substantial loss in 1962 because of the "impending bankruptcy of the EL," the company correctly gauged the potential of Erie-Lackawanna's main line: its wide clearances, uncongested operations, and strategic end points made it a natural artery for intermodal traffic.[53]

While Erie-Lackawanna could hardly be labeled a "dog" or a "transportation slum," railroads with financial resources expressed little interest in acquiring the newly created "Friendly Service Route." Said Milton McInnes, tongue-in-cheek, "Perhaps if we sliced off the main line at Port Jervis [New York], then we would have been more desirable [a reference to the high costs of operations in New Jersey and New York City]." At the time the company appeared, competing carriers contemplated merger, and this frightened management. "Several railroads in the East have been making overtures toward merging with each other," warned McInnes in his report to shareholders on February 21, 1961, "which, in some cases, would result in almost complete encirclement of the territory." The road worried about three threatening combinations: Chesapeake & Ohio and Baltimore & Ohio, New York Central and Pennsylvania, and Norfolk & Western and Nickel Plate. A marriage of the Central and Pennsy would be among the biggest in business history; the merged company would have assets of nearly $5.5 billion and 125,000 employees (Erie-Lackawanna had a work force of about 20,000.) Other "leftover" roads fretted, too. If the Interstate Commerce Commission approved a three-system plan, what would happen to "outcasts" like the Boston & Maine, Central Railroad of New Jersey, Delaware & Hudson, and the New Haven?[54]

Quickly, though, Erie-Lackawanna developed a sound strategy. It would seek inclusion with the Norfolk & Western and Nickel Plate. "The Erie-Lackawanna would be a logical component of that system since, to an appreciable extent, both lines serve the same territory, have a substantial amount of duplicate or parallel lines and connect at a number of common points, in addition to which the Erie-Lackawanna would provide the proposed Norfolk & Western System with an outlet to important traffic centers in New England and the Port of New York." Management seemed unified on this matter: no ex-Erie versus ex-Lackawanna battle erupted within the ranks of senior management or the board. "Our wagon was going to be surrounded by hostile Indians," reasoned Robert Fuller, "and we had to have a plan of defense."[55]

Why would Norfolk & Western assist Erie-Lackawanna? After all, the Friendly Service Route still retained those negative qualities that earlier had troubled the Delaware & Hudson, and its debt continued to grow. Nevertheless, Erie-Lackawanna possessed strategic value. President Stuart T. Saunders of the Norfolk & Western knew that it could flesh out his road's route structure, even though his senior vice president, John P. Fishwick, fervently believed that "there was too much trackage in the East." Still, the N&W sought access to eastern gateways and terminals. Much more significantly, N&W did not want Erie-Lackawanna to fight its merger application with the Nickel Plate, which it had filed earlier with the Interstate Commerce Commission. (The N&W had also asked the ICC on March 27, 1961, for authority to lease the Wabash Railroad and to carry out several other related transactions.) "We thought this [support for Erie-Lackawanna] would be in our interest in the long run," admitted Fishwick, "and we also were interested in getting our merger through, frankly."[56]

With some leverage, then, Erie-Lackawanna improved its position with the signing of two documents. The first session took place on October 12, 1961. Represented by Paul W. Johnston, chairman of the Executive Committee, the company agreed with Norfolk & Western and Nickel Plate that it would not protest their merger at the hearings already in progress. Erie-Lackawanna won this concession in return: "[The roads would] *forthwith, in good faith*, enter into consultations and negotiations in an attempt to agree upon a plan for some form of affiliation of E-L with the enlarged Norfolk system which would be mutually advantageous to the two companies."[57]

Erie-Lackawanna and the Norfolk & Western and Nickel Plate approved a second agreement twelve days later. To show their earnestness, N&W and Nickel Plate decided to make a modest financial investment in Erie-Lackawanna securities. By the end of 1962, the former would buy "not less than $1,000,000," and the latter "not less than $500,000." The Nickel Plate additionally agreed to acquire a 50 percent interest in Bison Yard, then under construction. This was a binding contract regardless of the outcome of the merger application.[58]

Contact between Erie-Lackawanna and Norfolk & Western and Nickel Plate continued. In anticipation of some type of affiliation between Erie-Lackawanna and an enlarged N&W system, the companies formed a committee in February 1962 to explore the potential savings that should accrue. "The study involves the selection of principal traffic routes, re-direction of duplicate lines, consolidation of trains, coordination of offices, yards, stations, shops and other facilities," explained McInnes to shareholders in February 1963, "as well as estimates of savings resulting from car-hire, switching charges, trackage charges and similar activities."[59]

The McInnes administration wisely chose to guard against the negative ramifications of what would become the merger madness of the 1960's. This company did not want to be surrounded by powerful and expanded systems. This jockeying eventually led to its affiliation with the powerful N&W system. But in the early sixties no one at Erie-Lackawanna knew the future. Understandably, then, the company filed a petition before the Interstate Commerce Commission in January 1963 in opposition to merger of the New York Central and Pennsylvania. Yet Erie-Lackawanna was flexible. It would alter its position only if it succeeded in entering the N&W fold. But if that failed, Erie-Lackawanna demanded to join the proposed Penn Central Railroad.[60]

In the interim Erie-Lackawanna grappled with the realities of hard times during the early 1960's. While its freight trains rolled at competitive speeds, 60 miles an hour on long sections of the main line, there were fewer of them and they were frequently shorter. As during previous depressions and recessions, the company felt the pain of declining traffic from steel, automobile, and other heavy-goods industries. Since so many factories depended upon one another, a chain reaction of sorts occurred, and it adversely affected the freight business. Steel production in the Mahoning Valley of Ohio, for example, dropped considerably during the early 1960's and that meant fewer shipments of iron ore from the Port of Cleveland to the mills as well as reduced coal and coke movements. This slump in steel production came as the result of reduced production of automobiles, household appliances, and the like. Carloadings for these commodities declined for Erie-Lackawanna and for competing carriers.[61]

Luckily, a bright spot appeared in the freight field: automobile traffic. While dampened by recession, growth of this business seemed assured. In May 1962, the company created a second section of train 100, its "hot-shot" eastbound manifest, to transport mostly Rambler automobiles, assembled at the American Motors Corporation plant in Kenosha, Wisconsin, from an interchange at Hammond, Indiana, to Croxton, New Jersey; East Cambridge, Massachusetts; Temple, Pennsylvania; and Watervliet, New York. A newly created subdepartment under the jurisdiction of the superintendent of Motor Transport Service coordinated these promising moves. No wonder management selected for the cover of the *1962 Annual Report* a photograph of flatcars with trailer rigs loaded with automobiles crossing the venerable Starrucca Viaduct, east of Binghamton. This image truly suggested the old and new on the Friendly Service Route.[62]

Still, Erie-Lackawanna remained seriously ill, and some expected its corporate death. But conditions both internally and externally improved; the prognosis for survival in some fashion soon looked better. A doctor of sorts, William White, would take charge, and his prescriptions would yield encouraging results. "Although our problems are numerous," White wrote in February 1964, "we are attacking them with vigor." The "White Revival" was just that: a life-saving renaissance.[63]

THE
WILLIAM WHITE REVIVAL,
1963–1967

"WHITE IS A RAILROAD man's railroad man," proclaimed *Tide*, the advertising trade journal. This was not an exaggeration; a list of the nation's best railroad executives in the twentieth century would surely include his name. This exceptional railroader, who headed four carriers during his 54-year career, left a positive mark on the industry. One of his notable accomplishments involved revitalization of the trouble-ridden Erie Lackawanna. Although William White labored only four years with the company, he showed how good leadership could bolster corporate morale and health.[1]

William "Bill" White was a remarkable individual. His life gave credence to the Horatio Alger story that an impoverished boy could realize the American dream. The oldest of seven children of struggling blue-collar, immigrant parents, he was born in the northern New Jersey community of Midland Park on February 3, 1897. As was common for poor lads of his generation, White left high school prematurely; he ended his formal education at age sixteen to assist his family financially. Finding work as a $20-a-month clerk in the freight auditor's office of the Erie Railroad in New York City, White advanced rapidly from that entry position. By the age of thirty he supervised the busy Mahoning Division, and nine years later he became general manager of the company's Eastern District. In February 1938, after a quarter of a century with "Old Reliable," White joined the Virginian Railway, the prosperous Pocahontas-region coal carrier, as its vice president and general manager. Then, three years later, he resigned to lead the Delaware, Lackawanna & Western Railroad. "White made the road come alive": he streamlined its debt

William White (*right*), chairman of the board of Erie Lackawanna, stands next to M. Cayley Smith, Jr., the railroad's general counsel, in Binghamton, New York, on March 1, 1965, while conferring with local business and civic leaders. (Broome County Historical Society)

structure and improved its efficiency. Although he liked the Lackawanna, he quit in August 1952 to head the immense New York Central Railroad. "I did not seek a change and I had no ambition other than to make the Lackawanna a better railroad, a better place to work, to restore its credit and to carry out to successful conclusion projects of which you are aware," he told the Lackawanna's Board of Managers. "Only two considerations have persuaded me to accept the Presidency of the New York Central System. One consideration is the challenge which it offers; the other is the opportunity that the Presidency of a larger railroad offers for a position of greater influence in the industry. The latter is important because of the problems which currently confront the railroad industry and to which I have given much time and attention, and which I shall continue to do with a broader scope."[2]

White clearly revealed his feelings to his colleagues at Lackawanna. He loved his work and cherished the challenges the railroad industry offered. "His business, his hobby, his life was railroading," aptly observed lawyer-writer Joseph Borken about the inner White.[3]

By the time William White came to power at the New York Central, he had gained the respect of the railroad and financial communities. One industry executive unabashedly proclaimed: "White was the best railroader who ever lived. He was the best administrator that I ever saw." He further recalled, "I remember seeing other railroad presidents and top brass who lined up in front of his office or at meetings to get his counsel." Others remembered similar happenings.[4]

There is ample evidence to support the "best railroader" label. For one thing, the hard-driving White was bright: "Quick as a wink," said one associate. He could easily master the complexities of most matters, including the world of money. "A lot of fellows can remember some things about finance," indicated Robert Fuller, senior vice president of the First National City Bank of New York, who as a Lackawanna board member and later an Erie Lackawanna director had known him well since the early 1940's. "Bill White grasped them quickly and he never forgot them. That's even more remarkable since he never finished high school."[5]

White also was a "fine judge of people," and he could deal with them effectively. He put together a remarkable organization during his eleven-year tenure at the Lackawanna and generally repeated this feat in his subsequent jobs. A clue to why he succeeded appears in the congratulatory letter he wrote to a former colleague who had been promoted to division superintendent on the Erie. "One thing to guard against is impulsiveness. Do not try to change everything in a hurry. . . . No one expects you to revolutionize the Division in a few weeks or even a few months. You will recall many instances of officers who went onto a new job displaying an attitude that everything was all wrong and had to be done all over. That is never true." White went on to argue, "With that attitude they immediately impress their staff and their men with the fact that they had not been doing a good job and get them discouraged and fearful that something is going to happen to them. The result is in every case that the Superintendent loses the confidence of the staff and the men and does not get the active cooperation which he must have, so I hope that you will take it easy in changing things around."[6]

Another positive characteristic Bill White possessed was his determination, whenever possible, to avoid making decisions on hearsay or inadequate information and to ferret out the facts. Illustrations abound. When White heard that there was "inaction" at the Lackawanna's Taylor Yard near Scranton, he ordered a young employee to watch the facility. White learned the reason for inactivity: workers were sleeping in a switch shanty. He then requested that an official join the watch for a second night. Once again crews slept. "But White didn't fire these employees until he had the facts." Another case of searching out facts occurred at the New York Central. Immediately after White took control, he examined the property carefully. "White wasn't an office railroader. He had a hands-on type of style," observed a writer for *Fortune Magazine*. During his initial inspection trip he realized that the company operated too many freights that were remarkably short in length. "None of the men with me," he told *Fortune*, "were even counting the cars. 'How do you count them?' they asked. I told them to count them by fives. I asked, 'Aren't you troubled by too damn many freight schedules?' They said, 'We sure are.' Then I pointed out that they had only to cut the freight schedules and increase the length of the trains." That soon happened. White liked "to needle people to be inquisitive." Apparently this became a trait common to members of his management team. "We became probing people," recalled an associate on the New York Central and Erie Lackawanna.[7]

Bill White, furthermore, possessed considerable vision. While he was trained in traditional railroad ways and refrained from brash actions, except when faced with a crisis, he realized that the industry needed to change and that this meant technological, administrative, and regulatory improvements. Early on White grasped the financial advantages of diesel-electric locomotives, even though his principal assistant at the Lackawanna, Perry Shoemaker, preferred steamers. When White led the Central, he pushed hard on a variety of fronts, including a fight for better freight divisions with western roads, removal of firemen from diesels, and repeal of anachronistic full-crew laws. "For a very brief period when Mr. White was in command," related a top Central official, "I had a glorious feeling we were going to win. Now with Mr. [Robert R.] Young at the helm, I was not so sure."[8]

The career of Bill White changed dramatically in 1954. A financial gadfly, Robert R. Young, "the canny populist of Wall Street," battled White and his supporters for control of the New York Central. Young erroneously charged White with ineffective management, and White, basing his charges on Young's past, asserted that his challenger planned to milk Central's assets. Young knew that if he were to seize the road, he needed to act before White revived it. After the smoke cleared from this hotly contested and expensive ($2.7 million) proxy fight, Young saw election of his fifteen-person slate. "I am sure Mr. Young had a lot of respect for Mr. White's abilities," wrote a Central officer, "and he did, in fact, offer him the opportunity to stay on as president." White, however, had no respect for Young and his associates. "Bill refused to work for Young and left the Central immediately after the results of the proxy contest were known."[9]

The former New York Central president did not leave railroading. Less than four months after Robert Young's smashing victory at the final session of the 1954 stockholders' meeting in Albany on June 14, White accepted the presidency of the Delaware & Hudson Company (which controlled the Delaware & Hudson Railroad Corporation) and later became its board chairman. Then, with Erie-Lackawanna on the ropes, the 66-year-old railroader assumed new responsibilities on June 18, 1963, as its chairman of the board and chief executive officer. (White resigned as D&H's chief executive officer, effective September 1, 1963, but not as board chairman; the Interstate Commerce Commission, in an extraordinary decision, allowed him to serve both carriers because of "special circumstances.") After agreeing to the $50,000-a-year job, White told journalists, "I want to make clear that I did not seek the position with Erie-Lackawanna. But on the board are old friends and associates who thought I could help them." He, of course, had strong ties to the ailing company, both from his previous employment with the Erie and the Lackawanna and his friendship with Robert Fuller, who served on the executive committee of the Erie-Lackawanna board of directors. Fuller, in fact, had told him flatly: "You are the best choice that we could possibly make." But there existed more than an emotional reason; White apparently "wanted that challenge, to show . . . that he could make a difference as a railway executive. . . . He was there on the back burner as head of the D&H and he wanted to remind people that Young had made a real mess of both the New York Central and his own personal life." (Young committed suicide on January 26, 1958, five days after Central directors omitted a quarterly dividend.)[10]

White, however, did not plan to remain at Erie-Lackawanna indefinitely. He originally thought that he would not stay past December 1, 1966, "or such shorter period as would meet the needs of Erie Lackawanna." White, who suffered from diabetes and angina, may have felt that physically he could not tolerate a large dosage of "Erie Lack-of-Money."[11]

When White agreed to join the Erie Lackawanna (he dropped the hyphen), he commanded solid support from board members. Likely he would never have accepted this demanding job had he lacked proper authority. The board's executive committee was "all-powerful," and White knew that he could count on it for allegiance and counsel. He received the ardent backing of Robert Fuller and Harland Forbes, who had supported him faithfully as members of the Lackawanna's board of managers. Raymond Wean, a former Erie board member, but "not pro-Erie," provided additional assistance. Even Harry Hagerty, who ardently endorsed the previous Erie-Lackawanna regime, realized that the railroad's fate and his Metropolitan Life Insurance Company's investments in it depended heavily on White's presence. In a letter to the Interstate Commerce Commission in which the company asked that White be permitted to serve two railroads, Hagerty urged approval: "[N]ew top level management is highly desirable, if not a downright necessity." Only the sixth member of the executive committee, John Thompson, a one-time Erie officer and then board member, "was not exactly in Bill's camp." Still, Thompson generally acquiesced to White's wishes.[12]

The Erie Lackawanna rank-and-file mostly applauded White's arrival. Former Lackawanna employees seemed relieved to have a previous Lackawanna man in charge. They remembered him fondly as a "very dynamic person," even though some called him "Mr. Ice Water," a reference to what some perceived to be his cold personality. Former Erie workers were also pleased; after all, "he was a long-time Erieman and knew our railroad." An ex-Erie electrician, who worked in the Marion diesel shops, put it this way: "We were heading for big, big trouble under McInnes. . . . White knew how to take charge and get things turned around."[13]

William White realized the magnitude of the financial emergency. He told his staff in Cleveland, "We haven't got two nickels to rub together," and warned publicly that he could not work miracles. "The deficits that have plagued the Erie Lackawanna for a number of years cannot be wiped out in one stroke." In an August 5, 1963, memorandum to a dozen of his top associates, White told them, "It is a huge task that faces all of us, individually and as a team. It is not a job for the 'other fellow'; it is a job for everybody, and how it is accomplished will separate the men from the boys." Reflecting the company's malaise were the trading ranges of its common stock: 13¼ to 7 before the merger but only 4½ to 2 by 1962. The immediate concern was not the price of securities, but payment of $4.5 million of real-estate taxes in New Jersey and $1.75 million of bond interest. Both obligations would shortly fall due.[14]

White responded promptly. In case the railroad failed to work out some means to solve its direct money woes, he ordered the law department to prepare a petition for voluntary bankruptcy and to select a jurisdiction in which to file it. The company would take action to forestall any threat of involuntary proceedings by disgruntled creditors. With this necessary but not-so-pleasant safeguard, White pushed forward with efforts to find funds.[15]

Help could come from a government-protected loan. The Transportation Act of 1958 gave the Interstate Commerce Commission authority to guarantee loans to railroads that encountered "temporary distress," and which could not find money at reasonable rates. The road, in fact, earlier had received $15 million of such monies, and that cash infusion had been crucial. Shortly before White assumed his duties, the executive committee, led by Robert Fuller and with White's blessings, moved to tap this possible source. Erie Lackawanna needed to act quickly; this provision of the law would soon expire.[16]

During the latter part of May, Erie Lackawanna asked the Interstate Commerce Commission for a government guarantee for a second $15-million loan. But the ICC declined, saying that the railroad offered inadequate collateral. Undaunted, Erie Lackawanna submitted another request; this time it would give as collateral $15 million of emergency bonds, which it could issue under terms of its First Consolidated Mortgage. Regulators, however, rendered another troubling decision: the company could have a loan guarantee for only $5 million. "[W]e did not consider [this] to be adequate for our needs," concluded White. Once more the company made a proposal; it would accept $8.5 million. The Commission refused. The intrepid railroad successfully demanded that the ICC consider a plan whereby the carrier carefully explained how it would increase revenues, reduce freight-car hire costs and generally cut expenses that would likely permit it to "turn the corner" and operate in the black during 1965. But a fourth rejection followed. With hat in hand, Erie Lackawanna pleaded for the $5 million. The answer from Washington was again no. This somewhat surprising decision was "surely based on a perception that the road was about to fail." The government, then, would grant nothing. "[T]his Commission has refused to guarantee any portion of a loan despite the fact the country's foreign aid program through grants and loans has financed railroad requirements in many foreign countries," charged an angry and dismayed White in his Interim Report to shareholders on November 1, 1963. "Unfortunately, American railroads do not qualify under foreign aid programs."[17]

Even though the Interstate Commerce Commission refused to endorse a government-guaranteed loan, White, nonetheless, effectively handled the immediate crisis. Knowing that the railroad needed to push New Jersey lawmakers toward a more equitable taxation policy, White and his colleagues realized, too, that the railroad could not dodge its $4.5 million tax bill. The company decided to pay what it could, namely $2.5 million; it would provide the remainder as soon as possible. In fact, the railroad paid another $750,000 within a few months. "We regret the inconvenience to the municipalities that result from the deferral of payment of a portion of the tax bill," White told the press. But the Erie Lackawanna head could not resist blasting the ICC again for refusal of the loan guarantee. "[This] points up the inconsistencies of federal policy in granting billions of dollars to aid railroads in foreign countries, spending billions to subsidize railroad competitors in this country, and granting millions in direct loans to finance such things as golf courses, motels, ski resorts, summer theaters, [and] bowling alleys."[18]

Solving the bond problem required more effort. While the railroad managed to pay interest on its immediate bonded indebtedness, it confronted the maturing of a major bond issue. In October 1964 $11.6 million of Erie Railroad Company First Consolidated Mortgage Series E 3¼ bonds would come due. White and the board knew that the company could not easily meet this obligation. Working closely with Robert Fuller, who headed a special committee to deal with maturity problems, White proposed that these securities be extended for a five-year period. To sweeten the request to bondholders, the company would raise the interest rate to 6 percent. But the railroad could not do so unilaterally; it needed Commission approval. At public hearings held on February 4, 1964, Erie Lackawanna presented its proposal. Although backed by the larger institutional holders, two smaller, noninstitutional investors objected. Yet this quest for bond modification ended in victory for the company. The ICC accepted the argument that the railroad deserved a chance to restore its financial health with this five-year extension. The Commission, however, required the company to win endorsement from holders of at least 80 percent of these bonds; it did so quickly and without difficulty.[19]

Part of the immediate strategy for survival involved finding funds to upgrade the property. White knew from personal inspections and data supplied by his staff that the railroad was in a state of decay. Maintenance had been heavily deferred for a half-dozen years, and this meant that freight and passenger cars, track, bridges, and structures needed to be repaired or replaced. The company had an atrociously high rate of "bad-order" freight cars, 14.5 percent as of June 18, 1963 (the national average was 7 percent), and its locomotive fleet exceeded its economic lifespan by approximately four years. "If equipment, track and structures are in good condition, maintenance can be deferred for a reasonable period without consequences too serious," argued White, "but it cannot continue for five or six years without adverse effect."[20]

To keep its trains running, the Erie Lackawanna desperately needed aid from lending institutions. Not surprisingly, White's appearance bolstered chances for funding: "Bankers who knew Bill felt much more comfortable dealing with him than with his predecessor. . . . They had confidence in his abilities and consequently with the future of the railroad." Still, many banks, especially those in New York City, were not anxious to assist a battered railroad. They would provide funds but at high rates of interest, perhaps several points above prime. White logically cultivated friendly members of the banking community. For example, he found George Gund, chairman of the board of the large and rapidly expanding Cleveland Trust Company, especially supportive.[21]

White aggressively sought money to upgrade the railroad's decrepit rolling stock and exploited his positive image in the financial world. He revealed his business savvy by sensibly avoiding equipment trusts and opting instead for conditional sales agreements. Although interest rates on the former were usually lower, the latter meant that purchases could be financed faster and easier since usually only one bank was involved. An example of White's success occurred in January 1964: Buffalo's Manufacturers and Traders Trust Company loaned $738,494 for acquisition of 50 bulkhead gondola cars. Additional financing with conditional sales contracts led to more and better equipment, and thus improved scheduling, reduced car-hire costs, and pleased shippers. Between August 28, 1963, and August 19, 1966, the company entered into 39 agreements, totalling $59,158,445, that financed 75 diesel-electric locomotives and 8,022 freight cars. The banks risked little: the equipment itself provided collateral and railroads, even hard-pressed carriers

An American Locomotive Company photographer catches the first "Century 424" (four axles and 2400 horsepower) diesel locomotive emerging from its Schenectady, New York, plant on May 23, 1963. Erie Lackawanna acquired fourteen of these second-generation, high-horsepower units from Alco. (Erie Lackawanna Inc.)

like Erie Lackawanna, fought to honor these commitments, for not to do so would severely damage their credit rating and sharply lessen possibilities for critical betterments.[22]

⌇

Another priority for William White involved changes in personnel. Most promotions, dismissals, and reassignments occurred early in his tenure. Some former Eriemen thought his actions were "sort of ruthless"; ex-Lackawanna people more commonly approved. Said one official, "He did the right thing. . . . He Lackawannized the place, and that's what it so badly needed." Soon most employees concurred that "Mr. White handled the whole matter of staffing the top executive posts pretty well," but they were less likely to endorse cutbacks in the lower ranks.[23]

The fate of Milton McInnes was decided quickly. Even before White took charge, Robert Fuller and the Executive Committee concluded that Mac should step down as president. "He was not capable of doing a good job" was the consensus. White and fellow board members agreed that McInnes should be demoted: he received a newly created post, vice president for staff. "I was put out to pasture," remarked McInnes. Assigned to the office in New York City, McInnes had limited responsibilities. He mostly represented the carrier on boards and at meetings of satellite firms, including several terminal properties and coal companies. In 1967 McInnes became a consultant, and three years later he retired with a good pension. McInnes admitted that "I felt bad about sneaking out," but harbored no grudges. "I had a wonderful relationship with Bill White. . . . The board wanted to get rid of the captain and I understood this."[24]

In a situation unusual for a major railroad, Erie Lackawanna officially lacked a president until September 1965. "Since Bill was such a superb railroader, the company really didn't need a president. He was after all the chief executive officer." White, of course, did not function alone. He had the able assistance of six individuals who comprised his corps of "general officers." These included four vice presidents (general counsel, operations and maintenance, sales, and staff), the comptroller, and the secretary-treasurer.[25]

Yet White paved the way for naming a president. Shortly after he assumed his duties, he hired Gregory W. Maxwell as the road's vice president for operations and maintenance. White had known Maxwell on the New York Central and Maxwell had contacted White about a job at Erie Lackawanna. Maxwell subsequently gained responsibilities: he became senior vice president on January 1, 1965, and learned from White eight months later that the board of directors would elect him president at its September meeting.[26]

White and the Board chose well. Maxwell was an intelligent, tough, and experienced railroader with a technical bent. Observed an associate, "He had

Gregory Maxwell, last president of Erie Lackawanna, poses for a formal portrait about the time he assumed his leadership position with the company. (Dorothy Maxwell)

that engineer's view of the world." Born in Toledo, Ohio, on July 21, 1917, the son of a physician, this third and final president of the Erie Lackawanna possessed a good education. After graduation from high school in Toledo, Maxwell entered the University of Michigan's highly acclaimed program in transportation engineering in 1934 and received his bachelor's degree five years later. Next he learned railroading the old-fashioned way, through first-hand experience. Maxwell joined the New York Central in July 1939, and for the next fourteen years, except for military service for four years in the Army's Transportation Corps during World War II, he held a variety of positions in the operating department, including stints as assistant trainmaster, trainmaster, and assistant superintendent.[27]

In 1953 Maxwell progressed to the higher level of management. He won appointment as division superintendent in Buffalo. The following year the Central named him general superintendent at New York, and soon he accepted a similar post in Cleveland. Another promotion came in 1956, when Maxwell took the job of general manager in Indianapolis. He stayed there for two years before he assumed expanded duties in Syracuse.[28]

Maxwell made a major career change in 1959. He left the New York Central for the bustling and strategically important Terminal Railroad Association of St. Louis (TRRA). He took this challenging job because "I needed broader railroad experience," for he had his eyes on a top-level managerial post. Until Maxwell joined Erie Lackawanna, he served simultaneously as TRRA's president, director, and chairman of its executive committee. He worked effectively; its owners, fifteen railroads that served St. Louis, liked his overall performance. But working for a company owned by a consortium of sometimes bickering interests taxed him greatly. "Why in the world did you ever take that job to get executive experience?" asked White. Maxwell, too, sometimes wondered.[29]

William White endorsed additional personnel changes, and he worked closely with Wyer, Dick & Co., recently hired by the Executive Committee to study this matter. Robert Fuller had told him: "We will try to clean up the place as much as we can before you take over." Not long thereafter Charles Shannon, who represented the consulting firm, assured White that he could reduce the work force by "at least 1,800." (When Wyer, Dick completed its assignment, it estimated the reduction almost perfectly: 1,801 positions were cut. The railroad's employment by the end of 1964 stood at 16,385, a sizable drop from the 21,068 at the time of merger.)[30]

The task of Wyer, Dick involved examination of the performance of all employees, including every corporate officer. An especially troubling situation involved the size of the work force assigned to station service. "The Erie Lackawanna was lousy with people here. . . . We had to cut there quickly because so many were involved." White backed Wyer, Dick's recommendation that the company terminate its less-than-carload business. "[T]he profitable freight of this type [has] gone to competitors who, in most instances, take only that which they wish to handle, on a selective basis, leaving the railroads with unprofitable, bulky and lightweight freight," explained White to shareholders in February 1964. At Wyer, Dick's insistence and with White's approval, the railroad also busily petitioned state regulatory authorities for permission to close scores of small-town depots. The work of these station agents "has dwindled to a few hours per day and neither the railroad's interest nor public interest is adversely affected." Fortunately, the Chicago & North Western Railway had blazed the legal trail in the late 1950's for agent removal, and Erie Lackawanna ended with comparative ease much of their agents' blatant featherbedding. Other increased efficiencies suggested by Wyer, Dick led to better deployment of personnel, including those engaged in shop work, track maintenance, and train service. Taking advantage of worker attrition, wherever practical, likewise meant fewer employees.[31]

In the process of making recommendations, Charles Shannon encountered a roadblock. "We were writing reports to tell the company to take off people, and these people were not being taken off or they were being put back on." The lack of implementation stemmed from the unwillingness of Gary White, vice president for operations, to cooperate. He viewed Wyer, Dick as a threat to his power and bitterly denounced its involvement in personnel matters. When Shannon arrived at headquarters in Cleveland to supervise these changes, Gary White, "a real tartar," fumed. But Shannon had no intention of retreating. "You have a nice big office," Shannon told him, "and I am going to have a desk brought in and it is going to set alongside of yours." His nemesis uttered a predictable response: "I'll be damned if you will!" The next day Gary White resigned. William White wholeheartedly approved of his younger brother's sudden departure. With this obstreperous executive gone, the process of trimming the payroll went more smoothly.[32]

Even after the initial round of personnel changes and the completion of Wyer, Dick's work, White continued to axe incompetent employees. The most notable firing involved M. Cayley Smith, Jr., the company's longtime attorney and then vice president and general counsel. Smith had a longstanding problem with alcohol abuse, but the Erie and Erie-Lackawanna before White generally tolerated "social drinkers." White discovered that his general counsel had failed to participate in important sessions of the merger hearings between the New York Central and Pennsylvania, which vitally affected the company. When he checked on why Smith missed them, he learned that his top in-house lawyer had been in a drunken stupor, riding back and forth in a roomette on the *Twentieth Century Limited* between New York and Chicago. White, who was always a tough enforcer of "Rule G" ("The use of intoxicants or narcotics by employees subject to duty, or their possession or use while on duty, is prohibited, and is sufficient cause for dismissal"), believed that it applied to *everyone*, even those who commanded an executive suite. He quickly dismissed this veteran of 27 years. White wanted responsible employees who were also honest, bright, and hard-working. These qualities were found among company executives after 1964, including White's closest associate, Gregory Maxwell.[33]

William White and Gregory Maxwell worked well together. Their effective collaboration is revealed in how they confronted the freight equipment crisis. "The Company has been short of freight car equipment of all kinds," White told members of the Board of Directors on August 27, 1963. "It has severely affected freight revenues and costs an excessive amount of money for equipment rentals." Although the railroad had succeeded in adding thousands of new cars, it still needed to embark on an aggressive program of repair and rehabilitation. In the late 1950's the Erie had constructed a $4 million, 187,296-square-foot car-repair shop in Meadville, Pennsylvania, but lack of money had prevented its operation on a full-capacity, full-time basis. White and Maxwell quickly executed a marvelous plan to energize repair work at Meadville. Likely at Robert Fuller's suggestion, the company used the moribund Erie Improvement Company (EIC), a non-carrier affiliate, to acquire title to 2,544 bad-order freight cars. White then convinced George Gund to have Cleveland Trust provide $3,712,500 for this rolling stock and the cost of repairs. With these funds Erie Lackawanna got the car facility functioning properly. The old subsidiary, which lacked the stigma of money problems, acted as the financial vehicle: the loan went to EIC and not to Erie Lackawanna. Fortunately, the bank accepted the rolling stock as collateral. The railroad then repurchased the cars from EIC over a ten-year period. And another benefit followed. "The success of this arrangement with George Gund and Cleveland Trust made it easier for us to get loans from other Cleveland banks," Maxwell recalled. "This was important since the railroad didn't really have many financial friends in New York."[34]

With Meadville on-line, the quality of Erie Lackawanna's car fleet improved markedly. At the end of 1964 the company held only 9 percent of its freight equipment for heavy repairs, and the percentage continued to decline. By January 1, 1967, more than 9,000 cars had received general repairs, and this exceeded 40 percent of its freight-car fleet.[35]

The creativity shown by management with the Meadville shops was one of various efforts to maximize earnings through imaginative business methods. Yet not every attempt to raise or save money produced wonderful results. A good example was Erilak Properties.

With the demise of intercity passenger trains, railroads, including Erie Lackawanna, retained ownership of stations that were truly white elephants. One such structure was the former Lackawanna terminal in Buffalo, New York. Historian Richard Saunders described it in the context of the 1950's: "The terminal building was a monument to the extravagances of an earlier day, its cavernous immensity a bit embarrassing when contrasted to its diminishing usefulness. The sweeping marble staircases that led to the second-story concourse, the seventy-five foot ceilings, magnificent in their decadence, symbolized the drafty discomforts of a bygone day." Saunders could have noted that this massive facility cost the Lackawanna and then Erie Lackawanna tens of thousands of dollars annually. By the mid-1960's, even though the building no longer served travelers, the company retained title and faced sizable tax obligations and maintenance expenses.[36]

William White recognized the financial drain caused by the abandoned Buffalo terminal and other surplus structures that dotted the system, and so he endorsed an imaginative scheme: the creation of Erilak Properties, Inc. This new corporation was not a subsidiary but rather a wholly independent entity. Its purpose was straightforward: "to hold title to properties which we might desire to permit to become tax delinquent because of the excessive taxes levied thereon." If legal problems developed, action would be taken against Erilak and not the railroad.[37]

The Erie Lackawanna soon sold the derelict Buffalo structure to Erilak Properties. The price was $30,000 plus $11,179.60 for taxes; Erilak gave a note for the combined amount. The properties company eventually found a buyer, but it received only $20,000 for the parcel, which it then used to reduce its debt. While Erilak Properties gave Erie Lackawanna legal protection, it still generated paperwork and expenses, mostly for payment of its franchise taxes. Yet the railroad kept the corporation alive until the early 1970's; management thought it might be useful eventually for its intended purpose. In fact, it was proposed in 1967 that the railroad use Erilak to acquire properties in Jersey City and Weehawken, again for the purpose of "using a dummy corporation to hold properties which created heavy tax burdens and could be foreclosed on tax liens without injury to the parent company." As it turned out, "Erilak was a lot of bother. It was a lot easier to sell unwanted properties directly rather than running them through Erilak." That became company policy after the Erilak experiment.[38]

Less complicated than employing conditional sales agreements and utilizing controlled or related nonrailroad firms were efforts to husband resources. White demanded better control of costs and willingly chopped off what he considered to be frivolous extras. An example of the former involved reduction of expenses in terminal operations in the New York City area. White correctly concluded that the costs of transporting cars of perishables by lighters to a Pennsylvania Railroad pier in New York were "clear out of sight." He ordered the company to seek regulatory approval to cancel this tariff, and it did so successfully. As for illustrations of the latter, White removed the perquisites that former management had bestowed on themselves: for instance, memberships were denied in country clubs for executives who had no good reason to have them. Even the format of the company's annual reports changed. Heretofore, these publications were printed on quality paper stock and sported numerous illustrations. But beginning in 1963, reports appeared on cheap paper, lacked illustrations, and were about one-third shorter.[39]

In what was probably a false economy, White ordered termination of the nation's oldest railroad employee publication, *Erie-Lackawanna Magazine*, née *Erie Railroad Magazine*. "I sure missed that magazine," recalled a freight conductor from Huntington, Indiana. "I always enjoyed reading it and keeping up on the people and happenings along the railroad." He was not alone. (After White's tenure, the company introduced *EL Digest*, an abbreviated version of its once-popular publication.)[40]

Although the end of *Erie-Lackawanna Magazine* dampened morale, White was not insensitive to how employees felt about the railroad. In an inspired move, early in his tenure he directed the removal from storage of the tavern-observation cars that once graced the Lackawanna's *Phoebe Snow* between Hoboken and Buffalo. Personnel renovated this equipment and it soon became part of the regular consist of the *Erie-Lackawanna Limited*, the road's premier passenger train between Hoboken and Chicago (the tavern-observation cars ran only between Hoboken and Meadville). "It is yours to use at no extra charge," touted a promotional folder. "You can enjoy the scenic beauty along the Erie Lackawanna route . . . and perhaps a refreshing beverage at the same time. Cigarettes, cigars and playing cards are also available here . . . all at moderate prices." White also asked that this refurbished train be rechristened the *Phoebe Snow*. Soon the company distributed thousands of pamphlets, "Miss Phoebe Again Welcomes You to the Erie Lackawanna," and advertised the train in other ways, including radio spots in various online communities. "It was a master stroke," concluded Richard Saunders. "The train flew the company's flag proudly and the morale of employees, customers and creditors rallied." White was acting in a fashion reminiscent of the shrewd Ralph Budd, president of the Chicago, Burlington & Quincy Railroad, when Budd in the early 1930's rejuvenated his company using the radically new *Zephyr*. This stainless-steel streamliner served as a symbol of hope not only for Burlington employees but also for Americans scourged by Depression and doubt.[41]

The appearance of Erie Lackawanna's *Phoebe Snow* did more than boost morale. It generated "considerable favorable publicity and some increased patronage." The railroad positioned itself for the additional riders who wished to attend the New York World's Fair in 1964. The presence of good equipment on a train running on convenient schedules for fair-goers and others with a New York City or Chicago destination helped to stabilize passenger earnings.[42]

William White, however, was not a sentimentalist about long-distance passenger service. With declining income from the passenger, mail, and express business (revenues dropped from $24,346,730 in 1963 to $21,475,219 in 1965), White pushed to eliminate money-losing trains. In 1965 the company won permission from the Interstate Commerce Commission to discontinue a daily train in each direction between Hoboken and Scranton and a daily train in each direction between Hornell and Buffalo. (The latter had involved a long fight with the Public Service Commission of New York.) The road also received authority to stop hauling passengers on two trains between Hoboken and Chicago, schedules designed principally for mail and express. "The handling of passengers necessitated stops that otherwise were not necessary and involved schedule rigidity," charged White. "Flexibility also permits us to change their schedules wherever necessary to suit the needs of Railway Mail Service and REA Express." When *Phoebe Snow* became a money

The New York–Chicago passenger train *Phoebe Snow*, pride of William White's Erie Lackawanna, pauses in Dover, New Jersey, on April 25, 1965, on its way west. (Railroad Avenue Enterprises)

loser, White endorsed its demise. Much to the amazement of other railroads, the ICC speedily approved the train's discontinuance, mostly "because the Erie was so weak financially." *Phoebe Snow* made its last run on November 27, 1966. To the strains of "Auld Lang Syne" the final westbound train departed from the Hoboken terminal on the Sunday after Thanksgiving Day. White rode in his private car attached to the regular consist, but he avoided attention. Rather, Bernice Yacka, a resident of Bound Brook, New Jersey, and a cashier for the railroad, captured the spotlight: "She was dressed all in white, just like the girl in the Phoebe Snow pictures that hung in each car." With the end of *Phoebe Snow* only one train, *The Lake Cities*, made the 977.8-mile run between Hoboken and Chicago.[43]

When it came to passenger operations, the worm in Erie Lackawanna's apple was its commuter and not its through-line service. Both the Erie and Lackawanna had once hauled patrons profitably in the New York City com-

The eastbound *Phoebe Snow*, with its smart observation lounge car from its Lackawanna namesake, rolls through Denville, New Jersey, on the former Lackawanna on
September 10, 1966. (Railroad Avenue Enterprises)

mutation zone. Historically the wealthier road, the Lackawanna committed
itself to efficient service when it spent more than $11 million between 1928
and 1931 to electrify most of its commuter trackage. Although the Public
Service Corporation of New Jersey developed a dense network of trolley lines
throughout the northern part of the state early in the twentieth century, its
electric cars, generally slow and uncomfortable, attracted only modest numbers of riders away from Erie and Lackawanna trains. Yet keen competition
eventually developed. The opening of the Holland Vehicular Tunnel on November 11, 1927, and subsequent construction of the George Washington
Bridge, Lincoln Tunnel, and an expanding network of paved roads, together
with increased automobile and bus usage, drained business. "We lost much of
the midday or casual travelers," observed Milton McInnes. This process continued, except during World War II when acute shortages of gasoline and
tires bolstered commuter patronage. The postwar figures for the Lackawanna illustrate the decline: an average in 1947 was 22,800 rush-hour, 38,000
weekday, 18,700 Saturday, and 7,800 Sunday passengers; a decade later there

An aging electrified commuter train runs on the former Lackawanna route near Mount Tabor, New Jersey, on July 1, 1975. By this date a state agency had assumed the costs of this essential public service. (Railroad Avenue Enterprises)

were an average of 18,900 rush-hour, 27,300 weekday, 5,200 Saturday, and 3,400 Sunday passengers. Concluded E. S. Root, chief of research at Erie, "[T]he 5-day [work] week and the increase in local shopping centers readily accessible by private automobiles are probably as important reasons as any for the decline in such demand."[44]

The Erie and Lackawanna realized that their commuter trains lost heavily after World War II. By the mid-1950's Erie's deficits exceeded $2 million annually and Lackawanna's $3 million annually. "Experience has demonstrated that this type of service cannot be operated at a profit under present-day conditions," explained Harry Von Willer to shareholders in 1958. "As commuter trains are concentrated in a short period during morning and evening rush hours, operating costs are extremely high and even if compensatory fares could be charged, they would be so prohibitive that passengers could not afford them and would be forced to seek other means of travel or make other plans."[45]

Both companies further faced demanding taxing authorities. The plethora of track, stations, coach yards, and other support facilities needed for commuter operations hiked their tax obligations. In the case of New Jersey, taxing bodies assessed railroad property at 100 percent of true value, while other real estate state-wide averaged an assessment rate of 28 percent. The Lackawanna, for example, paid $2,540,780 in 1958 for property taxes in Hudson County (Hoboken and Jersey City). Wrote Perry Shoemaker, "Confiscatory taxes [in New Jersey] have steadily depleted Lackawanna's cash and resources as tribute, to Hudson County in particular, has continued unabated."[46]

The Erie's response to an ever-worsening commuter problem differed strikingly from that of the Lackawanna. Old Reliable did amazingly little. This was likely an expression of management styles and personal experience. As Perry Shoemaker explained the latter: "Whereas Erie system officials were located in Cleveland, a long way from the reality of New Jersey problems, Lackawanna's top management lived—and voted—in New Jersey, and were daily users of commuter services." Only Paul Johnston, of Erie presidents during the post–World War II era, pushed for modest corrections. His administration convinced the New Jersey Board of Public Utility Commissioners in the early 1950's to allow abandonment of some money-losing trains, mostly on its Greenwood Lake Division, the former New York & Greenwood Lake Railway, between Jersey City and Wanaque-Midvale. Johnston, too, suggested that a regional authority might be a practical solution. But the company put much more faith in achieving savings on its commuter operations by consolidating terminal facilities with the Lackawanna at Hoboken than in persuading regulators to approve more train take-offs and fare hikes. As for the real-estate tax problems, "it was probably hopeless," concluded Milton McInnes. "There was no chance in New Jersey because that state had a long history of taxing utilities and railroads at the highest rate that was possible."[47]

The Lackawanna responded more forcibly. Initially Perry Shoemaker did what Paul Johnston sought, namely, reduced the scope of commuter operations. In 1953 the company won regulatory permission to eliminate 75 trains per week on its Boonton line, and subsequently asked to end all commuter service on this route. The state refused in 1956, but the railroad returned to request more train cuts. A year later the public authority granted its approval to remove more commuter runs on the Boonton line and also some on the Gladstone and Montclair branches. Shoemaker also welcomed the sharing of costs with the Erie at Hoboken, but he believed that more could be accomplished. He and his colleagues applauded creation of a public-study group, the Bi-State Metropolitan Transit Commission in 1954. (Shoemaker enthusiastically endorsed this approach—in part because he fancied such organizations. He served as vice chairman of the Committee of Hoover Commission Task Force Members and headed the Transportation Subcommittee of the Second Hoover Commission.) Ideally, an examination of the region's transportation problems might lead to an equitable way to protect both carriers and patrons. But by 1958 the crippling burden of commuter service remained. When he analyzed this and added the Lackawanna's acute cash problems, Shoemaker concluded that "the time is past for studies and discussions." It was time for a bombshell.[48]

Perry Shoemaker dropped his bomb on December 8, 1958. In "An Open Letter from the Lackawanna Railroad to Its Commuters, to the Communities It Serves, to the Legislature and to the Governor," published in pamphlet form and distributed widely, including copies to train riders, Shoemaker succinctly explained the problems continued commuter operations posed. His first paragraph caught everyone's attention: "It is the plan of the Lackawanna to initiate proceedings in the Spring of 1959 looking toward the progressive discontinuance of all suburban passenger and commutation service." Shoemaker wisely left an opening for public officials (which was the purpose of this strategy): "Should the State, before the end of next Spring, adopt a tax policy for railroads similar to that it now extends to the extensive waterfront and other property of the Port Authority, to highway property and to airport property, the Lackawanna will give every proper consideration and effort to working out with public authority a way to retain essential commutation service."[49]

The Shoemaker letter caused a stir. Letters, telegrams, and telephone calls flooded the Lackawanna's offices in New York City. Most respondents grasped the company's plight. After all, New Jersey's regressive and quiltwork taxation policies annoyed more than railroaders. "You have been setting forth a strong, factual story," concluded Irving T. Gumb, executive vice president of the New Jersey State Chamber of Commerce. "It should bring good results." Some comments were less supportive or expressed horror at the Lackawanna's publicly expressed intentions. "Many of us will be surprised at your plan to end the fine electric service in this State—probably one of the best such systems in the country," wrote William G. Fuller, a resident of Orange. "Only a few months ago, a substantial reduction in suburban service was allowed. . . . It was thought that the consolidated facilities that are shared with the Erie represent a considerable financial benefit to both roads. . . . Your tax problem may be open to some solution, but such a step as you propose may be a calamity from which this area will never recover."[50]

The media, too, reported the Lackawanna plan extensively. The pronouncement of December 8 hardly shocked the Fourth Estate; Shoemaker had spoken on the subject to members of the New Jersey Press Association at Rutgers University three days earlier. "In the absence of action by the State— and it would require political courage which our Governor and the Legislature could exercise—we have no alternative," concluded the Lackawanna president. "No management of a private enterprise can sit idly by and permit discriminatory taxation to bankrupt it. We have been contravened in the Courts. We have been frustrated in the Division of Tax Appeals. What would you do?"[51]

Fortunately, the Lackawanna was not alone in leading the charge for reform. While "Erie support was more difficult to activate," Shoemaker received strong backing from another struggling area commuter carrier, the Jersey Central. "My most active supporter," remembered Shoemaker, "was Earl Moore [president of the Jersey Central]."[52]

With Lackawanna and Jersey Central pressing hard for change, the New Jersey political process responded. Admittedly not much happened initially. Lawmakers considered but failed to pass a modest tax-relief measure, and Governor Robert B. Meyner showed less enthusiasm. He replied to the Lackawanna with the suggestion that the federal government join New Jersey and New York in seeking a solution to the commuter crisis. And he took this opportunity to jab carriers who complained about their commuter losses and tax payments. "The railroads cannot continue to take the stand that they should operate passenger services at a profit," Meyner told the *New York Times*. "They assume the obligation of carrying both passengers and freight in their respective franchises. The level of freight rates has been set to allow for passenger income losses."[53]

Governor Meyner's lack of sympathy and good sense did not preclude aid. During the 1960 legislative session, lawmakers, with the governor's blessing, authorized the state to contract with railroads to provide continuation of commuter trains and to appropriate funds for that purpose. Both the Erie and Lackawanna eagerly signed contracts for this support; they collectively received approximately $2 million for the ten-month period that began September 1, 1960. Although the newly formed Erie-Lackawanna entered into additional contracts, these were merely stopgaps or, as one official said, "at best Band-aids for the financial bleeding."[54]

Following creation of Erie-Lackawanna, management continued to speak of the need to end the financial drain. "There remains much to be done on a governmental level to eliminate the losses sustained in the operation of commuter service," noted Milton McInnes in February 1961. "[M]anagement hopes that further progress can be made in this regard." Unfortunately, except to urge lawmakers in Trenton to provide annual contracts for financial assistance, the McInnes administration accomplished nothing. (The amount paid by the state to Erie Lackawanna between 1960 and 1965 totaled $14 million, less than a third of the loss sustained by the company.)[55]

William White's arrival caused Erie Lackawanna to tackle the commuter problem head-on. "White was out to solve the damn thing," remembered consultant Charles Shannon. The railroad quickly hired Wyer, Dick & Co.

to examine the road's New Jersey and New York commuter operations in detail. "We wanted the amount of loss determined objectively by outside experts instead of Company employees to avoid dispute," announced White. He retained his longtime habit of seeking out facts before he pushed forward.[56]

Because of his experience, Corwin Dick headed the study team. His efforts, however, did not please Erie Lackawanna's chief executive officer. "White didn't like the Wyer, Dick work, in part because the state laughed at the Dick report." New Jersey officials thought that it inflated the cash drain.[57]

This setback did not deter White. After consultations with Wyer, Dick personnel, it was decided that Charles Shannon would make a second examination and that it would be based on "net avoidable costing" in ascertaining the financial impact commuter trains had on the road's financial health. This accounting formula involved determining the costs to which Erie Lackawanna would *not* be subjected if commuter trains stopped running, less the amount of revenues, including public monies, they generated. "You would save all of the passenger costs, labor and on the Morris & Essex line you could cut the three tracks down to one and only operate a slow way-freight," explained Shannon. "This avoidable costing produced some good hard numbers. That's what White wanted and the New Jersey people feared." On an avoidable-cost basis (complete discontinuance of commuter trains) the company would benefit enormously, in excess of $10 million annually.[58]

Even before Charles Shannon and Wyer, Dick & Co. completed their exhaustive studies, White took charge. He won approval from the Board of Directors on June 22, 1965, "to take whatever action was necessary to discontinue suburban passenger train service in the States of New Jersey and New York and to discontinue the operation of ferryboats between Hoboken and New York." Yet before the railroad filed a petition with the New Jersey Board of Public Utility Commissioners, under whose jurisdiction most of the money-losing trains operated, White advised public officials to take some initiative: either the states, an authority created by them, or an agency formed by the counties served must assume the deficit. He told everyone using or affected in some way by these trains that the railroad could not sustain additional losses and that it could not possibly finance the "$80.0 million required to be spent to modernize the service by replacing the equipment and rehabilitating the facilities if the service is not to suffer a breakdown—first occasionally and eventually complete."[59]

The official request to end commuter service came on January 5, 1966. White and his associates did not expect to win. "We knew that our request wouldn't be granted," related counsel Harry G. Silleck, Jr., of Nixon, Mudge, Guthrie, Rose and Alexander, "but it put great pressure on the Commission." As in the past the Board of Public Utility Commissioners thought that it protected the public interest by denying the railroad's full request. It based its position partially on a consulting study made by Peabody & Associates and "it was not good. . . . These people knew more about the coal industry than about railroads." But regulators finally recognized the severity of the company's financial plight; Peabody, too, confirmed the heavy losses. And commissioners realized that the White regime was "damn determined to rid itself of this awful burden." After the public hearings that began on January 26, the Board granted some major concessions. In its order of May 4, 1966, it permitted abandonment of trains on the Caldwell, Carlton Hill, Newark, and Northern branches and between Netcong and Branchville, Netcong and Washington, and Mountain View and Midvale, and also a number of trains that ran on other lines, mostly during off-peak hours. This meant a reduction in trains operated Monday through Friday from 298 to 155 per day, on Saturdays from 91 to 62, and on Sundays from 62 to 39. Although the Commission estimated savings of $2 million annually, Wyer, Dick & Co., assisted by members of the railroad's staff, determined savings at $2,065,708 per year but offset by revenue losses of $576,143, thus producing a net savings of $1,489,565.[60]

The state-endorsed retrenchment and the railroad's threat to pull the plug annoyed many. Two railroad labor unions, the Boards of Freeholders of Bergen and Morris Counties, and a commuters' group from Bergen County appealed the Commission's decision to the New Jersey Supreme Court. In an uncommonly swift response, the high court affirmed this vast reduction in suburban service.[61]

Good news for the Erie Lackawanna continued. New Jersey agreed to enter into a contract to subsidize those trains that remained. "That was worked out with the Governor's office and the State Department of Transportation," recalled Harry Silleck. With the backing of Governor Richard J. Hughes, in June 1966 lawmakers unanimously approved a public transit measure, including creation of the Commuter Operating Agency (COA). Located within the Division of Rail Transportation of the Department of Transportation, COA would have power to enter into long-term contracts with railroads for commuter operations. Erie Lackawanna signed an agreement in which it would receive payments of more than $4.2 million for the fiscal year that began on June 1, 1966. "[T]he State's Commuter Operating Agency will reimburse the railroad for deficits resulting from operating suburban rail passenger service in the State of New Jersey," noted a pleased White, "and that the deficits will be computed on the basis of avoidable cost under a formula to be agreed upon between the State and the railroad." Later, too, the company received permission to retire its vintage ferryboats that crossed the North River, erasing a deficit of about $600,000 a year.[62]

The White regime also overcame New Jersey's inequitable taxing policies. As the result of litigation brought early in 1966, Erie Lackawanna and other carriers who owned property in Hudson County secured a settlement that required assessors to place railroad real estate on a parity with other property. Governor Richard Hughes again provided assistance; he recognized "the inequalities of the past." Hughes convinced lawmakers to revise the tax code to conform to the terms of the earlier settlement. This reform dropped the company's real-estate tax bill from $4.4 million in 1965 to $2.9 million in 1966. The state additionally agreed that railroad property devoted to passenger transportation would be tax exempt after January 1, 1967.[63]

The easing of the financial drain from commuter operations and oppressive taxation soon bolstered Erie Lackawanna's money picture. Even before this vital victory, White's talents and those of his dedicated staff achieved the road's objectives: "to turn the corner" and "get in the black." The bottom line initially required red ink: the company lost $17,115,272 in 1963, but it reduced the amount to $8,268,194 in 1964. Net income for 1965 was a positive $3,290,788 and nearly doubled a year later. This encouraging trend elicited widespread favorable reaction. The *Value Line Survey*, a financial newsletter, commented on the railroad's gratifying first quarter of 1966: "This is not an impressive profit by most standards, but for Erie it is nothing less than sensational when one realizes that this was the first March quarter in which the company (or predecessor companies) had earned a profit since 1957." Remarked *Inside Story*, a publication of the International Stanley Corporation, in January 1967, "[T]he marked resurgence of the Erie Lackawanna is managerial achievement on the brink of disaster that can't help but bring a sigh of relief and blush of pride to railroaders everywhere."[64]

———

William White might have led an even stronger company had management's struggles against workers been more effective. White believed, and for good reason, that this was "almost an impossible battle," a much more difficult one to win than the fight to reduce commuter deficits. On the whole, railroads by the 1960's faced, in comparison to other industries, the most unionized work force, the most highly paid workers, the most restrictive work rules, and the most restrictions on maneuvering in labor squabbles.[65]

Erie Lackawanna reeled under the burden of labor costs. "We have so few options with our labor expenses," complained White. Few disagreed. The railroad industry had long negotiated wage pacts with the various unions, and individual carriers had to accept these settlements. Erie Lackawanna, for example, absorbed $11.5 million in additional employment costs between 1964 and 1965. Furthermore, payroll taxes for Railroad Retirement and those added for Medicare, the pride of President Lyndon B. Johnson's evolving Great Society, tacked on $1.3 million in 1966 with little likelihood for future reductions. The railroad's average employment cost per employee rose from $7,364 in 1963 to $8,927 in 1967, an increase of 21 percent.[66]

A more hopeful development occurred with the industry's efforts to alter archaic work rules. During the early 1960's several study groups investigated work-rule disputes and agreed that changes favoring carriers should be forthcoming. Yet the entrenched body of railroad labor consistently refused to accept these findings. When a national railroad strike loomed in August 1963, President John F. Kennedy won industry approval to withhold work-rule changes while he submitted to Congress a proposal that would provide for all outstanding issues to be arbitrated. These decisions would be final and binding. Congress, however, passed legislation, signed by President Kennedy, that required final and binding arbitration in only two areas: those involving firemen on diesel locomotives in road freight and yard service and those relating to train-crew consists. This measure directed that other issues in dispute be negotiated between the parties within six months.[67]

Unions opposed any binding decisions by arbitrators. They predictably took this matter to court, challenging the constitutional right of Congress to dictate binding arbitration in a labor dispute. Eventually a federal district court, the U.S. Court of Appeals, and the U.S. Supreme Court heard labor's pleas but the bodies repeatedly favored the defendants.[68]

The legislative and judicial victories produced less-than-perfect results. Although Erie Lackawanna realized hundreds of thousands of dollars in savings during White's tenure, failure to repeal or significantly modify full-crew laws in Indiana, New York, and Ohio prevented additional savings. The railroad was encouraged when New York lawmakers, prodded by Governor Nelson Rockefeller, in 1966 repealed that portion of the state's excess-crew law that required a third brakeman on freight trains handling more than 25 cars. But this victory occurred only after the carriers, including Erie Lackawanna, agreed that no person employed at the time of repeal would be terminated except through natural attrition. Moreover, the railroads accepted the concept of a five-person crew. Gregory Maxwell disagreed with White's willingness to back this pact. Maxwell did not want "set in concrete" that "now all freight trains would have to have a conductor and two trainmen." This turned out to be the only major rift between the two men.[69]

———

Notwithstanding the handicaps labor created, Erie Lackawanna sought to do its best. "We're in business to provide dependable service and to make money": this simple pronouncement by William White in 1965 explains why the company zealously expanded its Trailer-on-Flatcar (TOFC), or piggyback, operations. Impressive growth occurred. The railroad transported 111,550 loaded truck trailers in 1964, a 14.4 percent increase from the previous year and a 39 percent increase from 1961. Volume rose 10.8 percent in 1966, and the trend continued. This reflected the national boom in TOFC and the bright spot for carriers. Loadings for the industry soared from 207,783 in 1956 to 1,162,731 a decade later with the take-off coming after 1961.[70]

Although deferred maintenance prevented the Friendly Service Route from operating a speedway for its piggyback movements, the road still hauled them competitively. When Gregory Maxwell arrived, he found that freight trains ran too fast for track conditions. "We wanted to make the Erie Lackawanna a 50-miles-per-hour railroad," he remarked. This was a sensible decision. If a derailment occurred at 60 miles per hour, 25 to 30 cars would likely be damaged, but with a speed 10 miles per hour less, only 15 to 20 cars would probably be involved. "The savings in claims and repairs," argued Maxwell, "would be highly significant." Altering speeds downwards, however, would not ruin the company's competitive position. "We were speeding up and closing terminals, and so we still had a jump on cross-country trucks." Management closed or reduced operations in seventeen yards and terminals system-wide; this meant closures at Hammond and Huntington, Indiana; Kent, Ohio; and Jamestown, Salamanca, Hornell, East Binghamton, and Port Jervis, New York, on the main line.[71]

Even the magisterial Chesapeake & Ohio concurred that the White team performed well. When that road thought Erie Lackawanna might enter its fold as a result of its recently announced merger with Norfolk & Western, management sent an undercover surveillance team to scrutinize the property during the fall of 1965. The subsequent report concluded that the White regime was doing a good job considering its financial limitations. "Virtually the entire railroad is in good-excellent condition," noted these C&O investigators. "EL on-time performance is generally good," and they indicated that the road's best time for Chicago–New York freight traffic was 26½ hours, somewhat slower than New York Central's 25½ hours, but considerably better than the 28 hours for the Baltimore & Ohio–Reading–New Jersey Central route, or the 33 hours for the Norfolk & Western–Lehigh Valley combination or the 34 hours via the C&O–Lehigh Valley. Erie Lackawanna also competed effectively on both Chicago-to-Buffalo and Chicago-to-Boston runs.[72]

The William White agenda at Erie Lackawanna was primarily to end the ledgers' hemorrhage of red ink. Yet he believed from the start that the company must find a suitable merger partner. With the road's financial health considerably improved by 1966, White considered the Erie Lack-of-Money tag to be unfair. Unquestionably the company was weak, but White and his associates rightly disputed any contention that Erie Lackawanna was an unattractive property. "We're hardly a weed-covered shortline," snapped a ranking officer.[73]

The company had good reason to expect to find a merger partner. As part of the Norfolk & Western–Nickel Plate–Wabash merger proceedings begun in early 1961, N&W agreed that if the Interstate Commerce Commission sanctioned this union, the combined firm would negotiate "in good faith" for inclusion of Erie Lackawanna. When the ICC gave its approval, which became effective October 16, 1964, it announced that it would retain jurisdiction in the case for five years and encouraged Erie Lackawanna to join.[74]

Yet before the Commission gave the Norfolk & Western a green light for merger (technically merger of the N&W and Nickel Plate, lease of the Wabash and the Pittsburgh & West Virginia, control of the Akron, Canton & Youngstown, and purchase of the Pennsylvania's Sandusky-Columbus line linking the N&W and Nickel Plate) and opened the door for inclusion, the White administration worried about a marriage of the New York Central and Pennsylvania, the two largest railroads in the East and keen competitors. Even though the Central and Pennsy lacked the economic vitality of the past—one historian called them "the equally bad-off former monarchs of railroading," Milton McInnes remembered, "We thought that together they would cream us." These carriers filed their merger documents on March 9, 1962, and public hearings stretched from August 20, 1962, to September 16, 1964. During the merger testimony, Erie Lackawanna opposed unification unless it were included. If, however, N&W agreed to accept Erie Lackawanna, then Erie Lackawanna would support creation of Penn Central.[75]

The merger craze seemed unending. Numerous companies scrambled to position themselves in the best possible fashion. "If over the next decade the railroad map of America will be redrawn," observed John Fishwick, senior vice president of the Norfolk & Western, in a public address at the American University in Washington, D.C., in 1965, "we want to do everything we can to see that it is redrawn in a way that benefits us." Early in the decade the fast-moving developments among carriers in the East pointed to creation of three systems: N&W–Nickel Plate–Wabash, New York Central–Pennsylvania, and Chesapeake & Ohio–Baltimore & Ohio. For White's road the merger picture became muddied, when the enlarged N&W announced on August 31, 1965, that it would seek merger with another profitable coal-hauling giant, Chesapeake & Ohio. "Chessie's Road," which had won control of the B&O in early 1963, like the N&W, wished to protect itself from the possible Penn Central colossus. The expanded N&W, though, pushed this proposal. Fishwick explained its genesis: "I woke up in the middle of the night and I kept turning this thing over, and finally the idea of a merger of the N&W and the C&O seemed like a good idea."[76]

Jack Fishwick's vision meant that the combined Norfolk & Western–C&O could afford to take in outcast carriers like Erie Lackawanna, but perhaps it could delay their acquisition. Yet, expecting these properties, management of the N&W and C&O wanted protection. In its ruling in the N&W case, the Interstate Commerce Commission also permitted the Boston & Maine (now appropriately maligned as the "Busted & Maimed") and the Delaware & Hudson to petition for inclusion. Thus the N&W had several troubled railroads knocking at its door; the loudest was Erie Lackawanna. The C&O, too, foresaw potential problems. It inherited from the Baltimore & Ohio a substantial position in the dying Reading Company, a once prosperous anthracite road that sustained heavy losses from its commuter operations. The Reading, in turn, controlled the Jersey Central, another old anthracite carrier famous for a deficit-ridden commuter service. "We were strong and profitable roads," remarked Fishwick, "and we didn't want to be pulled down by any weak sisters."[77]

Details of how to protect the powerful railroads fell into the capable hands of a New York City investment banking firm, R. W. Pressprich & Company. Since its founding at the turn of the century, Pressprich had enjoyed a stellar reputation for its underwriting, distributing, and dealing in securities and also for providing advisory services to governmental authorities, public commissions, and corporations. Moreover, the Norfolk & Western was closely linked to the company; for instance, Pressprich commonly sold the N&W's equipment trust certificates. Out of this continuing relationship developed the blueprint for a "protective" holding company. Known as "Dereco," it was largely the handiwork of Charles L. Bergmann, "the best bond man on Wall Street," and his principal associate, Isabel H. Benham, a bright and experienced railroad financial expert and, incidentally, a close friend of the Fishwick family.[78]

Dereco, "a wonderfully kept secret" until announcement of the Norfolk & Western–Chesapeake & Ohio merger, took its name from the password on the work sheets at Pressprich: DERJCO. The D represented Delaware & Hudson, E for Erie Lackawanna, R for Reading, and J for Jersey Central. (The Boston & Maine name was not indicated.) "But Mr. Bergmann spit out Dereco," remembered Isabel Benham. "It can be pronounced." The Pressprich plan called for Dereco to be the corporate home of these troubled carriers, and all of their stock would be in its hands. The N&W-C&O, of course, would control Dereco. Neither the N&W-C&O nor Dereco, however, would assume any of the debt of these five companies. The benefits of this corporate arrangement were expected to be twofold: first, it had the potential of giving N&W-C&O considerable tax-loss carry-forwards, although the federal tax law needed modification; and second, if the captive roads failed, the heavy financial repercussions would be avoided.[79]

The day after the White administration heard officially of the Norfolk & Western–Chesapeake & Ohio merger plans and Dereco, Erie Lackawanna's Finance Committee, chaired by Robert Fuller, met with the courting couple.

(Because of White's ties to the D&H and his wish to avoid any charge of impropriety, Fuller assumed responsibility for Erie Lackawanna's merger work.) In discussions with Herman Pevler, N&W president, Walter Tuohy, C&O president, and several of their colleagues, Fuller and his associates learned that the fate of Erie Lackawanna had been decided and that it was a take-it-or-leave-it proposition. But White's road wanted direct inclusion. It disliked the N&W-C&O's condition that Dereco was "off" if the merged firm failed to win the tax change; if commuter problems were not solved for the Erie Lackawanna, Jersey Central, and Reading; and, especially, if "there is no substantial adverse change in the financial position of any of the five proposed subsidiaries."[80]

The Erie Lackawanna was intrepid. With the fervent backing of White, Fuller, and the Board of Directors, company attorneys filed a petition with the Interstate Commerce Commission on September 28, 1965, that sought inclusion in the present Norfolk & Western system. The Erie Lackawanna then submitted a detailed plan with the Commission on February 15, 1966. Developed with the help of financial advisor Kuhn, Loeb & Company, this document carefully outlined what the Erie Lackawanna sought. As White said, "The plan is designed to be in the best interest of all owners of Erie Lackawanna securities." Essentially the proposal called for creation of a "New Erie Lackawanna" (New EL) by the N&W and then merger of the Erie Lackawanna (Old EL) into the new corporation. The latter would assume the obligations of the former. N&W common stock would be exchanged for Old EL securities. Erie Lackawanna common, for example, would be traded for 0.128 of a share of N&W common. Erie Lackawanna obligingly agreed that the merger of Old EL into New EL would be subject to its ending commuter losses and enactment of a change to the federal tax code. The latter then would permit N&W, by filing consolidated federal income tax returns with New EL, to deduct a portion of Old EL's tax-loss carry-forward "equal to the fair market value of N&W common stock into which EL capital stock is to be converted and exchanged upon merger, plus the maturity value of all outstanding indebtedness of EL assumed or guaranteed by N&W."[81]

The Interstate Commerce Commission conducted hearings of the petition during spring and summer of 1966, and briefs and reply briefs followed. Throughout this process the Norfolk & Western objected strongly to any proposal that would require it to give stock or anything of value to the common or preferred shareholders of Erie Lackawanna or Boston & Maine. Furthermore, the Roanoke-based road did not want to protect Erie Lackawanna bondholders. "N&W was scared to death of EL's debt." And the N&W insisted that its merger application with Chesapeake & Ohio be approved before inclusion of other roads. (Hearings on the N&W-C&O merger application, though, did not begin until April 1967.)[82]

Finally, on December 22, 1966, ICC Commissioner Charles A. Webb, who served as examiner, made known his decisions. He reported to the Commission that inclusion of Erie Lackawanna and Delaware & Hudson in the Norfolk & Western system "be authorized and directed" and that inclusion of the Boston & Maine "be authorized but not directed." Webb endorsed Dereco, echoing the reasoning of the N&W-C&O. "Thus, N&W would acquire control of the petitioners without assuming the large debt of EL and B&M." To Webb, then, having the outcasts under the broad wing of a holding company made sense. But counter to the wishes of N&W, Webb concluded that "an exchange of stock as proposed by EL is equitable, *provided* that on or before the date of inclusion Congress has amended the Internal Revenue Code substantially as proposed in the so-called Koegh bill." He also set these important conditions: inclusion would be predicated upon final consummation of the Penn Central merger (the ICC had given its approval on April 6, 1966), and Erie Lackawanna stockholders needed to approve the financial changes. If they did not, the ICC would block Erie Lackawanna from pursuing its earlier petition for union with Penn Central.[83]

Commissioner Webb sensed that his judgments would safeguard the public interest. Most of all, sickly carriers needed protection in what seemed to be shaping up as two dominant, independent systems in the East, Norfolk & Western–Chesapeake & Ohio and Penn Central. (As one of the conditions of merger between the Central and Pennsy, the latter had to divest itself of a prized asset, a large block of N&W stock.) Many thought that the developing merger scenario was reasonably sound as long as the weaklings found homes. Even N&W's Herman Pevler admitted in February 1968, "We are confident that this expanded N&W-C&O-Dereco system will provide balanced competition with the great Penn Central system and will be of great benefit to our shareholders and the shipping public." Pevler could agree with Webb, but from a different perspective. If the weak roads had a safe haven, the government, especially the ICC, would likely endorse merger of the nation's two most powerful coal haulers.[84]

As Erie Lackawanna progressed toward association with a stronger carrier, shocking news came from Cleveland. On Thursday, April 6, 1967, about 10 o'clock in the morning, William White, who was two months and three days past his seventieth birthday, died suddenly in the office of the company's chief surgeon in the Midland Building. "The physician and another person attempted CPR but his heart attack proved fatal," recalled Gregory Maxwell. "He died in harness."[85]

There was much left to be done at Erie Lackawanna. Yet William White had battled the odds and within less than four years had "really turned the place around." The company's net income rose dramatically between 1963 and 1966, and its corporate culture changed wondrously as well. White's Lackawannization boosted morale, increased efficiency, and helped to end red ink. His creativity and drive left positive marks. Moreover, White's merger strategy seemed close to fruition; indeed, the New EL, Erie Lackawanna Rail*way*, debuted a year after his unexpected death. "It didn't hurt to have had one of the nation's best railroaders, even for a short time," concluded one officer. "His death was a real blow." Most agreed that William White had sparked a revival at Erie Lackawanna, but historical hindsight reveals that he had not "saved" it. The company was to seek court protection within five years for the fifth time.[86]

DERECO,
1968–1972

ON APRIL FOOL'S DAY of 1968, John Palmer Fishwick, better known as "Jack," arrived at his office on the thirteenth floor of the Midland Building in downtown Cleveland to oversee the Erie Lackawanna Railway, the Norfolk & Western's "booby prize." "I'm not superstitious, mind you," the N&W executive told a reporter from the Associated Press. "I did know I'd be moving to Cleveland on April 1. But I didn't know my office would be on the 13th floor until I dropped into Erie headquarters when I was house-hunting in Cleveland last week."[1]

Jack Fishwick spoke truthfully when he rejected evil omens. He was a rational, sensible, and some would say calculating individual. Fishwick always "wanted the facts." Observed an associate, "He would push a person with questions until he could not answer them and then that fellow would be forced to admit that he would have to check the material." While many at Erie Lackawanna considered him a "cold individual" (a wag commented, "Isn't he rather a cold fish-wick?"), virtually everyone agreed that, regardless of his personality, he was well organized, disciplined, and possessed of a prodigious appetite for work. "Jack certainly had the qualities of a great railroad executive," concluded a man who had been a colleague at both Norfolk & Western and Erie Lackawanna. "His fertile brain worked out much of the strategy the N&W followed over the years with considerable success."[2]

This new Clevelander with his many titles—president of Dereco, Inc., chairman and chief executive officer of Erie Lackawanna Railway, senior vice president and director of the Norfolk & Western Railway, and soon-to-be

A pensive John P. "Jack" Fishwick is captured on film during the Dereco years. (Erie Lackawanna Inc.)

president of the Delaware & Hudson Railway—benefited from a solid education. Born in Roanoke, Virginia, on September 29, 1916, the son of recent immigrants from London, Fishwick graduated third in his class from Roanoke High School in June 1933. He earned a Bachelor of Arts degree (with a major in English) from Roanoke College four years later. Fishwick then left his hometown to enter Harvard Law School "because I always wanted to be a lawyer." In 1940 he received his LL.B. degree. "Jack did very well at Harvard," remarked a close friend. "When he took an accounting course, he got the top grade. The final took all day but he finished it early."[3]

Fishwick immediately embarked on a legal career, but the outbreak of World War II caused him to postpone it. After a stint with the prestigious New York law firm of Cravath, Swaine & Moore, Fishwick entered the Navy and advanced rapidly, serving first as captain of a submarine chaser and then as commander of a destroyer. After his discharge in 1945 with the rank of lieutenant commander, Fishwick returned to Roanoke. "I had in mind practicing law right here," he told the *New York Times* in 1968. "One of the first things I did was call on Stuart Saunders [a fellow Roanoke College and Harvard Law School graduate] who then was assistant general solicitor here at N&W." Added Fishwick, "The upshot of my visit was that he offered me a job. From then on it seemed as if I was right behind Stuart." As Saunders advanced toward the N&W presidency, which he gained in 1958, so, too, did Fishwick win major promotions. He became the company's general counsel in 1956, and earned the coveted post of senior vice president twelve years later.[4]

Publicly Jack Fishwick said that he relished the challenge of heading Erie Lackawanna in Cleveland. "The Erie is my first charge," he told *Forbes Magazine*. "Hell, I'm determined not to end up with a dead horse." Privately, however, he and his family disliked leaving the Roanoke Valley. "I felt that I was being sent to Siberia." And in 1989 he reflected that it had been an "almost impossible assignment since the likelihood of doing anything with the Erie was slight."[5]

The politics at Norfolk & Western headquarters surely explain the presence of Jack Fishwick in Cleveland. Herman J. Pevler, who took command of the merging Norfolk & Western, Nickel Plate, and Wabash railroads in October 1963, when Stuart Saunders left to head the Pennsylvania, felt threatened by the talented Fishwick. "With Jack out of town, Pevler thought that he would be fully in charge." Naturally the N&W president projected a different notion. "He [Fishwick] is our best man," Pevler told the media, assuring everyone that N&W wished to help its new ward. Few would challenge this assessment of Fishwick's abilities. Indeed, his image in the railroad industry was "excellent . . . the man-on-the-make," while Pevler's, in fact, suffered. William White, for one, had once remarked in disgust, "Pevler is stupid!" But Fishwick did not ignore happenings in Roanoke, and he later engineered a coup against his boss.[6]

Although Jack Fishwick took charge of the executive suite in Cleveland, the leadership of Erie Lackawanna remained mostly intact. This meant that Gregory Maxwell kept the presidency. Robert Fuller, the veteran board member who became chairman following the death of William White, gladly surrendered that position to Fishwick, but he warned Herman Pevler that Dereco must retain Maxwell. The Erie Lackawanna board wanted an experienced operating executive, and Maxwell had "talent so different from that of Fishwick, the lawyer." Fuller was blunt: "The Erie Lackawanna board will resign if Maxwell is replaced and this will embarrass the N&W." Pevler understood. Fishwick, too, agreed: "I needed Maxwell." The pre-N&W Erie Lackawanna board also continued to function, but it coexisted with the Dereco body with its ranking N&W personnel. "The Erie Lackawanna board was not about to get into open conflict with the N&W," related Maxwell, "and neither was the N&W about to destroy it." To do so would be an invitation for watchful bondholders to demand that N&W guarantee their investments.

Understandably, the N&W felt compelled to keep the massive Erie Lacka-wanna debt separate from its own.[7]

⸺⸺

Dereco, Inc. expanded on July 1, 1968, when it officially acquired its sec-ond property, the Delaware & Hudson Company. Dereco did so through ac-quisition of the firm's outstanding common stock. Shareholders of the D&H had voted five weeks earlier to convey the railroad's assets to Norfolk & Western in exchange for a 6 percent five-year $1 million promissory note and 412,647 shares of N&W common stock. (Technically, this meant 0.2597 share of N&W per share of D&H Company stock.) The transaction added 737 route miles, 2,404 employees, and $107 million of assets to the 2,904 route miles, 13,775 employees, and $464 million of assets of Erie Lacka-wanna.[8]

The financial world took note of Dereco's activities. Investors who owned Erie Lackawanna Railroad common, "which was really worthless," benefited enormously; they received 0.128 shares of Dereco "B" preferred. Holders of Erie 5 percent preferred got 0.375 shares of Dereco "A" preferred, while those with 5 percent preferred "B" earned 0.385 shares of Dereco A. These shareholders could convert their Dereco A and B into N&W common on a share-for-share basis after five years. Ultimately they would be exchanging nearly valueless shares for securities then selling for about $90 each with a $6 annual dividend. If by chance earnings of Dereco exceeded those of Norfolk & Western, the holding company, at its option, could call in the A and B is-sues at $150 per share six years after their issuance. "Whatever approach one uses to evaluate Dereco shares," Shearson, Hammill & Company told its cus-tomers, "a substantial profit appears to be built in to the set-up for Dereco investors."[9]

Dereco, Inc., however, did not develop as most experts expected. While the Delaware & Hudson joined, the Boston & Maine refused. Although this 1,529-mile Boston-based carrier, with its lines mostly in Maine, Massachu-setts, and New Hampshire, got the green light from both the Interstate Com-merce Commission and the U.S. Supreme Court to enter the Norfolk & Western system, it disliked the financial arrangements. Under the plan of-fered by N&W, holders of B&M preferred stock would receive 0.175 share of Dereco A and those with B&M common would acquire 0.1 share of Dereco B. As with Erie Lackawanna shareholders, these new owners of the A and B stocks could convert them into N&W common five years after their issuance. Boston & Maine Industries, which held most of the railroad's equity, opposed these terms, "believing them to be inequitable to B&M shareholders." The B&M owners further felt that their company might prosper if they could im-prove efficiency and reduce labor costs. Similarly, the B&M "viewed itself as the core for an expanded system in New England," and that also meant independence from N&W.[10]

The refusal of the Boston & Maine to join did not necessarily negate Dereco's growth. This holding company expected to add two old Baltimore & Ohio affiliates, Reading Company and Jersey Central (the latter had entered bankruptcy on March 22, 1967), as part of the anticipated merger of Norfolk & Western and Chesapeake & Ohio. But these efforts at unification failed. Even though the N&W-C&O merger case proceeded steadily through the regulatory maze and the hearing examiner approved the application on March 20, 1969, the carriers ultimately canceled their wedding plans. "This decision is deemed to be in the best interest of both companies," said the terse joint statement early in 1971, "in view of drastic changes [in] the Eastern railroad [picture] since the plan of merger was entered into in 1965."[11]

Explanations for the failure of the Norfolk & Western and Chesapeake & Ohio merger and hence expansion of Dereco are complex. The financial collapse of the Penn Central in June 1970 sent shock waves through the railroad industry and the financial community. This was the biggest business failure in American history and predictably dampened merger mania. "We were always told that the N&W-Chessie merger died quickly as a result of the Penn Central bankruptcy, which suddenly cooled financial institutions and the ICC on the proclaimed benefits of railroad mergers," recalled a Chessie officer. "As we well know now, the chill didn't last too long, but it was quite severe at the time." Other factors, too, contributed to the official termination; indeed, the Penn Central debacle provided a degree of face-saving escape. For one thing, C&O's declining income at the end of the decade caused concern. The company struggled with the weaknesses of the Baltimore & Ohio, which it had controlled since 1963, and "some developing problems in the C&O's coal markets." Furthermore, a clash of personalities erupted. Apparently N&W's Herman Pevler and C&O's president and chief executive officer Gregory DeVine had agreed earlier that a C&O officer would head the unified road, although DeVine neared retirement and there was no heir apparent on the C&O side. When Jack Fishwick learned of this arrangement, "he went through the roof," and this helped to prompt Pevler's ouster, and "ended the N&W-C&O deal."[12]

When Jack Fishwick arrived in Cleveland to begin his "high-risk" assignment, he did not expect the Norfolk & Western–Chesapeake & Ohio merger to collapse, nor did he expect Dereco to be limited to two roads. He did foresee a challenge making Erie Lackawanna profitable. The railroad had slipped badly in 1967 when the national economy braked sharply; the company posted a net loss of $8.77 million. Fishwick recalled that his first impression of Erie Lackawanna was that "it was sort of unnecessary." And he added, "There was too much trackage in the East; the Erie had the New York Central on one side and the Pennsy on the other." Still, Fishwick thought that Erie Lackawanna possessed an attractiveness: its style of operations and wide clearances made it "look like a western, not an eastern road." Moreover, he discovered quickly that "people could make a railroad run without a lot of fancy equipment or lots of money." Fishwick particularly admired the company's employees. "They took great pride in the railroad, especially in their commuter service in New Jersey. . . . These people would be out clearing switches after a snow without anyone calling them out. It was an attitude that cannot be bought and it deserves real respect."[13]

Fishwick forged ahead. He received mostly loyal support from fellow executives. "When you are the boss," he remembered with a chuckle, "you get some cooperation." Veteran traffic officer M. Fred Coffman provided a common reaction to Fishwick and to several executives who arrived later from Roanoke: "They were a breath of fresh air. They were sophisticated." While Erie Lackawanna personnel jokingly referred to Fishwick and his N&W associates as the "Virginia mafia," they realized that these individuals represented hope for better times. "It was great to have a big and wealthy company like N&W getting into the picture," noted Wallace Steffen, Erie Lackawanna's general solicitor. "Remember, the EL mostly ran itself during the Dereco era. The Virginia mafia didn't really control us." And N&W domination meant little to the rank-and-file. "There was no difference that I could tell," reflected J. D. Allen, a locomotive engineer and brotherhood official, and his views were typical.[14]

The head of Dereco found an organization that was in "reasonably good shape," a legacy of the William White era. The budgeting process especially impressed Jack Fishwick. "I thought they were making better forecasts than we got on the N&W." Erie Lackawanna personnel knew what the company needed, he believed, although budgetary constraints restricted their creativity and effectiveness. Still, Fishwick discovered some aspects of the corporate culture annoying. When he asked officers to call him Jack, some refused. "Those of the old school like Harry Schmidt [Traffic Department] couldn't bring themselves to call me by that name." He added, "This inflexibility could be found elsewhere . . . and it took longer to alter."[15]

The tenure of Jack Fishwick in Cleveland lasted two years and produced some encouraging financial results. "I got lucky. . . . This was a major period of my career and my success at Erie helped me a lot." Net income reached $4.5 million for 1968, and it was a positive $1.6 million in 1969. The railroad also redeemed the entire $11,126,000 of outstanding Series E bonds of its Erie First Consolidated Mortgage and an additional $6,705,450 of other debts, including collateral notes and Ohio Division First Mortgage bonds; "this was unusual for the time." Everyone took heart with an impressive 10.3 percent jump in freight revenues in 1968 over the previous year and a 3 percent increase in 1969. While the company gained from the opening of a Chrysler automobile distribution facility at Mt. Pocono, Pennsylvania, and a Seatrain Lines container port at Weehawken, New Jersey, piggyback traffic remained the bright spot. The road registered a 6.4 percent rise in its annual trailer loadings in 1968. The hope prevailed that there was at last a way to recoup losses of long-haul freight traffic caused by the advent of trucks on interstate highways.[16]

The financial picture at Erie Lackawanna, however, changed dramatically in 1970. "The best thing that can be said about 1970 is that it is over," wrote Jack Fishwick to Dereco shareholders. "It was a year of disappointment and frustration for Dereco, Inc., and for the railroad industry in general." Erie Lackawanna lost $11.1 million and "everyone at headquarters was running around with an acid stomach." Fishwick predicted in February 1971 that "[T]he cash squeeze on EL will continue to be critical," and he was correct.[17]

The stunning decline of interchange traffic through the Maybrook Gateway in eastern New York contributed heavily to the dismal income statement. The Erie and then the Erie Lackawanna had annually transferred tens of thousands of cars to the New York, New Haven & Hartford Railroad; these shipments moved mostly to and from destinations in southern New England over what historically had been the most efficient route into the region. By the late 1960's tonnage from Erie Lackawanna typically arrived at Maybrook in the morning and then in Boston that evening. In 1968 Erie Lackawanna gave the New Haven 85,458 cars but only 63,899 in 1969; Erie Lackawanna received 32,594 cars in 1968 but only 14,491 in 1969. This interchange traffic dropped even more a year later: 42,460 cars eastbound and 6,486 cars westbound. When translated into dollars, these decreases meant an estimated loss of $17.8 million in gross revenues for 1969 and 1970.[18]

The explanation for the rapid decline in the number of cars passing through Maybrook stemmed directly from the merger of the New York Central and the Pennsylvania railroads. The 19,459-mile Penn Central Transportation Company emerged on February 1, 1968, and eleven months later the bankrupt New Haven, "a hopeless invalid," under an order from the Interstate Commerce Commission, entered the fold. Immediately, Penn Central sent an assistant general manager from its headquarters in Philadelphia to "dynamite the connection at Maybrook." This he did with dispatch. A slowdown policy began and cars took as long as a week to travel over the former New Haven's Maybrook Freight Line to Boston.[19]

The Penn Central strategy made sense. The new carrier, besieged with financial problems from day one, had no desire to short-haul itself. It wanted the long haul to Chicago instead of only to Maybrook. So Penn Central re-routed traffic from Boston westward over the old Boston & Albany (New York Central) to Selkirk Yard in Albany and hence over the former Central's Water Level Route to the Windy City. Traffic from Rhode Island and Connecticut generally moved through the former New Haven's Cedar Hill Yard in New Haven and northward over several arteries to the Selkirk hub.[20]

Understandably, Erie Lackawanna protested strenuously. A remedy, unfortunately, was not readily forthcoming. Since the company had accepted conditions of the Penn Central merger, it could not appeal to the federal courts for redress. "We were stuck with the regulatory process," lamented Gregory Maxwell. Erie Lackawanna dutifully filed a complaint against Penn Central in July 1969 with the Interstate Commerce Commission, claiming "violation of protective condition incident to the New Haven merger into Penn Central." Erie Lackawanna asked for damages of $6.6 million and restoration of service. But the ICC responded slowly; hearings were not held until year's end. When the Commission finally intervened, it ordered Penn Central to reestablish schedules, but it refused to award compensatory damages.[21]

Disruptions continued. In May 1970 Erie Lackawanna filed a second complaint with the Commission and demanded restoration of service through the Maybrook Gateway. This time the ICC directed the matter to arbitration. Unluckily for the company, the arbitrator was an opponent of Jack Fishwick. The referee lacked concern, alleging that motor carrier competition, and not practices of Penn Central, had ruined the interchange business. But Erie Lackawanna offered compelling evidence: "There had been no major change in truck volume between 1968 and 1970." This conclusion was based on motor vehicle records obtained from Pennsylvania's ports-of-entry.[22]

With the Interstate Commerce Commission unsympathetic, the matter of Maybrook seemed hopeless. Then on May 8, 1974, it became moot: Penn Central's massive and deteriorating Poughkeepsie Bridge over the Hudson River burned, permanently severing this once bustling gateway route. The remaining interchange traffic, consolidated into one daily train each way, moved via Utica, New York, and a connection with Penn Central, over the Binghamton-Utica branch.[23]

The regulatory structure created yet other examples of what historian Albro Martin has called "enterprise denied." The Interstate Commerce Commission, as it regulated almost every aspect of the railroads' operations, pursued policies during this period that hurt Erie Lackawanna as well as other carriers in the East. The ICC, for instance, raised per diem charges on "foreign" rolling stock. This dramatically increased car-hire costs, in part because Erie Lackawanna could not afford its own fleet of specialty equipment, particularly 86-foot auto-rack cars. In a similar fashion, a car service order from the Commission forced eastern roads to return 50-foot general-purpose box-cars owned by western carriers directly to those lines. This equipment, for example, could not be reloaded in New Jersey or New York and sent into the South, and so the railroad hauled these cars empty to western interchanges. The Southern Division Case likewise damaged earnings. The ICC required Erie Lackawanna to accept traffic that originated in the Southeast for points along its lines in New Jersey. The road lost about $1.5 million annually handling this business because of excessive terminal and switching costs. Management requested that a surcharge be added for each of these cars, but the Commission refused. The company hardly took solace that regulators rejected like demands from other carriers serving the Garden state.[24]

There also existed the matter of labor constraints. Since the Interstate Commerce Commission treated inclusion of Erie Lackawanna into the Norfolk & Western system as if it were a merger, the company encountered tough restrictions on employee numbers and compensation. "As of April 1, 1968," recalled Gregory Maxwell, "we had a frozen work force." And this labor-protection arrangement cost the company about $1 million annually. Admittedly, some of the blame rested with railroad executives. At the time of the Norfolk & Western–Nickel Plate–Wabash merger, Stuart Saunders foolishly agreed that Nickel Plate workers would have jobs until they reached 65 and that their earnings would not be reduced. Then Jack Fishwick approved a similar arrangement for Erie Lackawanna operatives once Dereco took charge.[25]

The labor guarantees under Dereco likely cost more per employee than did the Nickel Plate settlement. Erie Lackawanna also based workers' salaries, plus overtime pay, on the one-year "test period" prior to inclusion. That formula hurt. In the late 1960's the railroad had cut firemen as quickly as the courts allowed, and this retrenchment created a sizable shortage of qualified engineers. Some personnel, especially those who ran on the "West end," worked "sixteen hours a day and seven days a week." Their extraordinary overtime pay then went into their base salaries. "The test period was unrealistic," admitted a Brotherhood of Locomotive Engineers officer. "The protection of wages resulted in an artificially high rate of wages being paid these overworked engineers."[26]

The Interstate Commerce Commission further injured Erie Lackawanna with its response to the company's request to exit the long-distance passenger business. Although the ICC ruled on December 19, 1969, that "passenger trains Nos. 5 and 6 between Hoboken, N.J., and Chicago, Ill. . . . [are] not required by public convenience and necessity and that continued operations thereof will unduly burden interstate commerce," an expensive delay preceded this favorable decision. The railroad petitioned the Commission in early June 1969 to permit abandonment of *The Lake Cities*, their popular name, on August 31. But because of "numerous protests and complaints filed," the ICC ordered operations continued for at least four months. Public hearings then followed along the 977-mile route: in New York City; Scranton, Pennsylvania; Binghamton, Elmira, and Jamestown, New York; Youngstown, Kent, and Marion, Ohio; Huntington and Rochester, Indiana; and Chicago.[27]

The testimony revealed much about the passenger business and the regulatory process. Public usage of the trains, for one thing, was low. For example, a daily average of only 25.95 patrons boarded the train in Hoboken during the first six months of 1969 and then only 0.45 continued to Chicago. The statistics for Newark, New Jersey, were worse: 5.49 people boarded and 0.19 detrained in the Windy City.[28]

Similarly, *The Lake Cities* failed to earn adequate income from "head-end" traffic of mail and express. When the Post Office Department canceled contracts for Railway Post Office (RPO) service on most intercity trains in 1967, including Numbers 5 and 6, it removed the last pillar supporting passenger travel in the country. The decision so devastated passenger train income nationally that Congress passed the Rail Passenger Service Act in October 1970, creating the quasi-public National Railroad Passenger Corporation, initially called Railpax and then Amtrak, which debuted on May 1, 1971. But this federal action came too late for Erie Lackawanna. The Post Office's removal of RPO business from the two trains caused head-end revenue figures to plummet from $2,365,100 in 1967 to $1,314,600 in 1968.[29]

Although awash in red ink, Erie Lackawanna did not permit *The Lake Cities* to become shabby trains, staffed with surly employees. "If you are in the passenger business," argued Gregory Maxwell, "you had better do it right." The diners, for instance, always had fresh flower buds, linen tablecloths, and cloth napkins. Nothing suggests that this company intentionally drove passengers away as some carriers did in desperation. Witnesses at the discontinuance hearings commonly agreed that they found "the trains comfortable and dependable, the crews friendly, courteous and helpful, the service excellent, the schedules not too bad, . . . the meals very good, the sleeping cars clean, the cars well-maintained . . . and the overall service better than that provided by other railroads."[30]

The problem, of course, involved the inability of Numbers 5 and 6 to generate adequate income. In 1968 the trains brought in $2,359,000 in total revenues but cost $2,861,800 in direct expenses. Yet most witnesses, who either represented groups (chambers of commerce, government bodies, and labor unions) or themselves, regularly demanded that Erie Lackawanna continue these long-distance runs. Of the 128 witnesses who appeared in opposition to discontinuance, 16 admitted that they had never patronized the trains. Some who occasionally did wanted them as a "backup service in inclement weather." "The public liked the trains," recalled Wallace Steffen,

Only a few months before abandonment of long-distance Erie Lackawanna passenger service, *The Lake Cities* passes by the closed tower at Slateford Junction, Pennsylvania, in the Delaware Water Gap, on its way to Hoboken, New Jersey. The knife-sharp ballast, a hallmark of the older Lackawanna, remains in evidence. (Railroad Avenue Enterprises)

company attorney in the case, "but they didn't use them and this cost us a bundle after we lost the mail business."[31]

The Lake Cities finally made their last runs on January 6, 1970. When the westbound train rolled into Chicago's dingy Dearborn Street terminal, 48 minutes late, the end came officially to 83 years of continuous passenger service between New York and Chicago on the Erie. A few reporters gathered to cover this historic occasion, and Conductor George Coble seized this opportunity to tell them, "It's the company's own fault that this passenger train was discontinued. I think it is about time the government got on the backs of railroads so they will provide service to customers." Conductor Coble surely did not grasp the financial condition of his employer's last long-distance "varnish." Except for some rail workers, patrons, and enthusiasts, "Death of Erie's No. 5" meant little except to improve the balance sheet.[32]

By 1970 Erie Lackawanna had virtually solved its lengthy and expensive passenger problem. The road's New York–area commuter trains continued to receive substantial subsidies. Indeed, the New Jersey Department of Transportation greatly enhanced the quality of these runs in early 1971 when it took delivery of 105 sparkling, state-of-the-art commuter cars from the Pullman-Standard Company and 23 high-horsepower commuter locomotives from General Electric. The cost exceeded $26 million, "a price the railroad could never have afforded." "Whether he's a neurosurgeon or a plumber, whether he carries an attache or a tool box," crowed the transit body, "this commuter is special enough to have special new transportation technology brought to bear on his daily ride."[33]

These pieces of rolling stock and motive power were unusual in that they were designed for "push-pull" service. Explained an Erie Lackawanna press release on January 21, 1971: "This is the first time this kind of operation has been specifically designed into new equipment—both cars and locomotives— for use on a U.S. railroad and which will provide increased flexibility of operation, eliminate terminal switching and considerably reduce possibilities of delays in service." Based on innovative equipment developed by the Chicago & North Western in the late 1950's for its Chicago commuter territory, push-pull involved bidirectional operation: the locomotive pushed the train in one direction and pulled it in the other, with the locomotive always on the same end. In the case of Erie Lackawanna, locomotives pushed trains into the Hoboken terminal and pulled them on outbound runs.[34]

The only fly in the ointment involving passenger operations remained a money-losing commuter service in northeastern Ohio. Trains 28 and 29 traveled over the 66-mile, 13-station route between Youngstown and Cleveland with no head-end business and few paying passengers, although with ample railroad employees who used their complimentary passes.[35]

Erie Lackawanna had long battled the Public Utilities Commission of Ohio (PUCO) to end this annual drain of more than $200,000, but with no success. It failed to receive either meaningful rate increases or permission to annul the trains. The railroad encountered the formidable political clout of both the affluent Village of Aurora, 23 miles from Cleveland and the home of many riders, and its own workers, who manipulated the regulatory process to their advantage. This daily (except holiday and weekend) service operated at increasing losses. But PUCO rejected abandonment until after Erie Lackawanna's death. The last train, operated by Conrail, pulled into the Youngstown station the evening of January 14, 1977. Ironically, its three cars, which once adorned the Lackawanna's crack *Phoebe Snow*, had been full for much of the trip. Rail fans squeezed regular patrons, and one veteran rider who traveled between Cleveland and Aurora had to stand for the first time in his memory.[36]

The last commuter run on the Cleveland-Youngstown line was on January 14, 1977. David McKay, a Cleveland railroad enthusiast, photographed the three-car train shortly after it was brought into the Youngstown terminal by a former Erie Lackawanna locomotive with Conrail markings. (David McKay)

While bludgeoned by government action (or inaction in some cases), Erie Lackawanna under Dereco struggled to survive. Its ties to parent Norfolk & Western helped. Developments in the freight-traffic sector illustrate the positive impact of the N&W affiliation. In May 1970 Erie Lackawanna and N&W inaugurated *The Cannonball*, a joint through freight train that operated on a run-through basis daily except Sunday in each direction between New York and St. Louis via the roads' interchange at Huntington, Indiana. The roads pooled their locomotives and only changed cabooses and crews, reducing transfer time. These trains added $3.5 million to Erie Lackawanna's revenues in 1970 and nearly $7 million in 1971. The N&W deliberately short-hauled itself to favor its subsidiary with this service. The company could have had a longer haul by soliciting the traffic over the former Nickel Plate and Wabash lines via Buffalo or in conjunction with the Lehigh Valley at that same gateway.[37]

The *Cannonball* trains were not the sole cooperative freight efforts backed by Norfolk & Western. Prior to the first New York to St. Louis run, N&W, for example, participated in the movement of unit grain trains from its territory in the Midwest to the Port of Albany, New York, via the Dereco roads. While this traffic varied daily and seasonally, it competed effectively with rival service provided by Penn Central.[38]

With Norfolk & Western's blessings, Dereco fostered additional run-through operations, frequently in conjunction with the Boston & Maine. The principal linkages were piggyback and mixed-merchandise fast freights or "redballs." The former originated at B&M's ramp facility at East Cambridge, Massachusetts, near Boston, and terminated at the Erie Lackawanna intermodal ramp in Chicago. These "pigs" moved via the B&M–Delaware & Hudson interchange at Mechanicville, New York, and the D&H–Erie Lackawanna connection at Binghamton. The latter started at the B&M yard in East Deerfield, Massachusetts, where traffic from its diverging lines was gathered and distributed. Then these mixed-merchandise trains were assembled and broken up at the Erie Lackawanna's Marion classification facility for the road's various western rail connections, including the N&W interchange at Huntington. The D&H once again acted as intermediate carrier, and shipments that originated on the D&H were added and others destined for D&H points were set out, usually at Mechanicville.[39]

Although these run-through freight operations revealed a visible form of cooperative action, Jack Fishwick promoted other joint efforts to bolster Dereco's earnings. Significantly, he attempted to strengthen and better coordinate operations between the two carriers by selective transfer of key personnel. Examples abound. F. W. Hewitt, Jr., who helped to create Delaware & Hudson's online electronic data processing (EDP) system, left D&H headquarters in Albany for Cleveland where he upgraded Erie Lackawanna's "lagging" EDP efforts. J. H. O'Neill also relocated from Albany to Cleveland where he became vice president for finance and real estate for Erie Lackawanna. W. J. Slater moved from exclusive service at Erie Lackawanna to become engineer for maintenance-of-way at D&H. William Carlson, the talented chief mechanical officer of Erie Lackawanna, was made chief senior mechanical officer of D&H. (In most cases the railroads split salaries on an 80-20 basis, with D&H making the smaller contribution.) And Erie Lackawanna's vice president for sales, Herbert Simpson, maintained a close relationship with his counterpart at D&H and monitored joint solicitation of traffic, a vital job since the chief competitor of the Dereco roads, Penn Central, employed a large sales force. Fishwick could tell Dereco shareholders on

February 24, 1971, that "The companies now have joint officers in the executive, finance, operating, purchasing and stores, mechanical, medical, data processing and public relations departments." He could have added that there existed "a spirit of unified team effort, mutual cooperation and partnership."[40]

The presence of Dereco led to coordination of more than personnel. "The D&H needed to be shaken up," recalled Gregory Maxwell. "Its locomotive repair program, for one thing, was poor." Thereafter, the D&H made some of its heavy repairs to its motive power at the Erie Lackawanna's shops in Hornell; likewise the wheel shops in Meadville worked on D&H's car and locomotive wheel-sets. In October 1970, Dereco launched a "Power Control Center" in Cleveland to oversee deployment of D&H and Erie Lackawanna locomotives. "This 24-hour, seven-days-a-week operation has substantially improved utilization of power primarily by increasing the running-through of locomotives over the combined EL-D&H system."[41]

Cooperation and coordination between Norfolk & Western and the Dereco roads and between Erie Lackawanna and Delaware & Hudson represent only part of the critical happenings between 1968, when N&W control began, and 1972, when Erie Lackawanna entered bankruptcy. The "Friendly Service Route" attempted to be just that; it vigorously strove to generate income by meeting customers' needs.

The relationship between Erie Lackawanna and United Parcel Service of America (UPS), itself a service-oriented company, is a premier example. In 1970 Gregory Maxwell brilliantly encouraged the Traffic Department to contact UPS about the possibility of hauling its truck trailers in solid, dedicated trains. UPS resisted initially, "because it was unhappy with previous experiences on another railroad [Penn Central]." But then UPS relented, and its head, J. P. McLaughlin, asked Maxwell for a specific proposal for a train five days a week. UPS liked the idea of transporting loaded trailers between New York and Chicago with minimal delays and the opportunity to "deramp" them in Marion for easy delivery to Toledo, Fort Wayne, and other nearby destinations. And UPS examined the railroad closely; it assigned an employee to study operations. "He rode on our freight trains and talked to our crews," remembered M. Fred Coffman, vice president for traffic. "UPS quickly recognized the dedication of our employees and we got their business." Added Coffman: "One reason for winning the UPS was that we adjusted our schedules to suit them." Maxwell and Coffman cultivated UPS for the remaining years of the railroad and made this service a "joint endeavor." Erie Lackawanna also benefited from the UPS policy of remaining with a business partner permanently if its service met company standards.[42]

The gleaming metallic-gray United Parcel Service trailers became a fixture on Erie Lackawanna. The first UPS piggyback movement left Croxton, New Jersey, on September 11, 1970, and soon one train operated each way between the end points. The UPS traffic produced increasing revenues because UPS was expanding. In fact, it grew at the expense of competitors, including the Post Office and the ailing REA Express, Inc., successor to the giant Railway Express Agency. The railroad also claimed to have a better traffic balance. By 1974 it operated five UPS trains daily, three westbound and two eastbound, "which is what this eastbound railroad needed." Erie Lackawanna and its competitors were increasingly becoming inbound terminating routes for raw materials produced elsewhere; the East's output was moving more by trucks to various destinations.[43]

Determined to please United Parcel Service and other shippers, Erie Lackawanna struggled to keep its physical plant in decent condition. Yet track conditions worsened, especially after 1970. "We took shortcuts with track work," admitted Joseph R. Neikirk, a ranking N&W operating officer whom Jack Fishwick assigned to Cleveland on May 1, 1970, as senior vice president for operations and traffic. "With little money to buy new rail and ties, we bought lots of ballast!" While the company tried to bury its track problems, it still kept trains moving mostly at 50 miles per hour.[44]

The railroad likewise attended to its rolling stock and motive power as best it could. Unfortunately, by the early 1970's the company lost customers because "we just couldn't supply the specialized equipment that was needed." But before the severe money crunch, the firm in 1968 completed heavy repairs to nearly 2,000 freight cars and purchased 500 new 100-ton and 250 new 70-ton gondolas. The next year it made another sizable commitment to equipment: it bought 698 freight cars of all types and leased 600 piggyback trailers, 20 cabooses, and 28 locomotives. The Norfolk & Western acquired the latter and leased them to Erie Lackawanna at the market rate of interest. Erie Lackawanna also invested $2.6 million to modernize its piggyback yards and terminals in Chicago and Croxton.[45]

One creative, money-saving, and consumer-helping decision came in 1969 when the railroad spent $263,000 for a SEARCH (System Evaluation and Reliability Checker) unit for its Marion locomotive shops. (The Marion facility conducted regular maintenance on locomotives while the Hornell shops did major repairs.) This computer-harness device speedily detected electrical faults in diesel-electric locomotives, an important technological advance since defects often baffled mechanics. "On a steam locomotive it took five minutes to find a problem and five hours to fix it," went a common saying; "on a diesel it took five hours to find the problem and five minutes to fix it." The company was the third railroad in North America (Canadian Pacific was the first) to use the SEARCH machine, and it continued the Erie tradition for innovation. The device worked splendidly. "Before we used it," noted Gregory Maxwell, always an enthusiast of high technology, "we had between sixteen and eighteen road failures per month and then it dropped down to three or four monthly." The percentage of locomotives out-of-service likewise declined; the rate dropped from 15 to 18 percent to a scant 4 percent. To place this performance in perspective, the Union Pacific at any one time had approximately a quarter of its locomotive fleet down for repairs and the St. Louis–San Francisco (Frisco) about 20 percent.[46]

Periodic maintenance with modern equipment paid off nicely for Erie Lackawanna and its customers. "We kept our locomotives in service and our trains running," noted Gregory Maxwell. But management did much more to satisfy shippers. Most notably it overhauled freight operations between Chicago and the East in 1968, just when newly merged Penn Central was wallowing in confusion, its service in chaos. "Approximately 75 percent of the long-haul traffic formerly moved by regular train service is now moved in solid, through trains," wrote Jack Fishwick in February 1969. "This traffic arrives at final destinations 12 to 24 hours earlier than previously. By pre-classifying blocks of cars for single destinations, terminal delays have been cut by more than 8 hours on the average." And he continued, "EL's computer system is used to simulate train operations, and provides information for improved freight train schedules and locomotive assignments."[47]

Then in early 1969 the service picture brightened even more when the Brotherhood of Locomotive Engineers and the United Transportation Union endorsed interdivisional trips between Marion and Port Jervis, a distance of 640 miles. The agreement reduced the number of crew changes from 6 to 3 and cut approximately 90 minutes from running times for this stretch of main line. The company paid employees for extra mileage, but it saved on their lodging and related expenses and, more importantly, it saved time. Union members generally understood that if Erie Lackawanna lost competitiveness, business would go to trucks and other railroads and hence employment opportunities would diminish.[48]

In another notable schedule improvement, Erie Lackawanna negotiated a "Through Service Agreement" with the Jersey Central for run-through trains between Scranton and Elizabethport–Jersey City via an interchange at Lake Junction, New Jersey. When shippers discovered that the transit time between Erie Lackawanna's western gateways and points along the Jersey Central dropped by more than 24 hours, they heartily approved and business flourished. A strong negative response, however, came from competitors Lehigh Valley and Reading. These carriers howled at what they considered to be hurtful competition, but they could not stop it.[49]

This additional illustration of railroads profitably coordinating their freight operations suggests a practice that should have been implemented much earlier and more extensively. Although Erie Lackawanna participated in versions of run-throughs prior to Dereco, mostly delivering trains past congested terminals to connecting carriers, successes after 1968 indicated the benefits. Contended Richard Saunders in his examination of railroad mergers: "Coordination was probably a better avenue to savings than consolidation." While this is a questionable conclusion when the vast savings generated by the Erie-Lackawanna merger, for example, are considered, it is correct that cooperative efforts produced positive results.[50]

~~~

While encouraging events took place at Erie Lackawanna under Dereco, the company weakened steadily after 1970. These difficulties cannot be blamed on the quality of management. Even though Jack Fishwick returned to Roanoke in 1970 to head Norfolk & Western, the Dereco roads received able assistance from N&W officers Joseph Neikirk in operations and John R. Turbyfill in finance. The assignment of these accomplished men to Cleveland expressed the commitment by N&W to keep the properties alive. "I was told to run the railroad in the most efficient manner that I could," remarked Neikirk. The experienced Gregory Maxwell assumed the presidency of the Delaware & Hudson from Fishwick, and Fishwick remained as president and chief executive officer of Dereco.[51]

Erie Lackawanna suffered tremendously from forces beyond the control of management. The economics of the early 1970's were unsettling. Near the close of the Lyndon B. Johnson administration severe economic winds began to buffet the nation and they continued unrelentingly during much of Richard Nixon's presidency. The escalation of government expenditures, most of all for the Vietnam Conflict, boosted interest charges, increased inflation, and caused growing pessimism in business and financial circles. An indication of the malaise was the change in the prime rate, that is, the rate banks charge their best customers. It stood at 6 percent in January 1968, but climbed to 8.5 percent eighteen months later, and reached 9 percent by 1970. The impact of limiting or even eliminating access to credit for marginal borrowers became known as a "credit crunch," and it would strike again in the mid-1970's. Moreover, workers responded to the higher costs of living by demanding pay hikes, and this produced inflationary wage increases.[52]

Because they were always sensitive to economic downswings, the railroads saw the future darken considerably. Companies comprising what the Interstate Commerce Commission called the "Eastern District," including Erie Lackawanna, suffered the most. While they collectively reported a positive income of a modest $17 million in 1969, they experienced a staggering $376 million deficit in 1970, the first loss for this group since 1961. The rate of return on investments in the industry as a whole stood at a disappointing

1.73 percent in 1970, the lowest since the Great Depression. And national wage agreements negatively affected the industry. Carriers experienced a dramatic rise in the average earnings of their employees: $8,654 in 1968, $9,274 in 1969, $10,086 in 1970, and $10,826 in 1971, a 25 percent gain for this three-year period. The failure of giant Penn Central along with the smaller Boston & Maine, Jersey Central, and Lehigh Valley graphically revealed the crisis, especially in the East. "It looks like the 1930's over again," concluded a transportation consultant, and, in a way, he was right.[53]

Shifting economic forces, furthermore, hardly augured well for eastern railroads. By the early 1970's domestic businesses were becoming increasingly decentralized and specialized. Altered patterns of manufacturing meant expanded activities in the South and West, or (as pundits described it) the "sunbelt" came to eclipse the "snowbelt." Already tire-making in Akron, Ohio, the largest city on the Erie Lackawanna main line, was in steady decline. "It sure started to look bad for us [in Akron] by the early seventies," recalled traffic executive Fred Coffman. "B.F. Goodrich, Firestone and the others were closing down those old multi-story factories and moving their production elsewhere." The products of industry also changed. The decade of the 1970's was not so much the time of tires but of semiconductors. Goods of the postindustrial age tended to be smaller, lighter, more valuable, and moved over shorter distances. Unfortunately for rail carriers, they were ideally suited for truck transport.[54]

The raft of negative forces that Erie Lackawanna confronted aggravated its money situation and pointed toward insolvency if net income could not be increased. Although the railroad's gross revenues rose from $262.1 million in 1970 to $268.7 million in 1971, and net losses dropped, the deficit in working capital remained and the amount of cash and temporary investments plunged. "EL's cash position in 1971," explained Jack Fishwick, "was adversely affected by the payment of $5.9 million of retroactive wages relating to 1970." Once more the Dereco head turned pessimistic: "The Erie is on the brink of disaster," he concluded in early 1971.[55]

Others worried, too. An official of the Metropolitan Life Insurance Company, for one, urgently telephoned John Turbyfill in February 1971 to ask about Erie Lackawanna's immediate fate. He had heard a rumor that the company planned to seek court protection from its creditors. Realizing that the railroad was in poor financial health and concerned about negotiations on a bond extension, the insurance executive wanted information. As Turbyfill told the railroad's board of directors, "[The insurance executive] felt that Metropolitan would look rather silly if they agreed to the Ohio Division [bond] refinancing and then EL went into bankruptcy." Turbyfill reassured Metropolitan. Although he advised the company that the railroad's cash position was "critically tight," it was not preparing to file a bankruptcy petition. Moreover, he promised to keep Metropolitan apprised on the financial situation; after all, it owned the largest share of Erie Lackawanna debt.[56]

If John Turbyfill elaborated on the "critically tight" cash situation, he would surely have admitted the likelihood of postponed payrolls. Vouchers on hand, representing outstanding unpaid bills, rapidly accumulated in the treasurer's office; the amount approached $6.5 million by the end of January 1971. Some officers believed that bankruptcy was imminent or, at the least, that "this bad cold might turn quickly into fatal pneumonia."[57]

Conditions became so acute that management responded with varied emergency actions. "We were told to find every penny that we could," recalled a financial officer. Special teams of accounting and traffic personnel worked to accelerate collection of freight payments. The company canceled nearly $1 million worth of orders for new rail and decided that any replacements would be done with used steel. It cut 700 employees, approximately 5 percent of the work force, and suspended purchase of materials "unless absolutely required." Management also decided to postpone certain obligations, including payment of hundreds of thousands of dollars in back wages mandated by the federal government. Part of the response involved the "war-room" on the eighth floor of the Republic Building adjoining headquarters. This specially created place contained a large metal map of the system. "It had magnets to show locations of maintenance-of-way work, slow orders and so forth," remembered Joseph Neikirk. "We had to try to keep on top of every aspect of our operations to save money."[58]

Erie Lackawanna barely limped through 1971 and into mid-1972. This company in crisis felt the sting of a federal pay board when it ordered major wage increases in early 1972. And then the Interstate Commerce Commission refused to grant carriers a 4 percent increase in freight rates, which Gregory Maxwell predicted would "cost Erie Lackawanna at least $3 million in revenues this year." The railroad was essentially out of money by the spring of 1972. Banks would not make loans at reasonable charges, demanding a prohibitive 3 percent above the prime rate. "We were living on our cash flow," remarked Richard Hahn, a bright, Harvard-educated lawyer whom Jack Fishwick sent from Roanoke to Cleveland to succeed John Turbyfill as chief financial officer on April 1, 1972. The road continued to have a plethora of unpaid bills. "We did a lot of juggling," remembered Hahn, and "only the most demanding creditors got paid." Another disconcerting factor involved two large interest payments due on Erie and Delaware, Lackawanna & Western bonds on July 1, 1972. And the company's ability to liquidate excess real estate had been largely exhausted. Sales dropped from $3.1 million in 1968 to less than half a million three years later.[59]

Hahn, the sophisticated outsider, seemed troubled initially by the way

Erie Lackawanna coped with financial matters. He soon realized that the company's lack of money "boxed it in" to certain practices. Hahn could not expect the external assistance that the wealthy Norfork & Western enjoyed. For decades his former employer worked closely with Salomon Brothers and gained from its considerable resources. So Hahn embraced classic self-help. He sharpened the process of financial analysis by demanding research on every major expenditure and employing zero-based budgeting. "I wanted the historical background on each proposed expenditure," he recalled. "We had to manage our meager resources the best way that was humanly possible."[60]

No amount of enlightened financial practices could minimize the impact of a capricious act of nature. Hurricane Agnes axed the fragile Erie Lackawanna in June 1972, and this calamity led quickly to the second largest railroad bankruptcy since the Great Depression.

The first storm of the 1972 hurricane season was erratic. Residents of the Middle Atlantic states paid little attention to a tropical disturbance that developed near western Cuba and swept across Florida from the Gulf of Mexico. Although locally heavy rains fell over sections of the South Atlantic states on June 18 and 19, Agnes lost much of its punch. But rough weather lingered. As Agnes wandered up the Atlantic seaboard, it refused to act like other tropical storms; it neither broke apart nor veered out to sea. Agnes intensified instead. By the evening of June 20, the storm coupled with a cold front to produce torrential rains throughout large sections of New York's Southern Tier and northern Pennsylvania. Water poured from the heavens, at times an inch per hour, and the storm continued for nearly three days. The "Great Flood of 1972" swept rapidly through the valleys of the Allegheny, Chemung, Genesee, Susquehanna, and other rivers and tributaries. One hundred and eighteen people died, and property damages quickly soared past the $1.5 billion mark, making Agnes one of the most deadly and expensive hurricanes in the century.[61]

Area railroads suffered enormous losses. The concentrated and unbridled fury of Agnes caused an estimated $40 million in damages to facilities and millions more in lost revenues. The victims were hardly the strongest financially, and included such troubled roads as the Penn Central, Lehigh Valley, and Reading. Because of its location, Erie Lackawanna took a direct hit. Floodwaters washed out portions of roadbed along 200 miles of main line, especially between Elmira and Hornell. From Hornell to Owego, a distance of 95 miles, for example, 100 washouts occurred, measuring from 2 to 15 feet deep and up to 4,000 feet long. The company's appendages also suffered greatly; Agnes knocked out the Bloomsburg, Tioga, and Wayland branches. Major bridge damage occurred as well; sixteen spans were either damaged or destroyed. The longest bridge to be affected was the ancient 818-foot Portage Viaduct across the Genesee River near River Junction, New York. The swirling current undercut two of its enormous piers, which soared 235 feet above the riverbed. The railroad endured additional setbacks, for flood waters spoiled equipment, and forced the rerouting of through traffic. The main line did not reopen until July 16, and it took longer to restore service on the severed branches.[62]

Understandably, the loss was high for Erie Lackawanna; the bill exceeded $11 million. Repairs to tracks and structures and other facilities approached $5 million, loss of revenues exceeded $4.5 million, detour costs amounted to more than $1 million, and additional expenses totaled about $650,000.[63]

While Agnes clobbered Erie Lackawanna both physically and financially, hundreds of employees responded valiantly. During the height of the storm reports of heroism reached headquarters in Cleveland. One involved crewmen aboard an eastbound time-freight, NE-74. Receiving an order to halt at Wellsville, New York, because of a washout at Alfred, seventeen miles to the east, these trainmen decided to take only a locomotive to inspect the track. But before they had gone far, they learned of a nearby washout. On their return to Wellsville, crew members heard calls for help from two teenage girls who were trapped in waist-deep water near the right-of-way. The engineer immediately radioed the state police, who soon met the locomotive at a nearby road crossing and provided a rowboat, which these Good Samaritans loaded onto the outside walkway. They rolled down the track, and then rescued the potential victims, placing them in the cab for the trip to safety. In a less dramatic fashion, hundreds of maintenance-of-way workers, even before the skies cleared, plunged into action, fixing smaller washouts with tie cribbing and ballast and larger ones with tons of dirt and rock. And they tackled damaged bridges with stopgap measures and tidied up the property as best they could. Remarked Joseph Neikirk, "The Erie people didn't know the word quit!"[64]

The Norfolk & Western, however, knew when to throw in the proverbial towel. Jack Fishwick, from his office in Roanoke, ordered Erie Lackawanna to seek court protection. "We wanted out," recalled Fishwick. Gregory Maxwell, on the other hand, had for months openly opposed a bankruptcy. "Over my dead body!" he had shouted to a subordinate. Of course, Maxwell realized that his road was now at death's door and grasped Fishwick's terse message to Dereco shareholders: "The damage inflicted by Hurricane Agnes . . . was the final blow, and EL was forced to petition for reorganization on June 26, 1972." N&W expected to write off about $55.8 million as extraordinary charges to income for 1972 and "forget the whole episode with Erie."[65]

While at first glance the period of mandated control of Erie Lackawanna by Norfolk & Western appeared to have nightmarish qualities, N&W, in reality, benefited from this four-year relationship. Although the bankruptcy wiped out its equity of approximately $56 million, the company obtained tax credits amounting to nearly three times that amount, useful to any profit-making concern. Furthermore, N&W had not poured money into the coffers of its ward. After all, Erie Lackawanna was to stand on its own feet and function as an independent entity. Yet N&W had made contributions. Unlike the historic pattern of holding companies, Dereco never milked the controlled properties for its parent. Obviously, there was little to squeeze from the Cleveland company. The Delaware & Hudson, on the other hand, enjoyed more robust health. That firm generated modest annual dividends prior to a dramatic decline of its online freight revenues at about the time of the Erie Lackawanna bankruptcy. For several years Dereco took these D&H dividends and loaned them to Erie Lackawanna rather than keeping them in Roanoke. N&W also financed a fleet of badly needed road locomotives and during the money crisis accelerated its payments for current receivables due Erie Lack-of-Money. Concluded an Erie Lackawanna official, "All in all, N&W was much more of a builder than a wrecker of the Erie. N&W really deserved to get out with its shirt on."[66]

Not everyone agreed. Jervis Langdon, Jr., then president of the Rock Island and formerly head of the Baltimore & Ohio, thought, as did some others in railroad circles, that "Fishwick and N&W never tried to work hard for Erie Lackawanna. . . . Jack was a damn good lawyer, but he always took care of N&W first. He had no real industry outlook. Jack was not interested in a public interest." Langdon was correct that N&W's ties to Erie Lackawanna had been part of its strategy to win Interstate Commerce Commission approval of that ill-fated merger with Chesapeake & Ohio. The losers in the East, including Erie Lackawanna, had to find a home before these two powerful coal haulers could tie the knot. Still, Norfolk & Western hardly looted the property, and forces apart from the control of railroad leaders curtailed earnings.[67]

Once beyond the sway of Roanoke and protected by the court, Erie Lackawanna battled to maintain its independence. But by the mid-1970's management concluded that the cause was hopeless. Perhaps if N&W had lavished money on Erie Lackawanna and had truly taken it under its wing, the road might have survived mostly intact. In a somewhat parallel case, the Chesapeake & Ohio had bolstered the ailing Baltimore & Ohio, which it had controlled since February 5, 1963. The former's $232 million, five-year improvement program saved the latter. Yet no symbiotic relationship of that type developed between the N&W and Erie Lackawanna. "As an independent company," noted Gregory Maxwell, "we had to compete against the Penn Central and the N&W and that was exactly what Bill White had wanted to avoid!"[68]

"ERIE LACK-OF-MONEY" AND THE COMING OF CONRAIL, 1973–1976

A RAY OF SUNLIGHT penetrated the dark clouds of Erie Lackawanna's financial difficulties. On June 16, 1972, when attorneys for the company filed for reorganization under the Federal Bankruptcy Act in United States District Court for the Northern District of Ohio, Eastern Division, the petition came under supervision of the talented jurist Robert B. Krupansky. The court practice of the blind draw initially directed the case to Judge William Thomas, but he was on vacation in Japan. Next it was assigned to Chief Justice Frank Battisti. Battisti's "whereabouts were unknown," however, for he had gone on a fishing outing to Wyoming. The case then fell to Judge John Lambrose, who, too, was on holiday. The fourth choice, Judge Krupansky, a recent Richard Nixon appointee, was available. "As it turned out, we were really fortunate with what happened with the matter of a judge," remarked Thomas Patton, one of two soon-to-be appointed trustees. "Judge Krupansky . . . knew his stuff." Added Patton, "If Battisti had gotten hold of this case, it would have ended differently. He would have made it political, and all of his cronies would have had their hands on the railroad." As Patton further noted, "Judge Krupansky indicated from the start that there would be a businesslike and nonpolitical administration of the estate."[1]

Judge Krupansky worked well for Erie Lackawanna and his role contributed to the company's spectacularly successful liquidation by 1992. This native of Cleveland was hardworking ("I am a workaholic," he remarked of himself), honest, and knowledgeable about business bankruptcy. A graduate of Western Reserve University and its College of Law, he had served as trustee for the reorganization of a medium-size brokerage firm, Edward F. Sigler & Company. "As trustee I paid off both the secured and unsecured creditors," recalled Krupansky proudly, "and this was indeed unusual." Although the judge expected to give the Erie Lackawanna bankruptcy case to Judge Thomas when he returned, Krupansky knew from his experience with Sigler that "I had to launch the reorganization process at once." He did so with alacrity.[2]

A matter of priority for Judge Krupansky involved selection of competent trustees, two or possibly three. Almost immediately he received applications, including one from Gregory Maxwell. "Some of these people had considerable railroad experience," but Krupansky was not satisfied. He wanted individuals with business experience *and* financial connections. "I needed to have top-notch people and ideally ones who had a reputation—positive, of course—in the financial world. This was a national case with national significance." And the judge also sought trustees who could devote time to the bankruptcy. Rather than sifting through the unsolicited resumes, Krupansky "threw out feelers into the Cleveland business community," and this produced the names of two prominent local business executives, Thomas F. Patton and Ralph S. Tyler, Jr. "I didn't know these men until I interviewed them," but Krupansky realized that "They were big-league businessmen with national connections." He named them officially on July 31, 1972, and the Interstate Commerce Commission gave its approval two weeks later.[3]

Fortunately for the judge and the railroad, Thomas Patton and Ralph Tyler agreed to serve and to accept modest annual salaries. Their positive responses were related to the timing of the offers. Both men had mostly completed their business careers and wanted challenges. Patton had retired from his post as chairman of the board and chief executive officer of Republic Steel Corporation, Cleveland's largest employer, on September 15, 1971, and Tyler had stepped down as chairman of the board of Lubrizol Corporation on April 24, 1972.[4]

Although Patton and Tyler had both led Fortune 500 companies, their backgrounds and personalities differed noticeably. Patton, who was born on December 6, 1903, came from a struggling Irish-American family on the west side of Cleveland. This bright, diligent lad attended area parochial schools, including St. Ignatius High School, where teachers recognized his academic talents and urged him to further his education. He followed their advice and enrolled at Ohio State University in 1923, graduating from its law school three years later. Admitted to the Ohio bar shortly thereafter, Patton worked in the legal department of the Union Trust Company in Cleveland until he left in 1928 to become an associate in the Cleveland law firm of Andrews & Belden. He continued with its successor, Belden, Young & Veach, as a partner until 1936. That year Patton accepted the post of general counsel for Repub-

Thomas F. Patton (*left*) and Ralph Tyler, Jr., became co-trustees of the bankrupt Erie Lackawanna Railway in 1972. These talented businessmen and lawyers led the company into Conrail and contributed to a successful final liquidation. (Erie Lackawanna Inc.)

lic Steel Company, a locally based member of the nation's group of Little Steel producers. Soon after his arrival he aggressively fought the Steel Workers Organizing Committee, a Congress of Industrial Organizations affiliate (CIO), during several bitter labor-management confrontations. This pleased the company's union-hating president, Thomas Girdler, and insured Patton's future with the firm. His success at Republic Steel continued: he became vice president in 1956, president and chief executive officer in 1960, and chairman of the board in 1968. The rags-to-riches Patton possessed a likeable personality. He was gregarious and a "very good social mixer." His game was golf and he played as often as possible. Patton also relished the world of politics, and this "streetwise Irishman" grew close to scores of important Republicans at all levels of government. His stunningly successful fund-raising efforts for the presidential campaign of Richard Nixon in 1968 endeared him to the party faithful.[5]

Unlike the Roman Catholic Patton, Tyler, a Baptist, grew up in a family of greater means and enjoyed better collegiate training. Born on the affluent east side of Cleveland on July 28, 1906, he attended its public schools and those of neighboring Cleveland Heights. Following his graduation from Cleveland Heights High School in 1923, Tyler entered Adelbert College of Western Reserve University where he completed his studies in 1927 with highest honors and a Phi Beta Kappa key. He then chose Harvard Law

School, earning his bachelor of law degree in 1930. Tyler, too, returned to his hometown, passed the bar, and joined a law practice. But he worked for the prestigious firm of Squire, Sanders & Dempsey, specializing for 34 years in corporate and financial affairs. He did interrupt his tenure between December 1933 and March 1934 to become a special assistant counsel for the Federal Reserve Board in Cleveland. When Tyler left Squire, Sanders & Dempsey in 1964, for the Lubrizol Corporation, a multinational chemical company, he continued with similar tasks as its general counsel and vice president. He won elevation to the board chairmanship four years later. Tyler impressed everyone with his hard work and his abilities at structuring several overseas ventures and foreign patent-licensing programs. A "lawyer's lawyer," Tyler possessed a brilliant legal mind and was considered a "true craftsman of the art." His meticulous ways meant that he "refused to accept any and all sloppy ideas." But unlike the affable Patton, Tyler was more reserved.[6]

There was good chemistry between the three individuals who led Erie Lackawanna through the bankruptcy labyrinth. Judge Krupansky respected his appointees: "They were smart men and ones with great integrity." And he added, "They really knew how to use staff personnel effectively." Patton and Tyler likewise thought highly of Judge Krupansky, and the amiable Patton assisted the judge in joining an exclusive Cleveland country club. The trustees appreciated Krupansky's willingness to allow them to exercise considerable freedom in running the property. "The judge let us decide the business questions," noted Patton, "and he did the legal matters."[7]

Bonds between the trustees were also strong. Though somewhat of an odd couple, as had been trustees Charles Denney and John Hadden during Erie's fourth bankruptcy, Patton and Tyler valued each other's talents. "Ralph was a serious-minded individual with great abilities," Patton reflected. "I always felt very comfortable with him as a business associate." Another reason Patton and Tyler worked well together was that they relished their positions. "I wanted something that I could do that was important after I left Republic Steel," explained Patton. "I'm an active person and this [Erie Lackawanna] was a real challenge which I enjoyed very much." Tyler echoed these feelings. He told an associate that being co-trustee was "the most enjoyable work in [my] three-part career," and five weeks before his death from a cancerous blood disorder on August 5, 1986, he wrote colleagues at Erie Lackawanna that "My Erie Lackawanna years were very important to me and I believe represented the most worthwhile activity I could have had for that time of my life." A positive feature about the co-trustees was that they remained friends. Admittedly, disagreements took place over specific matters during the attempted reorganization and the eventual liquidation, but the men refrained from public displays of disharmony. Since Tyler "always cleared matters with Tom," that factor, too, helped their relationship. And these two talented trustees complemented each other's skills: Patton was the "people person who saw the bigger picture" and Tyler was the "legal whiz."[8]

━━━

While its fifth bankruptcy dampened spirits among the Erie Lackawanna railroad family, for the near term the company remained intact. The major difference, of course, was that a federal judge and two trustees rather than the Norfolk & Western guided the property. This change did not trigger a re-shuffling of corporate personnel. Most significantly, Gregory Maxwell remained as president and chief executive officer. "We saw no reason to remove the management team," explained Thomas Patton. "Greg was doing as well as could be expected considering the circumstances. Most of the problems were beyond his control." Two members of the former "Virginia mafia" also stayed in Cleveland: Joseph Neikirk served as senior vice president for operations and traffic and Richard Hahn was vice president for finance. (Erie Lackawanna reimbursed Norfolk & Western for their salaries and benefits until the two resigned from N&W on August 31, 1972; effective September 1, 1972, they joined the Erie Lackawanna payroll.) "It was really status quo ante bellum with the bankruptcy," concluded one official.[9]

The immediate major response of management following the decision to seek court protection involved the Agnes floods, the crisis that precipitated bankruptcy. This involved emergency, often temporary, repairs to the heavily damaged physical plant. Once the railroad regained a semblance of normalcy, more substantial reconstruction occurred. Most train operations, including those on the main line, returned to normal by late August, although the Wayland (New York) branch remained embargoed for another month. One lightly used appendage, the Tioga (Pennsylvania) branch, had been destroyed, and so the company launched abandonment proceedings for this expendable line. Remembered Gregory Maxwell, "This branch generated only a little coal and some local traffic. It was hardly vital to our operations by the early 1970's." The estimated rehabilitation cost of $1.2 million sealed the line's fate.[10]

The millions of dollars of storm-related damages required outside assistance. To ease the financial pain, the company (always with approval of the trustees and the court) borrowed $3.978 million from the federal government under terms of the recently passed Emergency Rail Facilities Restoration Act, which had created a $40 million fund for that purpose. The arrangement offered generous provisions: principal repayment would extend for twenty years at an annual rate of 5.5 percent interest and principal repayments were deferred for the first two years of the loan.[11]

With the water-inflicted damages mostly unpleasant memories, the court and the railroad focused on how to proceed with the bankruptcy. Not long into the process, Judge Krupansky sought to relinquish the case to Judge Thomas. The two conferred and during their discussions Thomas asked Krupansky how much time he was devoting to the case. "I told him that I was spending about fifteen hours per day and that I expected the case to take about seven or eight years to complete." Understandably Thomas urged Krupansky to remain in charge; Krupansky willingly accepted his colleague's request. Even before this conclave, Krupansky wisely sought legal counsel. He turned mostly to John P. Fullam, the Philadelphia federal district court judge who had been overseeing the reorganization of Penn Central since the summer of 1970. This was fortunate, for Fullam "was an able and astute judge who understood the situation of the Northeastern carriers," concluded Jervis Langdon, Jr., the longtime railroad executive who served as one of three court-appointed trustees for Penn Central and later was its president.[12]

With Judge Krupansky committed to the case and determined to employ his best legal skills, the trio of Thomas Patton, Ralph Tyler, and Gregory Maxwell sought to salvage Erie Lackawanna. When the Erie had gone down for the count in February 1938, court protection permitted it to fend off creditors and to restructure its debt. The feeling on the executive floor was that Erie Lackawanna might repeat the process of 1938–41. But the exact strategy was not shaped immediately. "[I]t [is] too early to speculate as to what kind of reorganization will be best suited for the exigencies of the railroad and of the economic climate at the time a plan can be formulated," Patton told representatives of the firm's leading creditor body, Institutional Investors Erie Group, in October 1972. "In this connection . . . we might have to take a long look at such proposals, as that of the Lehigh Valley [another bankrupt Eastern carrier] which proposes a merger of the companies—LV, CNJ, Reading, etc." Still, as Maxwell said early on, "Our principal concern [and his especially] is a successful reorganization of EL." When Judge Krupansky issued Order Number 1, which prohibited the company from paying principal, interest, and sinking fund payments on its debt (except for equipment obligations) and real-estate taxes, the breathing time offered an opportunity to consider future actions. Under the bankruptcy law, the company had six months to file a plan of reorganization, although the trustees realized that such a time constraint needed to be extended. Krupansky agreed.[13]

The judge and trustees quickly grasped the difficulty of reorganization, especially for a property like Erie Lackawanna. "Ralph and I knew that we had our hands full," recalled Patton. "Remember, inflation got out of control in 1973 and 1974 and that was driving up the cost of doing business and everybody was suffering." And as Krupansky explained to the railroad trade press, "The Northeast encompasses railroad problems of a magnitude and complexity few can comprehend." The three also realized that railroading had become largely an asset-rich, cash-poor, high labor-cost business that yielded grossly inadequate returns on investment. As such they knew that the company should seek outside experts to determine if Erie Lackawanna's income-generating power was strong enough for an independent reorganization. The alternatives would be sale or merger of the property or some sort of liquidation where pieces were sold to the highest bidders to settle claims of creditors.[14]

In September the trustees, with court approval, sought planning assistance from the Corporate Finance Department of Salomon Brothers, the investment-banking firm long associated with railroad money matters. (Salomon Brothers had aided Erie Lackawanna during the Dereco period and it also served as financial adviser to the Reading Company.) The principal liaison with Erie Lackawanna was Robert Hampton, a Salomon Brothers vice president. This experienced professional had spent five years with the Chesapeake & Ohio Railroad working in its finance offices and four years with the First National Bank of Chicago as its commercial lending representative to the transportation industry. He worked well with Erie Lackawanna officials, and the fees his firm charged were modest.[15]

Robert Hampton and several associates rapidly joined forces with Erie Lackawanna personnel to prepare a trustees' report on reorganization planning. They completed a preliminary study for Judge Krupansky in early July 1973. While this 80-page document covered a range of topics, it centered on how the company might generate more operating income, reduce costs, and increase productivity. The report involved various proposals, including petitioning the Interstate Commerce Commission to rescind labor protection obligations that occurred when Norfolk & Western gained control, seeking ICC approval for abandonment of 169 miles of branch lines and completing a study of long-term freight equipment needs. One recommendation promised to enhance efficiency and therefore boost income: modernization and rehabilitation of the classification yard at Marion, Ohio. "[This is] the most important step that can be taken this year toward a successful financial reorganization."[16]

Since the early part of the century the west-central Ohio community of Marion, famous as the hometown of Warren G. Harding, had contained a strategic yard. It was only one of many scattered between Illinois and New Jersey. Salomon Brothers and Erie Lackawanna agreed that this installation had become even more vital to the railroad's operations but that it was in poor and antiquated condition. Much needed to be built: additional tracks, automatic car retarders, control tower, and new signals, switches, and communication system. Even without these betterments, the Marion facility had emerged as the company's principal yard for both east and west traffic. "We have cut back on the yards at Chicago and are running more trains through directly to our western connections," explained Gregory Maxwell in October 1972, "but these trains have to be made up at Marion."[17]

Wonderful benefits were anticipated if a multimillion-dollar revitalization of the Marion facility became reality. The study expected the project to slash yard crews needed by sixteen workers per week, and to reduce the force of switch tenders, retarder operators, and trainmen. Shrinking the number of crews would save locomotive fuel and supplies. Upgrading the yard tracks would mean fewer derailments and would also cut per-diem and mileage payments. Furthermore, some classification work at Port Jervis and Meadville could end, resulting in additional reductions of yard crews and support personnel. Based upon an examination by the New York City firm of Ford, Bacon and Davis, Inc., "consulting engineers of outstanding reputation," Marion yard improvements would save nearly $3.5 million annually and would cover the estimated construction costs in less than two years. A retired Erie Lackawanna official, J. M. Moonshower, went so far as to conclude in 1975 that "Had this project been completed in 1969 and the resulting savings properly administered, Erie Lackawanna deficits between 1969 and 1973, as well as the bankruptcy in June 1972, would have been avoided."[18]

The upgrading of the Marion facility received widespread backing, but for lack of money, it never happened. Only the engineering and legal work and some financial planning were done. Notwithstanding the protection provided by the Krupansky court, Erie Lackawanna could not negotiate attractive loan agreements. "Some banks were willing to provide funds for the Marion yard," recalled company treasurer Harry A. Zilli, Jr., "but they demanded prohibitive rates." And he added, "There was no way that we could accept 3 percent above prime." Although bankers knew that postbankruptcy obligations took precedence over prebankruptcy ones, they nonetheless worried about whether reorganization was feasible within a reasonable period of time. Noted Zilli, "They really wondered if we could ever generate adequate revenues."[19]

The caution among members of the banking community was understandable. While operating income for 1973 neared $290 million, or $25.8 million more than the previous year, net income stood at a minus $18.6 million. The financial picture for 1974 failed to improve substantially. Although operating revenues rose to $322.7 million, red ink still flowed freely: the road posted a negative net income of $17.2 million for the year.[20]

Even though discouraging financial figures hardly boded well for the future, officialdom at Erie Lackawanna did not automatically conclude that reorganization in a traditional manner was impossible. More than any other individual, Gregory Maxwell pushed for renewal. Viewed by some as a "strong, autocratic leader," the company president had a powerful personal commitment to keeping the property alive. "Maxwell loved being a railroad president," concluded an associate, "and he wasn't about to let the railroad dissolve into nothingness." Maxwell and others truly believed that an independent and competitive Erie Lackawanna would be in the best interests of shippers in the Midwest and Northeast regions. After all, the road was even more vital when viewed in the context of the rapid deterioration of Penn Central's physical plant. With approximately 40 percent of its mileage operating under slow orders (reduced speed), many wondered if that vast property could ever again serve the public's needs.[21]

Following the bankruptcy Maxwell did what he could to energize Erie Lackawanna. For one thing, he pressed for further cost-cutting measures. The most conspicuous example involved downgrading most of the deteriorating Delaware Division (Port Jervis Route) and removing one of the parallel lines of track and the signaling system. The company then dispatched virtually all its through freights between Binghamton and the New York terminal area over the Scranton Division. The reasoning actually centered on more than the savings created by reduced maintenance, estimated at $2 million annually, and the considerable value of the scrapped rail, ties, and other materials. Expounded Maxwell: "The Lackawanna [Scranton Division] line was shorter [about twenty miles] and that meant fewer crew miles. There was more business on that line and it was in better physical condition. We could run 60 miles per hour through the cut-off [in northern New Jersey]. The old Erie [Delaware Division] main was full of curves and thus demanded slower speeds." He could have added that the latter offered more interchange points with other roads than did the former route.[22]

Other acts of belt-tightening were less apparent but generally were more controversial. "My operations by 1972 were already mean and lean," explained Curtis Bayer, vice president for purchases and stores and never a Maxwell ally. "I was working bare bones all of the time, and I told Maxwell that it will cost the company money to cut back any more. He didn't listen to me, or for that matter anyone else except Bill Carlson [chief mechanical officer]." Continued Bayer: "After we went down in flames, Maxwell made a major mistake when he ordered additional cost-cutting. The traffic department, for example, entertained customers modestly but it was told to cut out all entertaining. Other railroads like the Chessie and Penn Central continued to entertain, and at times in a big way. That hurt us with our competition." This policy of retrenchment increased stress through executive ranks. "Several fellows began to suffer health problems because of all of this slashing." Soon this pruning involved the careers of some at the top. In the spirit of economy, Maxwell, backed by Patton and Tyler, streamlined senior management by terminating several officers, including Bayer and Joseph Neikirk. Instead of twelve major executives, the company by 1975 had only six: Maxwell, presi-

An Erie Lackawanna freight, PO87, takes a sharp curve west of Cochecton, New Jersey, on August 10, 1974. The milepost marker in the foreground, JC 131, indicates that the location is 131 miles west of Jersey City. The company removed the rails from this portion of the formerly double-track Erie main line. (Railroad Avenue Enterprises)

dent and chief executive officer; Richard Hahn, vice president for finance and administration; Fred Coffman, vice president for traffic; Richard Jackson, vice president for law and corporate secretary; Joseph Keenan, comptroller; and Harry Zilli, treasurer.[23]

Cutbacks also affected blue-collar workers. Those at the Marion diesel and Meadville car facilities experienced several shutdowns. In late 1974 about 550 temporary maintenance-of-way personnel received pink slips. Then the company placed in effect a 5 percent across-the-board reduction of permanent employees on December 4, 1974, which cut the work force from approximately 11,800 to 10,700.[24]

Maxwell likewise sought to maximize income. "He kept wanting the traffic people to generate business, even though some of it was not profitable," remembered Harry Zilli. "He was always after gross revenues." Furthermore, Maxwell made it clear to subordinates that he expected "the right numbers" in their reports to him and to the trustees. But the difficulty, of course, was that the railroad's traffic base and other forces made it impossible to produce the needed cash flow. Fred Coffman told the firm's "chief number cruncher," Warren Barber of the research department, "You can use your numbers and get fired immediately or we can use the numbers that Maxwell expects and lose our jobs in a year or two." It was a troubling situation for everyone, including the president.[25]

By the spring of 1974, the determination of Gregory Maxwell to go it alone, coupled to the mostly positive report by Robert Hampton and Salomon Brothers, along with bondholders' opposition to being included under any government-sponsored plan for rail reorganization, prompted the trustees to ask the judge for approval to continue the process under the bankruptcy statute. "We really thought that we might pull out of it through a straight bankruptcy," remembered Patton. Yet this shrewd executive "sensed a problem with the data and Maxwell's intentions, but lacked the hard facts to change anything." The judge agreed that Erie Lackawanna could be reorganized on an income basis, and he gave the go-ahead on April 30, 1974.[26]

Erie Lackawanna was not the only railroad with financial woes. Six other regional railroads, most notably giant Penn Central, grappled with the process of reorganization. While talk in the nation's capital during 1973 focused on the shocking revelations of the burglary of Democratic National Committee headquarters, the possibilities of fuel shortages and gasoline rationing, and the overheating economy being spurred by accelerating worldwide inflation, some worried about the fate of the financially desperate carriers. A one-day strike by the United Transportation Union against Penn Central over sudden changes in work rules in early February caused uneasiness. Concern heightened in late June when Judge Fullam received a pessimistic report from the Penn Central trustees. They argued that the railroad could *not* be reorganized under Section 77 on an "income basis" and proposed liquidation instead. The questions then heard in various business and governmental circles were: should these bankrupt roads, including Penn Central and Erie Lackawanna, become part of a nationalized system or should they be restructured under private auspices without public monies?[27]

As the year 1973 ended, most Americans knew a great deal about the Watergate affair, and Sam Ervin, the folksy North Carolina senator who chaired the Senate Select Committee on Campaign Practices, became nearly as famous as the besieged Richard Nixon. The public also became painfully aware of the long lines and high prices at gasoline stations that developed in the wake of the Arab oil embargo. Hardly any Americans, however, paid attention to Congressional debate on how to manage the evolving "Great Railway Crisis." They should have, for in 1973 more than half of the railroad mileage in the Northeast belonged to the bankrupts, with nearly three-quarters of it owned by the dying Penn Central.[28]

While the public thought little about an impending railroad catastrophe, a few interested parties did. A powerful coalition of railroaders, unionists, bankers, and shippers, which operated mostly outside the limelight, spent much of 1973 preparing rescue legislation. These activists lobbied lawmakers with the message that the nation's commerce would choke if Penn Central, most of all, was shut down and liquidated. Hard work led to the Shoup-Adams bill, named for its two sponsors, Republican Representative Richard Shoup of Montana and Democratic Representative Brock Adams of Washington, which Congress approved on December 20. President Nixon signed it fifteen days later, although his administration complained. As the President had earlier told his secretary of treasury, George Schultz, "I want a private, free-enterprise solution to come out of this." However, Nixon and other fiscal conservatives liked the bill's feature of off-budget financing. This meant that millions of dollars of anticipated government-backed loans would not appear in annual federal budget totals. Furthermore, banks, and not Washington, would supply much of the capital, although it would be guaranteed by the federal government.[29]

Passage of the Shoup-Adams Act (or, officially, the Regional Rail Reorganization Act of 1973, shortened to 3R Act), with its estimated $2.7 billion price tag, fulfilled the desires of those groups that sought governmental intervention. Whatever format developed, industry executives expected continued operations over major routes between the Midwest and New England; union brotherhoods took comfort with generous job-protection provisions; financiers worried less about their securities; and shippers, particularly automobile, chemical, and steel manufacturers, contemplated reliable service. And in the abstract, most Americans, if asked, would undoubtedly endorse the act's purpose of forging "an economically viable system capable of providing adequate and efficient rail service to the region."[30]

Although what became the quasi-public Consolidated Rail Corporation, or "Conrail," eventually turned out to be only "temporary nationalization," or at least a pale version of it, contemporary pundits adroitly called it "special interest socialism." Some even saw the act as a financial Frankenstein capable of damaging the national treasury. Actually, the scheme never met the criteria of pure nationalization: it would hardly have satisfied the once vocal Populists and Socialists who demanded government ownership. The goal became a for-profit company or companies ultimately operating free of direct federal involvement.[31]

Before the first Conrail train turned a wheel, the federal bureaucracy expanded to meet its legislative mandate. The 3R Act called for three distinct units to resurrect the troubled carriers: the United States Railway Association (USRA), an independent entity within the Department of Transportation for policy development; Rail Services Planning Office, attached to the Interstate Commerce Commission for evaluating USRA proposals; and ultimately Conrail itself, the operating portion, analogous to the recently launched National Railroad Passenger Corporation (Amtrak) and the older Federal National Mortgage Association ("Fannie Mae"). And significantly, the 3R Act required that eight of the fifteen members of the Conrail board of directors be government-appointed as long as 50 percent or more of its debt was accountable to Washington.[32]

The process that preceded Conrail's start-up was hectic and complex. At times it resembled the frenzied activities leading to the relief and recovery programs during the "First 100 Days" of the New Deal. Critics of "Conjob" charged that various shortcomings existed, most of all insufficient or sloppy planning. "Perfect plans [for railroad consolidations] had eluded everyone for fifty years," concluded historian Richard Saunders, "and this was going to be no exception." Such charges have merit: "the inexorable pressure of time" greatly contributed to flaws in the work of the USRA. Still, preparation of a plan to create an economically self-sustaining regional rail system that would meet the public interest and compete effectively with entrenched carriers was a Herculean task. The USRA responded as best it could, with help from the staffs of the Department of Transportation and the Interstate Commerce Commission and contract consultants. The USRA released its *Preliminary System Plan* on February 26, 1975, and its *Final System Plan* five months later.[33]

Part of the problem was how to cope with Erie Lackawanna. While small potatoes when compared to Penn Central, the road was still the second-largest bankrupt carrier and served a number of principal gateways. USRA staff members knew that the Friendly Service Route wanted to remain outside the sphere of any federally sponsored rail network and planned accordingly. Similarly, the federal court that administered the bankruptcy case of the Boston & Maine decided that carrier could also be reorganized under Section 77.[34]

The *Preliminary System Plan* focused on Penn Central and five other bankrupt carriers, but excluded Erie Lackawanna and Boston & Maine. Two much-discussed proposals involved either a single "Big ConRail" (the initial spelling) or two or more medium-sized ones, called "Multi-ConRail." The latter concept emerged on the drawing board as the Mid-Atlantic Railroad

Company or MARC. It would consist of the four regional bankrupts—Jersey Central, Lehigh & Hudson River, Lehigh Valley, and Reading—while the other, "ConRail I" or "Unified ConRail," would include Penn Central and the Ann Arbor. The USRA also considered creating the Consolidated Facilities Corporation (or ConFac), a government-backed corporation that would own the tracks of the bankrupt carriers and lease them to Conrail or to other roads, and discussed "controlled liquidation," the auctioning of useful lines of these failed roads to the highest bidders.[35]

But not long before the *Preliminary System Plan* appeared, Erie Lackawanna notified the United States Railway Administration that it wanted to join the government system. That is, the company sought to have its status restored to a "railroad in reorganization" under terms of the 3R Act, and asked the USRA "to provide for the inclusion of Erie Lackawanna in its planning." It also wanted funds that Section 213 of the Act gave such roads, as it desperately needed an infusion of cash to meet near-term obligations. Patton and Tyler were straightforward in their announcement: "[We] regretfully came to the conclusion that Erie Lackawanna cannot be successfully reorganized under Section 77 on an income basis as an independent carrier within a reasonable time."[36]

This request for federal assistance on January 9, 1975, shocked no one who knew the railroad's financial condition. Continuing inflation and a growing recession "really clobbered us," noted Harry Zilli, "particularly during the last quarter of 1974." Prices for materials needed to run the road increased faster during the year than at any time since World War I. Wages to contract employees soared 54 percent between 1968 and 1974, and were scheduled to rise another 41 percent during the next three years. The Interstate Commerce Commission worsened these negatives by consistently refusing commensurate hikes in freight rates. Even Gregory Maxwell, the diehard go-it-alone advocate, agreed that "we had no other real choice but to get in with Conrail." The specific data for 1974 was simply dreadful. The company faced $22,248,195 of accumulated interest on long-term debt in default, and net equipment and joint facility rents reached exorbitant levels, amounting to nearly $35.5 million for the year. Furthermore, the economic outlook for 1975 appeared to be no better. The road's service territory had suffered greatly as the national economy soured, and seemed in places to be in rapid and possibly permanent decline.[37]

Likely the most depressed locale along the Friendly Service Route was the Mahoning Valley (Youngstown) of Ohio, which for decades had been aptly called the "Breadbasket of the Erie." Its mostly antiquated steel manufacturers and fabricators reeled from the faltering national economy, but even more so from the impact of foreign competition. European and Japanese steel producers sold large quantities of their products at below-production costs on the American market because of national subsidies, even though the Anti-Dumping Act of 1921 and the Trade Act of 1974 forbade the practice. Orders to the region's principal firms, Youngstown Sheet & Tube, Republic Steel, and United States Steel, plummeted as did corporate earnings, the number of workers, and consequently rail shipments. Erie Lackawanna, "the big hauler in Youngstown," handled fewer cars of coal, coke, and iron ore to the mills and fewer loads of finished goods. Residents understood the billboards sadly proclaiming: "Foreign Steel, It's a Job-robbing Deal."[38]

Joining the emerging federal rail network involved more than Thomas Patton and Ralph Tyler simply concluding that this was a wise decision. Erie Lackawanna had legally detached itself from the 3R Act when it announced during the previous spring that it would remain independent. The company thus faced the necessity of winning enabling legislation from Congress for inclusion, and it also needed approval from Judge Krupansky.[39]

The trustees wasted no time in their efforts to leap the hurdles for inclusion. After all, they did not want to see their ward cease operations. Patton, the consummate politician, immediately sprang into action. "I had Washington connections," he happily recalled. Although Patton's ties to Richard Nixon had ended for practical purposes when the thirty-seventh president resigned on August 9, 1974, he had friends in the new Ford administration and in Congress. Moreover, Patton could tap the lobbying resources of Republic Steel. "We [Republic Steel] operated an office in Washington, and it was through these contacts that we [Erie Lackawanna] found an ex-Congressman from Ohio [William E. Minshall, R-Lakewood] to help us." The lobbyist cost the railroad $25,000, but this expenditure paid off handsomely. (An earlier $10,000 payment to Washington attorney Clark Clifford had yielded little.) With legislation written largely by outside counsel, the railroad won Congressional approval for inclusion (along with the Boston & Maine), and President Gerald Ford signed this amendment to section 207(b) of the 3R Act, along with other modifications, on February 28, 1975. Lawmakers and the Chief Executive generally concurred with these remarks made by Representative Benjamin A. Gilman (R-N.Y.): "While I am distressed about Erie's dilatory action in first seeking to go it alone and then belatedly confronting Congress with an ultimatum . . . , I urge my colleagues to take the practical course . . . [to include Erie Lackawanna]." Following a hearing on an inclusion petition, Judge Krupansky reestablished Erie Lackawanna as a "railroad in reorganization" eighteen days after the measure became law. The judge also granted the trustees authority to receive grants authorized by the 3R Act.[40]

The flip-flop by Erie Lackawanna was not universally popular. A small group of creditors and the Commonwealth of Pennsylvania appealed the

Krupansky ruling to the special court created by the 3R Act to handle such matters. But this judicial body quickly upheld the judge. It argued that Krupansky did not keep these protesting creditors from seeking relief from a court of claims and that such a reorganization was not inconsistent with the public interest, as Pennsylvania charged, since the trustees "showed the E-L could not be reorganized under the Bankruptcy Act."[41]

While most of those associated with Erie Lackawanna felt relieved that inclusion meant a way to protect investors, creditors, and shippers, company officers took pleasure in collecting immediate financial benefits. Section 213 of the 3R Act, which the Department of Transportation administered directly, provided funds to defray certain costs of "essential transportation services," including the firm's maturing equipment debt, and carried no obligation for repayment. The company also qualified under Section 215, handled by the USRA board, to receive support for maintenance-of-way work in anticipation of transferring its property to the government or possibly to a private carrier. As with Section 213, Erie Lackawanna was not required to return Section 215 funds. The federal treasury fed the financially starved railway well; it poured nearly $50 million into the road's nearly empty coffers between March 1975 and April 1976.[42]

When Erie Lackawanna won its second chance for inclusion, nobody in Cleveland fully realized the long-term value of the enabling legislation. Harry G. Silleck, Jr., who shaped the bill, sought to cover the legal bases. A partner in the prestigious New York firm of Mudge, Rose, Guthrie & Alexander, he had spent much of his professional career dealing with railroad matters. Silleck had advised William White from 1946 until White's death in 1967, after which Silleck's ties with Erie Lackawanna continued. What this talented lawyer achieved with the 1975 measure was to allow Erie Lackawanna to *either* reorganize or liquidate its assets "subject to such terms and conditions that the Reorganization Court [Judge Krupansky] found reasonable." Argued Silleck, "This provision proved to be more useful than I ever thought it would be when I put in that proposed language." Later the estate of the railroad discovered that it avoided a flock of personal injury claims, stemming mostly from asbestos-related cases of former employees. A federal court would rule in 1986 that the other bankrupt railroads that entered Conrail were not discharged from these suits, even though they became reorganized as nonrailroad concerns. But in the case of Erie Lackawanna, as Silleck noted, "the Sixth Circuit ruled that what Erie effected by its plan was more of a liquidation than a reorganization, and under a liquidation such claims would be precluded." The U.S. Supreme Court agreed when it denied a petition for certiorari review. Perhaps the most significant legacy of the 1975 measure was that it allowed a timely and complete liquidation. "It would have been very difficult if not impossible for Judge Krupansky to determine what amount of funds would be needed to pay all such claims, including claims not yet known that might be brought in the future, and to have allowed an unconditional distribution of the rest of Erie's assets to its stockholders," contended Silleck. "While continuing businesses, like the Manville Corporation, might establish a trust fund in a specific amount for all asbestos-related or similar claims, and might be expected to replenish the fund in the future if need be, that solution would not work for a publicly held company seeking to liquidate completely. Thus Erie, in the absence of the Sixth Circuit's decision, would probably have been forced to continue in some new business rather than liquidate as most stockholders desired."[43]

While the handiwork of Harry Silleck paid both short-term and long-term dividends to Erie Lackawanna, personnel at the USRA and elsewhere in the Department of Transportation were hardly elated with the company's reentry. The deadline for the *Preliminary System Plan* was only six weeks away, and the road could not be meaningfully incorporated into this important planning document. More significantly, the feeling existed that the trustees got two chances to make up their minds, and that this was inherently unfair. Then there was the matter of money. The addition of Erie Lackawanna would substantially increase costs, including line rehabilitation, labor protection, and asset valuation. Deputy Secretary of Transportation John Barnum, for one, thought that inclusion would likely result in the government paying for betterments that would be useless in the final structuring.[44]

Still, Erie Lackawanna was in, and Congress made the necessary appropriations. In the end, lawmakers had agreed that federal intervention offered the last best hope for a solution to the railroad problem; a breakdown of the national economy would surely follow if Penn Central, in particular, shut down. There was a growing sense, too, that the malaise in the railroad industry was spreading. The Chicago, Rock Island & Pacific, a 7,385-mile "Granger road" that operated in thirteen Midwestern, Great Plains, and Southwestern states, having been unsuccessful in its prolonged attempt to merge with the robust Union Pacific, teetered on bankruptcy. The management of the Rock Island understandably came to Washington with hat in hand in mid-1974 to seek funds under Section 211 of the 3R Act, which the USRA board controlled. Initially, the Rock Island asked for a $9 million loan, but before long the company returned to explain that it actually needed $100 million. The railroad, however, failed to win funding because "there was no reasonable prospect that the loan could be repaid or that [federal funds] could prevent the Rock Island from going bankrupt." Yet the USRA approved a $19 million loan in March 1975 for the Missouri-Kansas-Texas, "Katy," another beleaguered carrier, but a company with a better chance for survival. These demands subsequently led Congress to pass the Railroad Revitalization and

Sporting a bicentennial color scheme and a patriotic number, a Conrail locomotive pulls modern coaches that New Jersey Transit had earlier acquired for the remaining Erie Lackawanna commuter trains in that state. (Grant)

Regulatory Reform Act (4R Act), with USRA support. This measure, which became law in 1976, helped to stabilize the industry, although the Rock Island failed on March 17, 1975, and later liquidated.[45]

A plan to cope with the Great Railway Crisis moved ahead nearly on schedule. Even though sentiment grew for a Unified ConRail, which became known as "Three Systems East" (a competitive network of the region's three dominant railroads: Conrail and the two solvent carriers, Chessie System and Norfolk & Western, both of which would be enlarged with lines from the bankrupts), support continued for a version of the Mid-Atlantic Railroad Company. The new twist involved grafting Erie Lackawanna onto MARC to create what planners dubbed "MARC/EL."[46]

Although an ill-fated concept, MARC/EL received some notable and enthusiastic support. Its messiah was Charles E. Bertrand, head of the Reading and formerly an operating officer with the Baltimore & Ohio. Bertrand believed that anticipated traffic from diversion of freight from the Washington to Boston passenger corridor "will enable [MARC/EL] . . . to stand alone and provide competition to Conrail." He zealously pressed for the "competitive alternative" to Three Systems East. Bertrand found a powerful and faithful ally in William Scranton, former governor of Pennsylvania and a member of the USRA board. Scranton likewise fought doggedly for the scheme. Gregory Maxwell also expressed his approval; he backed the plan even before Erie Lackawanna sought inclusion. Maxwell, in fact, suggested a way to make MARC/EL more potent. Specifically, he wanted access to the 465-mile former Big Four main line from Galion, Ohio (near Marion), a connection with Erie Lackawanna, to St. Louis via Indianapolis, given to this 6,200-mile hybrid system. MARC/EL would then gain entry to the nation's greatest freight gateways—Chicago and St. Louis—and "this would make a good fast-freight road with excellent connections."[47]

The proposal of MARC/EL was well crafted. What surprised people was that this amalgamation of frail roads might actually prosper! The USRA, in fact, received its own study in late April 1975, indicating that MARC/EL was a viable arrangement: "the first new financials were something of a shock because they showed MARC/EL coming out surprisingly well." Other factors also underscored its merit. As a second federally backed carrier, MARC/EL would mean a smaller and theoretically more efficient Conrail (Penn Central and Ann Arbor). And it would offer competition, maximize service, and lessen fear of government domination over a unified Conrail.[48]

Powerful forces, however, aborted the gestating MARC/EL. Many within and outside USRA sought to invalidate "Little ConRail," as some called it, by repeated and varied criticisms. Likely the most significant point centered on the political liabilities of MARC/EL. After all, government planners responded to such forces, and opponents sensed that *two* federally sponsored railroads would anger the Ford administration. Critics' antennae were on the right beam: Gerald Ford was the most conservative chief executive since Calvin Coolidge, and the Executive Branch repeatedly charged that excessive regulation was at the root of the nation's economic problems. Similarly, the initial investment costs and maintenance expenses of two systems would surely exceed the other options, the latter possibly draining the treasury for years. If one of the two quasi-public properties began to fail, for example, the government would surely increase its aid and then might discover that the other carrier was at a disadvantage, and so on ad infinitum. Furthermore, creation of two roads would preserve more trackage, and this was not considered desirable. Most USRA personnel sought retirement of thousands of miles of trackage, especially "light-density lines" and also "redundant" main and secondary arteries. "They didn't want to have a map of Conrail look like a bowl of noodles," remarked Harry Silleck. "They thought that there was just too much track around. Clearly rail-to-rail competition was no longer seen as important as rail-versus-truck competition. You could do that [latter] with a handful of strong freight lines." Finally, a single ConRail could be more readily defended than two systems. Logically, one *big* railroad would be stronger than two.[49]

～～～

Before the final maneuvering that created a single Conrail, Erie Lacka-wanna toyed with several options for its future affiliation, even though after January 1975, it officially sought inclusion. While these schemes were short-lived, they revealed that the company's commitment to Conrail was not per-manently set. Erie Lackawanna, after all, could again disengage itself from a government scheme.

The most bizarre proposal involved the Hunt brothers from Texas. In early 1975 an attorney who represented Nelson Bunker Hunt and William Herbert Hunt, the colorful oil barons who later attempted to corner the silver market, contacted Erie Lackawanna about "affiliation with a western carrier." Apparently the Hunts had become interested in railroads; they already con-trolled a shortline in Oklahoma. Although Maxwell sent an underling to Dal-las with a package of financial data, nothing materialized.[50]

A more plausible possibility embraced a form of self-help. While em-ployee ownership became much discussed in the 1980's and workers acquired control of several important manufacturing concerns, this type of corporate restructuring had little impact on railroad employees. Yet it was the Chicago & North Western Transportation Company that early on had embraced this concept. In 1972, the carrier became "employee owned," although this struc-ture was later dropped. "What the C&NW had done was known at Erie," re-marked a top official. Employee ownership was discussed internally in Cleve-land and more so among workers in Marion, location of both the major yard and diesel-maintenance facility. "If something can be worked out along the lines of the Chicago and North Western acquisition by its employees, there may still be a ray of hope," suggested a former employee to the *Marion Star* in August 1975. "Then again, it may now be too late. One thing is certain: if the C&NW employees did it, Erie Lackawanna people can do it better—if given a chance." Gregory Maxwell concurred: "We had good relations with our em-ployees, and it might have worked at an earlier point in time." But not every-one, even in Marion, showed enthusiasm. "I was afraid it [employee owner-ship] would go down the tubes," related a veteran electrician. "I wasn't about to invest any of my money in such a scheme, although I wanted the railroad to stay in Marion." Perhaps Maxwell and others were too optimistic.[51]

A much more promising alternative came from Santa Fe Industries, the holding company that controlled the vast (12,500 mile) and vigorous Atchi-son, Topeka & Santa Fe Railway. For years, the Santa Fe had been Erie Lack-awanna's largest interchange partner. In an 85-page confidential report,

"Erie-Lackawanna Railway Company, Proposal for Acquisition," made available for internal use on May 30, 1975, the assessment of the road was surprisingly positive. Once an extensive six-year rehabilitation program occurred, this study projected that Erie Lackawanna would be able to generate a net after-tax income of more than $28 million annually.[52]

The report grasped the impecunious state of the property, but it found much that it liked, especially three aspects. One was the company's physical and operating characteristics. "The E-L is the only Eastern railroad which has the right-of-way suitable for high-speed, long-haul service without superfluous, congested and expensive urban terminals every hundred miles," observed the document. "The absence of clearance restrictions, . . . extensive double track mainline and interdivisional crew districts (up to 244 miles) are indicative of the physical resources which are presently being utilized at a level far below capacity." Thus the Friendly Service Route was ideally suited for the growth of piggyback and container traffic. The latter was then showing signs of unprecedented expansion; the combining of land and ocean shipping using containers steadily became a major source of profits for the industry. The study also expected another important means of generating substantial income: movement of automobiles and automotive parts. "The E-L potentially offers the only serious competition to the Penn Central for this traffic to New York and the New England States. Low clearances east of Park Junction (Philadelphia), Pennsylvania, restrict the competition of the B&O (Chessie System); whereas, the N&W-WM-RDG-CNJ 'Alpha Jet' (Trains AJ-1 and AJ-2) routes are longer and slower than those of the E-L." A third attraction was the opportunity to forge the nation's first single-road transcontinental route. "[This] would permit the Santa Fe Railway to compete more strongly for transcontinental, inter-regional and intra-regional traffic not now accessible by the Santa Fe." For decades the Santa Fe held the distinction of being the only carrier to operate its own line from Chicago to California, and with this plan the Santa Fe could claim another first. The report anticipated more than increased status; the Santa Fe, of course, expected substantial economic gains.[53]

If the Santa Fe report viewed Erie Lackawanna as a diamond in the rough, why then did the company fail to push for acquisition? Likely the probable explanation was that the study did not carry great clout. Top management did not order it; rather, John Darling, head of the railroad's cost analysis and research section, spearheaded the project. John Reed, Santa Fe's president, however, subsequently talked with Gregory Maxwell about his company's involvement. Maxwell rightly expressed interest, but he explained that "We were too far along with our commitment to Conrail."[54]

On August 10, 1974, "hotshot pig" NY 100 rumbles past the old Cochecton–Lake Huntington station in New York's Southern Tier. By the final years of Erie Lackawanna operations, trailer-on-flatcar business represented the bright spot in the company's freight operations. (Railroad Avenue Enterprises)

The precise relationship of Erie Lackawanna to the evolving Conrail remained blurred at the time of the Santa Fe study. Staff members at USRA attempted to complete the *Final System Plan*, but they could not predict the future appearance of the railroad map. The degree of Chessie and Norfolk & Western participation was unclear; neither road had made a formal commitment to acquire trackage of the bankrupt carriers, including Erie Lackawanna. But the USRA wanted the two private firms involved. Planners generally favored the Three Systems East concept, not wanting all of the bankrupts placed into one gigantic system. Furthermore, entry by the private sector held considerable political value. Nationalization was an ugly word and acquisitions by Chessie and N&W would make a Conrail pill easier for many to swallow. In a related fashion, the goal of competition seemed more likely with these three rival systems: a sturdy Conrail competing against a Chessie and N&W held considerable appeal.[55]

The USRA had an ideal scenario in mind. It wanted Norfolk & Western to acquire Erie Lackawanna, in part because "there was a historical relationship between these two roads." And Chessie was to take most of the Reading since "there was a natural affinity here—the Chessie did $30 million worth of interchange business a year with the Reading."[56]

The Norfolk & Western kept no one in suspense. President Jack Fishwick adamantly opposed acquisition of trackage east of what he call the "firewall," an imaginary line from Albany, New York, to Harrisburg, Pennsylvania. His company had no stomach for the terminal complexities, high property taxes, and related problems associated with railroading in the metropolitan New York region. The N&W told the USRA that it would neither pay for Erie Lackawanna nor accept it without an annual subsidy to cover anticipated losses. Understandably, the agency rejected such severe conditions. At best only a "Two Systems East" scheme seemed possible; the Chessie System was more cooperative.[57]

Differing from Jack Fishwick, Chessie chairman and chief executive officer Hays T. Watkins, an "industry statesman," expressed concern about more than the bottom line of his 9,500-mile and heavily coal-carrying system. He showed a much greater willingness to work with the government. "Hays Watkins believed that Chessie needed to intervene because all of the railroads in the Northeast seemed to be going down," remembered an associate, "and the Chessie had an obligation to the industry and the free-enterprise system."[58]

Yet Watkins's interests in the Reading, parts of Penn Central ("Chessie had its eyes on the old New York Central [coal] line to Charleston, West Virginia"), and even Erie Lackawanna were not wholly altruistic. When properly rehabilitated, these lines, Watkins believed, offered the prospect for future profits. What primarily attracted the Chessie executive to the Friendly Service Route was its United Parcel Service operation. "UPS was considered the only plum." At this time Chessie particularly favored piggyback service, and it considered the main line of Erie Lackawanna ideally suited for this traffic. It liked the road's projected volume for 1976 of 246,400 trailers, nearly half of which would move between the end terminals of Chicago and Croxton; many of these would be UPS units.[59]

Not everyone at Chessie headquarters in Cleveland agreed that Watkins should encourage Two Systems East. The most vocal dissent came from president John W. Hanifin. Although Hanifin and Watkins had been close for years, they became estranged over the expansion issue. "Hanifin really believed that the Erie Lackawanna and Reading were dogs, and thought that Watkins was way off bounds on this." Then the Chessie president, considered widely by underlings to be a "wacky character," turned on Watkins and sought to depose him. But Watkins enjoyed strong support from the Board of

Directors, and he orchestrated Hanifin's dismissal in late 1975. Bad feelings continued, and the aftermath led tragically to police protection of the Watkins home, the suicide of Mrs. Hanifin, and a reclusive life for her widower.[60]

In early June 1975, Chessie agreed to buy most of the Reading, the Erie Lackawanna, and two smaller portions of trackage, including the West Virginia coal line, for the government's asking price of $114.1 million. It would also do so without federal assistance. This thrilled USRA employees, but their euphoria dissipated somewhat when Chessie expressed its first reservations about these acquisitions. The company wanted federal legislation to protect it against possible judgments granted to creditors of the bankrupt estates in anticipated future litigation. And Watkins told USRA chairman Arthur Lewis that he expected an assurance that "in no circumstances should our positive response or the other eastern solvent's [N&W] lack of participation be used by ConRail or any other government agency in the future to favor other roads or to 'even out' competition." Then, on June 19, 1975, the USRA Board approved the Chessie agreement and endorsed legislation that would protect the company against deficiency judgments.[61]

Nevertheless, the Chessie deal remained unsettled. Initial bickering on price led the United States Railway Association to lower the original amount by $10 million, but then Chessie announced that it would pay only $22.1 million in cash and the remainder with 6 percent Baltimore & Ohio bonds. More discussions ensued. This prompted Chessie to reduce further its financial pledge; it proposed either $60 million in cash or $62 million in cash and securities. This withering of financial commitment especially annoyed Deputy Secretary of Transportation John Barnum: "Every time I turned around we were getting paid less for that property." Chessie's growing unwillingness to pay prompted the USRA Board of Directors on July 14, 1975, to reject the final arrangement by a six-to-five vote. Support remained strong, however, for private sector participation, and the following day the Board, pushed by member Gale "Gus" B. Aydelott, president of the Denver & Rio Grande Western Railroad, reversed itself by a favorable margin of two votes.[62]

When the *Final System Plan* appeared on July 26, Chessie System played a prominent role in the grand design envisioned by the USRA. The report listed the specific acquisitions which would make Chessie an approximately 12,000 route-mile system, although somewhat smaller than the anticipated ConRail complex. The Chessie's Baltimore & Ohio unit would operate this new trackage:

The acquisition by Chessie of almost all of the Reading and present Erie Lackawanna lines between Sterling, Ohio (just west of Akron) [and a direct connection with the B&O's Chicago line] and Newark via Jamestown, Hornell (with connecting lines to Buffalo) and Binghamton would allow it to provide single-line competition to ConRail between east coast markets and the Midwest, as well as competitive connect-

ing service between the Midwest and South and New England via the Delaware &
Hudson and the Boston & Maine. Chessie also had been offered the Charleston, W.
Va., market of the Penn Central. . . . In addition, it is proposed that Chessie acquire
trackage rights over CNJ to the Elizabethport Yard and access to certain CNJ stations
switched by ConRail in the Elizabethport/Perth Amboy, N.J., area. It is also proposed
that Chessie acquire trackage rights on the LV between Wilkes Barre, and Greenville
Yard, N.J.[63]

The document also indicated other specific details, including what Erie
Lackawanna lines would not be conveyed to Chessie's B&O affiliate:

The EL offerings to Chessie include all trackage and related facilities, including
yards, shops and specified rolling stock and locomotives, etc., except for:

All lines from Sterling, Ohio, west.

Nonviable light-density lines except for the lines from Pittston to Avoca, Pa.,
Washington, N.J., to Phillipsburg, N.J., North Alexander to Caledonia, N.Y., the
New Castle branch, the Montgomery branch and the extension to Bath, Pa. These
lines are needed by Chessie for through route service.

All viable freight lines in the New York-New Jersey metropolitan areas on which
passenger services are operated. These lines will be transferred to ConRail. Chessie
would have trackage rights to provide through and local freight service. ConRail, under contract with commuter agencies, will provide the passenger services. Chessie
would acquire the EL line from Cleveland to Youngstown over which a nonsubsi-
dized commuter train is operated.[64]

The agreement between the USRA and Chessie System and publication
of the *Final System Plan* did not mean that the railroad map of the East would
actually jell as announced. Chessie grew increasingly uneasy about owning
Erie Lackawanna. In September Hays Watkins told the Senate Subcommittee on Surface Transportation, chaired by Vance Hartke (D-Indiana), that he
worried about the property. One red flag involved the potential cost of taking
thousands of Erie Lackawanna employees. While Section 509 of the 3R Act
stated that "acquiring railroads shall . . . be reimbursed for the actual amounts
paid to, or for the benefit of, protected employees," the measure limited the
government's commitment to $250 million. These funds might be exhausted
after a few years, and Chessie would then experience a sizable drain of its treasury. Watkins implied that he would like to avoid the Erie Lackawanna, and
take only the Reading and the Charleston coal line. This did not please
USRA's Arthur Lewis. "The deal had to be all or nothing at all," he wrote
Senator Hartke, and he told journalists the same thing: "[I]t is imperative, in
order to achieve an optimistic basic industry structure, that the Chessie acquire (all three)." Lewis indicated that the USRA would oppose protection
against deficiency judgments for the Chessie if the company refused the entire package.[65]

Chessie felt additional pressure not to renege. Congressman James Hastings (R-New York), whose Southern Tier district depended heavily upon Erie Lackawanna service, entered the fracas. He asked the House of Representatives to reject the *Final System Plan*, a vote required by the 3R Act. Even though his resolution died without being considered in committee, Hastings sought to muscle Chessie into cooperating. Yet he was not sanguine about this legislative tactic, although he thought it might have an impact. Perhaps the Chessie appreciated Hastings's concern.[66]

The Chessie seemingly remained committed to the takeover of lines described in the *Final System Plan*. In October the road's Traffic Department released a 56-page document, "Evaluation and Plan: Reading, Erie-Lackawanna, and PC Charleston Lines Acquisitions," an unmistakable preparation for "Acquisition Day." Watkins and his colleagues felt better about such a likelihood when the USRA Board on November 6 reduced the purchase price to $54.5 million. This concession to Chessie stemmed partly from the impact of an investigative piece, "USRA Rail-Pricing Story a Tangled Web," by *Washington Star* reporter Stephen Aug. He indicated that USRA officials had been "astounded" when Chessie first agreed to the $114.1 million amount and that the government "would probably have accepted a figure of approximately $40 to $50 million for the entire offering."[67]

The fatal blow to Chessie acquiring much of Erie Lackawanna, or for that matter any line from a bankrupt carrier, came not from the United States Railway Association, from an obstinate lawmaker, or from wrangling about price; rather, the seed had been sown in the 3R Act itself. A mostly ignored provision (Section 508) required labor and management to agree on employee protection and related matters *before* a railroad could finalize a purchase agreement under the law. This affected not only Chessie but also the Southern Railway, which belatedly agreed to buy 450 miles of Penn Central trackage on the Delmarva Peninsula between Wilmington, Delaware, and Newport News, Virginia. Unlike the emerging Conrail, where labor and management would hammer out detailed agreements *after* conveyance, Chessie and Southern needed to resolve these issues prior to their acquisitions. Both companies had their own labor agreements that in some respects were less generous than those in effect on Penn Central and the other bankrupts. These matters had to be settled by February 11, 1976, to make possible "Conveyance Day" on April 1, 1976.[68]

Though representatives of labor and management from Chessie and Southern had been meeting since mid-November 1975 to negotiate agreements, they had little to show for their efforts. Neither USRA head Edward Jordan nor Secretary of Transportation William T. Coleman reacted to the impasse; both men had other pressing problems. Coleman, in fact, said that he learned of this complication only after President Ford signed the 4R Act on February 5, 1976, and indicated that he would have asked the President to postpone approving the measure until an accord had been reached.[69]

The gulf between labor and management was probably too wide to bridge. The unions demanded that members be transferred with their existing wages and work rules; railroads, on the other hand, expected union members to accept agreements already in effect. Obviously, union leaders knew that they "couldn't sell their members down the river," especially since their benefits and rights would likely continue at Conrail. Similarly, railroad officials did not relish workers who would enjoy special, more favorable rights than current employees. This inequality would surely trigger demands for more generous provisions among their existing employees. Hays Watkins drove home the point, too, that "taking over the labor practices and agreements which contributed to the bankruptcy of the acquired lines would have resulted in our assuming a loss operation and would have seriously restricted the performance of efficient rail transportation services."[70]

A major effort to solve the labor problem did take place prior to the deadline. Negotiations conducted by the experienced federal labor mediator William J. Usery went on in Washington for more than 70 continuous hours. The most promising compromise during these marathon discussions came from Usery himself: the concept of a grandfather clause. If accepted by both sides, transferred workers would keep their old benefits for as long as they held their new jobs. When they left, however, the prevailing labor agreement would then take effect. Also, the acquiring carrier would not terminate these incoming workers or transfer them to other assignments. Since neither side cared for the Usery plan, nothing was resolved by February 11.[71]

A last-ditch attempt to end the stalemate followed. Some politicians from Maryland and New York, who found deadlock unacceptable, announced their intention to seek an extension for the date of conveyance. They hoped that saber-rattling would pressure both labor and management. A more forceful response came from Secretary Coleman. He scheduled a negotiating session for the last week of February, and once again the mediator Usery participated. These talks involved Chessie's Hays Watkins and his counterpart at the Southern, Graham Claytor, Jr.; C. L. Dennis, president of the Brotherhood of Railway and Airline Clerks (BRAC); and Al Chesser, president of the nation's largest rail body, the United Transportation Union (UTU). Involvement of the latter two men was essential; they headed unions "which really wanted no part of the Erie and Reading entering the Chessie." Especially intransigent were the firemen, whose union, the Brotherhood of Locomotive Firemen and Enginemen, had merged with several other operating brotherhoods in 1968 to form the UTU. Understandably, little positive movement occurred, and the talks terminated on the morning of February 27. Coleman's public statement that impasse was "unfortunate for the country, for labor, and for the railroads" pointed toward the ultimate outcome: "Big Conrail."[72]

Yet before Conrail debuted, efforts to resolve the labor dispute took place for a final time. Secretary Coleman, determined to achieve at least a partial victory, called a press conference on March 19 in which he blasted labor and management for their failure to reach an agreement. From his perspective, the "will of Congress has been thwarted and the public interest has not been served." Coleman had mostly given up on a Chessie deal, but he held out hope for Southern Railway participation, which would have symbolic value. The Secretary very much wanted to build up the size of private sector carriers, eventually creating only a handful of rail giants. He set a deadline of Monday morning, March 22, for the unions and the railroad to agree. Coleman also asked that negotiators from Chessie resume talks, and they did so with union representatives in a Baltimore hotel.[73]

What was past became prologue again. While twelve of the twenty unions agreed to a settlement with the Southern, stalemate still occurred. The UTU, most of all, refused to budge. Similarly, the Chessie talks produced nothing of substance. Announced an angry Coleman: "I have done everything I can. I have argued, I have pleaded, I have cajoled." But as one union official charged, "Coleman should have figured out early on that Title V of the [3R] Rail Act prevented much from happening." Generally speaking, the brotherhoods had nothing really to gain from their discussions with the Chessie and the Southern.[74]

There were those who did not especially like what seemed to be in the offing. The attitudes of management at Erie Lackawanna were typical. Patton, Tyler, and Maxwell wanted their property to be part of the Chessie System rather than Conrail. "We preferred to join a privately owned company," recalled Maxwell. "Conrail was a big unknown." Railroad executives, business leaders, and those who held a conservative perspective generally concurred.[75]

Not everyone disliked the turn of events. The ultimate shape of Conrail meant that it was "far bigger than its most enthusiastic sponsors ever dreamed it would be," and more monopolistic. While Chessie officials likely accepted Maxwell's point of view, they no longer needed to fret about whether their involvement with Erie Lackawanna was a good thing. (The company, in fact, would later expand; it merged with the Seaboard Coast Line in 1980 to form the prosperous CSX System.)[76]

Labor also felt a sense of relief. Workers realized that they would have "reasonable" work rules and job protection with Conrail, including guaranteed buyouts. "We knew Conrail would be o.k.," explained a representative of the Brotherhood of Locomotive Engineers, a union that showed far less rigidity than either BRAC or UTU. "About 500 [Erie Lackawanna] engineers would be taken by the Chessie, but our members on the west end would have

taken a beating [since Chessie did not want trackage west of Sterling, Ohio]."
He further noted, "Conrail would just mean better job protection, period.
This was not a merger [of Chessie and Erie Lackawanna], and so there was no
automatic blanket protection from Chessie. The best surprise, you know, is
no surprise at all."[77]

Even the United States Railway Association felt encouraged. Some personnel never wanted anything but a large Conrail and they certainly disliked
MARC/EL. They also found a last-minute way to lessen criticism of giving
birth to a quasi-public giant. The agency announced on March 9 that the
Delaware & Hudson agreed to operate over some of the lines earlier assigned
to Chessie, and in this way two-carrier service would be given to more local-
ities. Soon D&H freight trains rumbled into yards at Buffalo, Newark, and
Alexandria, Virginia. Since the accord with D&H involved only trackage
rights (D&H would pay rental fees to Conrail), no new labor agreements
were required. And to strengthen the financially weak D&H, the USRA endorsed a Section 211 (3R Act) loan for $28 million.[78]

———

The turn of events, nevertheless, eventually hurt individuals associated
with Erie Lackawanna, including some employees who qualified for the generous job-protection provisions of the 3R Act. Residents of Marion were
among the first to recognize that the coming of Conrail would likely cause
serious economic dislocations. The alarm sounded with publication of the *Final System Plan*. Since Chessie would ignore Erie Lackawanna facilities west
of Sterling, Ohio, and Conrail would take only pieces of the main line, the
future of this longtime railroad community, with its massive railroad complex, looked bleak. Asked "An Erie Lackawanna Employee" in a letter to the
local newspaper, "Can Marion afford to lose 1,600 employees and their fam-
ilies?" While some Marionites discussed the possibilities of employee ownership, most thought that pressuring Washington into protecting the classification yard, diesel shop, and at least the Marion-Lima segment of the main
line offered a better chance for preserving jobs.[79]

What happened in Marion was a reaction unique among communities
along the Erie Lackawanna, and perhaps anywhere in the country. By mid-
August the Marion County AFL-CIO and the Marion Chamber of Commerce jointly created an organization they called MONEY, an acronym for
"Marionites Opposed to the Negation of the Erie Yards." This quintessential
grass-roots movement, with its cross-class backing, immediately launched a
petition drive to influence decision makers to maintain local employment.
MONEY endorsed MARC/EL and if that company failed to materialize, it
wanted retention of as much of the rail activities in Marion as possible.

Within a few weeks the group had collected nearly 30,000 signatures, many from a booth placed in the area's largest shopping mall. Instead of mailing these stacks of petitions to the Rail Services Planning Office, representatives of MONEY took them personally when they testified before that body on October 6. MONEY's coordinator, DaLee Mounts, expressed "a good, positive feeling" about the hearings.[80]

But the efforts of MONEY were futile. "It was sort of like pissing into a strong wind," was the earthy remark of one backer. Marion had no place in the scheme of either Chessie involvement or a "Big Conrail." The former had ample facilities on its main line in Willard, Ohio, 48 miles to the northeast, and the latter could use the former Penn Central service installation in Columbus, 47 miles to the south. "We took another look at it [Marion]," commented Robert Hetherington, USRA's regional affairs manager, "but nothing is changed. The high rehabilitative costs of the Marion yard just don't permit its inclusion in the ConRail system." Unfortunately for MONEY, Hetherington was right.[81]

While MONEY strove to protect the status quo, Erie Lackawanna struggled to serve its freight and commuter customers. Even with court protection, infusion of federal funds, and a watchful management, the Friendly Service Route slipped during the final months before "Conveyance Day" or "C-Day." Some believed that "track conditions had just gone to hell," and no one denied that the property showed "plenty of wear and tear," the result of reduced maintenance. A crude barometer of the decline of the physical plant was the number of slow orders issued for the main lines. Before the bankruptcy the percentage usually stood at less than 3 percent, especially during the drier months. But they increased steadily after 1972, and then dramatically following the trustees' decision to enter Conrail. For example, a memorandum to the trustees from Robert Downing, manager of transportation, dated July 14, 1975, reported that "there are 271 slow orders in effect on main tracks. Mainline mileage affected amounts to 771.9 miles or 33.6 percent of total mainline mileage." At one point in 1975, the number of slow orders exceeded 40 percent of the main routes. The company also allowed its mainline signaling system to decay. Conditions became so bad on the "West end" that the Federal Railroad Administration levied a $70,000 fine (later reduced to $35,400) in 1975, for "failure to correct signal circuit conditions at several points [Lima, Ohio, and Decatur, Indiana] on the Marion Division."[82]

Although Erie Lackawanna trains ran over plenty of poor track protected by ancient signaling devices, the trains were hardly death traps for employees. Actually, the workplace was remarkably safe toward the end, much more so than it had been only a few years earlier. A low-budget, decentralized safety program developed by Joseph Neikirk in 1970 made a difference. The road's safety record improved so markedly that it won an E. H. Harriman Memorial Bronze Medal in 1974, a first for the railroad or its predecessors. Later it received the highest recognition, the coveted E. H. Harriman Gold Medal, in 1975. Named after railroader Edward H. Harriman, who had been relentless in his pursuit of safety early in the century, and endowed by his widow, Mary, in 1913, the award annually honored carriers with the best safety records. "This was an amazing accomplishment for a bankrupt line like the Erie," commented an industry consultant following the second presentation. In some ways it was more remarkable since the railroad "was well ensconced at the bottom" of major roads for workplace injuries and deaths when the William White regime began. No wonder, then, the 18×14–inch gold certificate, which the company received officially in a ceremony held in Washington, D.C., on May 11, 1976, remained conspicuously displayed in the Cleveland office until the last space was vacated in 1991.[83]

The Erie Lackawanna ended its life as a railroad with more of a whimper than a bang. There had been a few bright spots before C-Day on April 1, 1976, when much of the property entered Conrail. The road experienced a modest increase of intermodal activity and movements of unit grain and coal trains, the latter mostly from mines along the Brockway (Pennsylvania) and Lisbon (Ohio) branches. Still, this battered and bankrupt carrier had little hope for survival in the hostile climate of the mid-1970's: the tremendous fall-off in business caused by deep recession, high inflation, competition from vehicular, water, air, and other rail transport, and the constraints of nearly total regulation and unionization made life a seemingly impossible struggle.[84]

On the last day of independent operations, only a few indications of this historic event were evident. The media took some notice of the railroad's passing, and scattered handmade signs of the "Good-bye EL" variety appeared on rolling stock and at trackside. Generally, it was business as usual.[85] Employees at WR Tower in Huntington, Indiana, for example, duly recorded a normal flow of freight trains on March 31, but shortly before midnight operator Paul Michael copied this message for all train crews:

Effective 2301 hours CST Mar 31, 1976 and 0001 hours EST April 1, 1976 the line Decatur MP 96.09 to North Judson MP 199.4 will be operated by Conrail as part of the Western Region Fort Wayne Division. The line Lima MP 54.3 to Elgin MP 72.0 will be operated by Conrail as part of the Western Region Fort Wayne Division. The line Marion MP 305.1 to Richwood MP 319.4 and from Peoria MP 330.4 to Broadway MP 327.5 will be operated by Conrail as part of the Southern Region Columbus Division. These lines in the Western Region and in the Southern Region will be governed by the rules of the Operating Department Erie Lackawanna effective Oct 25, 1964 and by timetable No 4 of Erie Lackawanna Railway effective Feb 24, 1974.[86]

The order graphically revealed that April 1, 1976, would be a different day on the railroad; the main line from New York to Chicago would forever be broken. "The Erie as we knew it was finished," observed an employee from Huntington. "No more hot-shot freights, no more big Erie family, no more anything, really."[87]

THE ESTATE,
1977–1992

THE NEW CONSOLIDATED RAIL Corporation brought about immediate changes, particularly with the former Erie Lackawanna Railway and the other smaller component roads. Most obvious to casual viewers was the transformation of the physical landscape. Conrail's corporate policies swiftly led to the down-grading or abandonment of much of the Erie Lackawanna trackage and to the liquidation of many of its support facilities. The once teeming classification yard at Marion, Ohio, for example, soon became choked with weeds and littered with discarded equipment. These happenings hardly surprised informed observers. Griffith "Griff" Davis, a former Lackawanna trainman and United Transportation Union officer, correctly predicted in 1975 that "If the Erie Lackawanna is included under this [Regional Railroad Reorganization] Act, I am certain it will be emasculated and become a mere shadow of its present self." Added Davis, "It will be swallowed by a massive corporation and become nothing but a minor operation."[1]

The advent of Conrail altered the lives of workers who had operated the Friendly Service Route and shippers who had depended upon it. The former, however, likely faced the greater adjustments. Some employees retired, often to remain in their home towns; others accepted severance payments and left railroading. Those who joined Conrail usually did so with some discomfort. Since former Penn Central personnel dominated the new carrier, employees from other bankrupt roads repeatedly encountered discrimination. "If the company had agreed to enter Conrail from the beginning," opined an Erie Lackawanna lawyer, "EL management people might have had better jobs."

Long lengths of "ribbon" rail wait to be picked up along the former Erie Lackawanna main line west of Kingsland, Indiana, in December 1981. (Grant)

Those from blue-collar ranks especially felt the sting of prejudice. Yet this was not wholly unexpected. "We knew that we wouldn't be number one in this arrangement," voiced an electrician from the Marion diesel shops. "And we were right. Our guys got the royal shaft." He remembered that when Marion employees went to work at the maintenance facilities in Columbus, Indianapolis, and Toledo, "ex-Pennsy and New York Central men got ahead of our fellows even though they had less seniority." A trainmaster believed that "most of us Erie people were seen as unwelcome guests by Conrail workers." The desire of Conrail's managers to retain mostly Penn Central properties led to these problems, and the brotherhoods backed their decisions, "largely because Penn Central people had a majority in the unions."[2]

Former Erie Lackawanna personnel, moreover, generally were not proud of their new work environments. "The Marion shops were always spotlessly clean," remembered a mechanical department foreman, "but the roundhouse at Fort Wayne [former Pennsylvania Railroad] was a goddamn mess . . . with the doors off the hinges." Added an ex–Erie Lackawanna conductor, "We ran trains; Conrail was really a joke at first."[3]

Eventually, the difficulties caused by the formation of Conrail were mostly resolved. "The passage of time sort of healed all the open wounds," reflected an official who left Cleveland to join the Conrail headquarters staff in Philadelphia. But it was more than the passage of time that soothed the transition from Erie Lackawanna to Conrail; the talents of the former Erie Lackawanna workers were commonly needed. This was especially true for skilled operatives. "The people there in Columbus had never worked on GE locomotives before and we saved their asses," recalled one Marion shopman. "You bet we got respect . . . , and I personally felt a lot better about Conrail."[4]

Some shippers also found the adjustments troubling. Although long-distance customers such as United Parcel Service[5] merely switched to Conrail or to a competitor, those who used trackage that Conrail declined to acquire or subsequently sold or abandoned felt the effect of these massive changes. With service radically altered west of Akron, Ohio, former shippers either launched or patronized newly formed shortline carriers. Such corporate banners as the Ashland Railway, Erie Western Railway, and Spencerville & Elgin Railroad flew over sections of the former main line. Yet even these firms, with their nonunion crews and modest overhead costs, encountered financial difficulties. When Conrail stopped operating much of the former Erie Lackawanna main line across Indiana in September 1977 a new corporation, Erie Western, headed by shortline promoter Craig Burroughs, appeared, but the railroad failed in June 1979. A successor company, Chicago & Indiana railroad, fared even worse; its history can be measured in months rather than years. Begun on June 15, 1979, the Chicago & Indiana suspended operations at the end of December. Only a small portion of this 158-mile Hoosier state railroad remained, namely, 16 miles that linked Monterey with the Chessie System at North Judson. If owners of the Buckeye Feed & Supply Company and other shippers in Monterey were to remain rail users, they had no alternative but to organize their own pike. Fortunately, their self-help response, the Tippecanoe Railroad, proved to be financially viable. These backers subsequently sold their property; after 1990 it became known as JK Lines, Inc., and remained profitable.[6]

Shippers east of Akron enjoyed generally better service. Those who had access to the Buffalo, Binghamton, and Port Jervis route experienced little inconvenience; this artery became a Conrail secondary main line. Although Conrail allowed the property to deteriorate, it announced in the summer of 1992 plans to invest heavily in upgrading the Buffalo-to-Binghamton segment. This came in the wake of the Canadian Pacific's failed attempt to buy the line, an action that followed the Canadian road's acquisition of the Delaware & Hudson Railway in January 1991. Moreover, Conrail's attitudes toward this historic trackage had changed markedly. The company's operating department, which was no longer controlled by "anti-Erie" personnel who favored the former New York Central network, finally recognized the line's

Local train No. 34 of the Erie Western, a soon-to-fail shortline, hauls a tank car past the old interlocking tower in Kingsland, Indiana, on March 17, 1978. This portion of the former high-speed Erie Lackawanna main line was about to be junked. (Charles Willer)

strategic and utilitarian value. The route held the potential for handling high-priority traffic to and from New York City.[7]

Trains other than those owned by Conrail also rumbled over portions of the old Southern Tier line. The Interstate Commerce Commission had granted the Delaware & Hudson trackage rights between Binghamton and Buffalo at the time of Conrail's creation to "assure competitive rail service in the Northeast." Then traffic on the eastern segment increased noticeably after 1985 when the New York, Susquehanna & Western gained access to the line between Binghamton and Campbell Hall, New York. "Susie-Q's" double-stacked container trains became a common fixture of this trackage.[8]

While segments of former Erie Lackawanna main lines in the East, including the Lackawanna Cutoff in northwestern New Jersey, and branches were dismantled or slipped into out-of-service status, several shortlines preserved some rail service. The Honesdale line between the Pennsylvania communities of Honesdale and Lackawaxen is an example. Conrail rejected this 25-mile appendage, and so the Pennsylvania Department of Transportation leased the trackage from the Estate (its sale was finalized in 1982) and then arranged to have a Delaware Otsego Corporation subsidiary, Lackawaxen and Stourbridge Railroad, run it. When troubles arose with this lessee, state authorities engaged another operator in 1989, and the road became the Stourbridge Railroad Company. Carloads of chemicals, lumber, and paper, nevertheless, continued to move over the route.[9]

While the restructuring of onetime Erie Lackawanna lines attracted a modicum of attention, the activities of the surviving core corporation, Erie Lackawanna Railway, and its successor, Erie Lackawanna Inc., passed mostly unnoticed. But what took place regarding the Estate (1976–92) holds enormous significance. After the company ended its railroad operations, it had generated considerable sums from the sale of retained assets and from a settlement with the federal government for properties conveyed to Conrail. Plus, it settled with prereorganization claimants. The final chapter of Erie ranks as one of the great business closures. "We're driving to the cemetery in a Cadillac," remarked a director of the Estate in 1990.[10]

The happy ending, however, was never assured, or even anticipated. Few observers believed that a deficit-ridden, defunct railroad would pay its obligations to bondholders, taxing authorities, and the like. Such individuals wholly misjudged the Estate's abilities to exit in a brilliant fashion.[11]

Even before Conveyance Day ("C-Day") on April 1, 1976, Thomas Patton and Ralph Tyler had fashioned an effective postconveyance organization. As of December 1, 1976, 40 individuals, possessing an array of talents, remained active in the Midland Building. Full-time employees of the Estate numbered 33, and the others were either "loaned" from Conrail or affiliated with the consulting firm of Wyer, Dick & Co. The trustees selected Milford M. Adams, a veteran financial specialist and Wyer, Dick operative, as administrative officer. A general counsel, manager of properties, secretary-treasurer, and comptroller joined executive officer Harry A. Zilli, Jr., to guide the daily affairs of liquidation. This administrative structure functioned frugally. The trustees, for instance, swiftly removed the remaining employees from the Railroad Retirement system and substituted Social Security protection, which produced a considerable annual savings. And trustees trimmed the staff when conditions justified cutbacks; only 19 employees, including officers, served the Estate by the end of 1982 and the group numbered just 5 by 1990.[12]

While negotiations with federal officials on the value of assets transferred to Conrail constituted the most important task confronting the Estate, the process of disposing of other possessions vitally affected the ultimate settlement. The shell corporation retained approximately 568 route miles of rail line, although slightly more than half remained in operation under federal subsidies to state governments. These functioning lines initially contributed approximately $700,000 annually in rental payments to the Estate's coffers. After conveyances to Conrail, the Estate was also left with about 900 pieces of real estate, amounting to roughly 7,200 acres, which were not considered necessary for railroad purposes. Although the bulk of this surplus land was located in New Jersey, it dotted the company's old rights-of-way from the Bronx to Chicago. This real estate ranged from choice locations along the Hudson River to inaccessible back land in the Allegheny Mountains. Admittedly, Conrail knew what was valuable; former Erie Lackawanna personnel "cherry-picked" some parcels for their new employer. And there was a potpourri of miscellaneous assets, the most valuable of which consisted of rolling stock, marine equipment, track materials, and interests in nineteen subsidiary and affiliated firms, including the Northwestern Mining & Exchange Company, Pennsylvania Coal Company, and Trailer Train Company.[13]

The Estate embraced a sensible approach to liquidation, and with the luxury of time completed its many tasks. Harry Zilli helped to insure a propitious process when he backed creation of the Bankrupt Committee, suggested by John A. Brennan, Jr., a former executive with Trailer Train Company and vice president for finance for the Reading trustee. This informal group consisted of representatives from Erie Lackawanna, Jersey Central, Lehigh Valley, and Reading who regularly discussed their mutual interests, especially in dealing with Conrail. "The Penn Central because of its size felt above us," remembered Zilli, "but it got involved later when it was apparent that the little bankrupts generated some excellent ideas."[14]

Penn Central entered into discussions with the Bankrupt Committee too late on real estate matters. The little bankrupts decided against employing real estate brokers for land sales, but Penn Central did, "and it cost them a bundle." Rather than paying the substantial retainers and commissions, as high as 5 percent (in addition to commissions payable to cooperating brokers, frequently as high as 10 percent), Erie Lackawanna and the others hired their own personnel to sell parcels directly. Edward T. Butler, who originally conducted this work for the Erie Lackawanna Estate, "knew the [railroad's] real estate like the back of his hand" and then sold it intelligently. He and his associates, for instance, used catchall deeds to transfer the least desirable parcels.[15] It was hardly cost-effective to have this land surveyed and to employ the services of title bureaus. "Butler's skills made a lot of money for the Estate," related Eugene Murphy, who later handled the Estate's real-estate af-

The Estate sold hundreds of parcels of former railroad lands, including some that were hardly choice. The old Harlem Transfer property along East 135th Street in the Bronx had by the late 1970's become a dumping site. (Erie Lackawanna Inc.)

fairs. By December 1982, the Estate had sold about 85 percent of its property, and for certain parcels in New Jersey "the company got a premium over the appraised value." Moreover, commissions paid to brokers amounted to less than $200,000, or about 0.3 percent of the total sales of $67,092,000.[16]

The work of liquidation revealed that "there was much more meat on the carcass than anyone really imagined." Illustrations of the hidden worth of the Estate abound. They ran the gamut from its interests in the RESS Realty Company to its possession of historic stock and bond certificates, both of which the Estate adroitly sold.[17]

After the collapse of the Van Sweringen financial empire, part of the brothers' downtown Cleveland real-estate holdings emerged in 1950 as the RESS Realty Company. This firm leased the Guildhall, Republic, and Midland buildings. The latter had housed the headquarters of the railroad since the early 1930's. The four principal tenants of the complex—Republic Steel Corporation, Erie Railroad Company, Sherwin-Williams Company, and Standard Oil Company of Ohio—held the 10,000 outstanding shares of stock; hence the RESS acronym. When Erie Lackawanna entered Conrail, however, its sublease became void. Yet a loophole existed. Under terms of the original agreement, the other major tenants needed to acknowledge the invalidation within a year, but they did not. After the elapsed time, the Estate, namely Ralph Tyler and Harry Zilli, brought the matter to the attention of the other parties and offered them the former railroad's 1,985 shares for $1.9 million. The Estate initially received a submission for $15,000 from the lease-holders, which it rejected as an "insulting offer." Accordingly, the trustees (actually Tyler, because of Thomas Patton's long association with Republic Steel) filed a petition in Judge Robert Krupansky's court naming the principal tenants and RESS as defendants and seeking compensation for their "oppressive, illegal and inequitable action." But Tyler dropped the suit in November 1981, when Sherwin-Williams, which wished to expand its office space, agreed to the asking price. Tyler, who was then recovering from a horseback-riding accident, worked out the legal details from his hospital bed.[18]

The same resourcefulness arose with the sale of old stock and bond certificates. Over the years the company had accumulated thousands of these canceled documents, many of which dated from the nineteenth century and came from such obscure carriers as the Chicago & Erie, Morris & Essex, and Warren railroads. The Estate correctly realized that these certificates possessed more than curiosity value; they fascinated collectors of antique business paper and railroadiana. The Estate sold these artifacts in two gigantic lots by sealed bids and generated more than $100,000. "It was certainly a better deal than throwing them into the Dumpster," chuckled Harry Zilli.[19]

While RESS Realty and canceled certificates generated sizable amounts of cash for the Estate, nothing seemed too insignificant to sell. The company even cashed in on used track ballast. For example, it sold approximately seven miles of this material from the abandoned branch line between the Ohio communities of Marquis and Leetonia to a local contractor for $2,000 in 1980.[20]

⌇

The financial settlement with the federal government on assets transferred to Conrail made liquidation a smashing success. Yet the method of establishing monetary value proved to be complicated and took years to resolve. It was, as one jurist observed, "probably the most gigantic task ever confided to a court." Although the amended Regional Rail Reorganization Act of 1973 (3R Act) created a three-judge Special Court to set valuation of the conveyed properties, the statute had discernible shortcomings. It mandated that the amount of compensation would be based on the "constitutional minimum value," but according to one lawyer, "nobody knew exactly what that meant!" The 3R Act contained more murky stipulations. It required that the court consider "other benefits" that accrued to the bankrupts' estates under the law and told the court to weigh any "compensable unconstitutional erosion" of the estates' assets. Moreover, the measure failed to provide any rules of procedure for determining these valuation figures.[21]

In order to facilitate the process, the three judges, who were named by a multidistrict panel, met before Conveyance Day with a large committee of lawyers who represented both the railroads and the government. These participants worked out the basic procedures to cover matters of conveyance and valuation. The court adopted what Harry G. Silleck, Jr., principal counsel to Erie Lackawanna, described as "a unique procedure." "We were not asked to file a complaint or a petition for our value," noted Silleck. "We were asked to present what turned out to be a more informal document, a statement of position."[22]

The Erie Lackawanna and the other railroad estates responded with dispatch to the judges' request. Once these statements of position were collected, court members decided that they wanted arguments, both written and oral, addressing the fundamental question of what the 3R Act meant by a constitutional minimum value and how that objective might be determined. By the end of 1976 the jurists had received the appropriate briefs and they had heard oral arguments on the matter.[23]

Several important events in the valuation case took place in 1977. The Special Court decided in April that the likelihood of an estate winning compensation on the issue of compensable unconstitutional erosion was "almost hopeless." The court later rendered opinions, prior to the taking of evidence, on the meaning of constitutional minimum value and whether it exceeded "net liquidation value." It deferred clarification, however, on the term "other benefits." The important message that the court sent to the estates was that they would benefit more by *settlement* with the government than by protracted litigation. The court's actions, therefore, prompted preliminary negotiation between representatives of the estates and the government. Yet in the meantime, these estates directed their special counsels and consultants to prepare for the evidentiary hearings, which remained to be scheduled.[24]

The Erie Lackawanna estate toiled diligently for months on evidence to support its contention that it had transferred assets of considerable value to Conrail. At one point Harry Silleck and his principal assistant, John L. Altieri, Jr., whom railroad consultant Charles Shannon called "a terrific lawyer," worked with more than a score of fellow Mudge, Rose, Guthrie & Alexander employees on preparing data. "It was a mammoth job," remembered Silleck, "and we did it well." Indeed, no one in Cleveland quibbled about either the quality of work or the mounting legal bills. "When you hire a top gun in the legal field," argued an Estate associate, "you expect to pay for it." There is no evidence that Mudge, Rose abused the Estate; moreover, the cost of companion work provided by Wyer, Dick, another firm of distinction, hardly smacked of financial exploitation either.[25]

Estate personnel and their legal and consulting helpmates, "who all worked together beautifully," focused on the "rail-use" value of the conveyed property. The Special Court had requested such a determination; in fact, it wanted material in two basic categories, namely rail-use and non-rail-use values, and in that particular order. "One might wonder why companies that could not reorganize on their own as independent carriers would have any rail-use value," remarked Silleck, "but the Special Court concluded that that was not necessarily the case." He added, "We [Erie Lackawanna] could have had rail-use value to other railroads." The Estate subsequently set this figure at approximately $600 million. This amount dramatically exceeded the $53 million, later raised to $55.3 million, which the United States Railway Association claimed was the net liquidation worth.[26]

The Special Court never needed to use a formula to value the Erie Lackawanna's surrendered assets. A series of out-of-court settlements took place between the government and each railroad estate save the Jersey Central. (The Special Court did not terminate its dealings with that firm until 1985.) "Everybody, except CNJ, appreciated the idea of working out a settlement," revealed Harry Silleck, and this "really pleased the judges." This turn of events meant that the Erie Lackawanna Estate avoided an official presentation of a non-rail-use case. "We worked on it, but we never came before the court on this."[27]

Negotiations between the government and the residual estates began in earnest in late 1980, and they continued for more than a year. "The government had sort of a pecking order," argued Silleck. This, in fact, later benefited Erie Lackawanna. The government logically wanted to handle Penn Central first, because it was the largest Conrail component. Since the government had treated "rather kindly" the value assessments of the Lehigh Valley and the Reading, the other principal estates, it anticipated that mutually acceptable agreements would surely follow. Although Erie Lackawanna made known its readiness to enter discussions early, the major difference over price was readily apparent. "What we were asking was significantly higher than what the government had started to value our property," noted Silleck. Thus, the government placed the Erie Lackawanna and the recalcitrant Jersey Central on the back burner.[28]

The leaders of the government's bargaining team had an agenda when it came to conveyance arbitration; namely, they had privately established a dollar range for an acceptable overall settlement. "All the government was trying to do was to push the situation a bit within those limits," contended Silleck. And he made this crucial point: "Remember that the Penn Central case was 85 percent of the total, and they [government negotiators] got that within a range that I think that they were prepared to pay." Since the other estates constituted only a modest part of the whole, government officials showed a willingness to accommodate them, and "they probably paid more than they really wanted to." Thus the Penn Central agreement, reached in late 1980 and consummated on January 15, 1981, augured well for Erie Lackawanna.[29]

Despite this, Erie Lackawanna forces faced some disadvantages when they started to negotiate a dollar price with government representatives during the latter part of 1981. Two matters were troubling. The first might be called the "Chessie affair." Before the creation of Conrail, the Chessie System had expressed keen interest in the Erie Lackawanna east of Akron, and the government too had lobbied hard for such a sale. Although Chessie backed out at the eleventh hour, a cozy relationship had developed between the Chessie and the United States Railway Association. Neither party wanted to give the Erie Lackawanna property much value. Since Erie Lackawanna did not participate in such discussions, that, according to Harry Silleck, "stacked the deck against us as far as coming up with a fair value was concerned." He elaborated by saying, "The whole Chessie affair left a sour taste in our mouths even though it didn't ultimately do us any significant harm." Needless to say, Silleck and his associates worried about the government's use of its Chessie files, with their "wrong or unfair information."[30]

A more serious factor affecting negotiations involved the absence of major tax credits for the Erie Lackawanna Estate. Earlier, Penn Central's keen desire to exploit its considerable tax advantages had aided negotiations; a strong incentive existed for the company to make a deal. But Erie Lackawanna was different. Because the Erie Lackawanna was a wholly-owned subsidiary of the Norfolk & Western between 1968 and 1972, the profitable parent company had wisely used its affiliate's tax losses and investment tax credits in its consolidated federal returns. In fact, the N&W paid the Estate $5.5 million following a settlement on this tax issue in August 1976. "So Erie Lackawanna did not have any losses to give a value to and develop for the benefit of creditors," argued Silleck. "This had an impact on our thinking from day one as to what should happen to the company." Without major tax-loss carryforwards, and with no other property around with which to build an ongoing business, the Estate sought to liquidate. Yet the government did not initially make a distinction for Erie Lackawanna, "even though [it] knew very well that the Erie Lackawanna would not have that additional element of value." Eventually, however, the Estate prevailed. "It took a while in these settlement discussions to bring home to the government that we were somewhat of a different beast than the other companies," remembered Silleck, "and that we had to have a value that we could justify to pay off creditors."[31]

Actually, as Harry Silleck suggested, the Erie Lackawanna conceivably turned a couple of lemons into lemonade; that is, the Estate ultimately profited from both the Chessie affair and the tax issue. Government representatives likely became sensitive during the deliberations to the unfairness of their actions when they unsuccessfully attempted to sell part of the railroad at a fire-sale price. Also, they apparently failed to grasp fully the importance of the tax credit issue, and subsequently may have softened their position.[32]

While these matters probably aided the Estate, other factors came into play. The government's favorable conclusion in the Penn Central case meant much. The Estate profited from excellent legal and consulting assistance, and it did not wilt during the bargaining process. Thomas Patton wished to battle the government. "Tom was determined to get every penny that he thought the company deserved." Fortunately, his will prevailed. Fellow trustee Ralph Tyler was more anxious to compromise, in part "because he thought the value was not as great as Tom believed." If Tyler had his way, the Estate, according to Harry Zilli, "would have settled for considerably less."[33]

The Erie Lackawanna Estate scored a material victory, and those individuals who participated in its quest for monetary justice felt satisfied. On October 19, 1981, the Estate and the government agreed orally to a settlement of $361,128,000, which both parties formalized several weeks later. This substantial amount consisted of $229,007,000 in principal and $132,121,000 in interest, which was compounded at 8 percent from April 1, 1976. Still, these final figures were considerably less than the estimate made by Wyer, Dick. When based on the formula of original cost less depreciation and physical deterioration, the value exceeded $400 million.[34]

There were other monies that would be forthcoming to the Estate. The government also approved payment for two largely owned subsidiaries, Rochester & Genesee Valley Railroad and Lackawanna & Wyoming Valley Railway. The former generated $1,245,000 ($790,000 in principal and $455,000 in interest) for the Estate, and the latter produced $320,000 ($203,000 in principal and $117,000 in interest). No one questioned the fairness of these settlements.[35]

<hr />

Even with a favorable agreement with the federal government, the process of liquidation did not come to an end. The work of the Estate continued for another decade, although initially its leadership anticipated only a five-year period. These activities, however, would involve a new corporate framework. On November 30, 1982, Judge Krupansky, who retained jurisdiction over the case even though he by then served on the Sixth Circuit Court of Appeals in Cincinnati, approved the painstakingly crafted "Trustees' Plan of Reorganization." This document, originally submitted to the court on December 21, 1978, and revised a year later, required extensive hearings and judicial deliberation. It produced some important changes. Most evident was the Estate's altered name: Erie Lackawanna Railway Company became Erie Lackawanna Inc. The reorganization likewise adjusted the bureaucracy of this Delaware-chartered firm. Most notably, Thomas Patton and Ralph Tyler assumed titles of co-chairman and co–chief executive officer and director. Although they remained firmly in charge, their trusteeship formally closed with the corporate death of Erie Lackawanna Railway. Patton and Tyler also dominated the newly created board of directors, which included a third member, Walter H. MacDonald, retired senior vice president of the Federal Reserve Bank of Cleveland, who was described as a "team player." Harry Zilli remained as president.[36]

Adoption of the reorganization plan also meant an appropriate structure for satisfying creditors. At the heart of the arrangement, Erie Lackawanna Inc. would award secured holders, owners of first and second mortgage bonds, 100 cents on the dollar and *all* accrued interest from when payments had stopped in the early 1970's until December 1982. (Comparable holders of Penn Central bonds received only the face value of their securities.) In lieu of an early cash payment, unsecured creditors of the Estate, who were mostly possessed income debentures, received one share of Erie Lackawanna Inc. common for every $100 of obligation. At the end of 1984, the company had 1,520 shareholders who owned 91.5 percent of the shares issuable under the plan. The outstanding common stock of Erie Lackawanna Railway, which was owned totally by the Norfolk & Western, became worthless, but that did not prevent the Roanoke-based railroad from donating these shares to the graduate business school of the University of Virginia. The company did so both for tax purposes and to end officially its ties to Erie Lackawanna Railway.[37]

The start of this final chapter of Erie revealed that not all investors had played their financial cards in the same way. Some had been more skilled than others. Those who kept their senior bonds did well. This meant that a $1,000 bond typically paid its face value plus $300 to $400 of interest, depending when the railroad had stopped such payments. But five of the six principal institutional investors, all life-insurance companies, had liquidated their bond holdings in the mid-1970's, and they sustained major losses. "They unloaded for about ten cents on the dollar," noted an Estate director. Yet the largest bondholder, Metropolitan Life Insurance Company, held firm. It may have been more than coincidental that Thomas Patton served on its board of directors. Although Patton denied influencing the company's policy—"I never told Metropolitan Life what to do with its investments"—he may have conveyed the merits of retention. Irrespective of Patton's action, Metropolitan Life protected millions of dollars of its policyholders' assets and reaped the benefits of the successful liquidation.[38]

It was the speculator, not the traditional investor, who eventually profited the most from the Estate's good work. This breed of capitalist found Erie Lackawanna securities attractive. "Railroads, including the Erie, tend to be asset-heavy," noted one large player, "and these assets tend to be heavily undervalued." And there was another appealing feature. "Since bankruptcy is a process, it allows the speculator greater security, because he does not have to worry about some management change that would affect the whole condition of the company." Yet the recognition of a potential bonanza occurred slowly. Early on, Wall Street traders concluded that the unsecured securities were "under water." In fact, $1,000 income debentures as late as 1980 were selling for about ten cents on the dollar. "Nobody thought that either the face value or the interest on them would ever be paid." But under the 1982 reorganization plan the $1,000 debenture, with an accumulated interest of $700, yielded seventeen shares of Erie Lackawanna Inc. common.[39]

<hr />

Once Erie Lackawanna Inc. emerged, it moved with dispatch to meet its obligations. A priority was payment of back real-estate taxes. Although the Estate had avoided these bills during the bankruptcy, these responsibilities remained. On December 1, 1982, the first day the new Erie Lackawanna conducted business, it paid out of its master trust fund nearly $57 million in state and local tax claims. This positive action became front-page news throughout the former railroad's service territory—and rightfully so. Municipalities, school districts, and libraries in Cuyahoga County (Cleveland), Ohio, for example, received more than $2 million in obligations on 89 parcels of real estate dating back to the second half of the 1971 tax year.[40]

In addition to tax settlements, Erie Lackawanna Inc. pushed forward to satisfy creditors. As indicated, secured bondholders were to receive cash and unsecured ones were to have stock. Payments to the former began on December 21, 1982, and by the close of 1983, the company had settled claims of $403,858,000. This included outlays of $322,180,000 in cash and issuance of 816,781 shares of capital stock.[41]

Several tasks, however, remained to be completed after 1983. Additional bonds were outstanding and needed to be redeemed. There was also the task of disposing of the last assets, which were mostly pieces of real estate. The company sold 107 parcels in 1984 for $1,103,000, but continued to hold about 100 more with a book value of approximately $2.5 million. It was 1989 before all this land had been liquidated. Then there were lawsuits that stemmed largely from former employees of the railroad and subsidiary mining firms. They usually involved asbestosis, but also black lung disease and hearing damage. Yet they had little direct impact on the company's reserves. The courts emphasized that the Estate operated under a liquidating plan of reorganization and this precluded most claims. Still, the company lost on this matter. Conrail and certain post-consummation claimants argued before Judge Krupansky that the Estate was liable under "certain circumstances."

But Krupansky disagreed. The protesters, however, appealed his ruling in 1987. What troubled the Estate was the timing of this litigation. Explained Harry Silleck: "Under these circumstances, although [we were] confident that Erie would ultimately win approval, the Erie Board of Directors decided that a settlement would be in the best interest of Erie stockholders because it would permit a prompt distribution of $115 per share. Under the settlement Erie paid $2.4 million and the appeal was withdrawn. . . . [The Estate] estimated that, if it lost the appeal, post-consummation claims could ultimately entail a liability of more than $10 million, perhaps substantially more, particularly since no one could tell how many additional claims might be filed."[42]

The big challenge came not from claimants but from the Internal Revenue Service. Disputes between the Estate and the IRS lingered until nearly the final days. The principal contentions between the two parties centered on the tax consequences of the conveyance. The company pursued a sensible response, wisely employing the talent of Mudge, Rose lawyers. Specifically, disputes arose over the firm's federal income tax return for 1982. While agreements were soon struck on several points, two matters were not easily resolved. One involved the company taking a tax benefit of $14.7 million when it used certain tax credits granted it by special federal legislation in 1980. But the IRS later decided that the Estate could not make this deduction against interest income that it had received from the valuation settlement. Furthermore, the IRS sought to increase taxable income for 1982 on other grounds. According to the Estate, the IRS believed that it could do so "because of alleged income arising from the exchange of certain obligations of the Company and of claims for certain other expenses deducted from income in 1982 and prior years for stock of the Company." The tax implications of this reasoning meant an additional obligation of $14.1 million.[43]

Members of the Estate's Board of Directors responded prudently. Although the IRS's position troubled them, they complied with the monetary demands. But the directors then turned to the appeals process. "We don't intend to lose this," was the public pronouncement made by Harry Zilli, and the Estate did not. Its tax strategy eventually led to a sizable financial gain. In January 1991, shortly before the Estate's demise, it received an award from the government that boosted its net assets by $40.2 million. Remarked Richard M. Gotterman, who held nearly one percent of the stock, "[M]y compliments on the IRS settlement. You did everything the shareholders could have expected."[44]

⌒

The considerable progress made by the Estate attracted notice in investment circles. When shares of the new Erie Lackawanna Inc. first traded over the counter, the national business press highlighted the firm. The NASDAQ listing brought more than publicity; public trading allowed stockholders to "cash in" instead of waiting for a far-off time when an unknown amount of liquidating distributions would occur. Of course, observers remained interested in the affairs of the Estate. A feature story in *Barron's* in 1984 encouraged owners of these shares. "Now, what's caught the eye of . . . investment pros is that a whole lot of that cash—with luck, on a per share basis, considerably more than the current stock price—may be left over after everyone's paid off." But this writer offered a pertinent caveat: "It depends on how successful Erie Lackawanna is in doing battle with the Internal Revenue Service. And that's never a sure thing."[45]

The happenings at the Estate in the early 1980's lured a group of investors who wanted to redirect the process of liquidation. While this clique lacked an official name, it was occasionally identified as the "Hendry bunch," after its driving force, Bruce E. Hendry, senior vice president of Craig-Hallum, Inc., a small Minneapolis-based investment firm. "He was no genius," argued an associate, "but he was quick . . . , a sharp cookie." Shortly before the creation of Erie Lackawanna Inc., Hendry and his allies decided to "take a swing" at the Estate.[46]

The Hendry bunch first wanted to gain control or at least have muscle on the board of directors. The group claimed support of about 38 percent of the shareholders, although it was unlikely that it had even half that number. "Hendry had gone around to various owners of Erie securities and collected information about them on filing cards which he put into a recipe box." When Hendry confronted Thomas Patton and Ralph Tyler, "who weren't anxious for battle," an agreement was reached. "Tom, especially, because of his position in the community, didn't want publicity of a fight in the local newspapers." The deal Hendry cut in 1983 led to board expansion by two that year and added another position in 1984, which would guarantee his control. Although Patton and Tyler bitterly opposed one proposed candidate, "a real gadfly," whom the Hendry bunch then dropped, they endorsed William R. Dimeling and Bernard V. Donahue. Dimeling served as president of the Great Eastern Coal Corporation and had extensive business and investment experience. Indeed, because of his earlier dealings with the Estate, Harry Zilli had suggested his appointment. Dimeling, like Hendry, was a "real salesman," but he was also "politically great" and "well connected." Moreover, Dimeling impressed Patton and Tyler. Donahue, part of the Hendry bunch, was a former Internal Revenue Service agent and a private investor from St. Paul, Minnesota. He had begun to acquire the railroad's unsecured bonds on his own during the mid-1970's. Hendry himself joined the board in May 1984.[47]

Bruce Hendry seemed destined to have a major impact on Erie Lackawanna Inc. Quipped Bernard Donahue, "I told Hendry that he should have that recipe box gold-plated!" By 1985 Hendry not only controlled the board of directors, but served as president and chief executive officer. He replaced Harry Zilli, who took the title of executive vice president and treasurer. Thomas Patton and Ralph Tyler became vice presidents; they no longer served as co-chairmen and co–chief executive officers.[48]

Hendry wanted to keep the company alive. He believed that he could take the millions of dollars of the Estate's assets and leverage them by a factor of ten or so for business acquisitions and investments. "Hendry wanted money for fun," claimed an associate. Remarked another, "Hendry thought that he could simply make more money for the shareholders through various investments." Yet Hendry had no experience in such ventures; he was merely a promoter. But Hendry's game plan was common. The other bankrupt carriers, including Jersey Central, entered nonrailroad activities to exploit their considerable cash assets.[49]

The Hendry agenda fizzled in 1986. The greatest blow involved his unsuccessful effort to amend the charter to permit Erie Lackawanna Inc. to become something other than a company in liquidation. If 75 percent of the stockholders agreed, the change could be made. Proxies to permit continuation were printed, but "they were pulled at the last minute" before the annual stockholders' meeting in June because the scheme lacked support. Shareholders, however, approved additional seats to the board of directors. The body would then have seven members: William Dimeling, Bernard Donahue, Bruce Hendry, Walter MacDonald, Thomas Patton, Thomas H. Roulston, and Harry Zilli. Roulston headed Roulston & Company, a Cleveland brokerage firm, and his company represented several English insurance companies that held about 12 percent of the outstanding stock.[50]

The Hendry interlude subsequently ended. A special meeting of the Board of Directors on July 29, 1987, spearheaded by Thomas Roulston, voted to remove Hendry as president and chief executive officer because of his efforts to make Erie Lackawanna Inc. permanent. Harry Zilli became president again as well as chief executive officer and treasurer. The feeling shared by directors and officers was that it would be foolish for the company to remain in existence. "The assets belonged to people who knew how to manage money," argued Bernard Donahue, "and they wanted them." Furthermore, the firm lacked the tax credits the other estates enjoyed. The company then turned in its corporate charter to Delaware officials in 1988. Delaware law, however, required that a firm remain in existence for three years after such a surrender.[51]

Stockowners finally started to receive their payout checks in 1988. "The long march was about over." In 1988, 1990, and 1991, the company made three partial liquidating distributions, with court approval, which aggregated $179 per share. In order to terminate the firm's affairs by December 31, 1991, Judge Krupansky approved a fourth and final liquidating distribution in two parts. This included a $9.75 payment per share, which the firm made on January 2, 1992, and the conveyance of the remaining assets of Erie Lackawanna Inc. to the Erie Lackawanna Inc. Liquidating Trust "for the benefit of such stockholders, who thereupon became the holders of the beneficial interests in the Trust, subject to the payment of liabilities to the extent provided for in the Liquidating Trust Agreement and of the expenses of the Trust." The Trust then paid stockholders $1.47 per share on August 18, 1992, thus giving them a total compensation of $190.22 per share. The corporate arrangement had a single trustee, Harry Zilli, but no employees, and its place of business was no longer the Midland Building but the Zilli home in North Olmsted, Ohio, a Cleveland suburb.[52]

By the autumn of 1992, the remnants of the Erie Railroad had mostly disappeared. The Trust continued and only one claim remained to be settled. This unfinished business involved a steam locomotive (ex–Chicago, Burlington & Quincy 4-8-4, number 5632), which Richard Jensen, a Chicago railroad enthusiast, owned. A dispute between Jensen and officials of the Chicago & Western Indiana Railroad (C&WI), where number 5632 had been stored, led to the scrapping of the locomotive in the early 1970's. Jensen sued the C&WI for damages and won, but appeals and other legal machinations dragged on for years. Although Jensen died in 1991, the Erie Lackawanna Estate shared a small financial liability because of its former interest in the C&WI.[53]

When the Trust dissolves and the Jensen case is settled, the Erie Lackawanna will at last take its place in American railroad history. But its memory will likely continue for a long time. In a way, the Erie, the Lackawanna, and the Erie Lackawanna railroads have already been institutionalized. A group of rail buffs formed the Erie Lackawanna Historical Society (ELHS) in 1971, and soon the organization claimed hundreds of members and sponsored annual meetings. The ELHS also produced publications, including *The Diamond* magazine, and launched an archives. The appearance of pictorial books and videos and the preservation of former depots and rolling stock have further called attention to this "fallen flag" carrier.

While Erie Lackawanna ended its corporate life in grand style and its memory will surely survive, a vital question remains. Could the railroad, or at least its main line, have lived on? Evidence can be marshaled to suggest a positive answer *if* certain events had occurred earlier. The company's entry into Conrail took place several years before the impact of a monumental piece of federal legislation, the Staggers Act. This 1980 measure, which was the Carter administration's effort at partial deregulation of the railroad industry, created a better regulatory environment for carriers. Indeed, Conrail's losses ended almost immediately. Erie Lackawanna would likely have benefited from this statute as well. Surely, too, the firm would have gained from a recent technological revolution of sorts, containerization of shipments. This railroad, with its wide clearances and lack of major online points of congestion, was wonderfully suited for such traffic. In fact, it was initially the only line with double-stack clearances. The increasing numbers of stack (container) trains on the historic Southern Tier route indicate its physical and strategic desirability. Since the advent of Conrail there has also been a dramatic change in labor work rules. One trend has been toward smaller crews, often only two people operating freight trains. This phenomenon would have been a boon to the balance sheet. Even though "trucks put the railroads in the Northeast into a bind," increased instances of gridlock on roadways, including interstate highways, would likewise portend well for an Erie Lackawanna. Significantly, Conrail, an investor-owned corporation since 1987, was prospering by the early 1990's. "[The carrier] is starting to look like something rarely seen since the Roaring '20s: a growth-company railroad," concluded a reporter for the *Wall Street Journal* in late 1992. Deregulation, technological betterments, greater economy and efficiency, and marketing savvy explain this optimism. When related to Erie Lackawanna, the variable is timing; conditions in the 1990's hardly replicated those of the 1970's.[54]

The fate of Erie Lackawanna gladdened bondholders and other creditors, but it probably damaged the larger public interest. Conceivably, an independent Erie Lackawanna could have improved transportation in the East. Demise of the Friendly Service Route meant that the region may have lost a major catalyst for innovation. That had been, after all, the tradition of the railroad since its beginnings. "There is no doubt that EL, with its clearances, would have been first to put on stack trains," contended William D. Burt, an intermodal expert and longtime student of the Erie. "I can testify from personal knowledge that UPS was in the late 1970's and early 1980's extremely interested in finding a way to operate a New York–Chicago train consisting of RoadRailer equipment [truck trailers on flanged wheels] and was denied the opportunity to do so by Conrail."[55]

If the Erie Lackawanna had survived as a railroad into the 1990's, it would have been a different operation. Imaginably, stack and RoadRailer trains, handled by cost-efficient crews, would have raced between its two great terminals. But the company, of course, failed. Yet in the act of burial it shed forever its legendary image of Weary Erie and Erie Lack-of-Money. No wonder Thomas Patton concluded, "I don't see that we could have done anything differently. The story has a happy ending."[56]

REFERENCE MATTER

NOTES

Chapter 1

1. Charles F. Adams, Jr., and Henry Adams, *Chapters of Erie and Other Essays* (Boston: James R. Osgood, 1871), pp. 4, 137; "Charter of the New York & Erie Railroad Company," in *Miscellaneous Reports, Addresses & Papers, 1832–1845* (New York: New-York & Erie Railroad Company, 1832), pp. 1–6.

2. Carl W. Condit, *The Port of New York: A History of the Rail and Terminal System from the Beginnings to Pennsylvania Station* (Chicago: University of Chicago Press, 1980), pp. 57–59; Robert E. Woodruff, *Erie Railroad—Its Beginnings! 1851* (Princeton, N.J.: The Newcomen Society, 1945), pp. 9, 11. Although completion of the New-York & Erie marked a major achievement in development of long-distance rail service, other strategic routes soon opened. The Philadelphia-based Pennsylvania Railroad reached Pittsburgh and the Ohio River in 1852, and also in that year the Baltimore & Ohio Railroad connected Wheeling, also on the Ohio River, with Baltimore. Then in 1853, the New York Central Railroad emerged from consolidation of several smaller roads and offered service from New York City to Buffalo.

3. *Report of the Directors of the New-York & Erie Railroad Co. to the Stockholders, December 24, 1851* (New-York & Erie Railroad Company, 1851), p. 3; John S. Bell, "When Erie Was a Youngster," *The Erie Railroad Employees' Magazine* 1 (October 1905): 187–89; John F. Stover, *Iron Road to the West: American Railroads in the 1850's* (New York: Columbia University Press, 1978), p. 49; New York, Lake Erie & Western public timetable, July 1886; "Scenery on the Erie Railroad," *Harper's New Monthly Magazine* 1 (July 1850): 212–15.

4. *"Appendix" to Second Report of the Directors of the New-York and Erie Railroad Company, to the Stockholders* (New York: Egbert Hedge, 1841), p. 8. See also George

W. Hilton, *American Narrow Gauge Railroads* (Stanford, Calif.: Stanford University Press, 1990), p. 31.

5. Hilton, *American Narrow Gauge Railroads*, pp. 15–16; "*Appendix*," p. 8; Edward Hungerford, *Men of Erie: A Story of Human Effort* (New York: Random House, 1946), pp. 53–54.

The South Carolina Rail Road led in construction of a right-of-way on stilts. It installed 136 miles of trestle work between 1830 and 1833. "The structure deteriorated rapidly, and minor derailments almost by definition became disasters" (Hilton, *American Narrow Gauge Railroads*, p. 120).

6. Edward Harold Mott, *Between the Ocean and the Lakes: The Story of Erie* (New York: John S. Collins, 1899), pp. 323–24.

7. Hungerford, *Men of Erie*, pp. 93–94; C. R. Fitch to W. F. Merrill, February 3, 1896, Erie Lackawanna Railway papers, The University of Akron Archives, Akron, Ohio, hereafter cited as EL papers.

The company for decades flaunted "Famous Erie Firsts." In a brochure, *First in Freight: The Story of a Great Railroad*, published in 1940, they were noted as follows:

> First railroad in the world of over 400 miles in length—1851.
> First trunk line railroad to link the Atlantic seaboard and the Great Lakes.
> First railroad to use six-foot gauge track—the broadest on the American continent in 1851.
> First railroad to use the telegraph for directing train operations.
> First railroad to transport California fresh fruit to the New York market.
> First railroad to use air brakes.

8. Hungerford, *Men of Erie*, pp. 123–35; Adams, *Chapters of Erie*, p. 4; Condit, *The Port of New York*, p. 57; Julius Grodinsky, *Jay Gould: His Business Career, 1867–1892* (Philadelphia: University of Pennsylvania Press, 1957), p. 27; Robert Greenhalgh Albion, *The Rise of New York Port, 1815–1860* (New York: Charles Scribner's Sons, 1939), p. 385; Harry H. Pierce, *Railroads of New York: A Study of Government Aid, 1826–1875* (Cambridge, Mass.: Harvard University Press, 1953), p. 13; *Report of the Directors of the New York and Erie Railroad Company to The Stockholders* (New York: Printed by Order of the Directors, 1853), p. 8; interview with Milton G. McInnes, Southbury, Connecticut, June 5, 1989.

9. Maury Klein, *The Life and Legend of Jay Gould* (Baltimore: The Johns Hopkins University Press, 1986), p. 77; Hungerford, *Men of Erie*, pp. 143–48; Grodinsky, *Jay Gould*, p. 30.

10. Mott, *Between the Ocean and the Lakes*, pp. 147–62; Condit, *The Port of New York*, p. 61; Klein, *The Life and Legend of Jay Gould*, pp. 76–87, 92–98, quotation on p. 86.

11. Klein, *The Life and Legend of Jay Gould*, pp. 88–102, 115–16, 119–21; Grodinsky, *Jay Gould*, p. 46.

12. Klein, *The Life and Legend of Jay Gould*, pp. 121–26, 132–33; Grodinsky, *Jay Gould*, pp. 56–69; George H. Minor, *The Erie System* (New York: Erie Railroad Company, 1938), pp. 383–94.

13. *Taintor's Route & City Guides: Erie Railway* (New York: Taintor Brothers,

1872), n.p.; Andrew M. Modelski, *Railroad Maps of North America: The First Hundred Years* (Washington, D.C.: Library of Congress, 1984), pp. 98–99.

14. Hungerford, *Men of Erie*, pp. 200–210; *History of Allen County, Ohio* (Chicago: Warner, Beer & Company, 1885), p. 399.

15. Minor, *The Erie System*, p. 119–23; *Plan and Agreement for the Reorganization of the Erie System* (New York: J. P. Morgan & Co., 1895), pp. 419–24; *Poor's Manual of Railroads of the United States* (New York: H. V. & H. W. Poor, 1897), pp. 419–24; Mott, *Between the Ocean and the Lakes*, pp. 293, 484.

16. *First Annual Report of the Board of Directors of the Erie Railroad Company* (New York: Erie Railroad Company, 1896), p. 49; *Tenth Annual Report of the Board of Directors of the Erie Railroad Company* (New York: Erie Railroad Company, 1905), p. 47; George Heckman Burgess to Eben B. Thoman, June 19, 1900, EL papers.

17. *Fifth Annual Report of the Board of Directors of the Erie Railroad Company* (New York: Erie Railroad Company, 1900), pp. 67; *Third Annual Report of the Board of Directors of the Erie Railroad Company* (New York: Erie Railroad Company, 1898), p. 11; William D. Burt, "Erie's River Line: Leap for the Brass Ring," *The Diamond* 5 (1990): 5.

18. *Travelers' Official Guide to the Railway and Steam Navigation Lines in the United States, Canada and Mexico* (New York: National Railway Publication Company, June 1899), pp. 142–43, 190, 340; "The Erie's Service First Class," *The Erie Railroad Employees' Magazine* 3 (March 1907): 16; *Third Annual Report*, p. 7; New York, Lake Erie & Western public timetable, July 1886.

19. Elbert Hubbard, *The Romance of the Railroad* (East Aurora, N.Y.: The Roycrofters, 1910), pp. 18–19; James J. Hill to John K. Cowen, October 30, 1898, James J. Hill papers, James J. Hill Reference Library, St. Paul, Minnesota.

20. *A New Chapter of Erie* (New York: Jas. H. Oliphant, 1924), pp. 5–13; William D. Burt, "Erie's River Line: Long Summer on the Cutoff," *The Diamond* 6 (1991): 5–7; Hungerford, *Men of Erie*, pp. 224–34; *Erie Railroad: Showing Changes from 1901 to 1914, Inclusive* (n.d., n.p.), p. 3; William Pickett Helm, "You Got Another Papa on the Erie Line," *Collier's* 84 (December 28, 1929): 12.

Steam locomotives are classified by their wheel arrangement in a system created by F. M. Whyte of the New York Central Railroad at the turn of the century. The first digit represents the number of leading wheels, the second the number of driving wheels, and the third the number of trailing wheels. Thus a 2-6-0 is a locomotive with two leading wheels, six driving wheels, and no trailing wheels.

21. Maury Klein, *Union Pacific: The Rebirth, 1894–1969* (New York: Doubleday, 1989), p. 178; *Thirteenth Annual Report of the Board of Directors of the Erie Railroad Company* (New York: Erie Railroad Company, 1908), pp. 16–17; Hungerford, *Men of Erie*, p. 219; *Twenty-fourth Report of the Board of Directors of the Erie Railroad Company* (New York: Erie Railroad Company, 1919), pp. 10–11.

22. *Erie Railroad Company: Its Prospects under Van Sweringen Management* (New York: Wood, Struthers, 1927), pp. 1–2; McInnes interview.

23. Henry S. Sturgis to Frederick Underwood, March 27, 1926, EL papers.

24. Ibid.; Hungerford, *Men of Erie*, pp. 235–36.

25. Ian S. Haberman, *The Van Sweringens of Cleveland: The Biography of an Empire* (Cleveland: The Western Reserve Historical Society, 1979), pp. 50–64; James Toman, *The Shaker Heights Rapid Transit* (Glendale, Calif.: Interurban Press, 1990), pp. 11–12; Herbert H. Harwood, Jr., "Oris Paxton Van Sweringen [and] Mantis James Van Sweringen," in Keith L. Bryant, Jr., ed., *Railroads in the Age of Regulation, 1900–1980* (New York: Facts-on-File Publications, 1988), pp. 450–53.

The Van Swerigens did not coin the "Old Reliable" phrase. It was in use as early as the 1880's. See *Railway Conductors' Monthly* 1 (August 1, 1884): 382.

26. *The Erie Railroad Company*, pp. 1, 3; Helm, "You Got Another Papa on the Erie Line," pp. 12–13, 36.

27. Harwood, "Oris Paxton Van Sweringen [and] Mantis James Van Sweringen," pp. 454–56; Richard Saunders, *The Railroad Mergers and the Coming of Conrail* (Westport, Conn.: Greenwood Press, 1978), pp. 48–49.

28. John W. Barriger to Arthur E. Baylis, July 13, 1975, Barriger Collection, Mercantile Library, St. Louis, Missouri, hereafter cited as Barriger Collection.

29. "Memo on the Van Sweringen Railroads," (n.p., n.d.), pp. 1–6, Barriger Collection.

30. Harwood, "Oris Paxton Van Sweringen [and] Mantis James Van Sweringen," p. 465.

31. Ibid.; Haberman, *The Van Sweringens of Cleveland*, pp. 105–20.

The unusual spelling of Allegheny commemorated Alleghany, Virginia, the summit on the Chesapeake & Ohio main line over the Allegheny mountains and the highest point on the Van Sweringen system.

32. "Executive Changes in Van Sweringen System," *Railway Age* 81 (December 25, 1926): 1256–57; Hungerford, *Men of Erie*, p. 236.

33. *Erie Railroad Company*, pp. 4–6.

34. *Thirty-third Report of the Board of Directors of the Erie Railroad Company* (New York: Erie Railroad Company, 1928), p. 13.

35. Interview with Jervis Langdon, Jr., Akron, Ohio, April 26, 1990; Frederick Westing and Alvin F. Staufer, *Erie Power: Steam and Diesel Locomotives of the Erie Railroad from 1840 to 1970* (Medina, Ohio: Alvin F. Staufer, 1970), pp. 166–67, 169; Hungerford, *Men of Erie*, pp. 242–43; *Thirty-fourth Report of the Board of Directors of the Erie Railroad Company* (New York: Erie Railroad Company, 1929), p. 33.

36. Interview with M. Fred Coffman, Akron, Ohio, November 4, 1988; Erie public timetable, June 7, 1931, pp. 41–42.

37. "Erie Inaugurates 25-Hour New York–Chicago Passenger Service," *Railway Age* (June 8, 1929): 1331–33; Roger Reynolds, *Famous American Trains and Their Stories* (New York: Grosset and Dunlap, 1934), pp. 40–42; Peter T. Maiken, *Night Trains: The Pullman System in the Golden Years of American Rail Travel* (Chicago: Lakme Press, 1989), p. 27; interview with Thurmon Poe, Huntington, Indiana, May 15, 1990.

38. *Who's Who in Railroading in North America* (New York: Simmons-Boardman Publishing, 1946), p. 173; McInnes interview.

39. Interview with George C. Frank, Sr., Boca Raton, Florida, December 26, 1989; "Erie Railroad," February 1, 1938, pp. 2, 17–19, Barriger Collection; *Forty-*

second Report of the Board of Directors, Erie Railroad Company (New York and Cleveland: Erie Railroad Company, 1937), p. 14; *Forty-fourth Report of the Board of Directors of Erie Railroad Company* (New York and Cleveland: Erie Railroad Company, 1939), p. 18; Frank interview.

40. McInnes interview; *Thirty-eighth Report of the Board of Directors of Erie Railroad* (New York and Cleveland: Erie Railroad Company, 1933), pp. 6–7.

41. Coffman interview.

42. *Forty-first Report of the Board of Directors of Erie Railroad Company* (New York and Cleveland: Erie Railroad Company, 1936), pp. 6–7; *First in Freight.*

43. *Erie Railroad Company*, pp. 19–20; G. J. Weihofen to author, May 12, 1991; "Coach Luncheons at Popular Prices" (New York: Erie Railroad Company, n.d.), "4-Way Tours," (New York: Erie Railroad Company, n.d.), p. 4.

44. McInnes interview.

45. Hungerford, *Men of Erie*, p. 238; interview with J. D. Allen, Cleveland, Ohio, May 10, 1989; David M. Vrooman, *Daniel Willard and the Progressive Management on the Baltimore & Ohio Railroad* (Columbus: Ohio State University Press, 1991), pp. xi–xvi.

Chapter 2

1. *Erie Railroad Magazine* 33 (February 1938): 8.

2. Interview with Milton G. McInnes, Southbury, Connecticut, June 5, 1989; Patrick D. Reagon, "Recession of 1937–1938," in James S. Olson, ed., *Historical Dictionary of the New Deal: From Inauguration to Preparation for War* (Westport, Conn.: Greenwood Press, 1985), pp. 408–10; *Railway Age* 104 (January 22, 1938): 197.

3. *Forty-third Report of the Board of Directors of Erie Railroad Company* (New York and Cleveland: Erie Railroad Company, 1938), p. 6; *Forty-fourth Report of the Board of Directors of Erie Railroad Company* (New York and Cleveland: Erie Railroad Company, 1939), p. 8.

4. *Railway Age* 104 (January 22, 1938): 197; *Railway Age* 104 (January 8, 1938): 133.

5. Minutes of the Board of Directors, Erie Railroad Company, December 30, 1937, Pennsylvania State Archives, Harrisburg, Pennsylvania, hereafter cited as Erie minutes.

6. The Reconstruction Finance Corporation generously aided the Erie; RFC loans amounted to $20,183,000 during the 1930's.

7. Erie minutes, January 3, 1938.

8. Jesse H. Jones to Charles Denney, January 2, 1938, in Erie minutes.

9. Erie minutes, January 3, 1938.

10. Ibid.; Jesse H. Jones, *Fifty Billion Dollars: My Thirteen Years with the RFC, 1932–1945* (New York: Macmillan, 1951), p. 143.

11. Erie minutes, January 18, 1938; Jones, *Fifty Billion Dollars*, p. 143; *Railway Age* 104 (January 22, 1939): 197.

12. *Railway Age* 104 (January 15, 1938): 168; *Forty-fourth Report*, p. 7.

13. Interview with Marianne Millikin Hadden, Shaker Heights, Ohio, March 30, 1989.

14. George W. Hilton, *Monon Route* (San Diego, Calif.: Howell-North, 1978), p. 153.

15. *Historical Statistics of the United States: Colonial Times to 1957* (Washington, D.C.: U.S. Department of Commerce, 1960), p. 435; Joseph Borkin, *Robert R. Young, the Populist of Wall Street* (New York: Harper & Row, 1969), pp. 116–17; H. Craig Miner, *The Rebirth of Missouri Pacific, 1956–1983* (College Station: Texas A&M University Press, 1983), pp. 6–7.

16. Henry S. Sturgis, *A New Chapter of Erie: The Story of Erie's Reorganization, 1938–1941* (privately printed, 1948), pp. 3–4.

17. Ibid., pp. 7–8.

18. Ibid., pp. 8–9.

19. Ibid., pp. 10, 14; *Plan of Reorganization (Filed by Debtor), December 19, 1938* (Cleveland: Davis, Polk, Wardwell, Gardiner & Reed), pp. 27–54; *Stenographers' Minutes Before The Interstate Commerce Commission, Finance Docket No. 11915* (Washington, D.C.: Interstate Commerce Commission, 1939), pp. 1022–23.

20. Sturgis, *A New Chapter of Erie*, pp. 15–20.

21. Interview with Jervis Langdon, Jr., Akron, Ohio, April 26, 1990. See also Stuart Leuthner, *The Railroaders* (New York: Random House, 1983), p. 127.

22. *Summary of Erie Railroad Company Reorganization before the Interstate Commerce Commission, Finance Docket No. 11915* (Cleveland: Erie Railroad Company, 1942).

23. Ibid.; "Shareholders Share in Proposed Erie Plan," *Railway Age* 107 (November 18, 1939): 317–18; "I.C.C. Hears Erie Oral Argument," *Railway Age* 107 (November 18, 1939): 802–3; "Commission Approves Erie Reorganization Plan," *Railway Age* 108 (April 20, 1940): 712–14.

24. *Summary of Erie Railroad Company Reorganization*; Sturgis, *A New Chapter of Erie*, p. 29.

25. *Forty-sixth Report of the Board of Directors of Erie Railroad Company* (New York and Cleveland: Erie Railroad Company, 1941), pp. 15, 27; Sturgis, *A New Chapter of Erie*, p. 29.

26. Sturgis, *A New Chapter of Erie*, p. 29.

27. Ibid., pp. 30–31; *Railway Age* 111 (November 1, 1941): 725; *Erie Railroad Company, Reorganization Proceedings, in the United States District Court, Northern District of Ohio, Eastern Division, No. 45,839* (Cleveland: United States District Court, February 18, 1939, to November 21, 1939), Vol. 3, pp. 1641–42, 1805–9, 1901–9.

28. Sturgis, *A New Chapter of Erie*, pp. 33–34.

29. Ibid., pp. 33, 39; *Erie Railroad Company, Reorganization Proceedings, in the United States District Court, Northern District of Ohio, Eastern Division, No. 45,839* (Cleveland: United States District Court, December 30, 1940, to July 25, 1941), Vol. 6, pp. 3821–33, 3837–38; *Erie Railroad Company, Reorganization Proceedings, in the United States District Court, Northern District of Ohio, Eastern Division, No. 45,839* (Cleveland: United States District Court, July 29, 1941, to December 2, 1941), Vol. 7, pp. 4485–92.

30. Interview with Isabel H. Benham, New York, New York, June 6, 1989; Sturgis, *A New Chapter of Erie*, p. 55.

31. Sturgis, *A New Chapter of Erie.*

32. "Today's Erie: A Railroad for Tomorrow" (1941), EL papers; *Marion* (Ohio) *Star*, December 22, 1941.

33. *Forty-Fifth Report of the Board of Directors of Erie Railroad Company* (New York and Cleveland: Erie Railroad Company, 1940), p. 12; *Who's Who in Railroading* (New York: Simmons-Boardman Publishing, 1946), pp. 173, 768; Robert E. Woodruff, "I Worked on the Erie" (unpublished manuscript, ca. 1953), pp. 1–3.

34. Woodruff, "I Worked on the Erie," pp. 3–4; "R. E. Woodruff Elected President," *Erie Railroad Magazine* 37 (December 1941), 8–9; "Robert E. Woodruff Elected Erie President," *Railway Age* 111 (November 1, 1941): 712–13.

35. Langdon interview; interview with George C. Frank., Sr., Boca Raton, Florida, December 26, 1989.

36. Woodruff, "I Worked on the Erie," p. 98.

37. "Apprentice School," *Erie Railroad Magazine* 38 (September 1942): 6–7; interview with John H. Ray, Lakewood, Ohio, April 24, 1989.

Robert Woodruff wrote a strange book, *The Making of a Railroad Officer* (New York: Simmons-Boardman Publishing, 1925), in which he emphasized the importance of human faces, profiles, and head sizes in determining an individual's abilities. He argued, for example, that "A man with a convex forehead is a keen observer and quick thinker" (p. 51) and that "A man of concave type thinks slowly and acts slowly but is capable of great endurance" (p. 52).

Woodruff, however, was hardly an original thinker on character analysis. As early as 1913, Dr. Katherine Blackford argued that any individual's personality traits could be determined by examining various physical characteristics. Blonds, for example, were more aggressive than brunets and therefore they would make better salesmen and advertising men. Fortunately, this pseudo-scientific nonsense mostly disappeared by the 1930's. See Katherine M. H. Blackford, "Scientific Selection of Employees," *Iron Trade Review* 52 (February 20, 1913): 462–63, and Katherine M. H. Blackford and Arthur Newcomb, *The Job, The Man, The Boss* (New York: Doubleday, Page, 1916).

38. Robert Aldag to author, March 2, 1991; G. J. Weihofen to author, May 17, 1991.

39. Interview with Robert G. Fuller, Singer Island, Florida, December 26, 1989; Frank interview; interview with T. G. Hannemann, Cleveland, Ohio, September 11, 1989; confidential interview.

40. Frank interview; Woodruff, "I Worked on the Erie," pp. 86–87, "'I Worked on the Erie' Club," *Railway Age* 120 (February 9, 1946): 330.

During Woodruff's tenure as president and after, the Erie liked to call itself the "Little Red Schoolhouse for Railroad Presidents." By the mid-1950's 21 individuals who at one time worked for the company had become presidents of other roads.

41. Frank interview; Woodruff, "I Worked on the Erie," pp. 87–88.

42. *Railway Age* 109 (November 9, 1940): 682; "What Do You Know About the Erie?" (Cleveland: Erie Railroad Company, 1941), pp. 1–3; *Forty-sixth Report*, p. 28; *Erie Railroad Annual Report 1941* (New York and Cleveland: Erie Railroad Company, 1942), p. 32.

43. "Right-of-Way," 16-mm. film produced by Office of War Information, 1943, National Archives, Washington, D.C.; *Historical Statistics of the United States*, pp. 427, 430–31.

44. *Erie Railroad Company Annual Report 1943* (New York and Cleveland: Erie Railroad Company, 1944), pp. 4–5, 57.

45. Interview with John Michael, Huntington, Indiana, May 15, 1990; interview with W. J. Donnelly, Upland, Indiana, October 18, 1990.

46. John Grover, "Highballing Oil to the East," *Erie Railroad Magazine* 38 (October 1942): 8, 29.

47. *Erie Railroad Company Annual Report 1944* (New York and Cleveland: Erie Railroad Company, 1945), p. 4; *Railway Age* 118 (May 26, 1945): 948; *Railway Age* 118 (June 16, 1945): 1064; "Erie's 765th Railway Shop Battalion," *Erie Railroad Magazine* 40 (July 1944): 6–7; *Erie Railroad Company Annual Report 1942* (New York and Cleveland: Erie Railroad Company, 1943), p. 5; Ray interview.

48. "Alfred University Professors Help Erie Manpower Problem," *Erie Railroad Magazine* 39 (September 1943): 9; *Erie Railroad Magazine* 40 (May 1944): 29; *Erie Railroad Magazine* 40 (April 1944): 5; *Erie Railroad Magazine* 39 (April 1943): 31; Woodruff, "I Worked on the Erie," p. 140.

49. "Erie War Bond Campaign Points Toward Success," *Erie Railroad Magazine* 38 (February 1943): 10–11; *Erie Railroad Magazine* 40 (May 1944): 16.

50. Richard Polenberg, *War and Society: The United States, 1941–1945* (Philadelphia: J. B. Lippincott, 1972), pp. 30–31, 95–96; Richard R. Lingeman, *Don't You Know There's a War On? The American Home Front, 1941–1945* (New York: G. P. Putnam's Sons, 1970), p. 80–81; interview with "Chick" Herzeg, Upland, Indiana, October 18, 1990.

51. *Annual Report, 1943*, pp. 22–24.

52. *Annual Report, 1944*, pp. 4–5; Woodruff, "I Worked on the Erie," pp. 128, 133.

53. Claude Moore Feuss, *Joseph B. Eastman: Servant of the People* (New York: Columbia University Press, 1952), pp. 270–96; McInnes interview.

54. *Erie Railroad Magazine* 39 (October 1943): 8.

55. *Annual Report 1943*, pp. 10–11; "Erie Railroad Annual Report for Employes," *Erie Railroad Magazine* 40 (April 1944): 7; interview with Milford M. Adams, Perry, Ohio, March 18, 1988; McInnes interview; *Annual Report 1944*, pp. 7, 11; Langdon interview.

56. *Erie Railroad Magazine* 42 (March 1946): 2, 4–5; *Cleveland Press*, January 13, 1946.

Chapter 3

1. John A. Hadden, "The Erie Railroad Today," March 1, 1947, Erie Lackawanna papers, The University of Akron Archives, Akron, Ohio, hereafter cited as EL papers; Robert E. Woodruff, "Happy New Year [1946]," EL papers; Robert E. Woodruff, "The President's Page," *Erie Railroad Magazine* 43 (March 1947): 2.

2. *Erie Railroad Company Annual Report 1948* (New York and Cleveland: Erie

Railroad Company, 1949), pp. 4, 11; interview with George C. Frank, Sr., Boca Raton, Florida, December 26, 1989.

3. "Erie's Growing Power," *Erie Railroad Magazine* 43 (March 1947): 8–9; *The Lima* (Ohio) *News*, July 3 and 31, and August 3, 1947; Robert E. Woodruff, "I Worked on the Erie," unpublished manuscript, ca. 1953, p. 134, EL papers; Maury Klein, "Replacement Technology: The Diesel as a Case Study," *Railroad History* 162 (Spring 1990): 109. See also John B. McCall, "Dieselisation of American Railroads: A Case Study," *The Journal of Transport History* 6 (September 1985): 1–17.

After November 1952, the Erie used its remaining steam locomotives (4-6-2 Pacifics) exclusively on its New Jersey and New York Railroad subsidiary; they handled four weekday trains in each direction. Steam continued until March 17, 1954. See Lloyd Stagner, "A 'Date' Diary: 1952–1962," *National Railway Bulletin* 56 (1991): 19.

4. Frederick Westing and Alvin F. Staufer, *Erie Power: Steam and Diesel Locomotives of the Erie Railroad from 1840 to 1970* (Medina, Ohio: Alvin F. Staufer, 1970), pp. 346–50; Gerald M. Best, compiler, "All Time Erie Locomotive Roster," *Railroad History* 131 (Autumn 1974): 102; "Erie's Growing Power," p. 9; John F. Kirkland, *Dawn of the Diesel Age: The History of the Diesel Locomotive in America* (Glendale, Calif.: Interurban Press, 1983), pp. 89–92.

5. "Diesels to Conquer Heavy Erie Grades," *Erie Railroad Magazine* 40 (October 1944): 7.

6. *Erie Railroad Company Annual Report 1947* (New York and Cleveland: Erie Railroad Company, 1948), pp. 12–13; "Erie Dieselizes All Through Passenger Trains and Exhibits Ones," *Erie Railroad Magazine* 43 (September 1947): 10–13; *Annual Report 1948*, p. 10.

7. "Diesel Power Steps Up," *Erie Railroad Magazine* 46 (May 1950): 4–6; interview with Milton G. McInnes, Southbury, Connecticut, June 5, 1989.

8. "All Time Erie Locomotive Roster," pp. 92, 93–97; interview with Leonard Kellogg, Marion, Ohio, May 12, 1989.

9. "Dieselization Steps Up Erie Performance," *Modern Railroads* 6 (May 1951): 40–41, 43–44; *Erie Railroad Company Annual Report 1951* (New York and Cleveland: Erie Railroad Company, 1952), pp. 7–8; *Erie Railroad Company Annual Report 1952* (New York and Cleveland: Erie Railroad Company, 1953), pp. 7–8; *Erie Railroad Company Annual Report 1954* (New York and Cleveland: Erie Railroad Company, 1955), p. 11; *Erie Railroad Magazine* 48 (March 1952): 13; "End of an Era," *Erie Railroad Magazine* 50 (November 1954): 14; Gerald M. Best, "Erie Locomotive Notes," *Railroad History* 131 (Autumn 1974): 18.

The Erie donated a 4-6-2 K-1-type Pacific steam locomotive, one used on Jersey City–Chicago passenger runs and "in perfect operating condition," to the American-Korean Foundation in 1954. Several American carriers gave the war-damaged Korean National Railroad quantities of used equipment.

10. *Annual Report 1952*, p. 8; *Annual Report 1954*, p. 8; "One Afloat, 4 More to Come," *Erie Railroad Magazine* 48 (October 1952): 10–11; Brian J. Cudahy, *Over & Back: The History of Ferryboats in New York Harbor* (New York: Fordham University Press, 1990), pp. 388–89; interview with John H. Ray, Lakewood, Ohio, April 24, 1989.

11. *Annual Report 1947*, pp. 10, 12; McInnes interview.

12. "Maintain Versatile Fleet," *Modern Railroads* 6 (May 1951): 117–18, 120.

13. McInnes interview; *Annual Report 1948*, pp. 10–11; "New Luxury Coaches for Erie's Diesel Passenger Trains," *Erie Railroad Magazine* 42 (October 1946): 4–7; "The President's Page," *Erie Railroad Magazine* 43 (March 1947): 2; "Now in Service! All-Room Sleeping Cars," *Erie Railroad Magazine* 45 (July 1949): 11; "Give Cars Modern Styling," *Modern Railroads* 6 (May 1951): 111–12.

14. "Self-Improvement Strengthens Erie," *Modern Railroads* 6 (May 1951): 35, 39; interview with Milford M. Adams, Perry, Ohio, March 18, 1988.

15. *Erie Railroad Company Annual Report 1945* (New York and Cleveland: Erie Railroad Company, 1946), p. 9; McInnes interview.

16. "Erie Mechanizes Track Work," *Erie Railroad Magazine* 46 (October 1950): 10–12; "Cut Track Costs with Machines," *Modern Railroads* 6 (May 1951): 132–34; "Punch Card Pioneer Still Improving," *Modern Railroads* 6 (May 1951): 81, 85–86, 89–90.

17. "Erie Railroad's Four-Way Radio-Telephone System," (n.p., n.d.) in John W. Barriger III Railroad Collection, Mercantile Library, St. Louis, Missouri; "Calling All Trains at 50 Miles an Hour," *Erie Railroad Magazine* 44 (August 1948): 4–5; "Erie Radio Increases Operating Efficiency," *Railway Age* 125 (September 11, 1948): 56–59; "Radio Railroad," *Erie Railroad Magazine* 48 (August 1950): 12–14; *Cleveland Press*, June 23, 1950.

18. Frank interview.

19. *Akron Beacon Journal*, August 23, October 22, 1946; July 16, 1947.

20. "New Erie Passenger Station Exhibits Modern Motif at Its Best," *Railway Age* 123 (October 18, 1947): 48–51.

21. *Akron Beacon Journal*, July 16, 1947; *Erie Railroad Magazine* 43 (September 1947): 4–8.

22. *Annual Report 1951*, p. 7; interview with Charles Shannon, Arlington Heights, Illinois, October 1, 1988.

23. Interview with M. Fred Coffman, Akron, Ohio, November 4, 1988; "What It Takes to Be a Railroad Traffic VP," *Business Week* (February 7, 1953): 132.

24. *Erie Railroad Company Annual Report 1946* (New York and Cleveland: Erie Railroad Company, 1949), p. 41; *Annual Report 1948*, p. 39; *Erie Railroad Company Annual Report 1950* (New York and Cleveland: Erie Railroad Company, 1951), p. 39; *Annual Report 1951*, p. 39; *Erie Railroad: Its Beginning—and Today* (n.p., 1951), pp. 19–23.

25. Coffman interview; Minutes of the Board of Directors, Erie Railroad Company, April 10, 1956, p. 3, Pennsylvania State Archives, Harrisburg, Pennsylvania, hereafter cited as Erie minutes.

Anthracite traffic on the Erie was on a steep decline after World War II. It dropped from 78,000 cars in 1946 to only 16,000 a decade later and would eventually disappear.

26. Named after an Ohio industrial engineer, George J. Hulett, the first of these mechanical ore unloaders served the Conneaut, Ohio, docks of the Pittsburgh, Shen-

ango & Lake Erie Railroad in 1898. Between that date and 1950 77 Huletts were built, including the 3 used by the Erie. See "Unloaded in 7½ Hours," *Erie Railroad Magazine* 43 (October 1947): 21.

27. *Annual Report 1951*, pp. 23, 40.

28. *Annual Report 1949*, p. 11.

29. "Handling Perishable Traffic," *Erie Railroad Magazine* 40 (June 1944): 8–9, 24; "Erie Serves New York Tables," *Erie Railroad Magazine* 46 (September 1950): 4–6; Coffman interview; interview with John R. Michael, Huntington, Indiana, May 15, 1990.

30. *Annual Report 1951*, p. 40; Coffman interview.

31. Traffic density maps, Erie Railroad, H. H. Copeland & Company, 1937, 1947, EL papers.

32. Carson S. Duncan to Harry W. Von Willer, May 28, 1948, EL papers.

33. *Annual Report 1950*, pp. 7, 26, 39; "Faster Fast Freight," *Erie Railroad Magazine* 46 (July 1950): 10–13; Coffman interview.

34. "What It Takes to Be a Railroad Traffic VP," p. 13.

35. *The Official Guide of the Railways* (New York: National Railway Publication Co., October 1951), pp. 122, 279, 436; interview with Louis W. Goodwin, Northfield, Connecticut, June 4, 1989; "Take the Erie!" (ca. 1950), EL papers.

36. *Cleveland Press*, January 5, 1947; "'Steel King' Inaugurated," *Erie Railroad Magazine* 46 (June 1950): 4–5; Thomas T. Taber to Harry Von Willer, n.d., T. T. Taber papers, Railroad Museum of Pennsylvania, Strasburg, Pennsylvania.

37. *Historical Statistics of the United States: Colonial Times to 1957* (Washington, D.C.: U.S. Department of Commerce, 1960), p. 462; Mark H. Rose, *Interstate: Express Highway Politics, 1941–1956* (Lawrence: The Regents Press of Kansas, 1979), pp. 29–40; interview with Frank Warren, St. Louis, Missouri, April 7, 1989.

38. McInnes interview; *Annual Report 1951*, p. 17.

39. Adams interview; *Annual Report 1951*, p. 3; *Annual Report 1946*, p. 3; *Annual Report 1949*, p. 1.

40. Erie minutes, August 19, 1949, p. 40; McInnes interview.

41. Adams interview; McInnes interview; interview with Jervis Langdon, Jr., Akron, Ohio, April 26, 1990; Paul W. Johnston, Jr., to author, November 7, 1991; interview with Perry M. Shoemaker, Tampa, Florida, August 19, 1989.

42. "Paul W. Johnston: Erie's New President," *Erie Railroad Magazine* 45 (October 1949): 4, 22; "R. E. Woodruff Becomes Erie Chairman October 1; P. W. Johnston Will Be New President," *Railway Age* 127 (September 24, 1949): 56–57.

43. *Annual Report 1950*, p. 2; *Cleveland Plain Dealer*, October 2, 1949.

44. P. W. Johnston to G. C. Frank, June 29, 1950, EL papers.

45. "Chicago Railroad Fair," *Erie Railroad Magazine* 44 (July 1948): 18–19; Frank interview.

46. Frank interview.

47. Ibid.; G. C. Frank to H. W. Von Willer et al., November 29, 1950, EL papers.

48. G. C. Frank to T. J. Tobin, August 21, 1951, EL papers; Raymond J. Wean to George C. Frank, August 23, 1951, EL papers.

49. Frank interview; F. L. Stallman to G. C. Frank, n.d., EL papers; *Binghamton* (New York) *Sun*, May 14, 1951; *New York Times*, May 15, 1951; *New York Herald Tribune*, May 15, 1951.

50. G. C. Frank, "Final Report of E.C.T.," October 1, 1951, EL papers; *Akron Beacon Journal*, July 2, 1951.

51. T. J. Tobin to G. C. Frank, February 5, 1952, EL papers; Frank interview.

52. McInnes interview.

53. In a survey of employees' attitudes conducted in 1947, Erie Railroad officials learned the following: "Almost half—49 percent—felt the Erie was better than most companies as a place to work. Another 45 percent believe the Erie to be as good as the average, and 6 percent felt 'not so good.'" Clearly, the carrier did not face a morale crisis after the war. See "A Report on Employes' Questionnaire," *Erie Railroad Magazine* 43 (June 1947): 2.

54. Walter Licht, *Working for the Railroad: The Organization of Work in the Nineteenth Century* (Princeton, N.J.: Princeton University Press, 1983), p. 49; James H. Ducker, *Men of the Steel Rails: Workers on the Atchison, Topeka & Santa Fe Railroad, 1869–1900* (Lincoln: University of Nebraska Press, 1983), p. 25.

55. Interview with William J. Donnelly, Robert Eisenhower, Vic Kromer, John Michael, Paul Michael, Bart Paoletto, and Thurman Poe, Huntington, Indiana, May 15, 1990, hereafter cited as group interview; John Michael interview; Kellogg interview; Woodruff, "I Worked on the Erie," p. 38; interview with Robert G. Fuller, Singer Island, Florida, December 26, 1989.

56. Interview with "Chick" Herzeg, Upland, Indiana, October 18, 1990; interview with William J. Donnelly, Huntington, Indiana, May 15, 1990; interview with Dominic Carbone, Cleveland, Ohio, August 23, 1989; "A Report on Employes' Questionnaire," p. 2.

57. *Erie Railroad Magazine* 44 (October 1948): 18–21; interview with Barbara Armbruster, North Olmsted, Ohio, May 17, 1990; group interview; "Cleveland Ballplayers," *Erie Railroad Magazine* 45 (December 1949): 32; "System-Wide Bowling Tourney," *Erie Railroad Magazine* 43 (May 1947): 6–8.

58. Group interview; McInnes interview.

59. See H. Roger Grant, *The Corn Belt Route: A History of the Chicago Great Western Railroad Company* (DeKalb, Ill.: Northern Illinois University Press, 1984), pp. 146–49.

60. "Labor Files—Miscellaneous, 1941–1951," EL papers.

61. *Annual Report 1947*, p. 20; *Annual Report 1948*, p. 5; *Annual Report 1949*, p. 2; *Annual Report 1950*, pp. 15, 17; *Erie Railroad Company Annual Report 1953* (New York and Cleveland: Erie Railroad Company, 1954), p. 14.

62. *Annual Report 1948*, p. 5; *Annual Report 1947*, p. 15; *Annual Report 1949*, p. 12; *Annual Report 1953*, p. 5.

63. Maury Klein, *Union Pacific: The Rebirth, 1894–1969* (New York: Doubleday, 1989), p. 510; McInnes interview; memorandum on Canadian Royal Commission report on firemen, Nelson A. Rockefeller papers, Gubernatorial Office Records, Rockefeller Archive Center, North Tarrytown, New York.

64. Adams interview; Robert E. Woodruff, "The Erie Promotes Industrial

Growth" (speech of August 28, 1946), EL papers; Coffman interview; *Annual Report 1950*, p. 18.

65. Paul W. Johnston, "The Erie Serves Industry as Never Before" (speech of January 3, 1953), EL papers.

66. Hadden was surely correct about the "Ford people" enjoying their trip on an Erie business car. The company had a reputation for excellent food and ample drink. "They probably closed the blinds and got smashed," suggested one employee.

67. "There's a Ford in Our Future," *Erie Railroad Magazine* 49 (October 1953): 8–11, 13; "Huge Mahwah Ford Plant Opens," *Erie Railroad Magazine* 51 (November 1955): 4–6; John A. Hadden to P. W. Johnston, September 1, 1953, in Erie minutes, September 1, 1953; *Annual Report 1953*, p. 18; *Erie Railroad Company Annual Report 1955* (New York and Cleveland: Erie Railroad Company, 1956), p. 23.

The Mahwah plant eventually closed, but after Erie Lackawanna disappeared. Ford ended production at the sprawling facility on June 21, 1980, which meant a loss of 4,500 jobs and an $84.9 million annual payroll. See *New York Times*, June 21, 1980.

68. "Erie Welcomes 'Body by Fisher,'" *Erie Railroad Magazine* 51 (September 1955): 22–24; "Industrial Development," *Erie Railroad Magazine* 48 (June 1952): 6–9; Coffman interview; James J. Flink, *The Automobile Age* (Cambridge, Mass.: MIT Press, 1988), pp. 277–79.

69. "This Little Piggy *Did Not* Go to Market!" *Erie Railroad Magazine* 50 (July 1954): 10–12; "Piggyback Starts on Erie After I.C.C. OK," *Erie Railroad Magazine* 50 (August 1954): 9; "Piggyback Service Extended to New England, Midwest," *Erie Railroad Magazine* 51 (January 1956): 15; "Daniels Motor Freight Trailers First to Use New Erie Service," *Erie Railroad Magazine* 53 (March 1957): 15.

70. William Gregg White to author, September 28, 1989; telephone interview with William D. Burt, Newark, New Jersey, November 9, 1990.

71. *Annual Report 1954*, p. 3; *Annual Report 1955*, pp. 3, 10; *Erie Railroad Company Annual Report 1957* (New York and Cleveland: Erie Railroad Company, 1958), p. 3.

72. *Historical Statistics of the United States*, pp. 70, 73, 117, 139; Douglas T. Miller and Marion Nowak, *The Fifties: The Way We Really Were* (Garden City, N.Y.: Doubleday, 1977), pp. 106–23.

73. *Annual Report 1955*, pp. 2, 11, 14.

74. Adams interview; *Annual Report 1955*, p. 14.

75. *Annual Report 1952*, p. 5; *Annual Report 1953*, pp. 4–5; *Erie Railroad Company Annual Report 1956* (New York and Cleveland: Erie Railroad Company, 1957), p. 2; Karl A. Borntrager, *Keeping the Railroads Running: Fifty Years on the New York Central* (New York: Hastings House, 1964), pp. 152–55, 179.

76. McInnes interview.

Chapter 4

1. "The Team Moves Up," *Erie Railroad Magazine* 52 (November 1956): 4–5.

2. Interview with Charles Shannon, Arlington Heights, Illinois, October 1, 1988.

3. Russell F. Moore, ed., *Who's Who in Railroading in North America* (New York: Simmons-Boardman Publishing, 1959), pp. 650–51; "Harry W. Von Willer Elected

Erie President," *Railway Age* 141 (October 29, 1956): 35; *Cleveland Plain Dealer*, May 30, 1971.

4. "What It Takes to Be a Railroad Traffic VP," *Business Week* (February 7, 1953): 130–31, 134; Roberta Von Willer to author, February 18, 1991.

5. Telephone interview with John Drake, Rutherford, New Jersey, December 11, 1990; Minutes of the Board of Directors, Erie Railroad Company, April 10, 1956, p. 3, Pennsylvania State Archives, Harrisburg, Pennsylvania, hereafter cited as Erie minutes; Shannon interview.

6. Interview with Perry M. Shoemaker, Tampa, Florida, August 19, 1989.

7. *Erie Railroad Company Annual Report 1955* (New York and Cleveland: Erie Railroad Company, 1956), p. 10; *104th Annual Report for the Year Ended December 31, 1955* (New York: The Delaware, Lackawanna and Western Railroad Company), p. 12.

8. Minutes of the Board of Managers, Delaware, Lackawanna & Western Railroad Company, November 23, 1955, p. 222, Syracuse University Library, Syracuse, New York, hereafter cited as DL&W minutes; "First Out of Hoboken!" *Erie Railroad Magazine* 52 (November 1956): 21; Erie Railroad press release, September 27, 1956, Erie Lackawanna papers, The University of Akron Archives, Akron, Ohio, hereafter cited as EL papers; "Commuters! Head for Hoboken," n.d., EL papers; Raymond J. Baxter and Arthur G. Adams, *Railroad Ferries of the Hudson and Stories of a Deckhand* (Woodcliff Lake, N.J.: Lind Publications, 1987), pp. 169–70; "Chicago To Hoboken," *Erie Railroad Magazine* 51 (December 1955): 6–8; "Gull's Life Is Empty; Last Ferry Has Run," *Erie Railroad Magazine* 54 (December 1958): 5, 30.

9. DL&W minutes, April 25, 1957, p. 47; "Plan Track Cut to Do Better Job Faster for Less Money," *Erie Railroad Magazine* 53 (July 1957): 8–9; "Begin Work on Connection to Link Erie, DL&W Track," *Erie Railroad Magazine* 54 (November 1958): 5; Shoemaker interview.

10. Richard Saunders, *The Railroad Mergers and the Coming of Conrail* (Westport, Conn.: Greenwood Press, 1978), p. 104; "ICC Gives Erie, DL&W Clear Track on Plan," *Erie Railroad Magazine* 54 (August 1958): 5; *Erie Railroad Company Annual Report 1958* (New York and Cleveland: Erie Railroad Company, 1958), p. 10.

11. Shoemaker interview.

12. Larry Lowenthal and William T. Greenberg, Jr., *The Lackawanna Railroad in Northwest New Jersey* (Morristown, N.J.: The Tri-State Railway Historical Society, 1987), pp. 92–93; *Annual Report of The Delaware, Lackawanna & Western Railroad Company, 1914* (New York: Press of L. Middleditch Co., 1915), p. 4; Jules I. Bogen, *The Anthracite Railroads: A Study in American Railroad Enterprise* (New York: Ronald Press, 1927), p. 105; Rodney O. Davis, "Earnest Elmo Calkins and Phoebe Snow," *Railroad History* 163 (Autumn 1990): 89–92. See also Robert J. Casey and W. A. S. Douglas, *The Lackawanna Story* (New York: McGraw-Hill, 1951) and Thomas Townsend Taber and Thomas Townsend Taber III, *The Delaware, Lackawanna and Western Railroad, the Road of Anthracite, in the Twentieth Century, 1899–1960* (Muncy, Pennsylvania: privately printed, 1981).

13. *Annual Report of the Delaware, Lackawanna and Western Railroad Company, 1941* (New York: Delaware, Lackawanna and Western Railroad, 1942), p. 29; inter-

view with Robert G. Fuller, Singer Island, Florida, December 26, 1989; interview with Curtis F. Bayer, Moreland Hills, Ohio, November 11, 1989.

14. John Sherman Porter, ed., *Moody's Manual of Investments: Railroad Securities* (New York: Moody's Investors Service, 1949), pp. 619, 621–22; *Who's Who in Railroading in North America* (New York: Simmons-Boardman Publishing, 1946), p. 747; Fuller interview; Bayer interview.

15. "The Delaware, Lackawanna and Western Railroad Company, Earnings Appraisal of Lease Line Properties" (Newark, N.J.: Wm. Wyer & Co., March 8, 1943), pp. 1–18; *Annual Report of The Delaware, Lackawanna and Western Railroad Company, 1944* (New York: The Delaware, Lackawanna and Western Railroad Company, 1945), p. 8; telephone interview with Perry M. Shoemaker, Tampa, Florida, March 22, 1991.

16. "Lackawanna Railroad, Ten Years—1941–1950," n.d., pp. 1–6, EL papers; Fuller interview; Shoemaker interview.

17. Shoemaker interview; Russell F. Moore, ed., *Who's Who in Railroading* (New York: Simmons-Boardman Publishing, 1964), p. 482.

18. Shoemaker interview; DL&W minutes, May 18, 1956; ibid., September 29, 1955, pp. 173, 176; ibid., January 31, 1957; "Discussion of P. M. Shoemaker, President, The Delaware, Lackawanna and Western Railroad Company Before the Annual Meeting of Stockholders, May 12, 1959," EL papers; Perry M. Shoemaker to author, August 25, 1989; "Remarks of P. M. Shoemaker, President, The Delaware, Lackawanna and Western Railroad Company To Its Stockholders, at Their Annual Meeting, May 8, 1956," EL papers.

19. DL&W minutes, June 26, 1958; *104th Annual Report*, p. 9; *107th Annual Report, The Delaware, Lackawanna and Western Railroad Company* (New York: Delaware, Lackawanna and Western Railroad Co., 1959), p. 13.

20. Shoemaker interview; Bayer interview; Fuller interview.

21. Shannon interview.

22. Fuller interview; Perry M. Shoemaker to author, March 15, 1991; John Sherman Porter, ed., *Moody's Transportation Manual* (New York: Moody's Investors Service, 1956), pp. 122, 300, 1149.

23. DL&W minutes, September 5, 1956, p. 75; "Perry M. Shoemaker to Lackawanna Security Holders," September 11, 1956, EL papers; "Merger Study," *Erie Railroad Magazine* 52 (October 1956): 4–6.

24. "Wm. Wyer & Co. Organized in 1940" (ca. 1954), p. 1, EL papers; interview with Charles J. Meyer, Livingston, New Jersey, May 25, 1988.

25. "Wm. Wyer & Co.," p. 4; Shannon interview; Meyer interview.

26. "Wm. Wyer & Co.," p. 5; Meyer interview.

27. *Report on Economics of Proposed Merger: The Delaware and Hudson Railroad Corporation; Erie Railroad Company; The Delaware, Lackawanna and Western Railroad Company* (Upper Montclair, N.J.: Wyer, Dick & Co., July 1, 1958), p. 5; Meyer interview.

28. William Wyer to William White, P. W. Johnston, H. W. Von Willer, and P. M. Shoemaker, April 27, 1957, EL papers.

29. "Report by Wyer Firm Ends Merger Study's First Phase," *Erie Railroad Magazine* 54 (July 1958): 9; *Report on Economics of Proposed Merger*, pp. 1–3.

30. Merger meeting minutes, July 15, 1958, p. 1, EL papers; Shoemaker interview.

31. "[Report] . . . prepared in connection with a study of a proposed consolidation of Erie Railroad Company; the Delaware, Lackawanna and Western Railroad Company; the Delaware and Hudson Company" (Boston: The First Boston Corporation, December 1958), pp. 1–3, hereafter cited as First Boston report; William White to E. Roland Harriman, Frank W. McCabe, and Peter S. Paine, December 11, 1958, EL papers.

32. First Boston report, pp. 24, 80, 91–95; Shannon interview.

33. *Supplemental Report on Economics of Proposed Merger* (Upper Montclair, N.J.: Wyer, Dick & Co., September 28, 1958); Fuller interview; Shoemaker interview; Shannon interview.

34. *Supplemental Report on Economics of Proposed Merger*, pp. 1–2; William Wyer to William White, P. W. Johnston, P. M. Shoemaker, September 26, 1958, EL papers; Shannon interview.

35. *Wall Street Journal*, April 14, 1959; Shoemaker interview.

36. "Year of Aggressive Selling, Cost Reduction Seen Ahead," *Erie Railroad Magazine* 54 (April 1958): 5–7; Fuller interview; Shoemaker interview; *Wall Street Journal*, April 14, 1959.

37. Harry Von Willer to George C. Frank, Sr., April 19, 1958, EL papers; Perry M. Shoemaker to author, March 15, 1991; "D&H + DL&W + Erie Merger Off," *Railway Age* 146 (April 20, 1959): 42.

38. *Report on Proposed Merger: Erie Railroad Company* [and] *The Delaware, Lackawanna and Western Railroad Company* (Upper Montclair, N.J.: Wyer, Dick & Co., August 6, 1959), p. 1; Shoemaker interview.

39. *Report on Proposed Economics of Proposed Merger*, pp. 1–2; William Wyer to P. W. Johnston and P. M. Shoemaker, August 6, 1959, EL papers.

40. Shoemaker interview; Harry Von Willer to George C. Franks, Sr., August 17, 1959, EL papers.

41. Erie Railroad and Lackawanna Railroad press release, July 1, 1959, EL papers; "Erie, Lackawanna Directors Approve Plan for Merger," *Erie Railroad Magazine* 55 (May 1959): 5; "Erie, Lackawanna Chairmen Given Merger Plan Facts," *Erie Railroad Magazine* 55 (July 1959): 5, 30; *Wall Street Journal*, June 25, 1959.

42. Fuller interview; personal memorandum from P. M. Shoemaker to W. G. White et al., April 29, 1959, EL papers; "Memorandum concerning unification negotiations between Erie and Lackawanna," n.d., EL papers; interview with Milton G. McInnes, Southbury, Connecticut, June 5, 1989.

43. "Why the Proposed Erie-Lackawanna Merger Is in the Public Interest," *Erie Railroad Magazine* 55 (August 1959): 10, 25; Shannon interview; Meyer interview.

44. McInnes interview; "Another 'Natural,'" *Trains* 19 (September 1959): 6; *Erie Railroad Company Annual Report 1959* (New York and Cleveland: Erie Railroad Company, 1960), pp. 4–5; *108th Annual Report, The Delaware, Lackawanna and Western Railroad Company* (New York: Delaware, Lackawanna and Western Railroad Co., 1960), p. 1.

45. Erie Railroad and Lackawanna Railroad, press release, October 7, 1959, EL

papers; *Yearbook of Railroad Information* (Jersey City, N.J.: Eastern Railroad Presidents Conference, 1961), p. 4.

46. Shannon interview; Maury Klein, *Union Pacific: The Rebirth, 1894–1969* (New York: Doubleday, 1989), pp. 510–11; John F. Stover, "Wayne A. Johnson," in Keith L. Bryant, Jr., ed., *Encyclopaedia of American History and Biography: Railroads in the Age of Regulation, 1900–1980* (New York: Facts on File Publications, 1988), p. 245.

47. George W. Hilton, *The Transportation Act of 1958: A Decade of Experience* (Bloomington: Indiana University Press, 1969), pp. 3, 10–14, 186–207; Shannon interview; *New York Times,* January 16, 1958.

48. *Yearbook of Railroad Information* (New York: Eastern Railroad Presidents Conference, 1956), p. 1.

49. Gus Welty, ed., *Era of the Giants: The New Railroad Merger Movement* (Omaha: Simmons-Boardman Publishing, 1982), pp. 3, 86–91.

50. "Erie, DL&W Shareowners to Vote on September 22nd," *Erie Railroad Magazine* 55 (September 1959): 5; Shoemaker interview.

51. "Erie Railroad Company, Notice of Special Meeting of Stockholders," August 17, 1959, pp. 1–15, EL papers; *108th Annual Report*, pp. 2–3; Fuller interview.

52. McInnes interview; Richard L. Saunders, Jr., "Railroad Consolidation in the Eastern United States, 1940–1964" (Ph.D. dissertation, University of Illinois-Urbana, 1971), p. 450; "News release from G. C. Frank, Asst. to President, Erie Railroad, Midland Building, Cleveland, O.," n.d., EL papers; Harry Von Willer to George C. Frank, September 30, 1959, EL papers.

53. "Erie-Lackawanna Railroad Company, Merger Proceedings, 'Book of Facts,'" pp. 22–23, EL papers.

54. Ibid., p. 24.

55. "News release from G. C. Frank, Asst. to President, Erie Railroad, Midland Building, Cleveland, O." (n.d.), EL papers.

56. Ibid.

57. News release, October 7, 1959; Stephen Salsbury, *No Way to Run a Railroad: The Untold Story of the Penn Central Crisis* (New York: McGraw-Hill, 1982), p. 117.

58. McInnes interview; Shannon interview; Shoemaker interview.

59. Shannon interview; Shoemaker interview.

60. Shoemaker interview; "Wanted: 'Easier' Mergers," *Railway Age* 147 (November 16, 1959): 34; McInnes interview.

61. William C. Kessel, "How to Put the Hyphen into Erie-Lackawanna," *Trains* 20 (July 1960): 20.

62. D&LW minutes, special meeting, September 22, 1959; Saunders, *Railroad Mergers and Coming of Conrail*, p. 116; Fuller interview.

63. Interview with J. D. Allen, Cleveland, Ohio, May 10, 1989.

64. Saunders, *The Railroad Mergers and the Coming of Conrail*, pp. 111–12; McInnes interview.

65. *Erie Railroad Company Annual Report 1959*, p. 13.

66. Allen interview; McInnes interview; *Erie Railroad Company-Merger, etc., Delaware, Lackawanna & Western Railroad Company, Before the Interstate Commerce Com-*

Legal Publishing Co., 1960), pp. 26–27, hereafter cited as *Applicants' Replies to Exceptions*.

67. Shannon interview; *The Daily Plainsman* (Huron, S.D.), September 17, 1956; interview with Frank Koval, Wheaton, Illinois, September 9, 1988.

68. *Applicants' Replies to Exceptions*, pp. 26–27.

69. Shannon interview; interview with D. Keith Lawson, Rogers, Arkansas, October 18, 1980; Saunders, *The Railroad Mergers and the Coming of Conrail*, pp. 84–85, 111–12.

70. *Applicants' Replies to Exceptions*, pp. 34–35.

71. *Interstate Commerce Commission Reports* (Finance Docket No. 20707) (Washington, D.C.: Interstate Commerce Commission, 1961), p. 236.

72. Shoemaker interview; McInnes interview; *Interstate Commerce Commission Reports*, pp. 198–249.

73. *Interstate Commerce Commission Reports*, pp. 185–263; "Years of Study and Work Pay Off; Merger Approved," *Erie Railroad Magazine* 56 (October 1959): 8; "E-L: Merger Creates New Class 1 R.R.," *Railway Age* 149 (October 24, 1960): 24–25. See "Transcript of Record, Supreme Court of the United States, October Term, 1960, No. 681, Brotherhood of Maintenance of Way Employees, et al., Appellants, *vs.* United States, et al., Filed January 27, 1961," pp. 2–6, EL papers.

74. Shoemaker interview; *New York Times*, October 18, 1960.

75. "New Herald, Slogan Chosen for Erie-Lackawanna Road," *Erie Railroad Magazine* 56 (September 1959): 4; *Railway Age* 149 (September 19, 1960): 68.

The roads also asked employees to submit suitable advertising slogans. Based on three entries, a composite one, "The Friendly Service Route," was selected. "[It] being symbolic of what our customers have a right to expect of the merged company—a satisfactory service performed in a friendly manner." *Erie Railroad Magazine* 56 (September 1959): 5.

76. "News release from G. C. Frank, Asst. to President, Erie Railroad, Midland Building, Cleveland, O." (n.d.), EL papers.

Chapter 5

1. Interview with Perry M. Shoemaker, Tampa, Florida, August 19, 1989.

2. Interview with Milton G. McInnes, Southbury, Connecticut, June 5, 1989; Shoemaker interview; "McInnes Heads Erie-Lackawanna," *Railway Age* 149 (November 28, 1960): 9; M. C. Smith, Jr., to George W. Whittaker, October 25, 1961, Erie Lackawanna papers, The University of Akron Archives, Akron, Ohio, hereafter cited as EL papers; Lewis G. Harriman to P. M. Shoemaker, October 18, 1960, EL papers; M. G. McInnes to P. M. Shoemaker et al., September 26, 1961, EL papers.

3. Interview with Charles Shannon, Arlington Heights, Illinois, October 1, 1988.

4. McInnes interview; Russell F. Moore, ed., *Who's Who in Railroading in North America* (New York: Simmons-Boardman Publishing, 1959), p. 421.

5. Interview with Milford M. Adams, Perry, Ohio, March 18, 1988; McInnes interview; interview with M. Fred Coffman, Akron, Ohio, November 4, 1988.

6. McInnes interview; Moore, *Who's Who in Railroading*, p. 672; Adams inter-

view; Shoemaker interview; *Who's Who in America* (Chicago: A. N. Marquis Co., 1962), p. 1263; "Director Honored," *Erie Railroad Magazine* 47 (April 1951): 21.

7. Adams interview; interview with Robert G. Fuller, Singer Island, Florida, December 26, 1989; interview with Gregory W. Maxwell, Moreland Hills, Ohio, June 12, 1989; Shoemaker interview; interview with Curtis F. Bayer, Moreland Hills, Ohio, August 23, 1989.

8. "Court Rules Against Unions in Job Protection Dispute," *Erie-Lackawanna Magazine* 56 (December 1960): 4, 15; *Erie-Lackawanna Railroad Company 1960 Annual Report* (Cleveland: Erie-Lackawanna Railroad Co., 1962), pp. 4, 13.

9. *Erie-Lackawanna Railroad Company 1960 Annual Report*, p. 13; *Erie-Lackawanna Railroad Company 1961 Annual Report* (Cleveland: Erie-Lackawanna Railroad Co., 1962), p. 12; Bayer interview.

10. Bayer interview; McInnes interview.

11. *Wall Street Journal*, February 12, 1962; Shoemaker interview; Erie-Lackawanna Railroad press release, June 1, 1961, EL papers.

12. *Erie-Lackawanna Railroad Company 1962 Annual Report* (Cleveland: Erie-Lackawanna Railroad Co., 1963), pp. 19, 24–25.

13. Shoemaker interview.

14. P. M. Shoemaker, "Memorandum on Eastern Railroads and Erie-Lackawanna Situation," July 26, 1961, EL papers.

15. J. Handly Wright, "Railroads Need a Magna Carta," (n.p., n.d.), p. 3; Shoemaker, "Memorandum on Eastern Railroads and Erie-Lackawanna Situation."

16. McInnes interview.

17. Adams interview; Shoemaker interview.

18. Bayer interview; Curtis F. Bayer, "Did Someone Say Merger?" *Proceedings of the New England Railroad Club* (n.p., 1962), pp. 96, 98.

19. Bayer, "Did Someone Say Merger?" pp. 98–99.

20. Ibid., p. 100.   21. Ibid., pp. 100–101.

22. Adams interview.   23. Bayer interview.

24. Robert E. Woodruff, "Today's Modern Erie" [ca. 1946], EL papers.

25. Bayer interview; Shoemaker interview; Adams interview.

26. Bayer interview.

27. Coffman interview; Bayer interview.

28. Adams interview; Bayer interview; Shoemaker interview.

29. Bayer interview.

It was common for former Lackawanna employees to disparage the merger. "Then they merged us with the Erie and outright ruined the Lackawanna," charged Andrew Barbera, a locomotive engineer. "I think some of the officials on that Erie line were a bunch of crooks. Lackawanna men were stricter. The Erie was sloppy, and they just didn't care too much for our ways, the way we worked our railroad" (Stuart Leuthner, *The Railroaders* [New York: Random House, 1983], p. 97).

30. Shoemaker interview; Richard Saunders, *The Railroad Mergers and the Coming of Conrail* (Westport, Conn.: Greenwood Press, 1978), p. 119; Shannon interview.

Perry Shoemaker in a memorandum to Milton McInnes, dated November 2, 1961 [EL papers], argued that the company needed the "Preservation of competent personnel by assignment of real responsibilities." He noted that the carrier had lost several capable individuals:

W. E. Travis, former Lackawanna chief locomotive officer, who has gone to the D&H.

J. E. Mathews, Lackawanna's top insurance expert. He has gone into private business at New York.

D. J. McIntyre, who headed the Research Dept., and has gone to NYTA.

J. F. Mulligan, who was the second man in the Lackawanna Law Department, has left to take a position with Monroe Calculating.

F. F. Dayton, Trainmaster, who has gone to another railroad.

Others have been offered positions and are considering them.

31. McInnes interview; Shoemaker interview.

32. Saunders, *The Railroad Mergers and the Coming of Conrail*, p. 118; Shannon interview.

33. Shannon interview.

34. Ibid.

35. Adams interview.

36. Shannon interview; *A Year Book of Railroad Information* (New York: Eastern Railroad Presidents Conference, 1951), p. 26; *Yearbook of Railroad Information* (Jersey City, N.J.: Eastern Railroad Presidents Conference, 1964), pp. 27–28; *Erie-Lackawanna Railroad Company 1960 Annual Report*, p. 31; *Erie-Lackawanna Railroad Company 1962 Annual Report*, p. 31.

37. Adams interview; "Transfer of Employes Begins; Stronger Railroad in Future," *Erie-Lackawanna Magazine* 57 (May-June 1961): 7; Perry M. Shoemaker, "When Do Mergers Pay? Address of P. M. Shoemaker, Vice-Chairman of the Board Erie-Lackawanna Railroad Company Before the Conference on Transportation Mergers and Acquisitions, Northwestern University, Evanston, Illinois, August 28, 1961," EL papers.

38. Adams interview; Shoemaker, "When Do Mergers Pay?"; interview with Harry A. Zilli, Jr., Cleveland, Ohio, October 19, 1991; Shoemaker interview.

39. Interview with J. D. Allen, Cleveland, Ohio, May 10, 1989.

40. Ibid.; Shannon interview.

41. *Erie-Lackawanna Railroad Company 1962 Annual Report*, pp. 10–11; Maury Klein, *Union Pacific: The Rebirth, 1894–1969* (New York: Doubleday, 1989), p. 515.

42. Allen interview; *Erie-Lackawanna Railroad Company 1963 Annual Report* (Cleveland: Erie-Lackawanna Railroad Co., 1964), p. 4; *Erie-Lackawanna Railroad Company 1960 Annual Report*, p. 12; William White to Nelson A. Rockefeller, December 22, 1960, Gubernatorial Office Records, Rockefeller Archive Center, North Tarrytown, New York.

43. McInnes interview; *Erie-Lackawanna Railroad Company 1962 Annual Report*, p. 10; Shannon interview.

44. McInnes interview; *Erie-Lackawanna Railroad Company 1960 Annual Report*, p. 13; *Erie-Lackawanna Railroad Company 1962 Annual Report*, p. 12.

45. Shannon interview; McInnes interview.

46. "Report on Erie-Lackawanna Railroad Company Ticketing Procedures and Stations in the New York Suburban Area," October 9, 1963, EL papers.

47. Clipping from *Cleveland Press*, November [?], 1962, EL papers; McInnes interview; *Erie-Lackawanna Railroad Company 1962 Annual Report*, pp. 4, 9, 24–26; Shannon interview.

48. *Erie-Lackawanna Railroad Company 1960 Annual Report*, p. 9; "Work Begun on Piggy-Back Yards at Chicago, Croxton," *Erie-Lackawanna Magazine* 56 (January 1961): 6–7; *Erie-Lackawanna Railroad Company 1961 Annual Report*, p. 8; *Erie-Lackawanna Railroad Company 1962 Annual Report*, p. 7.

The rate of ties replaced dropped sharply after 1961. The company installed 123,905 in 1960, 57,003 in 1961, and only 3,386 in 1962. See *Moody's Transportation Manual 1964* (New York: Moody's Investors Service, 1964), p. 335. Suggested Charles Shannon, "Tie replacement might be viewed as a rough barometer of a railroad's economic health." Shannon interview.

49. Shannon interview; *Erie-Lackawanna Railroad Company 1961 Annual Report*, p. 8; *Erie-Lackawanna Railroad Company 1962 Annual Report*, p. 7; *Erie-Lackawanna Railroad Company 1963 Annual Report*, p. 5; McInnes interview.

50. McInnes interview; Bayer interview; *Erie-Lackawanna Railroad Company 1961 Annual Report*, p. 4; "Suspend New E-L College Scholarships," *Erie-Lackawanna Magazine* 56 (December 1960): 5, 13; "Magazine Distribution To Be Reduced," *Erie-Lackawanna Magazine* 57 (May-June 1961): 7.

51. Adams interview; *Erie-Lackawanna Railroad Company 1960 Annual Report*, p. 14; *Moody's Transportation Manual, 1961* (New York: Moody's Investors Service, 1961), p. 1376; *Erie-Lackawanna Railroad Company 1962 Annual Report*, p. 13; *Erie-Lackawanna Railroad Company 1961 Annual Report*, p. 14; Testimony of John I. Michael, Finance Docket 23879, p. 3, EL papers.

52. John W. Barriger III to Milton McInnes, January 2, 1963, EL papers; *Moody's Transportation Manual, 1961*, p. 1373; Maxwell interview.

53. K. A. Husoskey to author, May 31, 1991; *Railway Age* 144 (January 13, 1958): 36; *Railway Age* 149 (September 5, 1960): 12; Maxwell interview.

William D. Burt, an intermodal specialist, has commented extensively on the New York Central and Erie-Lackawanna approaches to intermodal service. As he writes: "Had EL learned from the success of NYC *Super-Van* trains it would have recognized that the crux of the matter was retailing. . . . By retailing directly to the market, the Central's motor carrier unit selectively targeted those shipments that would fill empty backhauls, and its pricing tended to bring corridors and terminals into traffic balance, to the extent that this was achievable. Not coincidentally, this shifted remaining overbalanced headhauls disproportionately onto EL and other rivals willing to handle them without requiring the traffic to bear its associated cost of empty return movement. Naively, they [Erie Lackawanna and other carriers] always rationalized that they could push their freight forwarder middlemen to find backhaul, little realizing that NYC had already grabbed those loads. Retailing also put NYC in direct communication with its real customers and avoided the buck-passing over freight damage claims that all too often typified wholesale piggyback" (William D. Burt to author, January 5, 1993).

54. McInnes interview; *Erie-Lackawanna Railroad Company 1960 Annual Report*, p. 4; *Erie-Lackawanna Railroad Company 1961 Annual Report*, p. 13; Saunders, *The Railroad Mergers and the Coming of Conrail*, pp. 181–200.

55. *Erie-Lackawanna Railroad Company 1961 Annual Report*, p. 13; Fuller interview.

56. Interview with John P. Fishwick, Roanoke, Virginia, May 9, 1989; "Brief of Petitioner Erie-Lackawanna Railroad Company, before the Interstate Commerce Commission, Finance Docket Nos. 21510 et al. . . . , September 19, 1965," p. 5, EL papers.

57. Ibid., p. 4.

58. *Erie-Lackawanna Railroad Company 1961 Annual Report*, p. 13.

59. *Erie-Lackawanna Railroad Company 1962 Annual Report*, p. 14.

60. Ibid.

61. *Erie-Lackawanna Railroad Company 1961 Annual Report*, p. 6.

62. *Erie-Lackawanna Railroad Company 1962 Annual Report*, p. 8.

63. *Erie Lackawanna Railroad Company 1963 Annual Report*, p. 6.

Chapter 6

1. *Tide*, May 22, 1956, p. 26; Richard Saunders, "William White," in Keith L. Bryant, Jr., ed., *Encyclopedia of American Business History and Biography: Railroads in the Age of Regulation, 1900–1980* (New York: Facts on File Publications, 1988), pp. 471–72; Russell F. Moore, ed., *Who's Who in Railroading in North America* (New York: Simmons-Boardman Publishing, 1959), p. 674; *New York Times*, April 7, 1967.

2. Moore, *Who's Who in Railroading in North America*, p. 674; Joseph Borkin, *Robert R. Young, the Populist of Wall Street* (New York: Harper & Row, 1969), p. 137; interview with Robert G. Fuller, Singer Island, Florida, December 26, 1989; Minutes of the Board of Managers, Delaware, Lackawanna & Western Railroad Company, January 26, 1952, p. 27, Delaware, Lackawanna & Western Railroad Company papers, Syracuse University Library, Syracuse, New York.

3. Borkin, *Robert R. Young*, p. 138.

4. Interview with Curtis F. Bayer, Moreland Hills, Ohio, August 23, 1989.

5. Fuller interview.

6. Telephone interview with John G. Drake, Morristown, New Jersey, December 11, 1990; William White to Arthur W. Baker, July 2, 1939, letter in possession of Barbara Armbruster, North Olmsted, Ohio.

7. Drake telephone interview; Herrymon Maurer, "The Central Rolls Again," *Fortune* 49 (May 1954): 90; telephone interview with Gregory W. Maxwell, St. Louis, Missouri, November 6, 1991.

8. Interview with Gregory W. Maxwell, Moreland Hills, Ohio, February 19, 1988; "Is White Right about Passengers?" *Trains & Travel* 14 (November 1953): 27–29; Karl A. Brontrager, *Keeping the Railroads Running: Fifty Years on the New York Central* (New York: Hastings House, 1974), p. 210.

9. Borkin, *Robert R. Young*, pp. 132–209; Robert Sobel, *The Fallen Colossus* (New York: Webright and Talley, 1977), p. 210; telephone interview with Gregory W. Maxwell, St. Louis, Missouri, January 10, 1992; Borntrager, *Keeping the Railroads Running*, p. 185.

10. Jim Shaughnessy, *Delaware & Hudson* (Berkeley, Calif.: Howell-North Books, 1967), p. 359; Saunders, "William White," p. 474; *Wall Street Journal*, June 14, 1963; Minutes of the Erie-Lackawanna Railroad Board of Directors, April 1963, Pennsylvania State Archives, Harrisburg, Pennsylvania, hereafter cited as EL minutes; Fuller interview.

11. Maxwell interview.

12. "White Would Head Erie-Lackawanna," *Railway Age* 154 (May 13, 1963): 36; Fuller interview.

13. Drake telephone interview; interview with Milford M. Adams, Perry, Ohio, March 18, 1988; interview with John H. Ray, Lakewood, Ohio, April 24, 1989; interview with Leonard Kellogg, Marion, Ohio, May 12, 1989.

14. Bayer interview; *Erie Lackawanna Railroad Company 1963 Annual Report* (Cleveland: Erie Lackawanna Railroad Co., 1964), pp. 3, 13; Inter-Office Memorandum from William White, August 5, 1963, in possession of George W. Maxwell, St. Louis, Missouri; Maxwell interview.

15. "Erie Lackawanna: Operation Upsurge," *Inside Story* (Winter 1966–67): 3.

16. George W. Hilton, *The Transportation Act of 1958: A Decade of Experience* (Bloomington: Indiana University Press, 1969), pp. 79–96; *Erie Lackawanna Railroad Company 1963 Annual Report*, p. 13; Fuller interview.

17. *Erie Lackawanna Railroad Company 1963 Annual Report*, pp. 3, 13–14; Fuller interview.

18. *Erie Lackawanna Railroad Company 1963 Annual Report*, p. 3; *Railway Age* 155 (December 9, 1963): 56.

19. "Erie-Lackawanna Railroad Company Bonds Modification," Interstate Commerce Commission, Finance Docket No. 22882, 1964, pp. 152–57; "Supplement to Application," Finance Docket No. 22882, September 1, 1964; *Erie Lackawanna Railroad Company 1964 Annual Report* (Cleveland: Erie Lackawanna Railroad Co., 1965), p. 13.

20. *Erie Lackawanna Railroad Company 1963 Annual Report*, p. 13.

21. Fuller interview; Adams interview; David D. Van Tassel and John J. Grabowski, eds., *The Encyclopedia of Cleveland History* (Bloomington: Indiana University Press, 1987), pp. 31–32, 479.

22. "Erie-Lackawanna Railroad Company Bonds Modification," pp. 186–87; Maxwell interview; *Moody's Transportation Manual* (New York: Moody's Investors Service, Inc., 1967), pp. 707–8.

23. Adams interview; Bayer interview; Ray interview; interview with John Michael, Upland, Indiana, October 18, 1990.

24. Fuller interview; interview with Milton McInnes, Southbury, Connecticut, June 5, 1989.

25. Maxwell telephone interview, November 6, 1991.

26. Ibid.

27. Confidential interview, April 3, 1989; Frederick C. Osthoff, ed., *Who's Who in Railroading* (New York: Simmons-Boardman Publishing, 1968), p. 325; Maxwell telephone interview, November 6, 1991.

28. Maxwell telephone interview, November 6, 1991.

29. Ibid.

30. Fuller interview; interview with Charles Shannon, Arlington Heights, Illinois, October 1, 1988; *Erie-Lackawanna Railroad Company 1961 Annual Report* (Cleveland: Erie-Lackawanna Railroad Co., 1962), p. 5; *Erie Lackawanna Railroad Company 1964 Annual Report*, p. 2.

31. Shannon interview; *Erie Lackawanna Railroad Company 1963 Annual Report*, p. 6.

32. Shannon interview; Maxwell interview; Fuller interview.

33. Interview with Gregory M. Maxwell, Moreland Hills, Ohio, June 12, 1989; *Rules of the Operating Department* (Cleveland: Erie Lackawanna Railroad Co., 1964), p. 6.

34. "Memorandum for Board of Directors," August 27, 1963, EL minutes; "Cars' Ills Cured by Men in $4,000,000 Erie Shop," *Erie Magazine* 54 (October 1958): 5–7; "Highlights of Meadville Car Shop," ca. 1959, pamphlet in Erie Lackawanna papers, The University of Akron Archives, Akron, Ohio, hereafter cited as EL papers; Maxwell interview of June 12, 1989.

35. *Erie Lackawanna Railroad Company 1964 Annual Report*, p. 4; *Erie Lackawanna Railroad Company 1966 Annual Report* (Cleveland: Erie Lackawanna Railroad Co., 1967), p. 12.

36. Richard Saunders, *The Railroad Mergers and the Coming of Conrail* (Westport, Conn.: Greenwood Press, 1978), p. 98; "Erilak Properties, Inc.," EL papers.

37. "Erilak Properties, Inc."

38. Ibid.

39. Maxwell interview; Bayer interview.

40. Interview with Vic Kromer, Huntington, Indiana, May 15, 1990.

41. *Erie Lackawanna Railroad Company 1963 Annual Report*, p. 13; "Miss Phoebe Again Welcomes You to the Erie Lackawanna," EL papers; Saunders, *The Railroad Mergers and the Coming of Conrail*, p. 121.

42. *Erie Lackawanna Railroad Company 1963 Annual Report*, p. 13.

43. Ibid., p. 7; *Erie Lackawanna Railroad Company 1965 Annual Report* (Cleveland: Erie Lackawanna Railroad Co., 1966), pp. 6–7, 9; interview with William F. Howes, El Paso, Texas, December 7, 1991; *The Times-Herald* (Dallas, Texas), November 28, 1966.

44. *Annual Report of the Delaware, Lackawanna and Western Railroad Company for the Year Ending December 31st, 1928* (New York: M. B. Brown Printing & Binding Co., 1929), p. 6; *Annual Report of The Delaware, Lackawanna and Western Railroad Company for the Year Ending December 31st, 1929* (New York: M. B. Brown Printing & Binding Co., 1930), p. 9; *Annual Report of The Delaware, Lackawanna and Western Railroad Company for the Year Ending December 31st, 1930* (New York: M. B. Brown Printing & Binding Co., 1931), p. 8; George W. Hilton and John F. Due, *The Electric Interurban Railways in America* (Stanford, Calif.: Stanford University Press, 1964), pp. 306–7;

McInnes interview; "Commuter Service, File 1," Delaware, Lackawanna & Western Railroad, EL papers; E. S. Root to Thomas T. Taber, March 2, 1960, T. T. Taber papers, Railroad Museum of Pennsylvania, Strasburg, Pennsylvania, hereafter cited as Taber papers.

45. *Erie Railroad Company Annual Report 1958* (New York and Cleveland: Erie Railroad Co., 1959), p. 11.

46. "Commuter Service"; "Address of P. M. Shoemaker, President, The Delaware, Lackawanna and Western Railroad Company before the New Jersey Press Association, Rutgers University, December 5, 1958," EL papers, hereafter cited as Rutgers speech.

47. Telephone interview with Perry M. Shoemaker, Tampa, Florida, November 3, 1991; *Erie Railroad Company Annual Report 1952* (New York and Cleveland: Erie Railroad Co., 1953), p. 17; Robert B. Carson, *Main Line to Oblivion: The Disintegration of New York Railroads in the Twentieth Century* (Port Washington, N.Y.: Kennikat Press, 1971), p. 168; Shannon interview; McInnes interview.

Concluded Erie president Von Willer, "Frankly, under conditions as they presently exist . . . the prospect for any improvement or revitalization of commuter service under private enterprise is not a pleasant one." H. W. Von Willer to Thomas T. Taber, March 30, 1959, Taber papers.

48. Shoemaker telephone interview; *The Delaware, Lackawanna and Western Railroad Company 102nd Annual Report for the Year Ended December 31, 1953* (New York: Delaware, Lackawanna & Western Railroad Co., 1954), p. 8; *The Delaware, Lackawanna and Western Railroad Company 103rd Annual Report for the Year Ended December 31, 1954* (New York: Delaware, Lackawanna & Western Railroad Co., 1955), pp. 9–10; *The Delaware, Lackawanna and Western Railroad Company 106th Annual Report for the Year Ended December 31, 1957* (New York: Delaware, Lackawanna & Western Railroad Co., 1958), p. 9; Rutgers speech.

49. "Commuter Service"; Shoemaker telephone interview.

50. "Commuter Service."   51. Rutgers speech.

52. Shoemaker telephone interview.   53. "Commuter Service."

54. Ibid.; *Erie-Lackawanna Railroad Company 1960 Annual Report* (Cleveland: Erie-Lackawanna Railroad Co., 1961), p. 13; Adams interview.

55. *Erie-Lackawanna Railroad Company 1960 Annual Report*, p. 13; Shannon interview; *Erie Lackawanna Railroad Company 1966 Annual Report*, p. 9.

56. Shannon interview; *Erie Lackawanna Railroad Company 1965 Annual Report* (Cleveland: Erie Lackawanna Railroad Co., 1966), p. 5.

57. Shannon interview.

58. Ibid.; "Report on Avoidable Revenues and Expenses: New Jersey Suburban Passenger Service," Wyer, Dick & Co., 1967.

59. EL minutes, vol. 64, p. 23; *Erie Lackawanna Railroad Company 1966 Annual Report*, p. 9.

60. Interview with Harry G. Silleck, Jr., Cleveland, Ohio, October 19, 1988; Shannon interview; *Erie Lackawanna Railroad Company 1966 Annual Report*, p. 9.

61. *Erie Lackawanna Railroad Company 1966 Annual Report*, p. 9; Silleck interview.

62. Silleck interview; *Erie Lackawanna Railroad Company 1966 Annual Report*,

p. 9; Shannon interview; *Erie Lackwanna Railroad Company 1967 Annual Report* (Cleveland: Erie Lackawanna Railroad Co., 1968), p. 6.

63. *Erie Lackawanna Railroad Company 1966 Annual Report*, pp. 10–11.

64. *Erie Lackawanna Railroad Company 1965 Annual Report*, pp. 2–3; *Erie Lackawanna Railroad Company 1966 Annual Report*, p. 2; "Inside Story," p. 3.

65. Maxwell interview; *New York Times*, January 28, 1960.

66. *Erie Lackawanna Railroad Company 1963 Annual Report*, pp. 3–4; *Erie Lackawanna Railroad Company 1966 Annual Report*, pp. 3–4; *Erie Lackawanna Railroad Company 1965 Annual Report*, p. 3; *Erie Lackawanna Railroad Company 1967 Annual Report*, p. 7.

67. Interview with J. D. Allen, Cleveland, Ohio, May 10, 1989; *Erie Lackawanna Railroad Company 1963 Annual Report*, p. 3.

68. *Erie Lackawanna Railroad Company 1963 Annual Report*, p. 3; *Erie Lackawanna Railroad Company 1964 Annual Report*, pp. 4–5.

69. *Erie Lackawanna Railroad Company 1966 Annual Report*, pp. 11–12; Maxwell interview.

70. William White to Robert F. Fuller, February 3, 1965, EL papers; *Erie Lackawanna Railroad Company 1964 Annual Report*, p. 3; *Erie Lackawanna Railroad Company 1966 Annual Report*, p. 3; *Yearbook of Railroad Facts* (Washington, D.C.: Association of American Railroads, 1967), p. 30.

71. Maxwell telephone interview, January 10, 1992.

72. Howes interview; "Erie Lackawanna Railroad—Preliminary Report," C&O Industrial Engineering Department, December 1, 1965, EL papers.

This report misstated the New York Central's best times. They were likely about 22 hours. And in 1966, the Central's SV-10 (*Super Van*-10) ran from Englewood (Chicago) to New York in 20 hours. William D. Burt to author, January 5, 1993.

73. Maxwell interview; Adams interview.

74. Fuller interview; *Erie Lackawanna Railroad Company 1964 Annual Report*, p. 13.

75. Fuller interview; Albro Martin, *Railroads Triumphant: The Growth, Rejection & Rebirth of a Vital American Force* (New York: Oxford University Press, 1992), p. 324; "Norfolk & Western Railway Co. and New York, Chicago & St. Louis Railroad Co.—Merger, Etc.," Finance Docket No. 21510, *Interstate Commerce Commission Reports*, p. 782; McInnes interview; *Erie Lackawanna Railroad Company 1964 Annual Report*, p. 13.

76. *New York Times*, March 17, 1968; Saunders, *The Railroad Mergers and the Coming of Conrail*, pp. 125–49, 246–62; John P. Fishwick, "Merger and Consolidation Potentials," Nineteenth Railroad Management Institute, School of Business Administration, The American University, January 13, 1965, EL papers; interview with John P. Fishwick, Roanoke, Virginia, May 9, 1989.

77. *New York Times*, March 17, 1968; Fishwick interview.

78. Interview with Isabel H. Benham, New York, New York, June 6, 1989.

79. Ibid.; Fishwick interview; Minutes of the Board of Directors of the Norfolk & Western Railway Company, August 31, 1965, pp. 2–4, EL papers.

80. *Erie Lackawanna Railroad Company 1965 Annual Report*, p. 4; Fuller interview;

Fishwick interview; "Reply of Erie-Lackawanna Railroad Company to Petition for Consolidation of Proceedings for Hearing and Decision," Finance Docket No. 21510 et al.; Saunders, *Railroad Mergers and the Coming of Conrail*, p. 253.

81. *Erie Lackawanna Railroad Company 1966 Annual Report*, pp. 5–9; Fuller interview.

82. Fishwick interview; Maxwell interview; Saunders, *Railroad Mergers and the Coming of Conrail*, p. 254.

83. *Erie Lackawanna Railroad Company 1966 Annual Report*, pp. 21–22; Fishwick interview; Gus Welty, ed., *Era of the Giants: The New Railroad Merger Movement* (Omaha: Simmons-Boardman Publishing, 1982), p. 89.

84. Saunders, *Railroad Mergers and the Coming of Conrail*, pp. 246–47; *Norfolk and Western Railway 1966 Annual Report* (Roanoke, Virginia: Norfolk & Western Railway Co., 1967), p. 17; Fishwick interview; *Norfolk and Western Railway 1967 Annual Report* (Roanoke, Virginia: Norfolk & Western Railway Co., 1968), p. 16.

85. Maxwell telephone interview, January 10, 1992; Fuller interview.

86. Fuller interview; Shannon interview; Bayer interview.

Chapter 7

1. *Cleveland Press*, April 1, 1968; *Virginian Pilot* (Norfolk, Virginia), March 31, 1968.

2. Interview with Wallace R. Steffen, Westlake, Ohio, January 9, 1990; *Jersey Journal* (Jersey City, New Jersey), March 26, 1968; interview with Richard H. Hahn, Cleveland, Ohio, March 31, 1989.

3. Keith L. Bryant, Jr., "John P. Fishwick," in Keith L. Bryant, Jr., ed., *Encyclopedia of American Business History and Biography: Railroads in the Age of Regulation, 1900–1980* (New York: Facts on File Publications, 1988), pp. 154–59; interview with John P. Fishwick, Roanoke, Virginia, May 9, 1989; interview with Isabel H. Benham, New York, New York, June 6, 1989.

4. Bryant, "John P. Fishwick," p. 154; *New York Times*, March 17, 1968; *Roanoke* (Virginia) *Times*, March 8, 1968.

5. "John P. Fishwick: Dream Deferred," *Forbes* 101 (April 1, 1968): 71; Fishwick interview.

6. Benham interview; *Cleveland Press*, March 15, 1968; *Roanoke Times*, March 8, 1968; Hahn interview; interview with Gregory W. Maxwell, Moreland Hills, Ohio, June 12, 1989.

When William White called Herman Pevler "stupid," he missed seeing that the former Wabash executive was probably an above-average operating person and that he knew how to manage employees. Edward Burkhardt, a former Wabash official, recalled fondly that when Pevler once passed through Decatur, Illinois, in his business car, he asked the local superintendent if he experienced any problems with the sprawling yard facility. "No sir!" came the response. "We have a perfect yard operation here." So Pevler told his traveling associates, "Pull the pin. I'm going to stay here for a couple of days to observe this perfect yard." Interview with Edward A. Burkhardt, Milwaukee, Wisconsin, September 25, 1992.

7. Interview with Robert G. Fuller, Singer Island, Florida, December 26, 1989; Fishwick interview; telephone interview with Gregory W. Maxwell, St. Louis, Missouri, January 10, 1992; *Roanoke World-News* (Roanoke, Virginia), March 26, 1968.

8. *Norfolk & Western Railway Company 1968 Annual Report* (Roanoke, Va.: Norfolk & Western Railway Co., 1969), pp. 19, 24.

9. Fishwick interview; Benham interview; Isabel H. Benham to Marjorie Fisher, November 13, 1968, Isabel H. Benham papers, Barriger Collection, Mercantile Library, St. Louis, Missouri; Isabel H. Benham to Leo Blum, January 29, 1969, I. H. Benham papers.

10. *Moody's Transportation Manual* (New York: Moody's Investors Service, Inc., 1968), p. 1; telephone interview with Gregory W. Maxwell, St. Louis, Missouri, March 25, 1992.

11. Gus Welty, ed., *Era of the Giants: The New Railroad Merger Movement* (Omaha: Simmons-Boardman Publishing, 1982), p. 91; *Moody's Transportation Manual* (New York: Moody's Investors Service, Inc., 1971), p. 797.

12. Herbert H. Harwood, Jr., to author, March 9, 1992, March 10, 1992; Joseph R. Daughen and Peter Binzen, *The Wreck of the Penn Central* (Boston: Little, Brown, 1971), pp. 252–307; *Moody's Transportation Manual, 1971*, p. 737; Maxwell telephone interview, January 10, 1992.

13. *Erie Lackawanna Railroad Company 1967 Annual Report* (Cleveland: Erie Lackawanna Railroad Co., 1968), p. 2; Fishwick interview; E. F. Striplin, *The Norfolk & Western: A History* (Roanoke, Va.: Norfolk & Western Railway Co., 1981), p. 344.

14. Fishwick interview; interview with M. Fred Coffman, Akron, Ohio, November 4, 1988; Steffen interview; interview with J. D. Allen, Cleveland, Ohio, May 10, 1989.

15. Fishwick interview.

16. Ibid.; *Dereco, Inc. 1968 Annual Report* (Roanoke, Va.: Dereco, Inc., 1969), pp. 3–4, 6–7; "Trustees' Report on Reorganization Planning," July 10, 1973, pp. 23–24; *New York Times*, June 16, 1969; Maxwell interview; *Dereco, Inc. 1969 Annual Report* (Roanoke, Va.: Dereco, Inc., 1970), p. 5.

17. *Dereco, Inc. 1970 Annual Report* (Roanoke, Va.: Dereco, Inc., 1971), p. 3; Steffen interview.

18. Maxwell interview; Research Department, Erie Lackawanna Railway Company, ca. 1971, Erie Lackawanna papers, The University of Akron Archives, Akron, Ohio, hereafter cited as EL papers.

19. Maxwell interview; Robert Sobel, *The Fallen Colossus* (New York: Weybright and Talley, 1977), pp. 251–52.

20. Maxwell interview; Richard Saunders, *The Railroad Mergers and the Coming of Conrail* (Westport, Conn.: Greenwood Press, 1978), p. 296.

21. Maxwell interview; Minutes of the Board of Directors, Erie Lackawanna Railway Company, November 25, 1969; *Dereco, Inc. 1969 Annual Report*, pp. 5–6; *Dereco, Inc. 1970 Annual Report*, p. 6.

22. Maxwell interview; Minutes of the Board of Directors, Erie Lackawanna Railway Company, May 22, 1972, pp. 50–51, EL papers.

23. Maxwell interview; Minutes of the Board of Directors, Erie Lackawanna Railway Company, May 20, 1974, p. 349.

24. Maxwell interview.

25. Ibid.; Steffen interview.

26. Telephone interview with J. D. Allen, Cleveland, Ohio, February 4, 1992.

27. *Newark Sunday News* (Newark, New Jersey), October 19, 1969; "Erie Lackawanna Railway Co. Discontinuance of Trains Nos. 5 and 6 Between Chicago, Ill., and Hoboken, N.J.," Interstate Commerce Commission, Finance Docket No. 25735, December 24, 1969, p. 206, hereafter cited as "Discontinuance of Trains Nos. 5 and 6"; Steffen interview; *Dereco, Inc. 1969 Annual Report*, p. 6.

28. "Discontinuance of Trains Nos. 5 and 6," p. 211.

During the final month of operations, patrons utilized only 17 percent of the available seats, and train crew occasionally outnumbered passengers.

29. "Discontinuance of Trains Nos. 5 and 6," pp. 214, 239.

30. Maxwell interview; "Discontinuance of Trains Nos. 5 and 6," p. 225.

31. "Discontinuance of Trains Nos. 5 and 6," pp. 224, 239; Steffen interview.

32. *Chicago Tribune*, January 6, 1970.

Those Erie Lackawanna employees who worked on *The Lake Cities* did not lose their jobs. Rather, the company reassigned them to freight service.

33. *Dereco, Inc. 1970 Annual Report*, p. 6; "New Cars & Locomotives, Erie Lackawanna Ry., Service Inaugurated," Bureau of Public Information, New Jersey Department of Transportation, January 21, 1971, EL papers.

34. "News: Erie Lackawanna Railway," January 21, 1971, EL papers; interview with Charles Shannon, Arlington Heights, Illinois, October 1, 1988.

35. *Erie Lackawanna Railway Company 1973 Annual Report* (Cleveland: Erie Lackawanna Railway Co., 1974), p. 5; Steffen interview.

36. Minutes of the Board of Directors, Erie Lackawanna Railway Company, August 24, 1970, p. 67; October 16, 1972, pp. 54–55; Steffen interview; interview with David McKay, Akron, Ohio, May 29, 1992; *Cleveland Plain Dealer*, January 15, 1977.

37. Telephone interview with Gregory W. Maxwell, St. Louis, Missouri, March 26, 1992; *Dereco, Inc. 1970 Annual Report*, p. 8.

38. Fishwick interview.

39. "D&H and Coordinations," statement by Carl B. Sterzing, n.d., EL papers; *Dereco, Inc. 1969 Annual Report*, p. 8.

40. Minutes of the Board of Directors, Erie Lackawanna Railway Company, June 22, 1970, p. 50, EL papers; *Norfolk & Western Railway Company 1970 Annual Report* (Roanoke, Va.: Norfolk & Western Railway Co., 1971), p. 11; *Dereco, Inc. 1970 Annual Report*, p. 7; *Dereco, Inc. 1971 Annual Report*, p. 8.

41. Maxwell telephone interview, January 10, 1992; *Dereco, Inc. 1970 Annual Report*, p. 7.

42. Maxwell telephone interview, March 25, 1992; Coffman interview; interview with David J. DeBoer, Milwaukee, Wisconsin, September 25, 1992.

43. Minutes of the Board of Directors, Erie Lackawanna Railway Company, October 26, 1970, p. 79, EL papers; Maxwell telephone interview, March 26, 1992.

44. Interview with Joseph R. Neikirk, Norfolk, Virginia, May 16, 1989.

45. Coffman interview; *Dereco, Inc. 1968 Annual Report*, 7; *Dereco, Inc. 1969 Annual Report*, p. 7; Minutes of the Board of Directors, Erie Lackawanna Railway Company, April 22, 1969, p. 1, EL papers.

46. Maxwell telephone interview, January 10, 1992; Maury Klein, "Replacement Technology: The Diesel as a Case Study," *Railroad History* 162 (Spring 1990): 116; *Dereco, Inc. 1969 Annual Report*, p. 8.

47. Maxwell telephone interview, January 10, 1992; *Dereco, Inc. 1968 Annual Report*, p. 8.

48. Maxwell interview; *Dereco, Inc. 1969 Annual Report*, p. 8.

49. Maxwell telephone interview, March 25, 1992; *Dereco, Inc. 1971 Annual Report*, p. 6.

50. Maxwell telephone interview, March 25, 1992; Saunders, *The Railroad Mergers and the Coming of Conrail*, p. 331.

51. Fishwick interview; Neikirk interview.

52. See *Wall Street Journal*, August 15, 1991.

53. *Railway Age* 170 (April 26, 1971): 13; ibid. (January 11, 1971): 19; ibid. (January 25, 1971): 170; *Yearbook of Railroad Facts* (Washington, D.C.: Association of American Railroads, 1972), p. 57.

54. *New York Times*, June 21, 1992; George W. Hilton, *The Northeast Railroad Problem* (Washington, D.C.: American Enterprise Institute for Public Policy Research, 1975), pp. 4–5; Coffman interview.

55. *Dereco, Inc. 1970 Annual Report*, p. 4; *Dereco, Inc. 1971 Annual Report*, pp. 4–5.

56. Minutes of the Board of Directors, Erie Lackawanna Railway Company, February 22, 1971, p. 14, EL papers.

57. Ibid., p. 11; interview with Milford M. Adams, Perry, Ohio, March 18, 1988; Maxwell interview.

58. Interview with Harry Zilli, Jr., Cleveland, Ohio, February 17, 1988; Minutes of the Board of Directors, Erie Lackawanna Railway Company, February 22, 1971, p. 11; Neikirk interview.

59. Adams interview; *Railway Age* 173 (July 10, 1972): 10; Zilli interview; Hahn interview; Minutes of the Board of Directors, Erie Lackawanna Railway Company, January 24, 1972, p. 12, EL papers.

60. Hahn interview.

61. *Flood: The Southern Tier's June 1972 Disaster, A Pictorial Review* (Hornell, N.Y.: W. H. Greenhow Co., 1972); *New York Times*, June 18, June 20, 1972; *Wall Street Journal*, June 27, 1972.

62. *Railway Age* 173 (July 10, 1972): 10, 13; ibid. (August 14, 1972): 26–30; Minutes of the Board of Directors, Erie Lackawanna Railway Company, June 26, 1972, p. 59, EL papers.

63. "News: Erie Lackawanna Railway," June 25, 1972, EL papers; *EL Digest*, September 1, 1972.

64. *EL Digest*, September 1, 1972; Neikirk interview.

65. Fishwick interview; Adams interview; *Dereco, Inc. 1972 Annual Report*, p. 3.

66. Hahn interview; Adams interview; Minutes of the Board of Directors, Erie

Lackawanna Railway Company, March 25, 1969, EL papers; Minutes of the Board of Directors, Erie Lackawanna Railway Company, February 22, 1972, EL papers; Steffen interview.

67. Interview with Jervis Langdon, Jr., Akron, Ohio, April 26, 1990.

68. Howard Skidmore, "Merger, Money, and Men: What Happened When NYC Fought C&O for B&O?" *Trains* 52 (October 1992): 49; Maxwell telephone interview, January 10, 1992.

Chapter 8

1. Interview with Robert B. Krupansky, Cleveland, Ohio, February 21, 1989; interview with Thomas F. Patton, Cleveland, Ohio, February 7, 1989.

2. Krupansky interview.

3. Ibid.; Patton interview; "News Release," Erie Lackawanna Railway Company, July 31, 1972, Erie Lackawanna papers, The University of Akron Archives, Akron, Ohio, hereafter cited as EL papers; *Wall Street Journal*, August 1, 1972; *Cleveland Press*, January 14, 1974.

4. Interview with Bernard V. Donahue, Cleveland, Ohio, March 9, 1988; Diana Tittle, *Rebuilding Cleveland: The Cleveland Foundation and Its Evolving Urban Strategy* (Columbus: Ohio State University Press, 1992), p. 101.

Patton and Tyler each received $50,000 annually from 1972 to 1982, and then they petitioned the court for additional compensation. Judge Krupansky subsequently awarded them each a $275,000 bonus. "They were really pleased," recalled Harry Zilli. "Tyler's joy nearly lifted the roof off the building." Patton and Tyler hardly made the Erie Lackawanna into their personal money machine. One Penn Central officer, for example, won a court-approved pension of a thousand dollars a day. Telephone interview with Harry A. Zilli, Jr., Olmsted Falls, Ohio, October 27, 1992.

5. *Who's Who in America, 1964–1965* (Chicago: A. N. Marquis Co., 1965), p. 1556; Donahue interview; Patton interview.

6. *Who's Who in America, 1964–1965*, p. 2318; *Cleveland Plain Dealer*, August 5, 1986; interview with Richard H. Hahn, Cleveland, Ohio, March 31, 1989; interview with Bernard V. Donahue, Cleveland, Ohio, February 7, 1989.

7. Krupansky interview; Patton interview.

8. Patton interview; Donahue interview, March 9, 1988; Ralph S. Tyler, Jr., to William R. Dimeling et al., July 1, 1986, EL papers.

9. Patton interview; Hahn interview.

10. Interview with Joseph R. Neikirk, Norfolk, Virginia, May 16, 1989; *EL Digest*, September 1, 1972; telephone interview with Gregory W. Maxwell, St. Louis, Missouri, July 22, 1992; Minutes of Trustees and Officers, Erie Lackawanna Railway Co., June 17, 1974, p. 359, EL papers.

11. *Erie Lackawanna Railway Company 1972 Annual Report* (Cleveland: Erie Lackawanna Railway Co., 1973), p. 2; Minutes of Trustees and Officers, Erie Lackawanna Railway Company, February 26, 1973, pp. 147–48, EL papers; Proceedings before U.S. District Court, Northern District of Ohio, Eastern Division, May 14, 1973, p. 21, EL papers.

12. Krupansky interview; interview with Jervis Langdon, Jr., Akron, Ohio, April 26, 1990.

13. Minutes of Trustees and Officers, Erie Lackawanna Railway Company, October 4, 1972, p. 1, EL papers; Order No. 1, June 1972, EL papers; *Cleveland Plain Dealer*, July 1, 1973.

14. Patton interview; "EL: 'Brightest future' among the bankrupts," *Railway Age* 174 (May 28, 1973): 12.

15. Telephone interview with Robert Hampton, Boulder, Colorado, July 24, 1989; Salomon Bros., Consultants file, EL papers, hereafter cited as Salomon Bros. file.

16. Salomon Bros. file.

17. Hampton telephone interview; Salomon Bros. file.

18. Salomon Bros. file; interview with Charles Shannon, Arlington Heights, Illinois, October 1, 1988; Minutes of Trustees and Directors, Erie Lackawanna Railway Company, July 23, 1973, p. 229, EL papers; *Marion* (Ohio) *Star*, August 16, 1975.

19. Interview with Harry A. Zilli, Jr., Cleveland, Ohio, June 12, 1989.

20. *Erie Lackawanna Railway Company 1973 Annual Report* (Cleveland: Erie Lackawanna Railway Co., 1974), p. 9; *Erie Lackawanna Railway Company 1974 Annual Report* (Cleveland: Erie Lackawanna Railway Co., 1974), p. 9.

21. Interview with Dominic Carbone, Cleveland, Ohio, August 23, 1989; confidential interview; interview with Gregory W. Maxwell, Moreland Hills, Ohio, June 12, 1989; George W. Hilton, *The Northeast Railroad Problem* (Washington, D.C.: American Enterprise Institute for Public Policy Research, 1975), p. 18.

22. Maxwell interview; Proceedings before U.S. District Court, Northern District of Ohio, Eastern Division, August 7, 1974, pp. 31–33, EL papers.

23. Interview with Curtis F. Bayer, Moreland Hills, Ohio, August 23, 1989; *Erie Lackawanna Railway Company Financial Reports for Year Ended December 31, 1975 and Three Months Ended March 31, 1976* (Cleveland: Erie Lackawanna Railway Co., 1976), p. 18.

24. Minutes of Trustees and Officers, Erie Lackawanna Railway Company, December 4, 1974, p. 427, EL papers.

25. Zilli interview; interview with M. Fred Coffman, Akron, Ohio, December 4, 1988.

26. Patton interview; Shannon interview; Zilli interview; *Erie Lackawanna Railway Company 1974 Annual Report*, p. 2.

27. Stephen Salsbury, *No Way to Run a Railroad: The Untold Story of the Penn Central Crisis* (New York: McGraw-Hill, 1982), p. 209; *Wall Street Journal*, August 15, 1991; *The Great Railway Crisis: An Administrative History of the United States Railway Administration* (Washington, D.C.: National Academy of Public Administration, 1978), pp. 64–66.

The bankruptcy of Erie Lackawanna on June 6, 1972, was preceded by the failure of the Jersey Central (March 22, 1967), Boston & Maine (March 12, 1970), Penn Central (June 21, 1970), Lehigh Valley (July 24, 1970), Reading (November 23, 1971), and Lehigh & Hudson River (March 18, 1972). The Ann Arbor collapsed on October 15, 1973.

28. Hilton, *The Northeast Railroad Problem*, pp. 30–33.

29. Joseph Albright, "The Penn Central: A Hell of a Way to Run a Government," *The New York Times Magazine*, November 3, 1974, pp. 16–17, 94, 96–98, 102–5, 110; Brook Adams, "Railroads: A Vital Link in the Northwest-Northeast Transportation Chain," Address to the National Association of Regulatory Utilities Commissioners, Seattle, Washington, September 17, 1973, EL papers.

30. Albright, "The Penn Central," p. 16; interview with Isabel H. Benham, New York, New York, June 6, 1989; Langdon interview.

31. Albright, "The Penn Central," p. 16; Langdon interview.

32. *Final System Plan* (Washington, D.C.: United States Railway Association, 1975, 2 vols.), vol. 1, pp. 2–3; *Compilation of Certain Railroad Laws within the Jurisdiction of the Committee on Interstate and Foreign Commerce* (Washington, D.C.: House Committee of Interstate and Foreign Commerce, 1976), pp. 8–29.

33. Richard Saunders, *The Railroad Mergers and the Coming of Conrail* (Westport, Conn.: Greenwood Press, 1978), p. 312; *The Great Railway Crisis*, p. 192; *Final System Plan*, vol 1, pp. i–iii.

34. Langdon interview; telephone interview with Gregory W. Maxwell, August 25, 1992.

35. *The Great Railway Crisis*, pp. 295–97, 358–59; Benham interview; Langdon interview.

36. Patton interview; "Press Release," Erie Lackawanna Railway Company, January 9, 1975, EL papers; *Erie Lackawanna Railway Company 1974 Annual Report*, p. 2; interview with Harry G. Silleck, Jr., Cleveland, Ohio, October 19, 1988; "Memorandum of the Trustees of Erie Lackawanna Railway Company as to 1) Its Need for Cash to Carry on Its Operations, 2) Its Related Expense Control Program," June 7, 1975, p. 1, EL papers, hereafter cited as Memorandum of June 7, 1975; *New York Times*, January 10, 1975.

37. Zilli interview; *Saint Paul Dispatch*, February 18, 1975; Maxwell interview; "Erie-Lackawanna Railway Company: Proposal for Acquisition," Cost Analysis and Research, Atchison, Topeka & Santa Fe Railway, May 30, 1975, pp. 14, 16, EL papers, hereafter cited as ATSF report.

38. Patton interview; Thomas G. Fuechtmann, *Steeples and Stacks: Religion and Steel Crisis in Youngstown* (New York: Cambridge University Press, 1989), pp. 19, 38–39.

39. Silleck interview.

40. Patton interview; confidential interview; Silleck interview; *Congressional Record, House*, February 19, 1975, p. H854.

41. Krupansky interview; ATSF report, p. 7.

42. *Erie Lackawanna Railway Financial Reports*, pp. 1–2.

43. Silleck interview; Donahue interview, March 9, 1988; Harry G. Silleck, Jr., to author, January 19, 1993; January 26, 1993.

44. *The Great Railway Crisis*, pp. 384–86; Silleck interview.

45. *The Great Railway Crisis*, p. 391; *Wall Street Journal*, February 5, 1975.

46. *The Great Railway Crisis*, p. 398; Maxwell interview.

47. Benham interview; Maxwell interview; Charles E. Bertrand to Gregory W.

Maxwell, February 2, 1975, EL papers; *The Great Railway Crisis*, pp. 401, 506; C. B. Sterzing, "An Alternative to the Octopus Concept of Northeast Rail Reorganization," *Railway Age* 175 (February 11, 1974): 30–32.

48. *The Great Railway Crisis*, p. 505; Maxwell interview.

49. Benham interview; Langdon interview; "The Shape of Things to Come in the Northeast and Midwest," *Railway Age* 176 (August 11, 1975): 17; Silleck interview.

50. Interview with Milford M. Adams, Perry, Ohio, March 18, 1988.

51. Ibid.; Maxwell interview; *Marion Star*, August 16, 1975; interview with Leonard Kellogg, Marion, Ohio, May 12, 1989.

52. ATSF report; Maxwell interview.

53. ATSF report, pp. 3, 33, 35.

54. Maxwell interview.

55. Langdon interview; interview with William F. Howes, Jr., El Paso, Texas, December 7, 1991.

56. *The Great Railway Crisis*, pp. 512–13.

57. Interview with John P. Fishwick, Roanoke, Virginia, May 9, 1989; Saunders, *The Railway Mergers and the Coming of Conrail*, p. 312.

58. Langdon interview; Howes interview.

59. Howes interview; Maxwell interview; "Anticipated TOFC Traffic for 1976," p. 2, EL papers.

60. Howes interview; *Wall Street Journal*, October 20, 1975.

61. *The Great Railway Crisis*, pp. 514–16; *Journal of Commerce*, June 27, 1975.

62. *Wall Street Journal*, November 18, 1975; *The Great Railway Crisis*, pp. 516–19.

63. *Final System Plan*, vol. 1, p. 18.

64. Ibid., p. 19.

65. *The Great Railway Crisis*, p. 565; *Compilation of Certain Railroad Laws*, p. 85; *Washington Post*, September 20, 1975; *Journal of Commerce*, September 22, 1975.

66. *The Great Railway Crisis*, p. 566.

67. "Evaluation and Plan: Reading, Erie-Lackawanna, and PC Charleston Lines Acquisition," Chessie System, EL papers; *The Great Railway Crisis*, p. 566; *Journal of Commerce*, November 7, 19, 1975; *Wall Street Journal*, November 7, 1975.

68. Maxwell telephone interview, August 25, 1992; Saunders, *The Railroad Mergers and the Coming of Conrail*, p. 319; *Wall Street Journal*, February 13, 1976.

69. *The Great Railway Crisis*, pp. 661, 663–65.

70. Telephone interview with J. D. Allen, Cleveland, Ohio, February 4, 1992; Silleck interview; "Why Chessie and the Southern Withdrew," *Railway Age* 177 (February 23, 1976): 3.

71. Allen telephone interview; *The Great Railway Crisis*, p. 666.

72. Allen telephone interview; *The Great Railway Crisis*, pp. 666–67; *Baltimore Sun*, February 13, 20, 1976; *Washington Star*, February 27, 1976.

73. *The Great Railway Crisis*, p. 669; *Washington Star*, March 19, 1975; "Bill Coleman Tries Harder," *Forbes* 117 (April 1, 1976): 43; Allen telephone interview.

74. *The Great Railway Crisis*, pp. 670–73; Allen telephone interview.

75. Maxwell telephone interview, August 25, 1992; Langdon interview.

76. *Journal of Commerce*, March 24, 1976; Howes interview.

77. Allen telephone interview.

78. Langdon interview; *The Great Railway Crisis*, p. 668.

79. Kellogg interview; *Marion Star*, August 7, 1975.

80. *Marion Star*, August 23, 26, September 6, October 7, 1975.

81. Ibid., September 6, 1975; Kellogg interview.

82. Memorandum of June 7, 1975; Minutes of Trustees and Officers, Erie Lackawanna Railway Company, March 24, 1975, Schedule D, EL papers; Minutes of the Trustees and Officers, Erie Lackawanna Railway Company, July 14, 1975, Schedule B, EL papers; Minutes of Trustees and Officers, Erie Lackawanna Railway Company, April 28, 1975, p. 472, EL papers.

83. Neikirk interview; *EL Digest*, July 1975, p. 1; Minutes of Trustees and Officers, Erie Lackawanna Railway Company, May 19, 1975, p. 474; *EL Digest*, March 1976, p. 1; Shannon interview; Maxwell telephone interview, August 25, 1992; "SF, EL, D&H win top safety awards," *Railway Age* 177 (May 31, 1976): 11.

84. "EL: Winning Strategy against Long Odds," *Railway Age* 175 (October 28, 1974): 24, 26, 29; Minutes of the Trustees and Officers, Erie Lackawanna Railway Company, September 9, 1974, p. 394, EL papers; *EL Digest*, October 1974, p. 2; *Final System Plan*, vol. 2, p. 1258.

85. *Cleveland Plain Dealer*, April 1, 1976; *Marion Star*, April 1, 1976; interview with former Erie Lackawanna Railway employees, home of John R. Michael, Huntington, Indiana, May 15, 1990.

86. Train Order No. 1, Erie-Lackawanna Railway Company, March 31, 1976, in possession of Paul Michael, Huntington, Indiana.

87. Interview with Robert Eisenhower, Huntington, Indiana, May 15, 1990.

Chapter 9

1. Interview with Leonard Kellogg, Marion, Ohio, May 12, 1989; unidentified court testimony [1975], Erie Lackawanna Railway Papers, The University of Akron Archives, Akron, Ohio, hereafter cited as EL papers.

2. Interview with Wallace R. Steffen, Westlake, Ohio, January 9, 1990; Kellogg interview; interview with William J. Donnelly, Huntington, Indiana, May 15, 1990; interview with J. D. Allen, Cleveland, Ohio, May 10, 1989.

Employees of the bankrupt carriers who lost their jobs because of the restructuring process and who had more than five years of service maintained their salaries until retirement age. Any employee who refused to accept a transfer received only severance pay and lost the right to this considerable protection.

3. Interview with Bart Paoletto, Huntington, Indiana, May 15, 1990; interview with Robert Eisenhower, Huntington, Indiana, May 15, 1990.

4. Interview with M. Fred Coffman, Akron, Ohio, November 4, 1988; Kellogg interview.

When Conrail began operations, it inherited a mixed fleet of more than 5,000 locomotives. On April 1, 1976, the Conrail roster had 90 different models from 4 manufacturers, including General Electric. It took years for Conrail to standardize its diverse fleet of motive power.

5. Apparently, United Parcel Service was "quite unhappy at having its traffic consolidated with ex–Penn Central piggyback schedules." William D. Burt to author, January 5, 1993.

6. Preston Cook, *Erie Lackawanna Memories: The Final Years* (Silver Spring, Md.: Old Line Graphics, 1987), pp. 80–81; Edward A. Lewis, *American Shortline Railway Guide* (Milwaukee: Kalmbach Publishing, 3d ed., 1986), pp. 23, 196, 208, 230; Edward A. Lewis, *American Shortline Railway Guide* (Waukesha, Wis.: Kalmbach Books, 4th ed., 1991), p. 131.

In 1992 a portion of the old Erie Lackawanna main line amazingly rose phoenix-like from an abandoned 3.1-mile section near Laketon, Indiana. The Laketon Refinery Corporation, an asphalt manufacturer, decided that it could no longer afford to rely solely on truck transport and so built this industrial shortline.

7. Cook, *Erie Lackawanna Memories*, pp. 80–81; *Buffalo News*, July 3, 1992; Bill Stephens, "Delaware & Hudson Thrives under CP Rail," *Trains* 52 (July 1992): 24–26; Scott Hartley, "New Life for Conrail's Southern Tier," *Trains* 53 (March 1993): 54–60; telephone interview with William D. Burt, Binghamton, New York, November 12, 1992.

Even the Erie Lackawanna's Bison Yard facility in Buffalo has made a comeback. Although it was a vacant sea of rail and grass by the mid-1980's, Norfolk Southern in the early 1990's oversaw a multimillion-dollar revitalization and expansion to allow it to handle expanding auto, intermodal, and lumber traffic.

8. Jim Boyd, "Stack Trains on the Susquehanna," *Railfan and Railroad* 6 (May 1987): 44–57; Scott Hartley, "The Delaware Otsego Story," *Trains* 48 (January 1988): 28–41.

9. Greg J. McDonnell, "Is There Life after Lackawanna?" *Trains* 45 (July 1985): 36–46; Greg J. McDonnell, "D&H and B&H, Suzie Q and Salt," *Trains* 45 (August 1985): 40–49; Lewis, *American Shortline Railway Guide*, 4th ed., p. 248.

10. Interview with Bernard V. Donahue, Cleveland, Ohio, March 7, 1990.

11. *Erie Lackawanna Railway Financial Report for Nine Months Ended December 31, 1976* (Cleveland: Erie Lackawanna Railway Co., 1977), pp. 1, 20; "Erie Lackawanna Railway Company, Organization Chart," December 1, 1976, EL papers; interview with Charles Shannon, Arlington Heights, Illinois, October 1, 1988.

12. Minutes of Trustees and Officers, Erie Lackawanna Railway Company, May 10, 1976, p. 570, EL papers; interview with Harry A. Zilli, Jr., February 4, 1992; Minutes of Trustees and Officers, Erie Lackawanna Railway Company, April 22, 1976, pp. 568–69, EL papers; *Erie Lackawanna Inc. 1982 Financial Report* (Cleveland: Erie Lackawanna Inc., 1983), p. 2.

13. *Erie Lackawanna Railway Financial Report . . . 1976*, p. 2; interview with Eugene D. Murphy, Cleveland, Ohio, May 18, 1989; interview with Curtis F. Bayer, Moreland Hills, Ohio, August 23, 1989.

14. Interview with Bernard V. Donahue, Cleveland, Ohio, November 14, 1990; interview with Harry A. Zilli, Jr., Cleveland, Ohio, February 4, 1992.

15. A catchall deed conveyed the rights, title, and interests in a parcel, and was used by the Estate to "get out from taxes and any environmental responsibilities." The

property likely had little or no value, but appealed to speculators in "junk" real estate. Interview with Harry A. Zilli, Jr., North Olmsted, Ohio, January 7, 1993.

16. Murphy interview; The United States District Court, The Northern District of Ohio, Eastern Division, Document No. 3566-1, pp. 12–13, hereafter cited as District Court Document No. 3566-1.

17. Donahue interview, November 14, 1990.

18. District Court Document No. 3566-1, pp. 2–5; "Erie Lackawanna Railway Company Subsidiaries and Affiliates, 1972," Finance Department, July 13, 1973, pp. 36–37, EL papers; Minutes of Trustees and Officers, Erie Lackawanna Railway Company, February 26, 1980, p. 720, EL papers; interview with Harry Zilli, Jr., Cleveland, Ohio, April 5, 1989.

19. Zilli interview, February 4, 1992.

The Estate sold the first lot of certificates in 1982 for $61,000 and the second one in 1989 for $46,210.

20. Ibid.; Minutes of Trustees and Officers, Erie Lackawanna Railway Company, July 23, 1980, p. 733, EL papers.

21. District Court Document No. 3566-1, p. 14; *Erie Lackawanna Railway Company 1977 Annual Report* (Cleveland: Erie Lackawanna Railway Co., 1978), p. 2; interview with Harry G. Silleck, Jr., Cleveland, Ohio, October 19, 1988.

22. Silleck interview.

23. Ibid.; District Court Document No. 3566-1, p. 16.

24. Silleck interview; District Court Document No. 3566-1, p. 16; Shannon interview.

25. Shannon interview; Silleck interview; Donahue interview, November 14, 1990; interview with Robert B. Krupansky, Cleveland, Ohio, February 21, 1989.

26. Krupansky interview; Silleck interview; Shannon interview; District Court Document No. 3566-1, p. 17.

27. Silleck interview; *CJI Industries, Inc. 1986 Annual Report* (New York: CJI Industries, Inc., 1987), p. 1.

28. Silleck interview.

29. Ibid.; "Penn Central: The Price Is Set," *Railway Age* 181 (December 8, 1980): 12.

30. Silleck interview.

31. Ibid.

32. Ibid.

33. Ibid.; Zilli interview, January 7, 1993; Zilli interview, April 5, 1989.

34. *Wall Street Journal*, November 19, 1981, February 26, 1982; *Erie Lackawanna Railway Company Annual Report 1981* (Cleveland: Erie Lackawanna Railway Co., 1982), p. 1; Shannon interview.

35. District Court Document No. 3566-1, p. 18.

36. *Wall Street Journal*, December 22, 1978; *Plan of Reorganization, Submitted by Thomas F. Patton and Ralph S. Tyler, Jr., Trustees of Erie Lackawanna Railway Company, Debtor, December 21, 1978*, EL papers; *Plan of Reorganization, Submitted by Thomas F. Patton and Ralph S. Tyler, Jr., Trustees of Erie Lackawanna Railway Company, Debtor, As*

Amended November 15, 1979, EL papers; *Erie Lackawanna Inc. Financial Report 1982*, p. 12; interview with Bernard V. Donahue, Cleveland, Ohio, April 19, 1990.

37. Interview with Bernard V. Donahue, Cleveland, Ohio, April 18, 1989; *Erie Lackawanna Inc. 1984 Annual Report* (Cleveland: Erie Lackawanna Inc., 1985), p. 1; *Cleveland Plain Dealer*, January 12, 1982; Zilli interview, January 7, 1993.

38. Interview with Bernard V. Donahue, Cleveland, Ohio, October 4, 1988; interview with Thomas F. Patton, Cleveland, Ohio, June 1, 1989.

As of 1973, the bond holdings of institutional investors in Erie Lackawanna were as follows: Metropolitan Life ($31,809,000), Prudential Life ($7,844,000), Northwestern Mutual Life ($6,080,000), Connecticut General Life ($4,790,000), Connecticut Mutual Life ($3,310,000), and New England Mutual Life ($1,675,000).

39. Donahue interview, March 7, 1990; *Erie Lackawanna Inc. 1982 Financial Report*, p. 1.

If an investor acquired a $1,000 bond in 1980 for $100, that purchase yielded 17 shares of Erie Lackawanna Inc. common stock in 1982. In 1984, these shares traded in a range of $68 to $88. If sold at the $88 bid, the original $100 investment produced $1,496. If, however, these 17 shares were kept to the end of the Estate, their value reached $3,234. Investors gained significantly because bondholders were allowed to accumulate interest in bankruptcy.

40. *Cleveland Plain Dealer*, December 2, 1982.

41. Ibid., December 12, 1982; *Erie Lackawanna Inc. 1983 Annual Report* (Cleveland: Erie Lackawanna Inc., 1984), p. 1.

42. *Erie Lackawanna Inc. 1984 Annual Report* (Cleveland: Erie Lackawanna Inc., 1985), p. 2; interview with Eugene D. Murphy, Cleveland, Ohio, February 2, 1986; Zilli interview, April 5, 1989; Harry G. Silleck, Jr., to author, January 19, 1993, hereafter cited as Silleck letter.

The Board of Directors wanted the prompt payment of the first major distribution to shareholders. Judge Krupansky ordered the Estate to place its funds only in low-yield, nonspeculative instruments. Stockholders, however, probably could have made a substantially higher return on their own. Argued Harry Silleck: "[T]ime was of the essence in making the distribution." Silleck letter.

43. *Journal of Commerce*, April 25, 1983; *Erie Lackawanna Inc. 1985 Annual Report* (Cleveland: Erie Lackawanna Inc., 1986), pp. 9–10; interview with Bernard V. Donahue, Cleveland, Ohio, March 9, 1988.

44. Hilary Rosenberg, "Taxing Problem: What Is Erie Lackawanna Worth?" *Barron's* 64 (November 26, 1984): 36; *Erie Lackawanna Inc. Liquidating Trust 1991 Annual Report* (Cleveland: Erie Lackawanna Inc. Liquidating Trust, 1992), n.p.; Richard M. Goltermann to Harry A. Zilli, Jr., November 20, 1990, EL papers.

45. Rosenberg, "Taxing Problem," p. 15.

46. Donahue interview, April 19, 1990.

47. Ibid.; Zilli interview, January 7, 1993.

48. Zilli interview; *Erie Lackawanna Inc. 1985 Annual Report*, p. 13.

49. Donahue interview, April 19, 1990; Zilli interview, January 7, 1993; *CJI Industries, Inc. 1986 Annual Report*, pp. 1, 19.

50. Donahue interview, April 19, 1990; telephone interview with Harry A. Zilli,

Jr., North Olmsted, Ohio, October 27, 1992; Zilli interview, January 7, 1993; *Erie Lackawanna Inc. 1986 Annual Report*, p. 13; *Erie Lackawanna Inc. 1987 Annual Report*, p. 13.

51. Zilli interview, January 7, 1993; Donahue interview, April 19, 1990.

Even though 75 percent of the stockholders could vote to continue Erie Lacka-wanna Inc., the Sixth Circuit held that the existence of this proviso did not alter the fact that under the plan the company had effected a restructuring that was more liq-uidation than reorganization. Silleck letter.

Thomas Patton became chairman of the board on September 24, 1986. And there were changes on the board of directors by 1988. Bruce Hendry left and so did Wil-liam Dimeling. The latter resigned because of conflict of interest. Dimeling served on the board of directors of Conrail "and since we [Estate] were negotiating with Conrail on several matters, his resignation was in order." Dimeling left Erie Lacka-wanna Inc. on April 28, 1987. The final composition of the board included Donahue, MacDonald, Patton, Roulston, and Zilli. Zilli interview, January 7, 1993.

52. Zilli interview, January 7, 1993; *Cleveland Plain Dealer*, September 5, 1991; *Erie Lackawanna Inc. Liquidating Trust 1991 Annual Report*, n.p.

53. Zilli telephone interview; Kevin P. Keefe, "Dick Jensen Remembered," *Trains* 51 (October 1991): 78, 80.

54. Silleck interview; *Wall Street Journal*, November 20, 1992.

55. William D. Burt to author, April 30, 1991.

56. Interview with Thomas F. Patton, Cleveland, Ohio, February 7, 1989.

CTED BOOKS

Henry Adams. *Chapters of Erie, and Other Essays*. Boston:
ny, 1871.

of the Lehigh Valley Railroad: "The Route of the Black Dia-
owell-North Books, 1977.

Backman, Jules. *Economics of New York State Full-Crew Laws*. New York: New York State Association of Railroads, 1964.

Biernacki, Daniel G. *Erie USRA Heavy Pacifics*. Columbia, N.J.: Erie Lackawanna Historical Society, 1992.

Bogen, Jules I. *The Anthracite Railroads: A Study in American Railroad Enterprise*. New York: Ronald Press, 1927.

Borkin, Joseph. *Robert R. Young, The Populist of Wall Street*. New York: Harper & Row, 1969.

Borntrager, Karl A. *Keeping the Railroads Running: Fifty Years on the New York Central*. New York: Hastings House, 1974.

Bryant, Keith L., Jr. *History of the Atchison, Topeka and Santa Fe Railway*. New York: Macmillan, 1975.

———, ed. *Railroads in the Age of Regulation, 1900–1980*. New York: Facts-on-File, 1988.

Burgess, George H., and Miles C. Kennedy. *Centennial History of the Pennsylvania Railroad Company*. Philadelphia: Pennsylvania Railroad Co., 1949.

Burnie, Nadreen A., ed. *Transportation Mergers and Acquisitions*. Evanston, Ill.: Northwestern University Transportation Center, 1962.

Campbell, E. G. *The Reorganization of the American Railroad System, 1893–1900*. New York: Columbia University Press, 1938.

Carleton, Paul. *The Erie Lackawanna Story*. River Vale, N.J.: D. Carleton Rail Books, 1974.

Carson, Clarence B. *Throttling the Railroads*. Indianapolis: Liberty Fund, 1971.

Carson, Robert B. *Main Line to Oblivion: The Disintegration of New York Railroads in the Twentieth Century*. Port Washington, N.Y.: Kennikat Press, 1971.

Casey, Robert J., and W. A. S. Douglas. *The Lackawanna Story: The First Hundred Years of the Delaware, Lackawanna and Western Railroad*. New York: McGraw-Hill, 1951.

Conant, Michael. *Railroad Mergers and Abandonments*. Berkeley, Calif.: University of California Press, 1965.

Condit, Carl W. *The Port of New York: A History of the Rail and Terminal System from the Beginnings to Pennsylvania Station*. Chicago: University of Chicago Press, 1980.

Cook, Preston. *Erie Lackawanna Memories: The Final Years*. Spring Hill, Md.: Old Line Graphics, 1987.

Cudahy, Brian J. *Over & Back: The History of Ferryboats in New York Harbor*. New York: Fordham University Press, 1990.

Daughen, Joseph R., and Peter Binzen. *The Wreck of the Penn Central*. Boston: Little, Brown, 1971.

Davis, Burke. *The Southern Railway: Road of the Innovators*. Chapel Hill, N.C.: University of North Carolina Press, 1985.

De Boer, David J. *Piggyback and Containers: A History of Rail Intermodal on America's Steel Highway*. San Marino, Calif.: Golden Western Books, 1992.

Delaware, Lackawanna & Western Railroad. *Suburban Electrification: 50th Anniversary, 1931–1981*. Clark, N.J.: privately printed, 1981.

DeYoung, Larry. *Erie Lackawanna in Color, Volume 1: The West End*. Edison, N.J.: Morning Sun Books, 1991.

———. *Erie Lackawanna in Color, Volume 2: New York*. Edison, N.J.: Morning Sun Books, 1992.

Dirkes, Rod, and John Krause. *The Route of the Erie Limited*. Hampton, Va.: Three Star Productions, 1986.

Douglas, George H. *All Aboard: The Railroad in American Life*. New York: Paragon House, 1992.

Dubin, Arthur D. *Some Classic Trains*. Milwaukee: Kalmbach, 1964.

Ducker, James H. *Men of the Steel Rails: Workers on the Atchison, Topeka & Santa Fe Railroad, 1869–1900*. Lincoln, Neb.: University of Nebraska Press, 1983.

Feuss, Claude. *Joseph B. Eastman: Servant of the People*. New York: Columbia University Press, 1952.

Gordon, John Steele. *The Scarlet Woman of Wall Street: Jay Gould, Jim Fisk, Cornelius Vanderbilt, The Erie Railways Wars, and the Birth of Wall Street*. New York: Weidenfeld & Nicolson, 1988.

Grant, H. Roger. *The Corn Belt Route: A History of the Chicago Great Western Railroad Company*. DeKalb, Ill.: Northern Illinois University Press, 1984.

Grodinsky, Julius. *Jay Gould: His Business Career, 1867–1892*. Philadelphia: University of Pennsylvania Press, 1957.

Haberman, Ian S. *The Van Sweringens of Cleveland: The Biography of an Empire*. Cleveland: Western Reserve Historical Society, 1979.

Harlow, Alvin F. *The Road of the Century: The Story of the New York Central*. New York: Creative Age Press, 1947.

Henderson, John. *4 Great Divisions of the New York Central, Erie Lackawanna and Northern Pacific*. Flushing, N.Y.: H&M Publications, 1992.

Hicks, Frederick C., ed. *High Finance in the Sixties: Chapters from the Early History of the Erie Railway*. New Haven, Conn.: Yale University Press, 1929.

Hilton, George W. *American Narrow Gauge Railroads*. Stanford, Calif.: Stanford University Press, 1990.

————. *The Northeast Railroad Problem*. Washington, D.C.: American Enterprise Institute for Public Policy Research, 1975.

————. *The Transportation Act of 1958: A Decade of Experience*. Bloomington, Ind.: Indiana University Press, 1969.

————, and John F. Due. *The Electric Interurban Railways in America*. Stanford, Calif.: Stanford University Press, 1964.

Hofsommer, Don L. *The Southern Pacific, 1901–1985*. College Station, Tex.: Texas A&M University Press, 1986.

Horowitz, Morris A. *Manpower Utilization in the Railroad Industry*. Boston: Northeastern University, 1960.

Hungerford, Edward. *Men of Erie*. New York: Random House, 1946.

Jones, Jesse H. *Fifty Billion Dollars: My Thirteen Years with the RFC, 1932–1945*. New York: Macmillan, 1951.

Kennedy, E. C., Jr. *One Day One Conductor*. Ironia, N.J.: A. & E. Photo Arts, 1981.

King, Shelden S. *The Route of Phoebe Snow: A Story of the Delaware, Lackawanna and Western Railroad*. Elmira Heights, N.Y.: King Publications, 1974.

Kirkland, John. *Dawn of the Diesel Age: The History of the Diesel Locomotive in America*. Glendale, Calif.: Interurban Publications, 1983.

Klein, Maury. *The Life and Legend of Jay Gould*. Baltimore, Md.: Johns Hopkins University Press, 1986.

————. *Union Pacific: The Rebirth, 1894–1969*. New York: Doubleday, 1990.

Krause, John, and Ed Crist. *Lackawanna Heritage, 1947–1952*. Newton, N.J.: Carstens Publications, 1986.

Leuthner, Stuart. *The Railroaders*. New York: Random House, 1983.

Licht, Walter. *Working for the Railroad: The Organization of Work in the Nineteenth Century*. Princeton, N.J.: Princeton University Press, 1983.

Lowenthal, Larry, and William T. Greenberg, Jr. *The Lackawanna Railroad in Northwest New Jersey*. Morristown, N.J.: Tri-State Railway Historical Society, 1987.

Lucas, Walter Arndt. *From the Hills to the Hudson: A History of the Paterson and Hudson River Rail Road and Its Associates the Paterson and Ramapo, and the Union Railroads*. New York: Mullens-Tutrone Co., 1944.

Maiken, Peter T. *Night Trains: The Pullman System in the Golden Years of American Rail Travel*. Chicago: Lakme Press, 1989.

Martin, Albro. *Railroads Triumphant: The Growth, Rejection, and Rebirth of a Vital American Force*. New York: Oxford University Press, 1992.

Miner, H. Craig. *The Rebirth of the Missouri Pacific, 1956–1983*. College Station, Tex.: Texas A&M University Press, 1983.

Minor, George H. *The Erie System*. New York: Erie Railroad Co., 1938.

Modelski, Andrew M. *Railroad Maps of North America: The First Hundred Years*. Washington, D.C.: Library of Congress, 1984.

Mott, Edward Harold. *Between the Ocean and the Lakes: The Story of Erie*. New York: John S. Collins, 1899.

Overton, Richard C. *Burlington Route: A History of the Burlington Lines*. New York: Knopf, 1965.

Pennisi, Bob. *The Northeast Railroad Scene: The Erie Lackawanna*. Flanders, N.J.: Railroad Avenue Enterprises, 1976.

Pierce, Harry H. *Railroads of New York: A Study of Government Aid, 1826–1875*. Cambridge, Mass.: Harvard University Press, 1953.

Reynolds, Roger. *Famous American Trains and Their Stories*. New York: Grosset and Dunlap, 1935.

Rose, Mark H. *Interstate: Express Highway Politics, 1941–1956*. Lawrence, Kans.: The Regents Press of Kansas, 1979.

Salsbury, Stephen. *No Way to Run a Railroad: The Untold Story of the Penn Central Crisis*. New York: McGraw-Hill, 1982.

Saunders, Richard. *The Railroad Mergers and the Coming of Conrail*. Westport, Conn.: Greenwood Press, 1978.

Scull, Theodore W. *Hoboken's Lackawanna Terminal*. New York: Quadrant Press, 1987.

Shaughnessy, Jim. *Delaware & Hudson*. Berkeley, Calif.: Howell-North Books, 1967.

Sobel, Robert. *The Fallen Colossus*. New York: Webright and Talley, 1977.

Stover, John F. *History of the Baltimore and Ohio Railroad*. West Lafayette, Ind.: Purdue University Press, 1987.

———. *Iron Road to the West: American Railroads in the 1850's*. New York: Columbia University Press, 1978.

———. *The Life and Decline of the American Railroads*. New York: Oxford University Press, 1970.

Striplin, E. F. Pat. *The Norfolk and Western: A History*. Roanoke, Va.: Norfolk & Western Railway Co., 1981.

Sturgis, Harry S. *A New Chapter of Erie: The Story of Erie's Reorganization, 1938–1941*. New York: privately printed, 1948.

Sweetland, David R. *Lackawanna Railroad in Color*. Edison, N.J.: Morning Sun Books, 1990.

Taber, Thomas Townsend, and Thomas Townsend Taber III. *The Delaware, Lackawanna & Western Railroad in the Twentieth Century, 1889–1960: Equipment and Marine*. Muncy, Pa.: privately printed, 1981.

———. *The Delaware, Lackawanna & Western Railroad in the Twentieth Century, 1899–1960: History and Operations*. Muncy, Pa.: privately printed, 1980.

Taylor, George Rogers. *The Transportation Revolution, 1815–1860*. New York: Rinehart, 1951.

———, and Irene Neu. *The American Railroad Network, 1861–1890*. Cambridge, Mass.: Harvard University Press, 1956.

Vrooman, David M. *Daniel Willard and Progressive Management on the Baltimore & Ohio Railroad.* Columbus, Ohio: Ohio State University Press, 1991.

Welty, Gus, ed. *Era of the Giants: The New Railroad Merger Movement.* Omaha, Neb.: Simmons-Boardman Publishing, 1982.

Westing, Frederick, and Alvin F. Staufer. *Erie Power: Steam and Diesel Locomotives of the Erie Railroad from 1840 to 1970.* Medina, Ohio: privately printed, 1970.

Woodruff, Robert. *The Making of a Railroad Officer.* New York: Simmons-Boardman Publishing, 1925.

Zimmerman, Karl R. *Erie Lackawanna East.* New York: Quadrant Press, 1975.

INDEX

In this index "f" after a number indicates a separate reference on the next page, and "ff" indicates separate references on the next two pages. A continuous discussion over two or more pages is indicated by a span of numbers. *Passim* is used for a cluster of references in close but not consecutive sequence.

Adams, Brock, 189
Adams, Milford M., 109, 114, 214
Akron, Canton & Youngstown Railroad, 150
Akron, Ohio, 52–54, 173
Aldag, Robert, 31f
Alleghany Corporation, 13, 23f
Allen, Joseph D., 114f, 160
Altieri, John L., Jr., 218
American Locomotive Company, 41, 44
Andrews & Belden, 179
Ann Arbor Railroad, 191, 262
Anti-Dumping Act of 1921, 192
Ashland Railway, 212
Association of American Railroads, 91
Atchison, Topeka & Santa Fe Railway, 197–98
Atlantic & Great Western Railway, 4, 6
Atlantic Express (passenger train), 44
Atlantic Leased Lines, Ltd., 28
Aug, Stephen, 203
Aurora, Ohio, 166
Avoca, Pennsylvania, 48
Aydelott, Gale B., 201

Baker, George F., 9
Baltimore & Ohio Railroad, 7, 19, 53, 58, 76, 79, 106, 119, 150f, 159, 177, 201, 231
Barber, Harold Dale, 61
Barber, Warren, 188
Barngrove, James L., Jr., 111
Barnum, John, 194, 201
Barriger, John D., III, 12, 118
Battisti, Judge Frank, 178
Bayer, Curtis F., 104, 108–9, 111, 186
Belden, Young & Veach, 179
Benham, Isabel H., 29, 151
Bergmann, Charles L., 151
Bernet, John H., 12, 14f, 33
Bertrand, Charles E., 195–96
Binghamton, New York, 77
Bi-State Metropolitan Transit Commission, 142
Blond, Hyman J., 92, 99
Bordon, Daniel C., 24
Borken, Joseph, 124
Boston & Maine Industries, 158
Boston & Maine Railroad, 119, 151ff, 158–59, 168, 173, 190, 192, 202, 262

Boyd, Dallas, 64
Bradley, Charles L., 22
Brennan, John A., Jr., 215
Brier Hill, Ohio, 48
Broadway Limited (passenger train), 15, 57
Brotherhood of Locomotive Engineers, 114f, 171, 205
Brotherhood of Locomotive Firemen and Enginemen, 204
Brotherhood of Maintenance of Way Employees, 99
Brotherhood of Railway and Airline Clerks, 204f
Buckeye Feed & Supply Company, 212
Budd, Ralph, 138
Buffalo, New York, 136
Burroughs, Craig, 212
Burt, William D., 228
Butler, Edward T., 215

Canadian Pacific Railway, 212
The Cannonball (freight train), 167f
Carlson, William, 168, 186
Cedar Hill Yard, Connecticut, 162
Central Railroad Company of New Jersey, 111, 119, 144, 151f, 159, 171, 173, 191, 198, 202, 215, 219, 262
Chesapeake & Ohio Railway, 12, 21–27 *passim*, 34, 93, 119, 149–53 *passim*, 159, 177, 184. *See also* Chessie System
Chesser, Al, 204
Chessie System, 186, 195–206 *passim*, 220
Chicago & Atlantic Railway, 6
Chicago & Indiana Railroad, 212
Chicago & North Western Railway, 75, 97, 134, 166, 197
Chicago & Western Indiana Railroad, 227
Chicago, Burlington & Quincy Railroad, 138
Chicago Express (passenger trains), 17
Chicago Great Western Railroad, 56, 68
Chicago Railroad Fair, 63
Chicago, Rock Island & Pacific Railroad, 194f
Chrysler Corporation, 161
Civilian Production Administration, 53
Claytor, Graham, Jr., 204
Cleveland & Mahoning Valley Railroad, 28f
Cleveland & Pittsburgh Railroad, 5
Cleveland Trust Company, 130, 136
Clifford, Clark, 192
Coble, George, 165
Coffman, M. Fred, 54, 57, 160, 169, 173, 187f
Coleman, William T., 203–5

Columbus, Chicago & Indiana Central Railroad, 5–6
Commuter Operating Agency, 146
Conneaut Lake Park, Pennsylvania, 68
Connecticut General Life Insurance Company, 268
Connecticut Mutual Life Insurance Company, 268
Conrail. *See* Consolidated Rail Corporation
Consolidated Facilities Corporation, 191
Consolidated Freightways, Inc., 111
Consolidated Rail Corporation, 166, 189ff, 195–217 *passim*, 228, 265
Craig-Hallum, Inc., 225
Cross, Major General C. P., 38
Crowley, Patrick, 33
CSX Corporation, 205

Darling, John, 198
Davis, Griffith, 210
Davis, John M., 33, 81
Davis, Rowland L., Jr., 96, 99, 111
Delaware & Hudson Company. *See* Delaware & Hudson Railroad
Delaware & Hudson Railroad, 81, 83–87 *passim*, 107, 119, 126, 151–58 *passim*, 168–72 *passim*, 177, 202, 206, 212f
Delaware, Lackawanna & Western Railroad, 57, 77f, 79–83, 87–90 *passim*, 110, 123, 140–44 *passim*, 152. *See also* Erie Railroad
Delaware Otsego Corporation, 214
Denney, Charles E., 15–23 *passim*, 30, 103, 181
Denney, Clark, 103
Dennis, C. L., 204
Dereco, Inc., 151, 153, 157–63 *passim*, 168–72 *passim*, 177
DeVine, Gregory, 159
Dick, Corwin, 84–85, 145
Dimeling, William R., 225f, 269
Donahue, Bernard V., 225f, 269
Donovan, Major General Richard, 32
Downing, Robert, 207
Drew, Daniel, 5
Ducker, James H., 67
Duncan, Carson S., 56
Dunkirk, New York, 1, 4
Dunmore, Pennsylvania, 48

East Binghamton, New York, 149
East Rutherford, New Jersey, 70
Eastman, Joseph B., 34
Edward F. Sigler & Company, 179

EL Digest, 137

Eldridge, John, 5

Electro-Motive Division of General Motors, 42ff

Elmira, New York, 4, 77, 114

Emergency Rail Facilities Restoration Act (1972), 182

Endicott-Johnson Corporation, 94

Erie Improvement Company, 136

Erie Lackawanna Historical Society, 227

Erie Lackawanna Inc.: organization, 214, 221–22, 226; liquidation of assets, 215–17, 223; financial settlement with federal government, 217–21; speculators' involvement, 222–23, 224–25; tax payments, 223f; payouts to creditors and claimants, 223–24, 226–27

Erie Lackwanna Inc. Liquidating Trust, 227

Erie-Lackawanna Limited (passenger train), 138

Erie-Lackawanna Magazine, 118, 137

Erie Lackawanna Railroad: corporate logo, 100f; leadership, 101–4 *passim*, 123, 132, 135; employees, 105, 134; finances, 106f, 117f, 128–30, 147, 154; differences between Erie and Lackawanna railroads, 107–9; corporate culture, 110–11; merger adjustments and difficulties, 111–14; less-than-carload service (LCL), 113, 134; "featherbedding," 115–16, 134, 147f; commuter operations, 116, 139–42, 144–47; rolling stock, 117, 130, 135–36; Bison Yard (Buffalo, New York), 117–20 *passim*, 266; betterments, 117; retrenchments, 118, 137; Spector Freight System, Inc., 119; Norfolk & Western ties and merger plans, 120–21, 150–53; freight operations, 121–22, 148–49; Meadville Car Shops, 135–36; Buffalo, New York, passenger terminal, 136–37; Erilak Properties, Inc., 136–37; passenger service, 138; taxation by state and local bodies, 141–42, 146–47; ferryboat operations, 145f; piggyback operations, 148–49; advertising slogan, 248

Erie Lackawanna Railway: finances, 159, 160–61, 173–75, 182, 185, 191, 193; corporate culture, 160; Maybrook Gateway controversy, 161–62; car-hire costs, 162; car-service order by ICC, 162–63; employee protection agreement, 163; passenger-train discontinuances, 163–65; commuter operations, 165–66;

freight-train operations, 167–68, 171–72, 208; coordination with Delaware & Hudson, 168–69; personnel changes, 168–69; United Parcel Service, 169–70, 200; rolling stock, 170; betterments, 170; physical condition, 170, 207; System Evaluation and Reliability Checker (SEARCH) equipment, 170–71; retrenchments, 174, 186–87; impact of Hurricane Agnes, 175–76, 182; bankruptcy, 176–79, 182–84, 188, 190; Tioga, Pennsylvania, branch, 182; Wayland, New York, branch, 182; Marion, Ohio, yard, 184–85; Conrail inclusion, 191–99 *passim*, 208–9; employee ownership plan, 197; Hunt brothers, 197; Santa Fe Industries, 197–98; Chessie System, 200–204 *passim*; safety record, 207–8; employees under Conrail, 210–12; abandonment of trackage, 210–14 *passim*; shippers under Conrail, 212. *See also* Dereco, Inc.

Erie Limited (passenger train), 15, 17, 43, 57

Erie Railroad: early history, 1–8; wide gauge of track, 2; pilings for roadbed, 2–3; bankruptcies, 4, 6, 16, 20, 23–29; innovation, 4, 9, 17–18, 41, 52, 54, 232; leadership, 5–6, 8–9, 14, 15–16, 30, 75–76; "Erie War," 5; finances, 7, 9–11, 16, 20–29, 33, 39, 59–63 *passim*, 72–74, 90; freight traffic, 7, 15ff, 28, 33–40 *passim*, 55–57, 71–72, 240; Underwood administration, 8–14; passenger traffic, 8, 15–18 *passim*, 38, 57–59; steam locomotives and rolling stock, 9, 14–15, 41, 46–49 *passim*, 239; Van Sweringen era, 12–16; merger with Chesapeake & Ohio, Nickel Plate and Pere Marquette, 13; management structure, 14; employees, 18–19, 31–32, 36ff, 67–70, 98, 110, 242; Debtor's Reorganization Committee (1938), 26; apprenticeship program, 31–32; World War II, 34–39; dieselization, 41–46, 51; betterments, 51–54; Research Department, 54; commuter service, 59, 140–44 *passim*, 255; centennial celebration (1951), 63–66; industrial development, 70–71; piggyback service, 71–72; eastern freight-rate division case, 73; ferryboat service, 77f; coordination with Delaware, Lackawanna & Western, 77–79, 83; merger studies with Delaware & Hudson and Delaware, Lackawanna & Western,

84–88; merger with Delaware,
Lackwanna & Western, 88–100;
corporate culture, 110; Greenwood Lake
Division, 142
Erie Railroad Employee Magazine, 18
Erie Railway, 4–6
Erie Veterans' Association, 68
Erie Western Railway, 212

Fairlawn, New Jersey, 70
Federal Bankruptcy Act (1933), 24
Federal Railroad Administration, 207
Fein, Arnold, 96
Fillmore, Millard, 2
Final System Plan (USRA), 190, 199–206
    passim
First Boston Corporation, 86–89 *passim*
First National Bank of Chicago, 184
Fisher Body Division of General Motors, 71
Fishwick, John (Jack) P., 120, 150f, 155–63
    passim, 168–77 *passim*, 200
Fisk, Jim, 5f
Fitzpatrick, Herbert, 21f
Flexi-Van service (New York Central),
    119
Flying Saucer (freight train), 56–57, 71
Forbes, Harland C., 102, 127
Ford, Bacon & Davis, Inc., 185
Ford, Gerald, 192, 196, 204
Ford Motor Company, 71, 243
Four (4) R Act, *see* Railroad Revitalization
    and Regulatory Reform Act of 1976
Frank, George C., Sr., 42–43, 63–66 *passim*
Friedman, William J., 119
Fullam, Judge John P., 183, 188
Fuller, Robert F., 81, 83, 89–92 *passim*, 96,
    104, 120, 125–36 *passim*, 151–52, 157
Fuller, William G., 143

Gary, Elbert, 10
General Electric Company, 44, 166
General Motors Corporation, 71; Electro-
    Motive Division, 42ff
George Washington Bridge, 140
Gilman, Benjamin A., 192
Girdler, Thomas, 180
Gotterman, Richard M., 224
Gould, Jay, 5–6
Great Eastern Coal Corporation, 225
Great Western Railway (England), 2
Group of Holders of Erie Refunding and
    Improvement Bonds, 24–29 *passim*
Gumb, Irving T., 143
Gund, George, 130, 136

Hadden, Alexander, 23
Hadden, John A., 23, 28, 40, 71, 181
Hagerty, Harry C., 103–6 *passim*, 111, 127
Hahn, Richard, 174–75, 182, 187
Hammond, Indiana, 149
Hampton, Robert, 184, 188
Hanifin, John W., 200–201
Hannigan, Steve, and Associates, 64
Harriman, Edward H., 9; E. H. Harriman
    Memorial Medals, 208
Harriman, Lewis G., 102
Harriman, Mary, 208
Harrington labor amendment, 98
Hartke, Senator Vance, 202
Hastings, Congressman James, 203
Heineman, Ben W., 75, 97
Hendry, Bruce E., 225–26, 269
Hetherington, Robert, 207
Hewitt, F. W., Jr., 168
Hill, James J., 8–9
Hilton, George W., 24
Hoboken, New Jersey, 77
Holland Vehicular Tunnel, 140
Hornell, New York, 112, 149
Hubbell, Charles, 81
Hudson & Manhattan Railroad, 77
Hughes, Governor Richard J., 146f
Hulett ore unloaders, 55, 240–41
Hungerford, Edward, 18
Hunt, Nelson Bunker, 197
Hunt, William Herbert, 197
Huntington, Indiana, 68, 149, 208
Hurricane Agnes, 175
Hurricane Diane, 72, 82

Inside Story, 147
Institutional Investors Erie Group, 183
Interstate Commerce Commission, 12–13,
    21–26 *passim*, 39, 69, 73, 79, 83, 89–99
    passim, 105, 120f, 127–30 *passim*, 138f,
    150–53 *passim*, 158–64 *passim*, 172–79
    passim, 184, 190f, 213

Jackson, Richard, 187
Jamestown, New York, 149
Jensen, Richard, 227
Jersey Central Railroad, *see* Central Railroad
    Company of New Jersey
Jersey City, New Jersey, 4, 77f
Jewett, Hugh, 6
JK Lines, Inc., 212
Johnston, Paul W., 36, 61–63, 70, 75, 79,
    84–88 *passim*, 116, 120, 142
Johnston, Paul W., Jr., 62

Jonas, P. D., 86
Jones, Jesse H., 21–22, 23
Jordan, Edward, 203
J. P. Morgan & Company, 7, 9

Keenan, Joseph, 187
Kennedy, John F., 148
Kent, Ohio, 149
King, John, 6
Klein, Maury, 41
Knight, Truman G., 100
Koval, Frank, 98
Krupansky, Judge Robert B., 178–83 *passim*,
    188, 192f, 221–26 *passim*, 261, 268
Kuhn, Loeb & Company, 152
Kurth, Wilfred, 24

Labor, *see individual unions by name and see
    under* Erie Lackawanna Railroad; Erie
    Lackawanna Railway; Erie Railroad
Lackawanna & Wyoming Valley Railway,
    221
Lackawanna Railroad, *see* Delaware,
    Lackawanna & Western Railroad
Lackawaxen and Stourbridge Railroad, 214
The Lake Cities (passenger train), 58, 139,
    163–65
Lake Erie & Western Railroad, 12
Lake Shore & Michigan Southern Railroad,
    6
Laketon Refinery Corporation, 266
Langdon, Jervis, Jr., 177, 183
Lehigh & Hudson River Railroad, 191, 262
Lehigh Valley Railroad, 7, 94–95, 168–75
    passim, 183, 191, 202, 215, 219, 262
Less-than-carload freight (LCL), 113, 134
Lewis, Arthur, 201f
Licht, Walter, 67
Lincoln Tunnel, 140
Loomis, Edward, 33
Lord, Eleanor, 2
Lubrizol Corporation, 179, 181

MacDonald, Walter H., 222, 226, 269
McFadden, James D., 100
McGranahan, Stanley F., 93
McInnes, Milton, 44, 66, 70–75 *passim*, 90,
    92, 97, 101–7 *passim*, 111–21 *passim*, 128,
    132, 140–44 *passim*, 150
McLaughlin, J. P., 169
Mahoney, William C., 97
Mahoning Valley, Ohio, 191–92
Mahwah, New Jersey, 71
Mansfield, Ohio, 71

Manufacturers and Traders Trust Company,
    130
MARC, *see* Mid-Atlantic Railroad Company
MARC-EL, *see* Mid-Atlantic Railroad
    Company–Erie Lackawanna Railroad
    Company
Marion, Ohio, 184, 197, 206–10 *passim*
Martin, Albro, 162
Massachusetts Life Insurance Company, 25
Maxwell, Gregory W., 132–36 *passim*, 148,
    153, 157, 162ff, 169–91 *passim*, 196f, 205
Meadville, Pennsylvania, 135–36
Medicare, 147
Metropolitan Life Insurance Company, 25,
    29, 103, 127, 173–74, 222, 268
Meyer, Charles J., 85
Meyner, Governor Robert B., 144
Michael, Paul, 208
Mid-Atlantic Railroad Company (MARC),
    190–91, 195
Mid-Atlantic Railroad Company–Erie
    Lackawanna Railway Company (MARC-
    EL), 195–97, 206
The Midlander (passenger train), 43–44
Minot, Charles, 4
Minshall, Congressman William E., 192
Missouri-Kansas-Texas Railroad, 194
Missouri Pacific Railroad, 24
MONEY ("Marionites Opposed to the
    Negation of the Erie Yards"), 206–7
Monterey, Indiana, 212
Moonshower, J. M., 185
Moore, Earl, 111, 144
Morgan, David P., Jr., 90
Mott, Edward Harold, 3, 7
Mounts, DaLee, 207
Mudge, Rose, Guthrie & Alexander, 193,
    218, 224
Murphy, Eugene, 215–16
Murray, Joseph C., 94

National Defense Highway Act (1956),
    113
National Mediation Board, 20
National Railroad Adjustment Board, 68
National Railroad Passenger Corporation
    (Amtrak), 164
Neikirk, Joseph R., 170–76 *passim*, 182, 186,
    207
New England Mutual Life Insurance
    Company, 268
New Haven Railroad, *see* New York, New
    Haven & Hartford Railroad
New Jersey & New York Railroad, 29

New Jersey Board of Public Utility Commissioners, 142–46 *passim*
New Jersey Department of Transportation, 146, 165–66
New Jersey Press Association, 143
New Orleans passenger terminal case, 98–99
New Orleans Union Passenger Terminal Company, 98
New York, New York, 1, 77–78
New-York & Erie Railway, 1–4
New York Central Railroad, 7, 11, 15, 17, 57, 72, 75, 81, 83, 94, 106, 119, 121, 124–27 *passim*, 150, 231, 251, 256
New York Central Transport Company, 72
New York, Chicago & St. Louis Railroad, 11f, 57, 79–83 *passim*, 88, 93–96 *passim*, 117–21 *passim*, 150, 157, 163
New York, Lake Erie & Western Railroad, 6
New York, New Haven & Hartford Railroad, 56, 72, 119, 161f
New York, Pennsylvania & Ohio Railroad (Nypano), 28
New York Public Service Commission, 115, 138
New York, Susquehanna & Western Railroad, 29, 213
New York World's Fair (1964), 138
Nickel Plate Road, *see* New York, Chicago & St. Louis Railroad
Nickel Plate Securities Corporation, 11, 13
Nixon, Richard, 189
Norfolk & Western Railway, 34, 55, 83, 96–97, 118–21 *passim*, 150–63 *passim*, 167–77 *passim*, 182, 184, 195–200 *passim*, 220, 222
Northwestern Mining & Exchange Company, 215
Northwestern Mutual Life Company, 25, 268
Nuelle, Joseph, 81

O'Brien, Edmund A., 93–94
Office of Defense Transportation, 38
Office of Price Administration, 37
Ohio & Mississippi Railroad, 6
Ohio Public Service Commission, 52, 166
O'Neill, J. H., 168

Pacific Express (passenger train), 44
Patton, Thomas F., 178–92 *passim*, 205, 214, 221–28 *passim*, 261, 269
Peabody & Associates, 146
Pence, William D., 30
Penn Central Transportation Company, 153,

159, 161, 168–77 *passim*, 183–94 *passim*, 198–203 *passim*, 210f, 215, 219–22 *passim*, 261f
Pennsylvania Coal Company, 41, 215
Pennsylvania Department of Transportation, 214
Pennsylvania Railroad, 7, 15, 17, 53, 57f, 71, 91–95 *passim*, 106, 119, 121, 137, 150, 157, 231
Pere Marquette Railroad, 12
Perlman, Alfred E., 75
Pevler, Herman J., 95, 152f, 157, 159, 257
Phoebe Snow (passenger train), 138–39, 166
Phoebe Snow, 80–81, 138f
Piermont, New York, 1, 4
Piggyback service, 148–49, 169–70, 200
Pittsburgh & Lake Erie Railroad, 58
Pittsburgh & West Virginia Railway, 150
Pittsburgh, Fort Wayne & Chicago Railroad, 6
Port Jervis, New York, 48, 149
Preliminary System Plan (USRA), 190–94 *passim*
Prudential Life Insurance Company, 25, 29, 268
Public Service Corporation of New Jersey, 140
Pullman-Standard Company, 166

Rail Passenger Service Act, 164
Railroad Credit Corporation, 16
Railroad Revitalization and Regulatory Reform Act of 1976 (4R Act), 194, 204
Railroads: Age of Reconstruction, 9; economic plight in 1930's, 24; economic plight in late 1950's, 90ff; merger studies, 91; difficulties in Northeast, 106–7; economic plight in late 1960's and early 1970's, 172–73; "Great Railway Crisis," 189; deregulation, 227–28
Rail Services Planning Office, 190, 207
Railway Labor Executives' Association, 96–100 *passim*, 105
Railway Mail Service, 138, 164
Ray, John H., 31
Reading Company, 151f, 159, 171, 175, 184, 191, 195, 198–202 *passim*, 215, 219, 262
REA Express, Inc., 138, 170
Reconstruction Finance Corporation, 16, 21, 23, 29
Reed, John, 198
Regional Rail Reorganization Act of 1973 (3R Act), 189–94 *passim*, 202–6 *passim*, 217–18

Republic Steel Corporation, 179ff, 192, 216
RESS Realty Company, 216f
Robbins, Franklin, 67
Rochester & Genesee Valley Railroad, 221
Rockefeller, Governor Nelson A., 115, 148
Root, Eugene S., 54, 141
Roulston, Thomas H., 226, 269
Roulston & Company, 226
R. W. Pressprich & Company, 151

St. Louis–San Francisco Railway, 171
Salamanca, New York, 149
Salomon Brothers, 175, 184, 188
Santa Fe Industries, 197
Santa Fe Railway, *see* Atchison, Topeka &
   Santa Fe Railway
Saunders, Richard, 136, 138, 172, 190
Saunders, Stuart T., 120, 156–57, 163
Schmidt, Harry, 160
Schultz, George, 189
Scranton, Governor William, 196
Scranton, Pennsylvania, 113
Seaboard Coast Railroad, 205
Seatrain Lines, Inc., 161
Secaucus, New Jersey, 70
Selkirk Yard, New York, 162
Serlin, Howard H., 92
Serlin Group, 92, 96
Shannon, Charles, 111–16 *passim*, 134–35,
   144f
Shearson, Hammill & Company, 158
Sherwin-Williams Company, 216f
Shoemaker, Perry M., 78–91 *passim*, 95–107
   passim, 111–14 *passim*, 126, 142–44
Shoup-Adams Act, *see* Regional Rail
   Reorganization Act of 1973
Shoup, Congressman Richard, 189
Sigler, Edward F., & Company, 179
Silleck, Harry G., Jr., 145f, 193–96 *passim*,
   218–20, 224, 268
Simpson, Herbert, 168
Slater, W. J., 168
Smith, A. H., 11f
Smith, M. Cayley, Jr., 99, 135
Southern Pacific Railroad, 91
Southern Railway, 203, 205
The Southern Tier Express (passenger train),
   15
Spector Freight System, Inc., 119
Spencerville & Elgin Railroad, 212
Squire, Sanders & Dempsey, 181
Staggers Act (1980), 227
Standard Oil Company (Ohio), 216
The Steel King (passenger train), 58

Steel Workers' Organizing Committee
   (CIO), 180
Steffen, Wallace, 160, 164–65
Steve Hannigan and Associates, 64
Sturgis, Henry S., 10–11, 24–29 *passim*
Susquehanna, Pennsylvania, 49
Symes, James M., 94f

Terminal Railroad Association of St. Louis,
   134
Teterboro, New Jersey, 70
Thomas, Judge William, 178f, 183
Thomas, William, 114f
Thompson, David, 75
Thompson, John K., 26, 127
Three (3) R Act, *see* Regional Rail
   Reorganization Act of 1973
Tide, 123
Tippecanoe Railroad, 212
Toledo, St. Louis & Western Railroad, 12
Trade Act of 1974, 192
Trailer-on-flatcar operations, *see* Piggyback
   service
Trailer Train Company, 215
Transportation Act of 1920, 13
Transportation Act of 1940, 98, 105
Transportation Act of 1958, 91, 128
Tuohy, Walter, 152
Turbyfill, John R., 172–74 *passim*
Twentieth Century Limited (passenger train),
   15, 57
Tyler, Ralph S., Jr., 179–86 *passim*, 191f,
   205, 214, 217, 221–26 *passim*, 261

Underwood, Frederick, 8–10, 14, 67
Union Carbide Corporation, 93–94
Union Pacific Railroad, 171, 194
Union Trust Company, 179
United Parcel Service, 169–70, 212, 228,
   266
United States Railway Association, 190–94
   passim, 199–202 *passim*, 206, 219f
United States Steel Corporation, 192
United Transportation Union, 171, 188,
   204f
University of Virginia Graduate School of
   Business, 222
U.S. Department of Transportation, 190,
   194
Usery, William J., 204
U.S. Post Office Department, 164, 170
U.S. Truck Lines, Inc., 118

Value Line Survey, 147

Vanderbilt, "Commodore" Cornelius, 5
Vaness Company, 13
Van Hook, Jasper, 110
Van Sweringen, Mantis James, 11–15
Van Sweringen, Oris Paxton, 11–15
The Vestibuled Limited (passenger train), 8
Virginian Railway, 96–97, 123
Von Willer, Harry, 75–79 *passim*, 86–95
 passim, 100f, 141, 255

Wabash Railroad, 82, 93ff, 118, 120, 150,
 157
Wackenfeld, Richard H., 111
Washington labor agreement, 98
Watkins, Hays T., 200–204 *passim*
Wean, Raymond, 127
Webb, Charles A., 153
Webster, Daniel, 2
Weihofen, G. J., 31
Wellsville, New York, 176
West, Judge S. W., 23, 27
Western Maryland Railway, 198

White, Garret (Gary) C., 67, 75, 103–6
 passim, 110–13 *passim*, 135
White, Lynne L., 83, 95
White, William, 67, 81–88 *passim*, 106, 122–
 39 *passim*, 144–57 *passim*, 177, 193
White, William Gregg, 111
Wilkin, Judge Robert, 27f
Willard, Daniel, 19, 33
Woodruff, Robert E., 30–41 *passim*, 49, 54,
 58, 61, 69f, 75, 110, 237
Wyer, Dick & Company, 84–89 *passim*, 94,
 112, 116, 134f, 144ff, 214, 218, 221
Wyer, William, 84–89 *passim*

Yacka, Bernice, 138
Young, Robert R., 83, 126f
Youngstown Sheet & Tube Company, 192

Zephyr (passenger train), 138
Zilli, Harry A., Jr., 114, 185–91 *passim*, 214–
 17 *passim*, 222–27 *passim*, 269

Library of Congress Cataloging-in-Publication Data

Grant, H. Roger.
  Erie Lackawanna : death of an American railroad, 1938–1992 / H.
Roger Grant.
      p.   cm.
  Includes bibliographical references and index.
  ISBN 0-8047-2357-5 (acid-free) :
  1. Erie-Lackawanna Railroad Company—Management—History. 2. Erie
Lackawanna Railway Company—Management—History. 3. Erie Lackawanna
Inc.—Management—History. 4. ConRail—Management—History.
5. Railroads—Northeastern States—Management—History. I. Title.
HE2791.E677G73   1994
385'.06'574—dc20   94-252
                                                                       CIP

♾ This book is printed on acid-free paper.